www.transworldireland.ie

'Roche delivers a fascinating warts-and-all insight into what it's like riding in a peloton of 200 riders for three weeks on a diet of "plain pasta from a roadside motel with some olive oil". The way he captures the glory, suffering and heroism of the sport make it a must-read this Christmas'   *Irish Examiner*, Books of the Year

'Autobiographies released in the middle of sporting careers are often dubious endeavours. How can one evaluate a life when it is still in the throes of being lived? However, *Inside the Peloton* is an exception. It is a fiercely honest book, which tells the life of a cyclist desperate for success in the present, not a grizzled old pro looking back on a career of success, or a bitter old pro looking back on a career of failure. It tells the story of a man who is skirting the environs of being a great sportsman and for that I commend its release . . . Fascinating . . . candid . . . his honesty is refreshing in an era of public relations sanitization . . . *Inside the Peloton* reveals Roche's character immensely clearly. It serves not only as a great book – it also serves as a great marketing tool. Anyone who reads it won't be able to want anything but the best for him. And, they'll be sure to read his Tour de France 2012 diary'
Tadgh Peavoy, www.rte.ie

'A lively, enjoyable read, which also features some fantastic picture sections . . . candid, fascinating'   *Cycle Sport*

'Nicolas' diaries tugged us so deep into Le Tour this year, it read like a redemption song . . . This is how sport should be, because it isn't some grand multiplex. It can't be something that just comes on for our convenience like a fridge light. Real sport makes the skin tingle because, at its best, it flies an ungovernable path'
Vincent Hogan

'Roche's columns have been fascinating over the past three weeks. They seem to be delivered immediately after each stage, with legs burning, mind racing, and thoughts still raw . . . Roche's honesty has brought a humanity to an event that has become known for dubiously superhuman feats'   Shane Hegarty, *Irish Times*

'Nicolas Roche is a man of distinction, honesty and decency. And no truer words have I ever spoken'   Johnny Lyons, 98FM

INSIDE THE PELOTON

My Life as a Professional Cyclist

NICOLAS ROCHE

with

GERARD CROMWELL

TRANSWORLD IRELAND

TRANSWORLD IRELAND
An imprint of The Random House Group Limited
20 Vauxhall Bridge Road, London SW1V 2SA
www.transworldbooks.co.uk

INSIDE THE PELOTON
A TRANSWORLD IRELAND BOOK: 9781848271111

First published in 2011 by Transworld Ireland,
a division of Transworld Publishers
Transworld Ireland paperback edition published 2012

Addresses for Random House Group Ltd companies outside the UK
can be found at: www.randomhouse.co.uk
The Random House Group Ltd Reg. No. 954009

The Random House Group Limited supports The Forest Stewardship Council
(FSC®), the leading international forest-certification organisation. Our books
carrying the FSC label are printed on FSC®-certified paper. FSC is the
only forest-certification scheme endorsed by the leading environmental
organisations, including Greenpeace. Our paper-procurement
policy can be found at www.randomhouse.co.uk/environment

Typeset in 11/14pt Minion by Falcon Oast Graphic Art Ltd.
Printed and bound by CPI Group (UK) Ltd, Croydon, CR0 4YY.

2 4 6 8 10 9 7 5 3 1

INSIDE THE PELOTON

CONTENTS

Acknowledgements

Mum and Dad, thanks for giving me a happy home, a solid education and the support I needed when I decided to make cycling my career. I know it must be hard seeing me forge my own path and make my own mistakes in life but, as you both know, I inherited that stubborn streak from somewhere, so thanks for letting me do things my way.

To Christel: thanks for always being there when I needed you, whether that was as a goalkeeper-cum-target during football practice, as a tackle bag during rugby, or just as a sister and a friend.

To Alexis and Florian: two of the strongest, bravest, brothers ever, thanks for the fantastic support and for always looking out for each other when I'm away. When this cycling malarkey is all over I will book us all a table at Florian's restaurant (which will no doubt be jam-packed every night), and we will celebrate Alexis's latest victory together.

Behind every good man there is a good woman and, luckily, I have the unwavering support of Chiara at home. Thanks for looking after me and for putting up with me in the good times and the bad.

To all my family and friends, especially my Nana and

Grandad Roche back in Ireland, for making the Irish championships a great family gathering every year. Thanks to Carol for the delicious Toblerone cheesecake, Pam for the trips to Enniskerry and Peter, Simon and Eric for being around all those years. Thanks also to the rest of the Roche clan for the texts and phone calls of support in the times I needed it most. Nana, I promise to stay under the speed limit. Thanks also to my Nana Arnaud and my Grandad Arnaud, who passed this year. I will miss you Papy.

I would like to express my appreciation for those who helped me tell my story. Gerard Cromwell has interviewed and written about me almost since I started racing. Thanks for spending so long putting my life so far in order and on to paper, thus making this book happen. To Sinead, Jack, Aoife and Katie, thanks for letting him spend so much time doing it. You can have your husband and daddy back now, for a while at least.

Thanks to Eoin McHugh and Brian Langan at Transworld Ireland and to my London editor Giles Elliott for all their help and advice in putting this book together and looking after everything behind the scenes. Thanks also to Faith O'Grady, who saw the potential in this story and now knows her polka-dot jersey from her yellow jersey.

Thanks to Eoin Brannigan at the *Irish Daily Star* for being the first one to take a gamble on a cyclist's diary at the Giro back in 2007. Thanks to David Courtney, Shane Scanlon and all the sports staff at the *Irish Independent* for putting cycling back on the sports pages and back in the mainstream with my Tour de France diaries.

On the bike, I have to thank Daniel Fusberty for driving me in a battered car full of youngsters around France when

ACKNOWLEDGEMENTS

I raced with CC Antibes. Frankie Campbell looked after me really well from underage level all the way up to the Beijing Olympics while he was in charge of the Irish team and I really appreciate it. Cycling Ireland and the Irish Sports Council have always supported me since I was an underage rider and without them I wouldn't have made it this far.

Thanks to all the 'crickets' around Nice where I spent many years training along the Côte d'Azur with Amaël, Goeffrey, Tristan, Maxime and my current training buddies Leigh Howard, Simon Clarke and Eduardo Girardi for making those long hours in the saddle go by that little bit quicker.

Thanks to Angelo, Yves, Julien, Jean-Charles and 'Bady', for their friendship and continuous support, on and off the bike, and a big thanks to Pierrot and the gang from Belgium for making life so much easier for me whenever I race nearby.

To Julien Jourdie and Eric Bouvat from Ag2r La Mondiale, thanks for constantly keeping my morale up and keeping me focussed over the past three years.

To the Irish brigade at VC La Pomme: Tim, Phil, Páidí and Daniel, we must be due an Xbox tournament by now?

To my agent, Andrew McQuaid, thanks for helping keep me in a job I love. By the way, I think you're barred from the team bus from now on, unless you bring your own coffee.

Finally, to all the Irish fans that make the trip to the continent each year with their tricolours, inflatable hammers and leprechaun hats to see me ride the Tour and other races. Thanks for the support and for making it feel like we had a half a dozen riders in the race instead of just me. Go raibh maith agaibh.

Foreword
by Sean Kelly

For five years I had been the only Irish professional cyclist in Europe, until a young Dubliner burst on to the scene with victory in Paris–Nice at his first attempt in 1981. Stephen Roche and I instantly became friends and while we never actually raced on the same team, apart from at the world championships each year, we never deliberately did anything to harm the other's chances of winning a race. Between us, we won almost every major race on the professional calendar and, at one point, the only two Irish pros were ranked number one and two in the world.

My earliest memory of Nicolas Roche is of some time in 1984, when he was just a baby, and I was asked to act as Godfather at his christening in Dublin. I remember he was a pudgy little chap with jet-black hair. After that I would see Nicolas every so often when his mother Lydia brought him to watch Stephen race. I saw him a bit more when they moved to Dublin in the mid-1980s but lost contact for a while when the Roches moved back to France in 1999.

When Nicolas began racing in the South of France as a junior we got reports back in Ireland that he was riding well and putting in some good performances. When he came home to win the Junior Tour of Ireland in 2002, people here immediately began to compare him to his father. Off the bike, they heard the same accent, saw the same blue eyes and the same cherubic smile. On the bike, they saw a familiar sight too; his legs pumping piston-like underneath as his upper body remained motionless, as if he were part of the machine.

In their heads, Irish cycling fans rolled the clock back to 1987 and saw a future Tour de France winner, a potential world champion. But the son of a famous father gets that in every sport. Having gone through the system myself and watched numerous others follow behind me, I was aware that winning the Junior Tour or riding well as a seventeen-year-old could give others a little bit of a false impression of his chances for the future. As Stephen Roche's son though, it was easy for people to pin their hopes on the teenager.

As Nicolas moved on to senior level, however, I soon realized that he really had potential. Slowly but surely he improved every year, winning good amateur races, moving to bigger teams, going on to the professional ranks, picking up wins here and there until he got to where he is now, not just riding but contesting the biggest races in the world.

With a former Tour winner for a father, it would have been easy for people to say that Nicolas was only on a certain team or riding a certain race because of his father. But I have seen first-hand that Nicolas has very much made his own way in the peloton. He got to where he is today under his own steam. Wary of drawing too much attention to his son by turning up at races or hovering in the background, even now, Stephen has pretty much stayed away from it all yet has always been there to offer advice when asked.

I know from speaking to others on the circuit that Nicolas is very well liked and respected by both his fellow riders and by the press and it was great to see him become the first rider ever to wear the Irish champion's jersey in the Tour de France in 2009. To have the shamrock jersey at the front of the peloton and on the TV all day, every day, was a great boost to Irish cycling and brought the sport back into the public eye.

His Tour de France diaries in the *Irish Independent* are of major importance to the sport of cycling in Ireland. Throughout the three-week Tour, people from all walks of life follow Nicolas up and down mountains, in and out of hotels, on to the team bus and into the thick of the Tour every day.

His daily reports from inside the peloton have opened up the sport to a whole new generation and rekindled the interest of an older one, one that forgot about cycling when Stephen and I retired. They have tugged cycling back into the mainstream, into the news, television, radio and even on to the factory floor again. That is a great thing for cycling in Ireland.

In the last two or three years, Nicolas has been making great progress and from his performances in the 2010 Tour de France and Vuelta a España, I think it is just a question of how far he can go.

In 2011, when he could possibly have broken into the top ten, if not the top five, in the Tour de France, he suffered big setbacks with early-season falls at Amstel Gold and Flèche-Wallonne followed by a much worse crash in the final pre-Tour tune-up, the Critérium du Dauphiné. Those crashes really knocked the carriage off the rails and he paid dearly for them at the 2011 Tour. But Nicolas is determined and focussed and I know he will be back.

I will be watching him closely, not just as a former professional rider or as a friend of the family but as a fan. He knows himself that he has room to improve and is keen to keep working hard to try to get into the top ten of the Tour de France.

If he can get into the top five at the Tour, the potential is there to aim even higher in years to come. He can start thinking about a podium place and at this point that is a distinct possibility. I think he has the ability to be a very strong one-day classic rider but at the moment he is focussed on preparing for the Tour de France. We haven't seen the best of him yet. There is still a lot of potential left in Nicolas Roche.

Prologue

For a Yellow Jersey

The Tour de France is the world's biggest bike race. Watched by a daily global audience of up to 900 million people as it winds its way up and over the Pyrenean and Alpine mountain ranges, through the towns and villages of France, its leader is easily distinguished by a yellow jersey.

To wear this *maillot jaune*, even for one day, is the pinnacle of many a rider's career. But there is only one day that really counts. The final stage always ends on the Champs-Elysées in Paris. If you still have the yellow jersey at the end of that stage, after 3,500km of racing, then you've just won the Tour de France.

The final stage ended only minutes ago and I have the coveted yellow jersey in my clutches. The Champs-Elysées is packed with cycling fans, race staff and journalists. I have never seen so many people anywhere before in my life. As I'm carried through the crowd in celebration, instinctively, I keep one hand on the yellow jersey.

I can see my mother standing just a few yards away. I stretch out my arms, but I can't get through the throng of television cameras, photographers and microphones to reach her. She starts to cry, tears of pride.

As the TV crews push their cameras closer to my face and the journalists stick an endless row of microphones under my nose, I too begin to well up. But I'm not crying out of pride. I'm crying out of fear.

'Stephen! Stephen? Stephen . . .' the journalists call out.

I turn to the man beside me. He is dressed in yellow and is carrying me, but his name's not Stephen . . . It's Daddy. My name is Nicolas Roche. I'm three years old and my daddy has just won the Tour de France.

1

Dream Come True

In June of 1980, Lydia Arnaud travelled with her parents and two brothers to a *critérium* – a town-centre, short-circuit race – in Longjumeau on the southern end of Paris. Born into a cycling-mad family in Conflans-Sainte-Honorine, a large suburb on the north-western outskirts of the French capital, fifteen-year-old Lydia was the only daughter of André and Marie-Louise Arnaud, and her weekends were invariably spent supporting her brothers, Thierry and Michel, at various amateur bike races around Paris.

That evening, as usual, Lydia's striking blond hair, deep brown eyes and dazzling smile drew plenty of admiring glances from the young cyclists who gathered together to race in Longjumeau. Although she didn't know it at the time, one of them, a young Irish rider from the ACBB club in Boulogne, had taken a particular interest in Lydia. Although she wouldn't admit it yet, she noticed he had dark hair, blue eyes and 'chubby cheeks' that gave him an almost cherubic smile. While getting ready to race, he had been watching Lydia from a distance and was wondering how to impress her.

Twenty-year-old Stephen Roche had only been in France for five months at that time. Having won the nine-day amateur Rás Tailteann in Ireland in 1979 and finished an apprenticeship as a fitter in a Dublin dairy, Stephen had taken leave of absence from a new job in Premier Dairies in Glasnevin to move to France in February 1980. He had been selected to represent Ireland at the Olympic Games later that year and, in preparation for Moscow 1980, he left his home in Dundrum to race full time in France against the best amateurs in the world. He had joined the powerful Parisian cycling club Athletic Club Boulogne-Bilancourt (ACBB) at the beginning of the season and would go on to win nineteen races that year. The following year he would turn the cycling world upside down by winning four major stage races, including the prestigious Paris–Nice, in his first year as a professional.

At Longjumeau, however, all Stephen Roche could think of was this girl with the blond hair and beautiful smile. He wanted to impress her and thought that if he won the race she'd have to notice him. He attacked continuously throughout the race, eventually staying clear of the peloton and winning on his own. Although he didn't get to speak to her that evening, Stephen found out from a French teammate, Pascal Cuvelier, that Lydia was Thierry Arnaud's sister and, as Thierry Arnaud would be riding another critérium in Mantes-la-Jolie the next night, Lydia would more than likely be there. The following evening, having persuaded Cuvelier to give him a lift in his old Peugeot 404 across Paris to Mantes-la-Jolie, the duo walked around the circuit until they met Lydia and a friend, who, coincidentally, was wearing an ACBB jersey.

Although it could be argued that it was love at first sight for both of my parents, my father's half-French, half-Dublin accent when answering my future mother's initial enquiry as to how many laps were left in the race almost threw a spanner in the works. As he tried to tell her there were fifteen laps – *quinze tours* – left, his Irish brogue made it sound more like *Caisse-toi*, meaning 'Go away.' The shocked expression on Lydia's face was enough to make my dad repeat himself clearly, though, and all was well. After the race, the Arnauds' car pulled alongside Cuvelier's at traffic lights on the way home.

Dad rolled down his window and asked if Lydia and her brother Thierry would like to go for a drink. It was only after they had ordered that he realized he hadn't any money with him. Thierry saved the day.

Shortly after that first meeting, my dad teamed up with the Irish national team for a race in Belgium, and from there went to the Olympics in Moscow, but a change in pedal position brought about by an ill-fitting new pair of shoes injured his knee and saw him perform well below par. On his return to France, he went on holiday with some of his ACBB teammates to a little town in the south of France, near Biarritz. As there were no English-speaking teammates available to talk to, Dad's French language skills greatly increased and now, armed with his enhanced French vocabulary, he set about wooing my mother.

Although they hadn't actually started dating at this stage, my dad had previously offered to teach young Lydia some English if she came to Dublin with him in the off season. He later admitted it was just a chat-up line, said half in jest, but Mum had taken him at his word, and one of the first things she told my surprised dad upon meeting him again was that she had been given permission by her parents to go to Ireland with him. Somehow, the fact that my dad could speak very little French and my mum could speak even less English didn't stop them having the time of their lives that winter in Dundrum and, two years later, they were married . . .

My dad was twenty-three and my mum was seventeen and a half, as she likes to say, when they married. Dad had just completed his second year as a professional rider with the French Peugeot team when the wedding took place in Conflans on 30 October 1982.

The young Lydia and Stephen registered at the town hall in Conflans and had a church wedding afterwards. All of Dad's family and friends came over from Ireland, many of them spending the night before the wedding sleeping on the floor of the bedsit Mum and Dad shared in my grandparents' attic in Conflans. Dad's Peugeot teammates, such as the Australian Phil Anderson and the late Pascal Jules, were there too, and a good time was had by all. Afterwards, Mum and Dad went to Lourdes for four days' honeymoon. It rained for the duration. Mum says the idea of jetting off to the Bahamas or sunnier climes never even entered their heads. They wandered around Lourdes, saw the sights, said a few prayers and went home. They were so young they didn't know what else to do.

A few months later, in early 1983, they renovated a house that my grandparents owned in Conflans-Sainte-Honorine and lived there while their new house was being built down the road in Saillancourt. At the end of Dad's third professional season that year, they went on holidays to Spain with Dad's friend and fellow Irish professional Sean Kelly and his wife, Linda. Now married just over a year, Mum and Dad had been trying for a baby for a while and, maybe with that playing on her mind, my mum had a dream one night whilst on holiday. She dreamt of a 'little baby boy in a big church'. The baby's name was Nicolas, and the next morning she turned to my father and told him that if they ever had a baby boy she was calling him Nicolas. By the beginning of the following season, she was pregnant with me.

I made my world debut on the fifth stage of the 1984 Tour de France from Béthune to Cergy-Pontoise. My dad was riding the race for the new La Redoute team and, unlike my mother, he had no idea that, by the end of the stage, he would be the proud father of a bouncing baby boy.

My nineteen-year-old mum secretly planned my Caesarean arrival to coincide with the local stage finish so it wouldn't interfere with my dad's chances of winning the Tour when the race hit the mountains a couple of weeks later. At the finish of the stage, my Nana Roche, who had gone over to France for the birth of her first grandchild, met my dad shortly after he crossed the line. 'Where's Lydia?' he asked. 'You've got a son,' Nana beamed back. Dad looked shocked. 'What do you mean I've got a son? I spoke to Lydia last night and everything was all right.' Dad bundled Nana into his team car and arrived at the hospital to greet me in his La Redoute team tracksuit shortly after.

I weighed 4 kilos, or just under 9 lbs, when I was born. My mother says I was a good baby. Although she had a few sleepless nights worrying about her new offspring, as any new parent does, she says I was the best sleeper of the four children she would eventually have, and I was a good grubber too.

By then my parents had built a new house in Saillancourt. It was out in the country, about half an hour's drive from the centre of Conflans. We had a nice little detached dormer bungalow with a garden in the front and back; nothing massive, but enough for me to be able to do laps around the house on my bike when I got a little bit older. When I was two, my little sister, Christel, came along, and Mum says I took to her straight away. We were a pretty normal family, except for the fact that my dad rode a bike for a living instead of working in an office or a factory. But when I was three years old, things changed a little bit. My dad became a superstar.

Before 1987, Dad already made a name for himself by winning prestigious stage races such as the Tour of Romandie, Paris–Nice and Critérium International. In 1985, when riding for La Redoute, he won his first stage of the Tour de France and went on to finish third overall behind five-time winner Bernard Hinault and his La Vie Claire teammate Greg LeMond, and one place ahead of his friend and compatriot Sean Kelly.

A crash while riding a six-day track race in the winter of 1985 resulted in a knee injury that ruined his 1986 season, but 1987 began well for him, with victory at the Tour of Valencia, a stage win and fourth overall in Paris–Nice and then second at the Liège–Bastogne–Liège classic. Dad confirmed his good form by winning the week-long Tour of Romandie in Switzerland for a third time just a couple of weeks before the Giro d'Italia, the second biggest stage race in the world. But what happened after that means that the 1987 cycling season will forever belong to Stephen Roche.

In most people's eyes, Dad's early-season form meant he

should have been a pre-race favourite for the 1987 Giro d'Italia but, going into the three-week race, his own team thought otherwise. Carrera was an Italian team so, for them, the Giro was the most important race of the season. But, for their sponsor, an Italian jeans manufacturer, it was just as important that they won the race with an Italian rider. So Roberto Visentini, winner of the 1986 Giro, was always going to be the team leader, despite what Dad had done all season.

Visentini won the opening 4km prologue time trial in San Remo and began the 1987 Giro as he had ended the previous year's edition, in the pink jersey of race leader. The following afternoon, Dad won the second of two split stages, an 8km downhill time trial, held on the twisting descent of the Poggio; famous for being the final, decisive climb of the Milan–San Remo classic every year.

A victory for his Carrera team in their speciality, the team time-trial, two days later, propelled Dad into the pink jersey as highest placed rider on the team. The first mountain stage saw Dad's loyal friend and teammate Eddy Schepers go clear with Frenchman Jean-Claude Bagot of the Fagor team on the climb to Terminillo. Instead of beating the Frenchman for the stage win, Eddy quietly enlisted Bagot and his Spanish team's help for later in the Giro, in case things got awkward at Carrera for Dad. They soon would.

When Visentini reclaimed 'his' pink jersey by winning the stage thirteen time trial to San Marino, Italian fans rejoiced, sensing another home victory. At the end of the rain-sodden stage, Dad was now two minutes and forty-six seconds behind the Italian playboy. Everybody presumed the Giro was over.

Although the 'team plan' was that Dad would ride for

Visentini in the Giro and Visentini would ride for Dad in the Tour de France, Visentini was telling all the journalists at the Giro that he would be on holiday in July, during the Tour de France, so Dad knew where he stood with him. When Visentini took the lead, Dad decided to ride for him but also made up his mind not to bury himself for him.

Things stayed tranquil in the Carrera camp for five or six days – until the infamous stage to Sappada. Here, Dad descended a mountain at breakneck speed and, at the bottom, had tagged on to a breakaway group about a minute ahead of the peloton. He said later that it was a once-in-a-lifetime descent where he didn't touch the brakes once on the way down. With Visentini in pink, it was a textbook move which should have forced the other teams to ride and give Visentini and their Carrera teammates an easy day. If the other teams rode to catch the break, then they would be tiring themselves out for nothing and Visentini would still be race leader. If they didn't chase, then Dad had a great chance of stage victory and, if the gap grew big enough to the peloton, he would take over the race lead. It was a win-win situation for Carrera. But they didn't see it like that.

After Dad refused to stop riding when his team manager asked him, Carrera sent Dad's mechanic and friend Patrick Valcke up to ask him again, but Patrick told Dad he should keep riding. Dad's escape group was eventually recaptured after an exhausting chase by his own team, but he still found the strength to follow another move on the final climb. Egged on and encouraged by Eddy Schepers, Dad hung on to the leaders and, with Visentini cracking and losing over six minutes on the final climb, took over in the pink jersey again. Although the team still held the race lead, Carrera was not happy and tried to send Dad home. Dad wouldn't budge, saying he was going to win the Giro. At one o'clock in the morning, the Carrera company boss, Tito Tachella, arrived and decided both Visentini and Dad would continue in the race.

Dad was branded a Judas by the Italian newspapers, while Schepers and Valcke were called the Rebel and the Devil. Listening only to Visentini's side of the story, the Italian fans were baying for Dad's blood in the final week. For his safety, he needed two police motorbikes to ride alongside him in the mountains after fans had previously spat at him, hurled abuse and thumped him from the roadside. The joke on the Giro at the time was 'What does Stephen Roche have for dinner?' The answer was 'Pancakes, because they are the only thing they can slide under the door.'

Dad got some help from Scottish rider Robert Millar, who rode for the rival Panasonic team at the time. Millar and Eddy rode either side of him on the climbs to protect him from the fans, while Eddy also called in the favour owed to him by the Fagor team after Jean-Claude Bagot's earlier stage win. Visentini wasn't happy, telling the press that he would 'try to mount an offensive to put Roche in difficulty'.

Eventually, though, Dad's results did the talking and, as Visentini fell by the wayside, the rest of his teammates realized Dad was going to win the Giro and began to help him. They also knew that if they didn't then they were highly unlikely to be offered a share of his prize money, which was probably a bigger incentive. Proving himself to be the strongest rider on the race, Dad finished second on the tough mountain stage to Pila and then won the final time trial to win the Giro in convincing style.

* * *

Dad's victory in Italy had made him one of the favourites for the 1987 Tour de France, although nobody really believed he was strong enough to do the double. Once again, his Carrera team – this time minus Visentini, who had gone on holidays – won the team time-trial and, the following day, Swiss rider Erich Maechler went clear in a long breakaway and took the race lead.

Maechler wore yellow for seven days, and Dad grew concerned at the amount of energy the team was expending to keep him in the race lead. Stage ten saw an extremely long time trial between Saumur and Futuroscope, where Dad took an impressive victory to move up to third overall as Maechler lost his race lead to Frenchman Charly Mottet.

Spaniard Pedro Delgado took victory at Villard-de-Lans nine days later and Dad went into yellow with six days to go. He lost the lead the following day to Delgado but, as he was a better time triallist than the Spaniard and there was another race against the clock on the penultimate day, Dad knew that if he could keep within reach of the little climber in the final mountains the Tour was all but his.

On the twenty-first stage, on the 18km climb to the summit finish at La Plagne, Delgado broke clear and took a minute and a half out of Dad. Knowing that he couldn't keep up with the Spaniard for the rest of the climb, Dad gambled on letting him go and waited until the final 5km before giving his all in chase. By the top, he had pulled Delgado back to within just four seconds, but famously collapsed and needed oxygen after crossing the line.

Delgado held on to the yellow jersey until the penultimate stage, where Dad took one minute and one second out of the

Spaniard to finish second in the time trial in Dijon and take over the race lead. My father went on to win the Tour de France the next day in Paris by a mere forty seconds.

The Irish Taoiseach, Charlie Haughey, held my dad's hand aloft on the podium on the Champs-Elysées, and Stephen Roche became a household name in Ireland. Both races were shown each day on RTE and, as would again happen during the 1990 World Cup, people had sneaked off work and factories had TVs installed so they could watch the final time trials of both races live. Immediately after the Tour, hundreds of thousands of people lined the streets from Dublin Airport to the Roche home in Dundrum, as Mum and Dad waved to the crowd and showed off his pink and yellow jerseys from an open-top bus. He was given a civic reception the next day.

Dad was later given the freedom of the city of Dublin, while both he and Mum appeared on every chat show on Irish television, from *Saturday Night Live* to *The Late Late Show*. The lovable boy next door and his glamorous young French wife were the original Posh and Becks. You couldn't get away from them. Soon Dad was starring in TV ads for Galtee cheese and, if you opened a bank account with AIB, you got a free poster of him in his yellow jersey, and a reflective armband. Dad even had a song written about him by the now late Dermot Morgan, more commonly known as Father Ted. The song was entitled 'Get Outta Dat Saddle, Stephen' and stayed in the Irish charts for most of the summer.

Dad completed the treble at the end of the season when he won the world road race championships in Villach, Austria. Riding on a numerically challenged Irish team alongside Sean Kelly, Martin Earley, Paul Kimmage and Alan McCormack, the plan was that Dad would be back-up to help Kelly win the title, as the finish suited his strong sprint. The tightly knit Irish team worked well against the twelve-man European squads and looked after its two leaders until they both found themselves in the breakaway that would decide the race. When the break split on the final lap, however, it was Dad who was in the front portion while Kelly was caught in the rear end of the split.

As the wind was coming from the right, Dad's group was riding along the barriers on the left-hand side so that whoever attacked would have to jump out into the wind. He waited until there was a little gap on the left, with 500–600m to go, and while everybody was looking to the right, attacked up the inside, along the barriers. There was only just enough room to get through. It was a long way out but there was nothing else he could do. He held on and became world champion. It was unbelievable, an incredible end to the year.

By then, I had grown accustomed to having television crews in our house, or reporters calling to the door. It didn't seem to matter what country we went to, or what language people spoke. Dad was on the front cover of magazines, he was in the papers, he was on television. Everywhere we went, everybody knew my dad.

After winning the Giro, Tour and Worlds treble, Dad was invited to a private audience with Pope John Paul II in the Vatican. But he ended up having a knee operation around the time he was supposed to meet the Pope, so it turned into a group audience much later on, with the whole Carrera team present.

The Pope had been to Ireland in 1979. The whole country

basically shut down for his visit. Dad went to see him in the Phoenix Park with his friends. Afterwards, they drove to Galway, slept in a field and went to see him again the next day. Now, here Dad was, face to face with the pontiff. The first thing he told the Pope was: 'The last time I saw you I waited for ten hours in the Phoenix Park in 1979.'

We all went. Christel was only a toddler at the time and had a dirty nappy, but because of the security controls, there were no bins in the place, so Mum kept it in her bag. Nobody mentioned the smell as Dad presented Pope John Paul II with his pink jersey from the Giro, while I held the yellow from the Tour. I was very shy, apparently, but I gave Stephen Roche's yellow jersey from the Tour de France to the Pope. It's something you never forget.

2

Bike Rider

As Christel and I grew up, we did most things together. Our garden in Saillancourt was surrounded by a huge, thick hedge, running all the way around on all four sides. When we were small and light, Christel and I used to crawl around the garden on the top of the hedge. Eventually, we got too big for the hedge to carry our weight and we would fall through it, ending up scraped and sore on the front lawn.

If I wanted to play football in the back garden, Christel was the goalkeeper. Actually, she was more like a target. She would stand in goal and I'd just lash the ball towards her. More often than not, we'd have to abandon the game because she'd run inside crying after I'd belted her with it. If we played cycling, I'd dress her up in one of my dad's Carrera jerseys and she would be Roberto Visentini and I would be my dad as we raced around the house on our bikes.

I always wanted to play Tour de France. We did so many laps around the house that Christel often pretended to crash or to be injured so that she wouldn't have to race any more. I was very competitive, and Christel bore the brunt of it. When I got older, I even used to practise my rugby tackles on her.

As we got older, Christel and I were inseparable, although we also had our rows. As a kid, I was always getting into trouble and, a lot of the time, I roped Christel into it too. She became my partner in crime. One of my favourite things to do back then was to climb out of the dormer windows of our house on to the roof and then climb up and sit on the apex of the dormer. One day, Mum heard the dog barking and came out to see what he was barking at. She looked up to see me, Christel and one of my schoolfriends sitting on the roof. She nearly had a heart attack. It was bad enough that I brought Christel up on the roof, but bringing my friend up as well was the last straw. I remember her asking me how she would explain to his mother if he fell off the roof.

When I was growing up, we moved house a lot, alternating between France and Ireland. As the cycling season ended in September or October, we would spend our winters in Dublin. When Christel and I were toddlers, Mum would also bring us to Dundrum a few times a year during the cycling season, where we stayed for a couple of months at a time in my Nana and Grandad Roche's house while my dad was away racing. Nana's house in the Meadowmount estate was only a three-bedroom bungalow, and whenever we arrived we took up half the house, so in 1985 my parents bought another little house on the estate so that we would have somewhere of our own to stay when we came home to Ireland. My dad had grown up in Meadowmount, and his parents and some of his siblings still live there now. When he won the Tour de France in 1987, his open-top-bus trip through Dublin ended up at the estate, and thousands of people thronged the roads around for miles. Nowadays, a critérium called the Stephen Roche Grand Prix is held around the estate every June and passes by my granny's door.

In 1988, the year after my dad became world champion, Mum, Christel and I moved to Ireland full time while my dad continued to race on the continent, coming home to Dublin whenever he could. It didn't seem strange to us as kids to be living in a different country from our dad for most of the year because, no matter where we lived, Dad's job took him away a lot. In the early months of the year there were training camps to go to. Then there were week-long stage races, ten-day tours and eventually the big three-week tours of France, Italy and Spain to ride. Add to those the regular one-day classic races, which would always turn out to be longer with travel, and maybe half the year was spent away from home racing. Even if Dad was at home, he would often spend four or five hours training in the morning, have a nap in the afternoon and go training again in the evening. For us, it was just a normal life. And, for me, it still is.

I went to playschool while in Dundrum before beginning primary school in 1988 at an international school in Foxrock, where the teachers spoke both French and English. I had no problem with school in Ireland and enjoyed it until we returned to France and the house in Saillancourt in September 1989.

While I had loved school in Ireland, my new school in France was a different story and I put up a fight every day not to go. I'd pull and drag Mum away from the school door every morning. I don't think there was a single day in almost two years that I didn't cry. I suppose that is where my stubborn streak was born. When I was six or seven, we came back from school one day and, as punishment for being bold on the way home, I was informed by my mother that I was getting a bath. Like most kids of that age, I didn't like getting a bath at all and refused point blank. But Mum was having none of it and, as she filled the tub, I knew that sooner or later I was getting a good scrubbing, so I carried out the only form of protest I could think of at the time. She went out of the room for a minute and came back to find me in the bath with all of my clothes on. 'You just told me to get into the bath,' I said in a huff. 'You never told me to take my clothes off.'

By the time I was eleven, Dad had been retired two years and things weren't going so well between him and Mum. I think both of them had simply got so used to being apart when Dad was racing that they didn't know what to do when they were together all the time. Towards the end of 1995, they had a trial separation and Christel and I moved into a two-bed apartment in Osny with my mum. Osny was 10km from where we originally lived and moving into an apartment for the first time was a big change. It was a lot smaller than our previous house, but that wasn't the problem. Moving house also meant moving schools. After a whinge-filled first couple of years, I had since managed to settle well into the school in Saillancourt and had made plenty of friends. Now, halfway through term, I was suddenly going to be leaving all of those friends from school behind. I hated it. That was a hard time for me, and I hated my new, very strict Catholic school.

I was pretty average at school and I got into trouble a lot. I got into fights in the playground and, whenever I had a problem, using my fists was the way to resolve it. With eleven-year-old me, there was no such thing as 'sticks and stones'. If you called me names, you got a thump. I remember one winter being slagged or hassled by someone in school. I filled a snowball with gravel and fired it at him. It blew the ear off him – it poured blood – and I got into even more trouble. Another time I went into an area of the school that was off limits. Just because it was off limits, it was the only place I wanted to go, and I got caught for playing around in there and my mum was called in again.

Six months later, Mum and Dad decided to give their marriage another go and, in August 1996, the whole family moved back to Ireland, as Dad was involved in the build-up to the 1998 Tour de France, which was starting in Dublin. Although the move meant I would be moving into my third school of the year, I was delighted. We moved into a four-bedroom detached house on Hereford Lane, and in September I went back to school in Foxrock, which I loved.

I can remember organizing inter-class soccer tournaments in the playground with another guy. I was still big into football, even if I was the only Paris-Saint-Germain fan in school. One of my classmates invited me to play with his team and I went along to training with him in Marlay Park. I started off in my usual position on the wing, but the team thought I would make a better centre forward so I started to play there. I was a pretty good striker, quick and agile, and I scored a lot of goals that year. One of the Irish national newspapers, the *Evening Herald*, had a schoolboy soccer section every week at the time. All the league fixtures and results would be in the paper, and you got your name in it if you scored. Sometimes they even did a match report on your team if you were lucky. Best of all, though, was the Coca-Cola Hat Trick Hero section. Any kid who scored three goals in a schoolboy game got a Hat Trick Hero certificate from the paper. I remember getting one when I was around thirteen years old and sticking it to my bedroom wall. Another thing I can remember about playing football was my dad making me clean my boots. I had to clean them every time after training and before and after each match. They would always be the cleanest on the team.

The last time I ever got into trouble in school was in Foxrock. We were playing soccer during lunch break one day and I was the goalkeeper. Being really competitive, as usual, I was throwing myself around the goal mouth and stopping everything. I was priding myself on keeping a clean sheet when, towards the end of the game, somebody finally scored. 'Ha Roche, you're shit in nets,' someone shouted. I reacted immediately and instinctively gave my tormenter a dig in the ribs for his trouble.

One of the teachers in Foxrock saw me. He was fairly young, and I found out later that somebody he knew had been a victim of playground violence and fell and banged their head, causing them brain damage. He immediately banned me from having school breaks for the rest of the year. There were still about three months left. Not only that but every day after school he made me write about violence and the causes of violence. I had to research the different forms it could take, its moral and physical aspects, and its causes and consequences. I ended up writing a forty- or fifty-page essay on the subject. It was a good lesson for me and, looking back on it now, his punishment worked. It did me good. After that, there wasn't a peep out of me in whatever school I went to.

Up until then, I had played football and hadn't really paid much attention to cycling, so I was a bit surprised when, a few weeks later, my dad asked me, out of the blue, if I'd like to ride a race the following Sunday.

Dad had been asked to present the prizes to the kids after the final event of an under-age summer cycling league at the Boot Inn, around the back of Dublin Airport. He asked me if I wanted to ride the under-twelve race. I was a bit surprised as, even though my dad was a former world champion and Tour de France winner, I didn't even have a racing bike. I agreed, however, and I consequently rode my first ever bike race on an old Gios bike belonging to my mother. It was a cheap replica of the bike used by my dad when riding for the Tonton Tapis professional team in 1993. Now, my mum is pretty small, but I remember having to lower the saddle until it was sitting on the crossbar so that I could reach the pedals. The day before the race, Dad brought me to Joe Daly's bike shop in Dundrum for my first pair of cycling shoes, and I spent ages practising clicking my feet in and out of the pedals that afternoon.

I don't remember much about the race itself, apart from the fact that I came second. As it was the final event of a summer league, I don't think I got a prize afterwards, as I had only ridden one event and therefore hadn't scored any other points. I liked cycling straight away though, even if I was tired after it, and was keen to have another go. Second place in that first race must have ignited the until then dormant Roche cycling gene, and soon it would take over, leading me on a new path, one of blood, sweat and gears.

I continued to play football but also began to race a little bit more, and began the following season as an under-fourteen riding with the Orwell Wheelers club in Dundrum, the same club my dad had started his cycling career with.

Sometimes Dad would bring me on spins up the back of the Dublin Mountains. Like most kids of that age, I hated going up but I loved coming back down. I would also go out on the bike with my uncles, Peter and Lawrence, and when I eventually started to race properly the whole family would come to see me a lot of the time. Like my football boots, Dad made sure my cycling shoes and my bike were cleaned properly at all times. If I didn't clean them, I wasn't allowed to race. I later learned that this originated from his amateur days in France, when the boss of his ACBB club, Maurice de Muer, would insist on all of his riders presenting themselves to the start with clean bikes and equipment. It was de Muer's way of instilling a bit of discipline in his riders and, to this day, Dad looks after his equipment in the same way.

Like most newcomers to the sport, in my first full season at under-fourteen I was dropped in almost every race. I would hang on at the back of the bunch for as long as I could, my little legs spinning my restricted gears as fast as I could but, sooner or later, the wheel in front would drift away from me, my head would drop and that was it: they were gone.

My Uncle Lawrence used to tell me that it was harder to ride at the back of the bunch than it was at the front. It's a well-known saying in cycling and is true in many ways, because as riders attack up front or as they sprint out of a corner it has a whiplash effect on the rest of the bunch, and by the time it gets to the last man he has to sprint twice as hard to stay in contact. The problem, though, is that to avoid the whiplash effect you have to be strong enough to be able to ride at the front of the bunch in the first place.

Even though I was getting dropped in those races, I never

thought about giving it up. I enjoyed cycling. It gave me a sense of freedom. I loved travelling all over Ireland to race and meeting new people and making new friends and after a while I got fitter and stronger and more used to riding in a group of riders. Towards the second half of the season I wasn't getting dropped any more, but now I had another problem: tactics.

It took me a while to discover how to win races. I would attack too early or sprint too late. I'd ride too hard only to be beaten by fresher riders in the sprint to the line. But it was all part of the learning process, and my first ever win came at the very end of that season in Dundalk. I remember there was a downhill finish with a false flat towards the line. There were six or seven of us in the front group and it came down to a sprint. I sprinted as fast as I could, my legs going like the clappers, and I held on to win by inches. I had taken my first victory. I was a cyclist.

That Christmas, I got a new racing bike. It was a blue and white Stephen Roche model with a little bit of orange on the frame, and it had chrome forks and rear stays. If you look at kids' bikes now, they have all the top gear on them, the lightest frames, the fastest wheels, the best gears. Some under-twelves have the top spec on their machines, even though they only race for a few kilometres. I often wonder how they can improve as they get older. At least if you start off on a moderate bike, you have room to improve as your bike gets better each year, until you get the top model when you are old enough. My first bike had the basics, and that was it. Although it wasn't much smaller than my mum's Gios bike, the most important thing to me at the time was that it was mine.

By then I knew a lot of the other guys in my age category, as we met up every Sunday in various parts of the country to race against each other. I first met Páidí O'Brien at a race in Bohermeen, just outside Navan. Páidí is from Banteer, in Cork, and is one of the nicest lads you could ever meet, always smiling and full of chat. Even though we were competitors on the bike, we became good friends straight away.

In September 1997, I started secondary school in Blackrock College, a prestigious school on the south side of Dublin with a great pedigree in rugby. I liked Blackrock. My new-found pacifism meant that the teachers there liked me too. Although I wasn't too keen on playing rugby initially, it was a rite of passage in Blackrock College and I grew to love the game. As fly half, I scored plenty of tries that year. Dad remembers me being the cleanest player on the pitch, as nobody could catch me.

As well as playing soccer and rugby, I continued to race and, as an under-fourteen, was selected for Ireland for the first time. I had been picked alongside Páidí O'Brien, Stephen Adair and Michael Concannon for the Manchester Youth Tour in England. Although I didn't do anything in the race itself, riding for Ireland was all new to me and very exciting at the time. We were up at 5 a.m. to get the bus to Dun Laoghaire to catch the ferry. We got off the boat about nine and headed straight for McDonald's. It was like a school trip with bikes.

In 1998, my little brother Alexis came along. He is the only one of us four children to be born in Ireland. I was fourteen years old when Alexis arrived, so it was a big change for me suddenly to have a little brother. I used to close my bedroom door at night so I wouldn't hear him when he woke for a bottle, but I was old enough to be trusted to feed him sometimes during the day, and I enjoyed that. Alexis was really, really blond, with a big head of curly hair, and he was a great laugh as a toddler. We had a dog in Dublin and, when Alexis was one, he would roll around on the ground with him. I also remember him always wanting to play on the PlayStation with me. He used to crawl over and press the off button in the middle of a game. I soon realized that if I disconnected the second remote and gave it to him, Alexis would happily sit there thinking he was playing with me.

At the end of the 1998 season, my parents decided we were going to move back to France the following summer so, in preparation for the French education system and the upcoming move, I changed schools again that year, leaving Blackrock College to rejoin the international school in Foxrock.

While I was there, I was invited to the birthday party of one of my classmates, Benjamin Poudret. There were about a dozen of us at the party and, as we were all soccer mad, we had a game of football in Benjamin's garden. We had great fun, until Benjamin tackled me near the end of the game. Whatever way he caught me, I completely lost my balance and twisted my knee. The pain was excruciating and my knee swelled up like a balloon.

My parents knew there was something seriously wrong and they brought me to the local hospital, where the doctors told me I had torn a ligament. I was too young to operate on, so they just told me to rest and it would heal itself. It took two months for the swelling to go down, and that was the end of my rugby and football careers.

Instead, it was the beginning of my cycling career. The

following season, with no other sports to distract me, I really began to improve on the bike, winning a good few races in Ireland. In June of 1999, I took a silver medal behind Páidí O'Brien in the Irish under-fifteen national championships in Dunboyne and was selected for the Irish team for the Manchester Youth Tour again.

This time around, I had a bit more of an idea what to expect and also had pretty good form going into the Manchester race. I won the opening time trial, which was held on a motorbike circuit, and became the first leader of the race. I was second or third in the road race and won the next time trial too. Páidí won a stage, and I finished second again, and third or fourth on the last day, and won the race outright, my first international victory. I had been in yellow for the whole week and was quite proud of myself.

Now living in Antibes, 15km away from Nice and just down the road from the coastal town of Villeneuve-Loubet, where Dad had bought a hotel on the seafront, Christel, Alexis and I were joined by my youngest brother, Florian, in 2000. Florian had dark, curly hair and was a bit more like me, stubborn in his ways but good fun. In the space of two years, I had gone from having a relatively quiet life to having two funny little dudes running around wrecking the place.

Not long after we arrived in Antibes, a guy called John Escavi turned up and dropped a note into reception with his phone number on it. He said if I was interested in going training, he would go with me, and he'd also show me around the town of Antibes. John was the same age as me, and through him I joined the local cycling club, CC Antibes, as an under-fifteen rider.

At the time, CC Antibes had about two hundred riders, but

only maybe ten of them were our age. That summer, John and I went to every single race together and became good friends. We travelled to the races in the club car, an old seven-seater Peugeot 505, driven by either Daniel or Lionel, our coaches. The car was so old that sometimes we reckoned we would have been quicker cycling to the races.

I started off well with my new club, winning my first three races in the French *cadet* or under-sixteen age group at the end of that season. In my second-year under-sixteen, I won eighteen races out of thirty-five. At that time, I was an all-rounder and could do everything in those races. I could sprint, climb and time trial. John was a great little climber, always in the breakaway, but he wasn't a very good sprinter so he didn't get as many wins, but results to us were just an added bonus. The most important thing was that we were getting to travel to races and train together and having a laugh doing it. We enjoyed every minute of it, and although John stopped cycling as a junior we still remain good friends to this day.

There were a few good riders in the area that I came up against regularly. My nemesis was a guy called Alex Cabrera, who lived on the Montpellier side of Nice. Whenever we met, we always had a hard battle. We didn't know it then but four years later we would end up sharing the same room while we were both on trial with a top French team vying for a professional contract.

3

Team Stephen Roche

I stayed with CC Antibes for my first year as a junior, or under-eighteen, winning eight races in the region. In August 2001, I went back to Ireland for the Irish junior championships and finished second in the time trial. A few days later, I was fifth in the road race behind Niall O'Shea of the Cycleways team. He finished twenty seconds ahead of Cian Power, while Páidí O'Brien and his Kanturk teammate Brian Meade outsprinted me for the bronze medal. Niall later went on to become an accomplished TV and film actor, starring in the popular Irish soaps *Fair City* and *Ballykissangel.*

At the end of that month, the five-day Junior Tour of Ireland was due to begin in Dublin. The Junior Tour was, and still is, the biggest stage race for under-eighteens in Ireland. An international race, it attracts teams from all over the world, and plenty of former winners and stage winners of the Junior Tour are now household names in the world of cycling. David Millar, Mark Cavendish, Kai Reus, Geraint Thomas, Martin Earley, Mark Scanlon and Richard Groenendaal are just some of those that have gone on to have very good professional careers.

I had been going pretty well in France that year, and I hoped that my eight wins with the club in Antibes would be enough to see me selected for the Irish team for the Junior Tour. I called up the Irish Cycling Federation, as it was known at the time, to ask if there would be a place for me on the Irish team, but they told me that priority was given to the riders racing in Ireland, and that my results in France were not enough to earn selection.

So I asked another of my good friends from Antibes, Julien Plumer, to come over and ride the Junior Tour with me. I told him it would be a holiday-type thing and persuaded him that he would get to discover Ireland and have fun. Julien was eventually persuaded, and we named our two-man 'team' after the region in which we lived in France: Côte d'Azur.

The two of us travelled to Dublin with Julien's father Yves and my dad, who left the race after the opening prologue and then returned on the second-last day for the Wicklow mountain stage. The race that year was based in a school near Liffey Valley, and each night Julien and I slept in a dormitory in the school along with other Irish riders, and some Dutch riders.

We were all between the ages of sixteen and eighteen, and, staying in the same dorm for five days with very little adult supervision at night, you can imagine the mess the place got into. The Irish lads played one type of music one side of the dorm, while the Dutch played their music the other side. The place was nearly always in uproar, with a full-scale water fight breaking out between all of us at one stage.

The race itself was pretty good, and it was a great experience to be able to race for five consecutive days as a junior.

Unfortunately, Julien got sick, but I was still going reasonably well.

On the Roundwood stage, my dad was driving behind me as I tried to get across a gap to the lead group in fog and pouring rain. I could hear lots of shouting from the car and turned round to see Yves standing out through the sunroof with a video camera. It was lashing down, and I noticed he was wearing my training hat to keep his head dry. While I wasn't impressed with his choice of headgear, I could have handled a wet hat after the stage. But the next time I looked round I saw it blowing off his head on to the road. That was my favourite hat.

I finished the race in fourth place overall and won the white jersey for best first-year junior. Shortly afterwards, I was selected for the Irish team for the junior world championships in Portugal. Our team arrived in Lisbon five days before the world championships, and it was a totally new experience for me. I was sharing a room with Páidí O'Brien, and the two of us were so nervous it was unbelievable. I can remember waking up in the middle of the night every night for five nights and looking across to Páidí's bed. 'Páidí, can you sleep?' I'd ask. He'd answer, 'No.' Later on, it would be his turn: 'Nicolas, can you sleep?' And I'd answer, 'No.'

Before the race, Dad told us a story about his win in the '87 worlds. A few weeks beforehand, he was ten minutes down in a race. Even though his hotel was a kilometre before the finish line, he rode to the finish and then turned round and went back to his hotel. He drilled it into me that you must never abandon a race with a national jersey on your shoulders.

Páidí and I both crashed on the first lap. Even though I

was sore from the crash and fairly fatigued from the sheer lack of sleep and nerves in the whole build-up to my first worlds, I struggled on. I had been chosen to represent my country and, although I'd no chance of doing anything in the race after the crash, I wanted to respect the green jersey. I finished last in that world championship, almost getting lapped. But I knew it was very important to finish.

By 2002, my parents had officially divorced, and I lived with my mum, Christel and my brothers Alexis and Florian in Juan-les-Pins, near Antibes, while my dad lived in Paris with his new partner. On the bike, I changed clubs, moving with some of my friends to CC Draguignan, which was about an hour's drive away, and I continued to improve, winning twelve races in France that season.

In July, I went home for the Irish national championships in Monaghan, where I tussled with an in-form Páidí O'Brien for the title. Páidí was flying in 2002, and lived up to his pre-race-favourite tag in Monaghan when he rode away from the rest of us in the final kilometres to take the title, while I outsprinted Barry Woods of Killorglin to take the silver. Nine years later, Páidí has the enviable record of being the only Irish rider ever to win every national road race championships from under-eleven to under-twenty-three. He is just missing the senior title for the full set and, remarkably, he has never finished out of the top three in that race in four attempts.

A month later, I was back in Ireland for the twenty-fifth anniversary edition of the Junior Tour, which had moved its base to Waterford and had found a new sponsor in Martin Donnelly, a supplier of power tools and accessories. Having been ignored for the Irish national team the previous year, I turned down selection for the 2002 edition and instead formed a composite team with two French riders that I had been competing with all season. Anthony Esposito had been on the French national team twice that year and was going really well, and Jack Servetto had been on the same under-age team as me in Antibes and was a good friend. My dad had just started running his cycling holidays and training camps in Mallorca at the time, and he gave us jerseys and shorts with his name on them and we became Team Stephen Roche.

I had won a big mountain time trial in France two weeks before the Junior Tour, so when I heard there was a hilly time trial in Waterford to start the race, I thought I had a good chance. Having looked at the course in Dunmore East and spoken to my dad before the stage, I knew I had a good opportunity to win the stage and take the first yellow jersey. Dad reminded me that the time trial was a race against the clock. He'd noticed other riders freewheeling, but I was to 'chase the pedals' on the downhill section.

I completed the 3km time trial in three minutes forty seconds and became the first leader of the Junior Tour of Ireland. Before the stage start, it had been announced that one of the local shops was offering a digital camera to the first Irish rider on the stage. As I was waiting on the podium after being presented with my yellow jersey of race leader, the race announcer spoke: 'And now the winner of a digital camera for the first Irish rider on the stage goes to . . . Theo Hardwicke of the Irish national team.' I had forgotten all about the extra prize, but was incensed when they gave it to someone else. I reminded the announcer that, as I had won the stage, I was obviously the first Irish rider on the stage and therefore should be getting the prize, but he just picked up the microphone and said, 'The prize for first Irish rider . . . *on an Irish team*, goes to Theo Hardwicke of the Irish national team.' It was to be the start of a week-long battle with the Irish team for me.

I was keen to bring the final yellow jersey back to France a week later but, with just a one-second lead, I knew it would be difficult for my three-man Team Stephen Roche squad to defend my yellow jersey for six days against national teams and a couple of good continental outfits, so I was quite prepared to lose it the following day on the opening road stage. In fact, I thought it would be to my advantage to lose the lead by a few seconds and thereby force another team to defend it, until nearer the end of the race, when I planned to attack and get it back.

My plans for the race changed when I found out after stage two that only three riders had ever led the Junior Tour from start to finish. If I had been willing to give up my yellow jersey momentarily the day before, at the beginning of stage three, I was determined to hold on to it until the end and become only the fourth rider ever to do so.

As the rain lashed down during the stage, I was getting increasingly frustrated by the Irish team, which was marking me closely and wouldn't let me jump clear at all. I couldn't understand it. Every time I moved, one of them was on my wheel. I knew they wanted to have the winner on the national team, but surely they would have been better off letting one of the foreign teams chase me if I attacked and then hitting out after that team had tired itself out. It made me even more determined to get away from them.

With 50km to go on the 100km stage, I jumped hard and

opened a gap. At the time, I thought I was a lot closer to the finish than I actually was. Behind me, there was panic, but I just rode as hard as I could into the wind and rain and slowly went clear. Despite the whole of the national team and several others forming a chase group behind me, I had opened up a gap of two minutes at one point, before I started to suffer. The last 10km or so were really hard, with a lot of drags and a strong headwind. I began to falter near the end but hung on to win the stage alone, finishing thirty seconds clear of the chasers. My teammate Anthony Esposito was third on the stage, and I had opened up an overall lead of forty-one seconds and was also leader in the points and mountains competitions. It had been a very successful day for Team Stephen Roche, who also led the team competition, but my lingering memory of that particular stage is one of disappointment afterwards at the fact that I had only gained a handful of seconds after such a difficult stage.

Team Stephen Roche continued where we left off when Anthony Esposito outsprinted nine others to win stage four the following day into Sean Kelly's hometown of Carrick-on-Suir. Normally a non-sprinter, even Anthony was surprised to win in a group sprint. Team Stephen Roche had now won three out of the first four stages. Rivals for the rest of the season in France, our little three-man team was working well together, and we now held every jersey in the race. I still led the overall, the points and the mountains classifications, while Anthony had moved into the lead in the first-year junior competition. We also led the team competition. We were cleaning up.

With just forty seconds' lead overall and two stages remaining, I wanted a bigger cushion. I was feeling good and attacked after just 12km on the penultimate stage. I was hoping a small group would come across to me and that maybe, if we worked hard enough, we could stay clear to the finish and I would consolidate my advantage.

After a few hundred metres of riding hard, I turned round to see if I was making progress. The whole Irish national team was on the front of the peloton chasing me down. It didn't surprise me, as they had been doing it all week. Any time I flinched, one of them was behind me. As far as I was concerned, they were playing into the hands of the foreign teams, who didn't have to do any work at all and would eventually get out of the armchair they had been sitting in all week, attack the living daylights out of us and bring the race home with them. Exasperated, I sat up and let them catch me. I also let them know what I thought of their tactics.

A few kilometres later, Páidí O'Brien of the national team attacked. The bunch was strung out in one long line, with everyone gritting their teeth to hold on to the wheel in front of them. Just then I heard a ping. I had broken a spoke. I was worried, as I would have to change my wheel at the fastest part of the race and I knew I would have a hard time getting back on to the peloton. I stopped and got a new wheel from the car, and my teammates came back for me, to help pace me back up. As we neared the back of the bunch, I saw a green jersey. It was Páidí.

There is an unwritten rule in cycling that you don't attack the race leader if he is having mechanical difficulty. Although the rule is unwritten, it usually causes controversy if you ignore it, especially among the pros. You only have to look back to the 2010 Tour de France, when Alberto Contador attacked Andy Schleck on a climb just as he unshipped his chain. The arguments are still going on to this day as to whether Contador should have stopped his attack or whether he actually saw Schleck's chain coming off at all. In a junior race, though, it is normally every man for himself, so I was grateful to Páidí for his sporting behaviour and didn't contest the next King of the Mountains sprint, allowing Páidí to move closer to my lead.

A seven-man group went clear inside the last 20km of the stage and as one of them, a Dutch rider, was only a minute and a half off my jersey and the Irish team wasn't interested, our three-man Stephen Roche team had to chase. After some very hard riding, we managed to close the gap to forty-seven seconds on the line, and I was still in yellow with one day to go. Ironically, the winner of the stage was a British rider named Steven Roach.

The final stage covered three laps of a 20km circuit, with a King of the Mountains prime each time. That stage was the one and only time I have ever argued with Páidí O'Brien. As he had begun the day just one point behind me in the King of the Mountains competition and we had three climbs to contest that day, I knew we would be battling for the overall classification. Páidí is a great sprinter, and I narrowly beat him to the top of the first hill, earning an extra point. Afterwards, though, he wasn't happy that I was still sprinting for the mountain points even though I had almost certainly won the race outright. He felt that the yellow jersey was enough for me to be bringing back to France and, probably under a bit of pressure from the Irish camp, he wanted me to let him win the King of the Mountains competition.

I disagreed. 'Why should I give it to you?' I asked him. 'Every time I moved this week, your team, the Irish national team, chased me down. How come you didn't chase down the foreign riders when they attacked? If you want the jersey, you're going to have to win it yourself. I'm not giving it to you.'

The stage was won by Geraint Thomas of Wales, with Mark Cavendish of the Isle of Man third. I rolled across the line in thirteenth place, with my arms in the air and my forty-one seconds advantage over Joost van Leijen of Holland intact. I was happy to have taken what I considered a very big victory.

Some more good performances in France saw me selected for both the time trial and the road race at the junior world road championships in Belgium in October 2002. A week before the event, I won the GP Ashenes in Belgium and was looking forward to doing a good ride at the worlds. My dad had told me beforehand that, while the worlds were always a bit of a lottery, I had nothing to lose by giving it a go in the last few laps if I got the chance, so that's what I did.

To try and shake things up a bit and get rid of some of the weaker riders, I attacked my thirteen-man breakaway group with 16km to go. I was hoping two or three guys would come with me and we would ride flat out to the finish and stay away, but I was soon reeled in. I still thought our group would survive to the line, especially when we were still dangling clear going through the finish for the bell. Half a lap later, I was very disappointed to be back in the bunch and even more pissed off to get caught up in a crash soon after and lose my place at the head of the field. When I finally got back up, I was caught up behind yet another crash and had lost so much energy chasing that there was no way I was going to get up in the sprint. I crossed the line in the middle of the peloton in eighty-eighth place, nine seconds behind winner Arnaud Gérard of France.

I was eighteen that year and had another year to do in school but I thrived on the adrenaline rush I felt during those world championships and wanted to feel it again. I knew I was as strong as any of the other guys in the race and, only for a bit of bad luck, could have taken a medal in the road race. That race was my revelation. I wanted to be a professional cyclist.

4

Little Apples

I had intended to begin my first year as an under-twenty-three with the powerful VC (Vélo Club) La Pomme team in Marseille. One of the top amateur clubs in France, La Pomme was very well organized, rode all the best under-twenty-three races and had a reputation for being a feeder club for the best French professional teams. All the top teams kept an eye on VC La Pomme's riders, and drafted the best ones into the paid ranks each year. They also had a large Irish contingent at the time, as Cycling Ireland had set up a system whereby the top Irish riders would go to Marseille and race with them. Sligo rider Mark Scanlon, a former junior world champion, had ridden with La Pomme before turning professional with Ag2r the year before, so I had more than one reason to want to race with them.

My final secondary school exams were to be undertaken in June 2003, however, which meant that my parents weren't keen on me joining La Pomme. Marseille was a two-hour trip each way, and Dad figured that those four hours would be put to better use by me studying for my exams. He was adamant that I needed to get a good education behind me, no matter what, and so I began the season instead with the Sprinter Club de Nice.

The club in Nice was a little bit bigger than my two previous clubs. At the beginning of the year, the club promised me that it would take me to all the big national races outside of Nice. But even though I had won four races for my new club before June 2003, I was still riding the regional races. The Sprinter Club was happy with the local publicity my victories brought and knew that I would struggle to win the bigger races. Whereas they were content to have a big fish in a little pond, I knew I had to move further afield if I was to improve.

Although I cut down a bit, I still trained, and even raced locally for the three-week duration of my exams. My last three years of school were probably my best years, and so I did pretty well in the French equivalent of Ireland's Leaving Certificate. Afterwards, though, I decided to take a year out. While some teenagers take a year off to go and travel the world, I planned to take a year to try and earn a professional contract.

Fed up with the club in Nice, I contacted La Pomme to see if I could race with them after my exams for the rest of the season, and they agreed. I would drive down to Aubagne every Thursday evening until the end of the season and stay in one of the club's apartments for the weekend. As all the other riders, including the Irish guys, were living full time at the team base, I just bunked in wherever there was room.

Páidí had already joined La Pomme that season, and Tim Cassidy from Dublin, Philip Deignan from Letterkenny and Denis Lynch from Kanturk were also there. Tim and Philip had been on the worlds team in Lisbon and I knew Denis from the Irish scene too. We had great craic at the time. French trio Rémi Pauriol, Clément Lhotellerie, Rémy di Gregorio and Japanese rider Fumi Beppu were also riding for La Pomme at the time and all went on to turn professional. There were six or seven of us in bunk beds in one apartment at any given time, and it was pretty chaotic in that first year, but I have some great memories from back then.

Every Friday, the Irish contingent would have a pre-race spin to the port of Cassis, where we would lean our bikes against the café wall and sit and drink coffee in the sunshine outside. We had the perfect surroundings and the perfect weather. We would relax and chat as we watched the girls go by. I think Páidí and Philip spent half the summer there. In the evening, we would organize soccer tournaments on the Xbox. Tim and Philip were my toughest opponents, and sometimes we would stay up half the night trying to beat each other so that we could have bragging rights the next day.

Now that I was finished with my schooling, I was sure that my dad would allow me to concentrate on my cycling full time in 2004. Again, I was wrong. Dad knew how hard and cruel cycling could be and was worried I would have nothing to fall back on if it all went pear-shaped. He didn't want me to stop my studies to be a full-time bike rider. He was also convinced that his own meteoric rise upon turning pro was down to the fact that it was the first time he had ever concentrated fully on the bike. He had been able to juggle winning races and riding for Ireland as an amateur with his full-time apprenticeship as a fitter at a dairy in Dublin. I can remember the conversation clearly: 'Well, if you're not going to go to university, and you're not a professional, then you can't just spend all day on the bike. You're going to have to work.'

I worked in Dad's Roche Marina Hotel in Villeneuve-Loubet for the year. That was the deal. I did everything. I worked at reception. I was a waiter. I tidied the rooms. I swept the sand from the front of the hotel. I either worked early in the morning or in the evening, so I could always spend a couple of hours training. I got a good grounding in the everyday running of a hotel, and I even thought about going into the business myself if I didn't make it as a cyclist.

I was getting plenty of top tens and riding aggressively in my second year with La Pomme but, against the more organized and stronger professional teams, it was a lot harder to get a win. I spent a lot of the season off the front in long breakaways but often would have nothing to show for my constant attacking but sore legs. It took me a while to get used to the different style of racing, but I ended the season with two wins, the most satisfying of which was a team time-trial victory at the French Cup. Whoever won the French Cup team time-trial that year would be widely regarded as the best team in France, and La Pomme pulled out all the stops for the event. They even held a special team time-trial training camp beforehand, where we spent a few days getting used to the time-trial bikes again, settling into a good rhythm and sorting the team formation out. The camp paid off and for the second year in a row, this time with me playing an integral part in the team, La Pomme took victory.

Although I had only two time-trial wins that year, I got a phone call just after the team time-trial victory asking if I would like to attend a four-day mountain training camp with French professional team Cofidis. I travelled straight to the camp in Clermont-Ferrand, where some of the riders were getting ready for the Tour of Spain a few weeks later. The only other non-Cofidis rider to be invited there was Alex Cabrera, the French amateur I had spent much of my underage and junior racing career in France battling against. I don't remember anything special about the camp itself. We just rode up and down mountains all day. Some days I was going well, some days not so good, but I remember them telling me I had a good position on the bike and that I was riding well.

After each spin, we had a massage and a team dinner. Dad warned me that it's in these kinds of situation that you can win or lose a professional contract. Teams want to see that you can integrate into their squad at the dinner table without causing problems. They look at how you interact with other members of the team and whether you complain about this or that, maybe to the masseur or the mechanics. By now, I had moved house and changed schools more times than I cared to remember and was well used to meeting new people and staying in different places, and I chatted freely with everybody and anybody, and they seemed to be a nice bunch of guys. One thing I do remember from that camp is a trip to a go-karting track. I might have been suffering with the pros on the bike, but I was in my element on the race track and had a great time.

After the camp, Cofidis asked me to write out a CV and a letter telling them why I wanted to be a professional cyclist. I wrote that I felt I was ready to turn professional, that having a father who was previously a professional rider meant that I knew from his experiences how hard it was and that I thought Cofidis was the perfect team to give me a chance to learn the ropes and become a good professional.

On 1 August every year, professional teams are allowed to take on a handful of amateur riders on trial. The triallists, or *stagiaires*, get the chance to ride the pro races until the end of the season. If you do well, you are more than likely to be offered a professional contract for the next year. If not, you are dismissed back to the amateurs. It's a win-win situation for the pro teams. They can test out riders without having to pay them, and fill in rosters as the long, hard season begins to take its toll on their own riders. A few weeks after the mountain training camp, Cofidis contacted me and offered me a place as a *stagiaire*. I was delighted at the prospect of riding some of the biggest races in the world and accepted immediately.

At the same time, La Pomme had spoken with Ag2r, and they had already agreed to offer me a *stagiaire* place. Their only Irishman, Mark Scanlon, had already proven to be a very good pro, taking a stage win and wearing the yellow jersey at the Tour of Denmark in his first year with them. Up until then, I don't think I had ever written a letter in my life. But as I had already agreed to the Cofidis offer, I was soon writing my second letter in a week. This time, though, it was one of apology, saying that I couldn't accept Ag2r's offer but that maybe our paths would cross in the future. I did later sign for Ag2r, in 2009, and have ridden for them ever since.

My arrival at Cofidis was seen as fresh blood to some of the older riders, who had a hard season of racing in their legs. After each race, most of the team would go home and rest up for a few days. As a *stagiaire*, I'd move from one hotel to another for the various races in Belgium and France. I would join up with other members of the squad and, apart from me, there would be a completely different team for the next race. In that ten-day period, some of the pros did three or four races, but I was the only one to do all six. I was racing every second day. My kit was second-hand. It was only when the Italian riders began to slag me in the races that I noticed the green, white and red bands of former Italian champion Massimiliano Lelli on the sleeves.

My orders in each of the races were the same: Go from the gun and try and get in the early breakaway. This meant that I had no chance to catch my breath, constantly attacking until the break went clear, maybe 50km later. Although I was up the road plenty of times in those races, any move I managed to get into was always brought back. After that, I had to carry out the usual team duties like dropping back to the team car and fetching bottles for other riders and sheltering the team leaders from the wind. By the end of the first five races, when the pros really put the hammer down and the speed went up dramatically, I wasn't strong enough to stay in the peloton, let alone be able to try anything for myself, and I got dropped near the end of every one of them.

At the end of the ten days, the GP d'Isbergues was the final race of my trial. Having done nothing out of the ordinary in my previous five races, I knew that a good performance at Isbergues was crucial in proving to Cofidis that I could hold my own in the pro peloton. I really wanted to do something special and, as usual, tried to go with some of the early attacks. I managed to get into a fifteen-man breakaway group very early on in the race. This time, we opened a big lead on the peloton.

After a while, my *directeur sportif*, Alain Deloeil, pulled up alongside me in the Cofidis team car. He seemed surprised that I had made it into the break. He wound down the window and leaned towards me. 'Don't ride too hard, Nicolas,' he said. 'The end of the race is very difficult, with a lot of rolling hills.' But I knew that if I had the legs, I was capable of riding hard in the break and still being there at the end. I remember thinking at the time that if it had been an amateur race, it would have been ideal for me.

We had all been contributing to the break all day but had probably eased up a little and settled into a more controlled rhythm after our initial efforts had opened a big gap. With about 50km to go, the peloton began to close in on us and our lead was reduced to just under two minutes with over an hour's racing left. When we heard the new time gap, though, the shock of thinking we were going to get caught made us really put the hammer down again.

In the final 20km or so, there was constant attacking from our group, but nobody had the legs to stay out on their own for more than a few hundred metres or so. Deloeil drove alongside me again and asked how I felt. I told him I was okay, and he said to me: 'Nicolas, you have nothing to lose. If it comes to a sprint, you're not going to win anyway, so you might as well have a go if you have the legs.'

With 8 or 9 kilometres to go, there was a bit of a stall in the group and I attacked with all the power I could muster. I opened a gap and rode as hard as I could. It was true: I had nothing to lose. To me, finishing fifth or sixth in a sprint was the same as finishing last in the group. At least if I attacked, I had a chance of winning. This was the way I had ridden all through my amateur career, but riding with the pros was proving much harder. This was the first time I had made it into the breakaway, never mind being able to attack them. I stayed out front, dangling ahead of the rest of the break for ages, but there was no fairytale ending for me at Isbergues. I was caught just 1,500 metres from the line and finished tenth. But my late attack, the longest solo attack of the race, combined with my strong riding in the break, had shown Cofidis that I was capable of mixing it with the big boys and, more importantly, that I wasn't afraid to have a go.

Afterwards, Alain Deloeil and the other *directeur sportif* of the team, Francis van Londersele, called me into the team car and asked me if I would like to sign for Cofidis as a professional. On the other side of the road was the Mr Bookmaker truck. Mr Bookmaker was a good Belgian team and had also offered me a pro contract, on better money, although it was unsure of its place in the new ProTour and Dad reckoned they were more interested in my name than my results.

At Isbergues, the Cofidis masseur had met me at the finish. He'd collected my flowers, given me a towel, took my bike, found my suitcase and brought it to the shower, brought it back out to the truck for me, and everything else. Cofidis also had a team bus, camper van and mechanics van at the finish. Dad pointed out the Mr Bookmaker riders. Still in their cycling gear, they were dragging their own cases from the truck to the shower and from there back to the truck. He nodded towards them and said, 'Nicolas, there you are. It doesn't matter what I tell you. You can take the money off Mr Bookmaker, or you can take the comfort and professionalism of Cofidis.' I didn't take more than a couple of seconds to answer and about a month later I signed a two-year contract with Cofidis for 2005 and 2006.

* * *

For the 2005 season, Cofidis had been accepted as part of the new UCI ProTour which was due to be introduced in my first year as a professional. The ProTour idea was based somewhat on the success of Formula One. All of the world's top teams would have to compete for twenty ProTour licences, which would automatically enable them to take part in the most prestigious races in the world, such as the Tour de France. Smaller second- and third-division teams, or continental professional and continental teams, as they were to be known, would be left to vie for the few remaining wild-card places on the start line. An initial four-year licence would entice sponsors to stay in the sport longer, while all teams had to lodge a bank guarantee with the UCI (the International Cycling Union) so that riders would still get paid if sponsors withdrew their support or the team fell apart midway through the season.

Luckily for me, a new minimum wage was also introduced for ProTour teams. This meant that I would be earning just under €600 a week. Although my monthly take-home pay was probably twenty times less than some professional foot-ballers were earning in a week at the time, it was enough to pay the bills, and I didn't need much reading through the contract before I put pen to paper.

Although there were plenty of teething troubles along the way, and it was eventually replaced in 2011 by the new WorldTour, the all-new UCI ProTour seemed like a good idea at the time. Philip Deignan had also signed a two-year pro-fessional contract, and would be joining fellow Irishman Mark Scanlon at Ag2r in 2005. But Ag2r were not in the ProTour initially. Instead, they found themselves in the second tier of professional continental teams, fighting for the right to ride in the big races. Even though Mark and Philip would still be riding many of the same races as me with Ag2r, bringing the number of Irish professionals up to three, I was about to become the first ever Irish rider on a top-level ProTour team. Or so I thought. By the time the 2005 season came around, just a few months later, I wasn't the only Irish rider in the UCI ProTour. In fact, I wasn't even an Irish rider.

5

Pro

The Cofidis team I joined in 2005 was very different to that of the previous year. The boss of the team's sponsors was François Migraine – appropriately named, given some of the headaches the team must have given him up until then. In January 2004, nine members had been placed under investigation by French police for doping. Migraine banned the team from racing for a month and set up an investigation.

Of the nine personnel accused, six riders and a *directeur sportif* were given fines or suspended jail sentences, with a Polish soigneur spending three months in jail for supplying banned products. After debating whether to continue their support for the squad for the following year, Cofidis realized that cycling was still the best advertising vehicle it could find for its company and vowed to continue, but on Migraine's terms. He ordered a clear-out. Gone were all of the riders and backroom staff involved in the doping controversy. Former pro Eric Boyer would take over as general manager later in the year, and a new internal anti-doping programme was set up immediately.

My first rendezvous with my new teammates was at a

three-day get-together in Amiens in northern France in December 2004. In that time, we went from one meeting to another, getting all our new racing clothing, team bikes and other equipment. We planned training camps and race programmes. We met the mechanics, masseurs, managers, sports psychologists – everybody. I think my only time on the bike was when myself and another new professional, Hervé Duclos-Lassalle, went for a short spin to have our individual photographs taken. I remember Hervé had no gloves and I had no hat, and it was so cold that my ears were freezing.

As part of the team's new approach to anti-doping, we had our first drug tests in Amiens as well. In 2005, everybody had heard rumours and read stories in the press of teams doping and riders being encouraged to take drugs, so for me to be dope-tested on one of my very first days with Cofidis was very reassuring. I'd already made up my mind that, while I couldn't do much about what anybody else did, I would be racing clean. If I couldn't make it as a pro, then I would simply go and work in the hotel industry. The fact that the team itself, and not one of the governing bodies, had gone to the expense of carrying out the tests showed that Cofidis was really changed, and even though I had to get a needle stuck in me for blood tests and moaned about having to get my hair snipped in five places for DNA tests, I was secretly relieved. Although I had only just joined the team, things seemed to have changed at Cofidis from the previous year and that, to me, was a good thing.

At this first get-together, I also filled out my licence application form for the following year. Every cyclist, whether amateur or professional, needs a licence to race. In Ireland, thousands of domestic riders across the country send their application form and licence fee into Cycling Ireland in December or early January. The applications are inspected and graded according to age or ability, and some time before the season begins in March the applicants receive their racing licence through the post or from their club secretary.

Each racing licence carries the rider's name, address, date of birth and racing category, as well as their UCI nationality code, which is made up of the first three letters of the rider's home country and their date of birth. If you are Irish and were born on 17 January 1998, your UCI code would be IRL17011998, irrespective of your racing category.

Years ago, there used to be a part on Irish cycling licences where race referees, or commissaires, marked up any points you received for placings during the season. Once you reached a predetermined number of points, the commissaire would take your licence off you and send it away to be upgraded. If you were a third-category senior rider, for instance, and you reached a certain number of points during the year, you would be upgraded to second category and then, eventually, to first category, which meant you would have to ride longer and harder races. There were ways around this, of course. Guys would say they forgot their licence at the sign-on or the commissaires, in a hurry to get home, would forget to mark the points in after the races. Some riders would remain in the same category for ages, racking up wins and taking home prize money. Nowadays, it's all done by computer. A grading officer in Dublin gets the results of every domestic race each week, marks up everybody's points, and a new licence is automatically dispensed as soon as a rider moves up a grade.

As an amateur, I had simply sent in my form and my fee to the respective cycling federation and, depending on whether I was living in Ireland or France at the time, either Cycling Ireland or the Fédération Française de Cyclisme would send my licence out before the start of the year. There were never any problems. Until I turned professional.

By the time I turned pro in 2005, I had been living in France for almost six years. I'd finished secondary school in Antibes and had new friends there. I also had family on my mother's side in Paris and therefore had, and still have, very strong links to France. My dad once told a journalist who asked him about his nationality a few years ago that he felt 50 per cent French but 100 per cent Irish, and now I know what he meant.

As I was born in France, in order to travel to watch my dad race, or go on family holidays as a toddler, my first passport was French. When I first moved back to Ireland as a kid, I took out an Irish passport, and have held one ever since. I have always regarded myself as being Irish. I suppose I'm a bit more cosmopolitan than some Irish people in that I have a French mother and am currently based in Italy. I also speak French and Italian, although English is still the language I use every day.

But I had begun my cycling career at the back of Dublin Airport at the age of eleven, and by 2005 had represented Ireland in numerous international races, including three world championships. Although I had raced with VC La Pomme in France the year before and applied to the French federation for my racing licence, my UCI code was still IRL and I still rode internationally for Ireland. Even though I could have walked into the French embassy and got a French passport at any time, I never felt the need. As far as I was concerned, I was Irish.

Even though my parents live in France now, I love getting back to Ireland whenever I'm not racing. I love going to the odd rugby match in Lansdowne Road and having a proper pint of Guinness afterwards. My French teammates take the piss when I cheer on Leinster or one of the other provinces against Toulouse or Biarritz in the Heineken Cup, and it's even worse when the Irish rugby or soccer team play France. Although it's getting harder with all the travelling involved in cycling, I try to keep an eye on the Dubs in the All-Ireland football championship whenever I can. I had been given a mainly French education and so was steeped in all the culture and history of France but, for some reason, I've always felt like an Irishman with a French culture, rather than the other way round.

At that first team gathering, the guys at Cofidis were putting a bit of pressure on me to declare for France. It's a well-known fact that it is harder for a foreign rider to earn a living as a cyclist in France, Belgium, Spain or Italy than it is for a home rider. It's not much good to a French sponsor if their best rider comes from Listowel or Leixlip. Nobody from Roscommon is going to buy their DIY tools from Castorama, and nobody from Dundrum is going to do their weekly shopping in Super U. The top French teams want to associate themselves with the top French riders and, although I was far from being a top rider, I think Cofidis was hoping I might become one in the future. It would also be far easier for team management to explain to Cofidis that the team sponsor was spending its money on a young French signing rather than on a relatively unknown young Irish rider.

Although I still lived with my mum and Christel, Alexis and Florian in Antibes, by then I had moved to an apartment in the basement, while Christel had taken over my room in the central tower of the house. After my parents' divorce, my grandad Arnaud was very bitter towards my dad. Although I tried not to get involved in my parents' split and never took sides, I suppose, from my grandfather's point of view, it was the second time he had seen his only daughter hurt. To Grandad, Mum had gone to live in Ireland with an Irishman and, shortly afterwards, he had left her. Although it wasn't as simple as that, my grandad somehow saw Ireland as being the cause of everything bad in the world, and he wanted me to have nothing to do with my dad or Ireland any more. We argued a bit, as families do, but at the time, he couldn't understand why I wanted to ride for Ireland and he put a lot of pressure on me to change my nationality to French and to stop racing for Ireland.

To confuse things even more, when I did finally apply for my licence, I was told that I couldn't hold an Irish passport and get a French licence, even though that's exactly what I had been doing since I was twelve. I didn't know what to do and, as the 2005 season drew nearer and nearer, more and more people were urging me to declare for France. At twenty years old, all I wanted to do was be a professional cyclist and, looking back, I was too easily persuaded.

Reluctantly, I filled out the forms for France, which meant I could no longer race for Ireland. At the time, some people thought it was a snub, that I had turned my back on Ireland in order to better my career. But that made no sense. I knew that if I stayed Irish, because we had smaller numbers racing and I was one of only a handful of professionals, it would be easier for me to get on the national team than it would be in France, even if it was for only one race a year. I was also throwing away the Irish Sports Council grant that had helped me stay afloat while I trained and raced as an amateur. As an Irish professional, I felt that I could be an ambassador for Irish cycling and help raise the profile of cycling at home. In France, I would just be another pro bike rider, a nobody. As a first-year professional with nothing to show for myself, I hadn't a hope of getting on the French national team in the foreseeable future. But none of that really bothered me.

What bothered me most of all about leaving Irish cycling was that I felt I was part of a family. I knew everybody in the Irish set-up, as we had grown up racing with and against each other. The parochial nature of Irish sport meant that I also knew most of the race organizers, team managers, commissaires, sponsors, safety marshals – everybody. That's what I missed most.

But, at the time, I felt it was the only option. After listening to Cofidis, my grandad and others, I convinced myself that it was different for the other Irish guys racing in France, because they all had a background in Ireland, with their families and everything else there. If cycling didn't work out for them, they could go back to Ireland to live and work. But, for me, if cycling didn't work out, I was going to stay in France, as my family lived there. Back then, it was definitely easier to get work in France if you were French. So, instead of bringing the number of Irish pros up to three, alongside Philip Deignan and Mark Scanlon, I anonymously joined the ever-growing ranks of French riders in the pro peloton.

In January 2005, I received my first professional licence.

But for me the dream was not just to turn professional. Turning professional was one thing. Doing well enough in my first two years to stay professional was another thing altogether. At least on the ProTour I was beginning my professional career with a two-year contract. Some riders turning pro for some of the smaller teams only get a one-year deal. In one year they are expected to stay healthy, stay upright and win races in order to prove they have a future in the sport. If they don't, they are let go and in a lot of cases are never heard of again.

I didn't want to be one of those guys. I wanted to be able to perform well. I didn't want to turn pro and get my arse kicked every weekend. I knew I had a lot to learn about being a professional cyclist but, as far as I was concerned, turning pro early just meant that I was able to start learning the ropes sooner. In my head, I wanted to get a win in my first two years as a pro, but I knew that would be easier said than done.

At our second pre-season training camp in Montpellier, I got to know my new Cofidis teammates a little better. You get to know people pretty well when you spend five hours riding side by side, with no TV, internet or anything else to distract you. Cyclists out training are a bit like old women. We love to have a chat. It's amazing what you talk about over five hours. Most of the time, it's just gossip: what films you've seen lately, where you're going on holidays, cars, the next hill, the last hill – anything. I've often spent five or six hours training with someone, talking all the time, only to forget the whole conversation minutes after I get home; but it's a good way of bonding.

The Cofidis team's biggest stars at the time were French

sprinter Jimmy Casper, his compatriots Cédric Vasseur and David Moncoutié, and Australian Stuart O'Grady. Twenty-two-year-old Amaël Moinard and twenty-six-year-old Hervé Duclos-Lassalle, son of former Paris–Roubaix winner Gilbert Duclos-Lassalle, were the other two first-year professionals, while up-and-coming French star Sylvain Chavanel had transferred from the Bonjour team for 2005.

O'Grady had been a hero of mine growing up, and both he and Moncoutié went on to win stages of the Tour de France that year. He was a similar build to me, and I loved his aggressive style of racing. To be in the same team as him at barely twenty years of age was unbelievable, even if I only got to race with him once. I roomed with Stuey at the Tour of the Algarve in Portugal, my second race of the season, and that was it. From then on, he had a different race programme from me. Even though we only spent a few days as room mates, we got on well together and, six years later, Stuey still has time for a chat whenever we race together.

As a team, we did four- or five-hour training spins each morning in Montpellier, and then did fun stuff like laser games and go-karting in the afternoons. If you think Sylvain Chavanel is quick on a bike, you should see him in a go-kart! I finished third, behind 'Mimo' and team sprinter Jimmy Casper. Then a fourth-year pro with twenty victories to his name, Jimmy was the prankster of the team. One night, as part of our team bonding – or whatever you'd like to call it – Jimmy decided that everyone should stand up on their chair and introduce themselves at the dinner table. Oblivious to the other hotel guests, who expected to be having a quiet dinner, one by one we did it, rattling off a brief history of ourselves, including our names, ages and a list of qualities and faults. We each finished by singing a song. I can't remember for sure, but I think I sang the nursery rhyme 'Frère Jacques'.

Jimmy then decided to hold an initiation for the three neo-pros. Once again, this happened in the middle of a packed restaurant. 'Okay, we know you guys are only starting off and you could do with a bit of money in your pockets,' he announced. 'So we have each put 20 euro into a pot. The three of you can share it among yourselves if you take the challenge. The challenge is simple. You each have to let us break three eggs on your heads.'

Myself, Hervé and Amaël looked at each other, and agreed. We had probably been expecting a lot worse, so having three eggs broken over your head and then getting money for it didn't seem too bad. We sat on three chairs, a little bit away from the table, and were told to take off our T-shirts. If the standing on the chairs and singing hadn't already drawn plenty of attention to us, everybody in the restaurant was now staring, and I was dreading the thought of what was coming next. Somebody then produced a carton of raw eggs. Just as the first egg began to dribble down our necks on to our chests, the next one smashed on our scalps. By now, the waiters were getting a bit worried as to what was going on, while we just sat there, each of us waiting for the third egg. The guys threw the last three eggs, but they didn't make contact, smashing instead on the floor behind us, to guffaws of laughter. It took us a few minutes to figure out what they were laughing at. As the final egg hadn't smashed on our heads, we wouldn't be getting any money. Jimmy Casper walked over to us. 'Lesson number one: don't do something just for the money.'

The rest of the team was in hysterics, but it could have been worse. I had heard stories of other team initiations and knew we got off lightly, but the mess we left behind us meant that the team was barred from the restaurant the next time they went back to Montpellier.

As I was seven or eight years younger than almost everybody else on the team, I was starting on the bottom rung of the cycling ladder, as a team helper, or *domestique*. To give me a chance to develop, I was told I'd be mostly riding the French Cup races at the beginning of the year and would get to ride some of the big ProTour races later on. As riders got tired after the Giro and others trained for the Tour, I would be fitting into the empty spaces. I was very much regarded as the kid of the team.

My season began pretty well. In February, at my very first race, the three-day French stage race Etoile de Bessèges, I was in a long breakaway on stage two, and on the final day I attacked inside the final 10km and then helped set Jimmy up for the bunch sprint finish, where he took our first victory of the 2005 season. Jimmy was always appreciative of any little bit of help I could give him during a race and was one who gave me a lot of good advice as a young pro.

In April, I went clear with eleven others in the one-day Tour du Finistère in Brittany, and was going well. Moncoutié then came across to the break and, as he was one of my team leaders at Cofidis, I had to look after him. In an effort to better Moncoutié's odds at the end of the race, I attacked and whittled the group down to just six before the finish. Moncoutié, though, was unexpectedly beaten in the sprint by Aussie Simon Gerrans, and I took sixth place, my first result as a pro.

A month later, having attacked out of the breakaway group three times, I was fourth in another one-day race, the Tour de Vendée, and could feel myself coming into good form. My hopes of building on it, though, were obliterated when I hit a signpost at 50kph in the Tour of Luxembourg in June and dislocated my elbow.

I had been suffering in the gutter, trying to get some shelter from the strong crosswind, when the guy in front of me suddenly flicked around the sign at the last moment. I was on the wrong side of his wheel and had nowhere to go. For the split second that I saw the sign coming, I thought I was dead. I hit it head on, bounced off it and spun like a top across the road. I was hoping nobody would hit me as the rest of the peloton whizzed by either side of me. After a quick once-over from the race doctor, I remounted and started riding again, but the pain from my elbow made me stop a few kilometres later and get into the ambulance.

The ambulance driver was a lunatic. As he tore down the road, swaying from left to right in what looked like one of those vans out of the film *Ghostbusters*, I was sliding across the seat cursing at him to slow down as I bounced off the sides. I probably got more injuries in the ambulance than I did from the crash. The medic didn't bother putting cream or anything on my cuts and just stuck plasters all over me. By the time I got to the finish, they were welded to me, and it felt as if my skin was coming off with them when the team physio checked my wounds after the stage.

The rest of my season mainly consisted of four- to five-day stage races where I rode for whichever of our leaders was in form at the time. If they punctured and I was riding beside them, I'd give them my wheel to save time. If it rained,

I'd drop back for rain capes, and when it stopped, I'd get rid of them into the team car again. If Casper stopped for a piss on a flat stage, a couple of us would wait on him and pace him back into the peloton. Jimmy would tuck into our slipstream, saving as much energy as possible for his speciality, the 200m gallop to the line at the end of the stage. If any of my teammates needed a drink, I would slow down, drop back to the team car and get some bottles. I'd load them into my pockets, squash them up my jersey and then, a few kilos heavier, I'd ride as hard as I could back up through the cavalcade into the peloton, handing them out to my teammates as I weaved back up through the throng of riders. It didn't take long to figure out that it was a whole lot easier to get bottles if you asked if they were thirsty during a period of calm in the race instead of when the racing was flat out.

I remember we had to ride hard for Chavanel in the Tour du Poitou-Charentes. It was his home race, and Mimo absolutely wanted to win it. Once he took the race lead, we had to defend it, chasing down dangerous breakaways and setting a tempo at the head of the peloton that would discourage others from attacking. While it is physically tough, sometimes it's mentally easier to ride for a teammate than for yourself. It's easy to give up when it's just you. But when somebody else is depending on you, especially the race leader, you find that little bit of motivation and dig a little bit deeper. In the end, we pulled it off, and I went away as happy as if Chavanel's victory was my own.

As the year went by, I also noticed that in the ProTour races I was still Irish on the results sheets. The UCI code beside my stage placing each day still read IRL. Even though the French federation had told me I was registered as being

French, it wasn't true. I checked around to see what the full story was, and it turned out that my paperwork hadn't been changed properly and I was still Irish in the eyes of the UCI. After speaking to some people in Cycling Ireland and the UCI, I soon realized that I had the opportunity to continue to ride for Ireland. At first, I wasn't sure if Cycling Ireland would even want me back, but once they assured me that they did I was delighted. That was my biggest result of the season.

6

Tour of the Future

Looking back, taking tenth place in the GP d'Isbergues as a *stagiaire* at the end of 2004 had given me false hope. I had just turned twenty at the time and was still a bit naive. That one result had made me think I would be able to kick ass in the pro races every week in my first year as a professional. I didn't take into account the fact that some of the guys I had been racing against then were just going through the motions, mentally drained and physically worn out after another tough season. For me, getting a chance to race with them was a whole new world. I was excited going into it and keen to impress. At the beginning of 2005, though, I soon realized that when everybody was fit and fresh things were not so easy. I wanted to be much more consistent in my second year and to try to win a race.

My 2006 race programme was to begin with the new Tour of Qatar, a five-day stage race in the United Arab Emirates. Run in the middle of a desert, with mainly camels for spectators, the Tour of Qatar had come on to the cycling calendar the year before and is a race mainly for the sprinters. The pan-flat stages are often run up and down big, wide main roads, and with absolutely no trees, hedges or even buildings to protect you from the buffeting winds. It is perfect preparation for the big Belgian and Dutch riders, the strongmen of the cobbled classics who profit most as the peloton splits into diagonal echelons across the road in search of shelter. The rest of us, though, were just along for the ride. As my main goal for the year, the ten-day Tour de l'Avenir stage race, wasn't to be held until September, I was just using the race to gain fitness and to get back into the rhythm of racing again.

As it was the first race of the new season, I arrived in Qatar a little off my optimum racing weight, maybe two kilos or so over, and I really struggled in the crosswinds, as did three quarters of the peloton. I was dropped towards the end of every stage apart from one, where I punctured with 3km to go and finished behind the peloton anyway. That mightn't have been too bad if it hadn't been for the glorious buffet meals we were served after each stage. A lot of the time, we stay in hotels where the food leaves a lot to be desired, but in Qatar, the food was first class, and I tucked in. I remember they had this fantastic macadamia cake, and I helped myself to extra portions each day, something I wouldn't even allow myself to think about today. I put on another two kilos that week.

The general manager of my Cofidis team at the time, Eric Boyer, didn't usually travel with the team to races. He was normally busy doing office and logistical work. But he was in Qatar that year and wasn't impressed with my performance on the bike or off it. He berated me for being unprofessional and overweight. Only five days of racing into the 2006 season, and I had already had an argument with the team boss. Not a very good start.

Two weeks later, at the Tour of the Algarve, I crashed and injured my knee, which forced me out of the race. I don't know if Boyer thought I was just being lazy but, as punishment, he sent me to a training camp in the south of France. One evening, it was one of the guys' birthdays so we went out for a drink to celebrate. We didn't go home rolling drunk or anything, simply had a beer and a chat and went back to the team hotel. Boyer somehow found out about it, though, and because the camp was in Nice, near where I lived, I got the blame. Ten days later, I was sent to another training camp in Belgium, and I was flying, so they told me I was going to ride the Tour of Flanders, the biggest one-day cobbled classic in Belgium. I told team management that I hadn't ridden a race in seven or eight weeks, and I couldn't be expected to ride the Tour of Flanders, possibly the hardest one-day classic on the calendar.

I flew home to Antibes on the Monday night but was on a plane back to Belgium the following morning. On the Wednesday, we did a reconnaissance ride of the Tour of Flanders route and did another six-hour spin on the Thursday. On Friday, I rode the Route Adélie in France, took a five-hour train ride to Ghent on Saturday and rode Flanders on the Sunday. They told me to try and get in the early break and not to worry if it didn't work out. But, after about 80km, the guys gave me their jackets and I dropped back to the car with them and climbed in.

That night, I wanted to go home, but I was told I had to stay in Belgium, as I was riding another classic, Ghent–Wevelgem, in a couple of days. It made no sense for me to ride Ghent–Wevelgem, as it didn't suit me at all. It was just more of the same: cobbles, wind and echelons. That night in the hotel, I sat at the bar with Bradley Wiggins, who had just joined Cofidis that year. We sat and chatted, and I was so pissed off with the team that I ordered a crêpe with Nutella in it. In France, teams can be very stubborn regarding some things – stupid things. Whereas the American- and British-backed teams have a more open outlook, in France it's still very traditional and old school. They don't mind you putting olive oil and Parmesan on your pasta but you can't have Nutella at the breakfast table. You can have jam and butter, but you can't have Nutella. To me, it's not going to make any difference if you have some spread on a couple of slices of bread. It's the same for other things. They go crazy because you had 25ml of beer, but you can have the occasional glass of wine with your dinner. Things like that crack me up sometimes, to be honest. That night in the bar, one of the mechanics saw me eating my 'crêpes Nutella' and took a picture on his mobile. He sent it to Boyer and I was in the shit again.

In Ghent–Wevelgem, I was dropped out of the front echelon midway through the race and was left with a group of about eighty guys. Knowing we were just wasting our time in the wind, we all abandoned after about 30km of chasing. Boyer was furious. After the race, on the team bus, he had a real go at me in front of the rest of the team. 'Roche, you're useless. You're five kilos too heavy and you're eating crêpes. You're only here because of your father. You'd be better off giving your place to somebody else.' We had a big argument in front of everybody and didn't speak for ages afterwards.

In May, I came into good form, taking twentieth in the Trophée des Grimpeurs, tenth at Paris–Camembert and coming within 500m of winning a stage of the Four Days of Dunkirk. Boyer was all over me, telling me how good I was and how his reprimand had spurred me into action. My contract was up at the end of the year, and he spoke about my re-signing with the team for 2007. I asked Boyer for an increase for the following year, but even though everybody else was getting one, he refused, telling me I didn't deserve a pay rise. He said that as the Tour de l'Avenir in September was my main target for the season, he would speak to me then.

In June, I went home for the national championships in Westport. Keen to make the most of my good form, I went clear with David McCann, Ciarán Power, Páidí O'Brien, David O'Loughlin and John Dempsey. We were soon joined by my cousin Dan Martin, who was now riding for my old club, VC La Pomme, and it looked as if our breakaway group was going to be the move of the day. But a large group came across to us on the sixth of fourteen laps, and it unravelled everything.

With the group now too big to ride as a cohesive unit, Power and Páidí were the first to jump clear again, and McCann and O'Loughlin soon followed. I tried to get McCann's wheel but missed it by about a metre, and my head went. I cracked. They opened up a good gap and were riding away with the medals. I waited for Dan and the others, as I didn't want to spend the next 60km on my own. I thought that our group might have been able to get back on to the leaders, but we didn't. They were too strong and, once again, I finished just out of the medals in fourth, coming in alone just under three minutes later, while my old VC La Pomme teammate Tim Cassidy beat Dan for fifth.

A few days later, I was fourth overall in Paris–Corrèze in France and Boyer phoned to say he had a new contract ready for me to sign. I asked if I was getting a pay rise, but he said no. I told him I wouldn't be signing if I didn't, and again we agreed to see how I got on at the Tour de l'Avenir that September. I'd just hired an agent to try and get me some rides in the summer critériums, where you earn some extra money in appearance fees, and only two days later, Boyer phoned my new agent and told him, 'Roche has two days to sign, and that's it.' I'd had enough of it by then, and asked the agent to have a look for another team for me.

Once again, Ag2r was interested in signing me, but had to wait a couple of weeks before anything could be decided. In the meantime, I took eighth place in the Poly Normande one-day race at the end of July and went on to the Eneco Tour of Benelux. At the Eneco Tour, my good form had garnered the interest of another French ProTour team, Crédit Agricole, and I was approached during the week-long stage race to sign for them for the next two years.

While debating the move, I spoke to Australian rider Mark Renshaw, who lived in Nice and trained with me at the time. He assured me it was a good set-up, as did another Crédit Agricole pro, Rémi Pauriol, who rode with me at VC La Pomme as an amateur. I already knew some of the riders there, and they seemed to be well organized, had a good team structure and would be in the ProTour in 2007. I decided to go with the only concrete offer I had. Crédit Agricole faxed me a two-year contract during the race and I signed it and sent it back. The next day, Cofidis came to me with a contract, but it was too late. Boyer was fuming again.

The Tour de l'Avenir translates as the 'Tour of the Future'.

An under-twenty-five version of the Tour de France, the ten-day stage race covers much of the same roads and mountains used by the Tour and has come to be known as a breeding ground for future Tour winners. The race has been won by the likes of Greg LeMond, Miguel Indurain and the late Laurent Fignon, all of whom have dominated the Tour de France. Going into the race, Cofidis had three good riders for the General Classification (GC): Amaël Moinard, Maxime Monfort and me. While we were all friends and wouldn't be racing against each other, it was pretty much a case of whoever got the highest placing early on, the rest of the team would ride for him. I had no problems with that, as I didn't expect to win the race outright anyway. My main goal in 2006 was to win a stage of the Tour de l'Avenir and get a high placing overall, maybe finish in the top ten. My form had been pretty decent going into the race, and I knew I had a chance of a stage win if I got a bit of luck.

On the opening day's circuit race in Charleroi, Belgium, Amaël got clear in a group of eleven and ended the stage in third place overall, behind Mickaël Delage of Française des Jeux. He had signalled his intentions early and, with the rest of the team finishing over a minute and a half down, had already become team leader.

The following day, I went clear in a twelve-man breakaway group that took the race by surprise and built up a maximum lead of eight minutes on the peloton at one point during the stage. Soon after we had begun to establish a lead, I had a look around the group to see who I had for company. I noticed that I was one of the better climbers in the move. I knew that if we built up a good lead and stayed away until the end of the stage, it would mean that when we hit the mountains later in the race, the other non-climbers in the group were sure to lose time and it would greatly enhance my chances of taking a high overall placing, maybe even winning l'Avenir outright. Having a rider in the break also meant that Cofidis could play my card up front and relax in the bunch, forcing the three or four teams that had missed the move to chase.

My team couldn't lose either way. If the other teams didn't chase, I would finish the day, at the very worst, in the top twelve overall and had a great chance of winning the stage. If they did catch us, Moinard, Monfort and the rest of my team would have had a handy day in the peloton and could attack towards the end of the stage or simply save their energy for when they needed it most, in the mountains later on in the race. But with our lead increasing to eight minutes over the peloton, Boyer wasn't happy. I was going to be leaving Cofidis at the end of the season and he could see Moinard and Monfort's chances of winning the race disappearing up the road with me. He didn't want me to be the leader of the team for the rest of the race so he ordered my teammates to the front of the peloton to help the chase.

He told me afterwards that he didn't want us to get twenty minutes or something like that, but his excuse didn't make any sense to me. If we had gained twenty minutes, it would have been impossible for anybody in the peloton to make inroads into that, even if we had eight stages left. The race would have been decided between the dozen riders in the break, meaning we would only have to watch eleven guys for the rest of the race. There were three or four other teams in the peloton with nobody in the break, so when Cofidis rode behind me I wasn't too happy, and I certainly wasn't giving up without a fight.

As we crossed a climb after 105km of the 180km stage, I attacked and five of us pulled clear, opening a forty-second gap on the rest of the break with the concerted chase by the peloton – including my own teammates – now bringing them to within four minutes of our lead. By the next climb of Croix-Rouge, our quintet had a two-minute advantage over the peloton, who had reeled in the rest of the break on the climb. I kept attacking, trying to whittle the group down a bit and, for the last 30km, I only had French rider Vincent Jérôme and Edvald Boasson Hagen of the Norwegian national team for company. As Boasson Hagen was still an amateur at the time, he refused to work with us and, with the bunch closing fast, he attacked us with 2km to go. We knew that whoever brought him back would have no legs left for the final kilometre and a half uphill finish into Mont-Saint-Martin. Frustrated, and annoyed at my own team having helped close the gap behind me, I jumped after Boasson Hagen and got to within 200m of him, but it was too late. At the bottom of the climb, the whole peloton swept past us, but Boasson Hagen just hung on for the stage win. I would have got across the gap if it had been a flat finish and was really angry and very tired after having such a hard ride all day.

Stage four was always going to be the first really difficult day, with six mountains to be climbed in 150km. After a very fast start, four guys went away about 10km into proceedings. On the first climb, about 15km in, Spanish rider Iván Melero of Orbea attacked, and I decided to go with him. We both rode hard in the valley and, by the top of the next climb, the

Côte de Manderen, we had made contact with the four leaders. Although I was the best placed rider on General Classification in the group, there was no real reaction from the peloton, as I had started the stage two minutes down and was deemed out of reach of the race lead. Soon we had built up a lead of almost five minutes, making me virtual leader on the road.

Russian Alexander Khatuntsev crashed out of the break on the Côte de Luttange after 65km, and we were down to five riders. I was feeling good on the climbs and, keen to get rid of some dead weight, I attacked with 15km to go and dropped another two riders, leaving three up front. On the final ascent of the Côte de Pierrevillers, with about 6km to go, I put on the pressure and crested the summit first. Estonian Rene Mandri got dropped, so I was left out front with Melero. I felt strong, but I was pretty nervous too. To win a stage of that Tour de l'Avenir had been my main goal of 2006, and this was my best chance yet.

I jumped hard with 800m to go, and Melero counter-attacked me. I gritted my teeth and got his wheel, and had just enough left to come around him in the sprint. I had taken my first professional win for Cofidis. I screamed with delight as I crossed the line, clapping my hands and pumping my fists. Not only had I won a stage of the prestigious Tour de l'Avenir, but I had finished two minutes and twenty-three seconds ahead of the peloton, enough of a gap to see me become race leader.

For the first time as a professional, I made my way to the top step of the podium, where I was presented with, first, the stage winner's prize and then the race leader's yellow jersey, an exact replica of the Tour de France leader's jersey. I even got a cuddly Crédit Lyonnais lion, the same one as the Tour de France leader gets each day. I was beaming. To get my first pro win in any race would have been fantastic, but to get it at such a prestigious race and also to go into the yellow jersey of race leader was really special.

With Moinard now third overall, Cofidis should have been happy, as they now had a couple of cards to play. Personally, I was delighted. I had finally won my first pro race and felt it was an important notch on my belt. It was a big step up, incomparable to amateur racing and training, and it took a lot of pressure off me to prove that I could win when I got the chance.

The following day, in Nancy, I took to the start line feeling like a million dollars. But as the start neared I became increasingly nervous in my new yellow jersey. For the first time as a professional, I wouldn't have to do anything but keep an eye on the dangermen and try to follow them if they attacked. I had moved a few steps up the team ladder, and it would be someone else's turn to get me bottles and pace me back up to the peloton if I had to stop for anything. But I was conscious of not wanting to let anybody down that day. There was no point in everybody working hard for me if I couldn't follow the important wheels at the finish and retain my jersey for another day. It was the first time since turning professional that I had the full backing of the team. Well, almost.

Amaël and Maxime had told me before the start that Boyer had phoned them and warned them not to ride for me at all. They apologized in advance but said that they were told that if they helped me they wouldn't be getting a contract for the following year. In the end, Boasson Hagen took his second stage win of the race, but thanks to some good riding by my other teammates – Tyler Farrar, Damien Monier and Mathieu Heijboer – his four-man group only finished thirty-three seconds clear and didn't affect the over-all standings. We had successfully defended the race lead for another day.

Stage six to La Bresse featured another four climbs along the way and, after about 25km, an eight-man group went clear. They soon opened a five-minute advantage and, with me and my yellow jersey in their slipstream, my Cofidis teammates went to the front to close the gap. Forty kilo-metres later we had brought it down to three minutes and, eventually, on the final climb of the day, we got some help from some of the other teams and the front group was caught 2km from the summit. Here, though, the little Spanish climber Moisés Dueñas from Agritubel jumped clear. As Dueñas danced on the pedals and began to open a gap, I knew my yellow jersey was under threat. Dutchman Robert Gesink also rode away from me, with two more rivals, Belgian duo Tom Stubbe and Serge Pauwels. The Spaniard had started the day just thirty-three seconds behind me, but finished a minute and thirty-three seconds ahead of me on the stage, putting him into my yellow jersey. The other three had also leapfrogged me in the overall standings and, at the finish, I had dropped to fifth place overall.

On the Thursday, another tough mountain stage, I managed to make it across to a twelve-man breakaway group after 30km. Philip Deignan, the only other Irish rider in the race, was also in the move, and was climbing really well. At first, nobody would ride with me in the group, as I was still only a minute behind the race leader, and they expected a backlash from the peloton in response to my attack. After hovering around thirty seconds up the road for what seemed like ages, we began to pull clear on the Côte du Voisinal after 43km, and the gap opened enough that soon I had taken back enough time to become virtual leader on the road again.

I wasn't climbing as well as Philip, though, and on the 25km-long Col de la Vie Neuve Mairie, with 60km to go, Philip went clear, with only Rémi di Gregorio of Française des Jeux able to follow his pace. By the top, our group had blown to bits. I was with four others and had lost a minute and a half, while the peloton was three minutes and ten seconds down but closing. My quartet continued to ride pretty hard, but the two pure climbers just kept edging away.

Philip had missed much of the 2006 season with, first, a broken collarbone and then glandular fever. Two months before the race, he couldn't even do an hour on the bike, and at l'Avenir he was probably only about 60 per cent fit, but his ride that day was sheer class. Even though we were on different teams, he had tried to help me keep my yellow jersey the day before, but hadn't got the legs.

In the final sprint, di Gregorio used his local knowledge to cut the final corner on a tight left-hand bend and got 5m on Philip and took the win. Unfortunately for me, about twenty-five riders caught me on the climb to the finish. I took seventh on the stage, but didn't gain any time in the overall standings, so once again I had ridden very aggressively but had nothing to show but sore legs.

Unlike most stage races, where the final stage is almost a procession to the finish, the 2006 Tour de l'Avenir finished with a seriously tough mountain test from Saint-Nicolas-la-Chapelle to Marcinelle-en-Montagne. On the final 145km stage, we had no fewer than ten mountains to climb, including the Col de la Croix de Fer, the Col des Aravais and the Col des Saisies, all popular climbs of the Tour de France. The first mountain came after just 5km and, straight away, the attacks started, setting the tone for the rest of the stage. Thirty-two riders abandoned the race that day. I finished nineteenth on the stage, but lost six and a half minutes and dropped to tenth overall. I was disappointed, but I couldn't be too hard on myself afterwards. I had gone into the Tour de l'Avenir with the aim of getting a stage win and possibly finishing in the top ten. I had achieved both, and came away from the race satisfied that I had proven to myself and others that I was capable of riding well and winning stages of big events.

The world championships in Salzburg, Austria, followed and I was firmly back in the green jersey of Ireland. It was nineteen years after my dad had won his world title in the same country and, although I was still only twenty-one, and in good enough form to be in with a chance of an under-medal, a new UCI ruling meant that, as I was a member of a ProTour team, I wasn't allowed to ride the under-twenty-three world championships alongside my cousin Dan but would have to line out in the elite race instead.

I lined up alongside Philip and Irish road champion David McCann in my first ever elite worlds, and it was decided that I would try to go clear in an early break in the hope that David could have a go at the end of the race. I got into a twelve-strong group after 44km of the 265km race, and we stayed away for over 160km, but the gradual wearing-down process of the worlds meant that I was so tired afterwards that I ignored my dad's advice about wearing the national jersey and abandoned towards the end. My contract with Cofidis had come to an end, and it was time for a breath of fresh air.

7

In Credit

In 1989, the Carrera professional team signed my uncle, Lawrence Roche, to ride alongside his brother Stephen in the pro peloton. Lawrence was a good amateur rider, with the same riding style as my dad, and Carrera was probably hoping it would unearth another Irish superstar. Lawrence took a few top tens in one-day races, and even went on to ride the Tour de France three years later with the Tonton Tapis team. But he hadn't set the cycling world alight like my dad had and, by 1992, had reverted to amateur status.

The fact that I was Nicolas Roche, son of Stephen Roche, meant that Cofidis was expecting me to be like my dad and to be able to win a lot of the big races straight away as a twenty-year-old. Throughout my career, I've been slowly but consistently improving, and I will be happy enough if I continue to do so every year, but Cofidis had been expecting more. They weren't judging me on a par with any other first-year professional. For them, I was Stephen Roche's son, and I should be winning Paris–Nice and other big races at twenty years of age, like he had done. But Cofidis found out in 2006, as Carrera had found out in 1989, that there's not a Stephen Roche around every corner.

Having spent two years in the professional peloton, I now had even more respect for Dad's achievements. Although he had warned me plenty of times when I was growing up and expressing a desire to turn professional, I now realized how hard life as a professional cyclist was. I knew how many kilometres I had done and how many sacrifices I had made to get to my level. And I knew I was a long way off the highest level. My dad would tell me how many kilometres he did in his day and, at twenty-one, I couldn't even manage to do that many if I tried.

Although I missed out on selection for Paris–Nice, I got my first ride in a ProTour race for Crédit Agricole in 2007 in Tirreno–Adriatico, which was on at the same time in Italy. But that came to an abrupt halt when I crashed out with 50km remaining on the opening stage. As a race motorbike was overtaking the bunch, his pillion box clipped a rider on the side and sent him flying into the rest of us, causing a bowling-ball effect and taking a heap of others down. I ended up sandwiched between two riders, with one underneath me, another guy on top of me, and bits of bikes in between. After the impact, my knee had swollen up so much I couldn't bend it, and I was carted off to hospital with a suspected broken kneecap. I was really disappointed, as I was very motivated to do well and excited to be riding with some of the big names.

At the hospital, a scan revealed no broken bones, and they patched me up and sent me home. When I arrived back at the team hotel, however, the team doctor took the bandages off to have a look at my knee, and it was still bleeding profusely. I needed stitches.

I asked for an anaesthetic but, as he began to take out his equipment, he told me it wasn't worth it as I only needed five stitches! The doctor lifted my leg up on to the bedside locker and brought a lamp over to get a better view of the gash in my knee. While all this was going on, my roommate Yannick Talabardon was looking on. While I lay on my bed, biting my pillow in agony as the doctor proceeded to stitch my knee, Yannick calmly took out his phone and videoed the whole operation. He even gave a running commentary on the procedure, although he had to stop a couple of times when it got a bit too gruesome for him. Although Yannick doesn't ride on the same team as me any more, that video is always the first thing he talks about whenever we meet up.

I'd been hoping to be selected to ride my first three-week Grand Tour in 2007 and was on the long list of twelve riders for the Giro d'Italia. Out of this dozen, Crédit Agricole would pick their nine-man team for the world's second biggest stage race. I was feeling strong, and had a great run of form over the next week or so, taking ninth in Paris–Camembert, then sixth in the GP Denain two days later. Two days after that, I took thirteenth in the Tour du Finistère and topped it off with ninth in the bunch sprint that ended the Tro-Bro Léon the following day. Those four one-day races were part of the 1.1-ranked French Cup series and, despite missing several events in the series, I had moved up to twelfth overall and fifth in the young-rider ranking. Those results also secured my place on the Crédit Agricole team for the Giro.

On the Thursday evening before the Tour of Italy, I rode

behind a motorbike for an hour and a half to mimic race pace and get a bit of speed in my legs. I'd already done two and a half hours that morning and felt really strong on my final hard spin before the Giro. But then my mind started to play tricks on me. In the middle of thoughts such as, If I keep going like this for three weeks I'll have no problem, came thoughts such as, What if my good legs are already gone? and, Will I be able to get up the Monte Zoncolan climb? I had read that Italian rider and pre-race favourite Danilo di Luca was going to be using a 39x26 gearing on the biggest mountain of the race. If he needed that type of gearing on the climb, I'd need a bloody ladder!

As I packed my suitcase on the Wednesday before the Giro for my flight to Paris and on to Sardinia, I realized that I didn't even know what I would need to bring on a three-week tour. Okay, my iPod, mobile phone and laptop were certainties – I'm a bit of a gadget freak – but how many shorts, leg warmers, arm warmers, jerseys (short and long sleeves) would I need for three weeks? I had to phone some of the other guys on the team to find out.

Any time I mentioned that I was riding the Giro, somebody reminded me that it had been twenty years since my dad's victory in the race, so there was a bit of pressure on me going into it. But I was also putting a bit of pressure on myself. At twenty-two, I was never going to win the Giro, or anything like that, but I'd been looking forward to riding a three-week stage race since I turned pro and wanted to prove I could ride a good race.

But I hadn't a clue what to expect. I'd never ridden anything longer than the ten-day Tour de l'Avenir. I didn't know if I would get stronger or weaker – which was more likely –

as the race went on. My Crédit Agricole team for the Giro was made up of four guys to look after Norwegian Thor Hushovd in the sprints, and we had Patrice Halgand and Pietro Caucchioli for the overall. I hadn't been told what my role would be, but I had been warned that the team expected me to finish.

Before the start, a lot of people told me to calm down a bit and not to be as aggressive as usual. I'd shown in earlier races that I was capable of riding in a breakaway for 200km, but everyone knew I couldn't do that every day for three weeks. 'This is the Giro,' they told me. 'It's three weeks long. Pick your moments. Keep something in reserve.' I wanted to try and get up the road at least one day, but I knew I'd have to do it carefully. I couldn't afford to spend all day attacking one day and then have to ride a tough mountain stage the next. If I did, it would be extremely hard to recover and I might be in danger of not finishing the race.

Before the Giro, I had been approached by a national newspaper in Ireland, the *Irish Daily Star*, to keep a diary for their readers. Mark Scanlon had kept one during the 2005 Tour de France, and it had gone down very well with the readers. Since my dad and Sean Kelly had retired in the nineties, cycling hadn't got a lot of publicity in Ireland, and it was getting harder to attract young people into the sport, so I was happy to do it. It was the start of something that I have kept doing to this day, and I hope it gives some insight into the life of a professional cyclist.

8

Giro d'Italia 2007

Stage 1 – Saturday 12 May: Team Time Trial, Caprera–La Maddalena, 25.6km

Welcome to Caprera – Stress City. I don't normally get nerves, but before the start this evening I thought I was going to spontaneously combust! The reconnaissance of the team time-trial course didn't help much, as it felt pretty dangerous when we practised over it.

The actual race itself was a lot better. Now that it's over, I feel relieved. Beforehand, we thought a top-ten finish would be good for my Crédit Agricole team. We finished eighth. The stage went okay for me. The time stops on the fifth rider across the line, so you can afford to lose somebody along the way. I just hoped I wouldn't be one of them. Actually, I was pretty strong, and we finished with six out of our eight riders together. Some teams only got five.

Stage 2 – Sunday 13 May: Tempio Pausania–Bosa, 205km

Today was very hot. It was 38 degrees at one stage. It

was so hot that everyone on the team took turns going back to the team car for bottles. I went back twice, so I guess we drank a lot. The stage itself was a lot hillier than I expected, and the final climb with about 8km to go caught a lot of people out – me included. Up until then, I tried to stay near the front, in the third or fourth row.

This tactic worked fine until the final ascent, where both the pace and my heart rate went through the roof. I found myself drifting down the field, but was still in the front group on the descent. Then somebody let a wheel go and that was it, game over. I rolled in with a group of about fifteen guys and we lost around a minute and a half. As I have no intentions of winning the Giro, that didn't worry me. In fact, by finishing in this group I missed a crash with a kilometre to go that brought down about ten guys and saw the front portion of the bunch ride away to contest the sprint. It's an ill wind . . .

Tonight we are changing hotels and moving down the south of the island. I can't wait! We had no phone, no internet, nothing for the past three days. I don't know what's been going on in the outside world. It was like being in an episode of *Lost*. Hopefully, we can get back to civilization tonight.

Stage 3 – Monday 14 May: Barumini–Cagliari, 181km

The heat over the past few days has been killing me, and my feet especially have been getting a good toasting. I'm like a poor man's Michael Flatley. I have feet of flames, but it's not from dancing. The trouble with hot feet is that they swell up inside your shoes. Some people pour water on them, but if you do that, you can get corns and calluses. Last night I made an attempt to drill the soles of my racing shoes to let more air in, but I still got blisters today.

The first part of today's stage was pretty calm. The peloton let a group away early on and then just rode tempo for most of the day. Then, with about 50km to go, the rest of the race realized that the breakaway group was really strong and might steal the stage win. The bunch got all excited and began to put the hammer down to reel the leaders in.

The peloton's reaction happened to coincide with some really lumpy, hilly roads, and at one point I didn't feel too good at all. Once we got over that part of the stage, I started to feel a bit better and moved up to help our Crédit Agricole sprinters, Julian Dean and Thor Hushovd.

With 2km to go, I was in a good position, about fifteen or twenty from the front. I was on the wheel of our four sprinters, who were getting ready to lead out Hushovd. I wasn't much good behind them, so I moved out a bit and went to lead the four guys out. A heave in the bunch saw them move to the other side, so I thought if I went to the front they would be able to follow me, but they didn't. As we passed under the 1km kite, I turned round and saw that I had a little gap.

I was off the front with about 900m to go. Jesus, I could win the stage! I put my head down, gritted my teeth and ignored the pain. I was flying along the tarmac. Everything looked good until we hit a section of marble cobbles with about 500m to go. If you were riding to the shop, you wouldn't even notice them, but when you're on your absolute limit, any little thing can affect you. It was like I'd just hit a wall. Each bump and jolt drained the power out of my legs, and I drifted backwards as the sprinters surged for the line. Unfortunately for my team, Thor crashed in the gallop too.

Tomorrow, we have a rest day. Normally, rest days come at the end of the first and second weeks of a big tour, but the transfer to the mainland means that, tomorrow morning, we will board a plane and head to Italy. It doesn't mean we can lie around all day, though. We will arrive at our hotel about 3 p.m., get something to eat and go training. Because it's late in the afternoon, we will probably only do an hour or two before dinner and a massage. Then it's time to put the feet up and apply the blister cream before stage four!

Stage 4 – Wednesday 16 May: Salerno–Montevergine di Mercogliano, 153km

I knew I should have kept my mouth shut about the heat. Today it rained. At first it was refreshing, but then the road surface turned treacherous and guys started hitting the deck like it was going out of fashion.

Today I witnessed the biggest crash I have ever seen in a race. Going through a small town, the road surface was like a wet bar of soap. The whole peloton took it really gingerly and slowed down to a crawl. Suddenly, pink jersey Enrico Gasparotto's wheel went from under him, and he brought down world champion Paolo Bettini. Everything seemed like it was in slow motion, as the rest of the peloton slid into the back of each other and spread across the whole road. It was like we were riding on a big, wet tablecloth and a giant hand came and jerked it from under us. A cycling version of *Dancing on Ice*. Only the guys in front of Gasparotto escaped but, to be fair, they realized the scale of the devastation behind and sat up and waited for everyone to regain contact.

Today was the first mountain-top finish, but I didn't get the chance to see if I would get up the climb with the leaders as I crashed with Eddy Merckx's son Axel and a few others with 25km to go. After getting a new wheel from the team mechanic, I was sprinting back to the peloton while also looking down at my bike to check everything was working. The guy in front of me slammed on suddenly and I hit the ejector seat again. After a few seconds of ground, sky, ground, I ended up with a sore elbow and a bruised ego.

After a fruitless chase to regain contact with the leaders, I ended up in a group of over fifty riders and finished fourteen minutes down. Bring back the sunshine!

Stage 5 – Thursday 17 May: Teano–Frascati, 173km

Today is like St Patrick's day in Norway, or at least that's what my teammate Thor Hushovd told me this morning as he explained why he was wearing a pair of socks with the Norwegian flag on them instead of our team-issue Crédit Agricole ones.

Thor was pretty motivated for the win today, as it looked like it could come down to a bunch sprint. My job is to keep him out of the wind all day. In the final 10km or so, if he drifts back, I have to go back and get him, keeping him sheltered in my slipstream so he doesn't use up any more energy than he has to before the final sprint.

It was pretty stressful for myself, Angelo Furlan, Julian Dean and Laszlo Bodrogi, as everyone was pushing and shoving for position, but it's all good experience, and I'm enjoying the responsibility of having a job to do.

I deposited Thor behind Julian and Angelo with about 1,200m to go. Angelo led out the sprint, and it looked like Thor had the stage won, until Robert Förster of Gerolsteiner saw a bit of daylight in between him and stage-three winner Petacchi and dived into the gap for the win, with Thor second. The twisting finish didn't help us, but there are plenty more chances to get it right and, hopefully, Thor can win a stage.

Stage 6 – Friday 18 May: Tivoli–Spoleto, 177km

When a fellow cyclist asks about your health, the question always centres on two things: your legs. A seasoned rider will know what sort of day he is going to have almost as soon as he stands up in the morning. Nerves can make your legs tingle slightly, maybe go a bit wobbly, but they vanish once the race begins. Lactic acid comes from riding above your threshold. It burns, but after years of training and racing, you ignore the pain; you know it's good pain. Cramps can stop you in your tracks, force you to stretch and shake out your calves and thighs. Pain comes in varying degrees, from the short, sharp bursts of a sprint to the stinging of cold, hard hailstones hopping off your thighs. Most of these sensations you can ignore, and some of them are even a good sign, but if you find, as I did today, that you can't feel anything, then you're in trouble.

I was fine for about 30km. Then I went and attacked twice. For some reason, I never recovered from those efforts and, as the day went by, I had what the French call *un jour sans*, 'a day without'. I could feel nothing in my legs. It was as if they were hollow. I had been getting dropped on the climbs and having to ride hard on the descents to make contact. This pattern repeated itself throughout the stage until the final mountain, where I found myself in a group of sprinters who'd been dropped by the peloton. What really demoralized me was that these guys, sprinters like McEwan and Petacchi, who normally can't climb out of bed, were riding away from me. I was fighting to stay in contact. I can't explain why it happened, but I hope I recover tonight. Tomorrow's stage is a mammoth 254km (158 miles), the longest stage of this year's Giro and the longest I will have raced so far in my career.

Stage 7 – Saturday 19 May: Spoleto–Scarperia, 254km

Six hours and seventeen minutes. That's how long I was

in the saddle for today, and I'm exhausted. I racked my brains to see what could have caused yesterday's demoralizing ride. Having had problems with my feet earlier in the week, yesterday I changed back to my old insoles, which are a little bit thinner. I also had a new saddle, having ruined my old one in a crash. With the saddle slightly higher, due to it not being worn in yet, and my insoles slightly thinner, it made my pedal stroke a few millimetres longer, so I lowered it by 2mm this morning before the start. It doesn't sound much, but sometimes even the slightest change to your set-up can cause problems.

Happily, it seemed to do the trick, and I felt much better today. Our orders were to stay in the bunch and work for Thor. Once there is a chance of a bunch sprint finish, we all look after our sprinter, get him bottles, keep him out of the wind and help him over the climbs. There was only one big climb today, with 50km to go. I was riding in the middle of the bunch when the Quickstep team put the hammer down at the front in an effort to shed a few top-heavy sprinters, leaving their man Paolo Bettini fastest of the rest. They did a good job, and soon most of the gallopers were dropped, including Thor. I drifted back for him and nursed him over the climb. Near the top, my team-mates Christophe Kern and Angelo Furlan joined the effort to get Thor back in contention. What we weren't counting on was Thor leaving us behind as he descended like a stone off the mountain.

At the bottom, he was in the second group, while we were in the third. The two groups merged, and our manager radioed Laszlo Bodrogi out of the front group to wait for Thor, and the four of us rode eyeballs out for 20km to regain contact with the leaders. We got on with 20km to go, and I brought Thor up to the front before drifting down the bunch – job done. I sat up with 3km to go and coasted in while Thor got second on the stage behind Petacchi.

It's better for me to do my job today and then try to recover and do it again tomorrow than try to get maybe twentieth on the stage and be tired all day tomorrow. That's no good to the team. At the moment, I'm wrecked, but happy that today went well. Patrice Halgand has gone home with a broken collar bone, so tonight I am sharing a rustic hotel room with our New Zealand champion Julian Dean. I usually have trouble sleeping on stage races, but this Giro has seen me conk out every night. As I listen to my soothing *Gardens of Ireland* CD, Julian tells me he snores. It's 9.40 p.m. The fake chandelier on the ceiling is getting blurred. I doubt I'll hear him.

Stage 8 – Sunday 20 May: Barberino di Mugello– Fiorano Modenese, 200km

I got dropped with 2km to go on the first big mountain today, halfway through the stage, but I wasn't too far off the back at the top, and thought I would get back on the descent. Instead, the group rode away from me and even guys that were behind me flew past on the way down. At the bottom, I was alone.

Eventually, a group of about a dozen sprinters, including Robbie McEwan and Max van Heeswijk, rode up to me, and I got in with them. Up front, we had a worst-case scenario unfolding for our group. Sometimes, with a break up the road, the peloton just settles down into a rhythm and there's a good chance you'll get back on if you're in a big group behind. Today, though, a large group of twenty-two riders, including world champion Paolo Bettini and some of the favourites, got up the road and built up a gap of over seven minutes.

When Marco Pinotti and his T-Mobile team realized they could lose the pink jersey, they went to the front with the Saunier Duval team and tore after the leaders. With anyone outside a certain percentage of the winner's time taken out of the race, for us, the faster they rode, the faster we had to ride, or we would be outside the time limit and eliminated. We were like a donkey chasing another donkey chasing a carrot. And whoever was holding the carrot must have been on a motorbike! All my group rode together to the finish. It was like a 120km time trial, but we made it.

Tomorrow shouldn't be too bad, but the following day has a lot of climbs, and the next day, to Briançon, will be hard. The problem is, we don't have another rest day until Monday week, and I don't seem to have any power any more. To have two bad days in a week is not good. I can't explain it. I'm really disappointed in my form, but at least it can't get much worse!

Stage 9 – Monday 21 May: Reggio nell'Emilia–Lido di Camaiore, 177km

Today we had the first 'piano' of the Giro. The peloton

took it easy for once. Nobody really said anything, but when you see all the top guys chatting at the front, riding the full width of the road, you don't attack. In Italy, they call it riding 'piano'. We had a piano for a couple of hours after the start and, while I'm more of a U2 fan, I was more than happy to play that tune!

I just sat in the bunch and tried to save energy. I didn't actually have much to do until the last 30km, where we kept our sprinter Thor in contention over the only real climb of the day. I then brought him up to the front with 3km to go. The finish was very twisty and dangerous, with a lot of cars and stuff on the side of the road. Julian and Angelo led Thor out, but they went a bit early into a headwind. But they seemed happy to have some practice for the Tour de France. I just coasted in, finishing thirty-sixth.

Stage 10 – Tuesday 22 May: Lido di Camaiore–Santuario Nostra Signora della Guardia, 250km

Today was one of the days I feared most. The first two climbs weren't too bad, and I got over them okay, but on the third one, the Passo del Biscia, I thought it was all over for me. I was very far back on the ascent, and on the descent a group of guys let the wheel go on a dangerous corner and I was left in no-man's-land. I eventually caught the group ahead of me, and the next climb was a bit better.

The past few days, I have been asking myself whether I had come into form too early, or if I should have been in better form before the Giro but, to be honest, I think it's just the heat that's doing a lot of damage. Today I drank between ten and fifteen bottles. With about an hour and a half left, our manager drove alongside and gave me a can of Coke. To some teams, this is not a big thing, but at Crédit Agricole and a lot of other teams it's a big deal, because we're not allowed to drink Coke. If you have a can, everyone is your friend. Some guys will even try to buy it off you, but the ethical thing to do is take a few big swigs and then share it around. Next time, you could be the guy asking for the drink.

On the 17km final climb to the mountain-top finish, my legs were feeling sore, but I'm happy that at least they were feeling something, which is a good sign. I stayed with the group until 5km to go and then just rode at my own rhythm and finished five or six minutes ahead of the sprinters' gruppetto.

Stage 11 – Wednesday 23 May: Serravalle Scrivia–Pinerolo, 198km

Today was another flat day. I just tried to use the early part of the stage to rest and recover. There was only one escapee, Cofidis rider Mikaël Buffaz. One rider alone against the whole peloton doesn't stand a chance, especially when he's been out there all day, as Buffaz had. It was always going to be a bunch sprint finish and, after I helped Thor into position, I decided to keep riding hard and got twenty-fourth on the stage. The only problem with that was that my bike probably made it into the top twenty, as we crossed the line separately. A combination of wet roads and fresh paint saw half the bunch fall just before the line. I never touched the brakes. My front wheel just went from under me, and I crossed the line on my arse – another first for me! The only thing about falling in the wet is that you tend to slide, rather than come to a grinding halt, and I ended up with just a few bruises and a sore hip.

Stage 12 – Thursday 24 May: Scalenghe–Briançon (Francia), 163km

Last night, my dad arrived at the Giro. It was great to see him, and today he travelled in the team car for the whole stage. With two big mountains, one of them the highest of the whole Giro, the Colle d'Angelo, en route to Briançon, I was under a bit of pressure to do a good ride. My teammate Christophe Kern didn't make it any easier when a French TV crew arrived to film a short documentary about my dad and me. He kept reminding me the whole of France would see me if I got dropped.

Today turned out all right. I was up near the front for most of the first mountain, giving myself some room to drift down the bunch if I started to falter. Halfway up, I started going backwards and rode a lot of the climb at my own tempo as riders passed me or I passed them on the way up. I got into a group of about twenty, including Axel Merckx and Rinaldo Nocentini, on the descent, and we rode the Col d'Izoard together. We just rode steady up it, and then steady again on the descent. There was no panic to stay inside the time limit today, so it wasn't too bad, and we finished twenty-two minutes behind stage winner Danilo di Luca. At least today, when I got dropped, my legs were hurting me. I'm feeling a bit more like my old self now, and hopefully things will stay like that until Sunday week in Milan. Dad had to rush for the train back to Paris after the stage, but he was pretty pleased with me and it was great for my morale to see him.

I'm sharing with Christophe tonight as Julian is sick. He's been coughing, spluttering and complaining of a sore throat. Thor abandoned today, so Julian is quarantined in a room of his own. At least I won't have to listen to his snoring any more!

Stage 13 – Friday 25 May: Mountain Time Trial, Biella–Santuario di Oropa, 12.6km

I was in two minds today whether to ride the mountain time trial hard or use it as an easier day. In the end, I didn't have much choice. We arrived too late to reconnoitre the course, and I even had to rush to get ready to make my start time. I was fuming! Normally, we arrive at the stage starts too early. I usually like time trials and, although I wasn't going to win or anything, I wanted to see what sort of time I could post. During the stage, I found myself distracted and, while I rode hard, I didn't ride fast, and a stronger rider could have unleashed a lot of power on the flatter part at the bottom. I've two weeks behind me now, and tomorrow is another hard day. As Taoiseach Bertie Ahern might say, I've a lot done, but a lot more to do!

Stage 14 – Saturday 26 May:
Cantù–Bergamo, 192km

Today, the race started as if everyone's shorts were on fire! We were full pelt from the off. With the climb of Passo di San Marco at 112km, followed by the smaller but equally tough La Trinità-Dossena 40km later, a lot of guys were scared of the stage and wanted to get ahead before the climbs to give themselves some sliding room.

I was worried about the fast start, but when we hit the climbs the race exploded. The big hitters absolutely tore the legs off each other, but it actually worked out better for me. With the top guys battling it out for honours, the rest of the peloton were content to simply let them at it and rode the rest of the stage at a good tempo into Bergamo.

I was climbing pretty well and wasn't really in trouble all day, but tomorrow is going to be tough.

Stage 15 – Sunday 27 May:
Trento–Tre Cime di Lavaredo, 184km

In every major tour, you have a group of dropped riders, mainly top-heavy sprinters who can't climb with the best and form a large group at the back of the race, working collectively to ensure everyone gets inside the time limit and can start the next stage. There is always a leader in this 'gruppetto' and on this Giro it's Alessandro Petacchi. The Milram sprinter has already won three stages and wants to get to Milan on Sunday to win the final leg.

Halfway up a climb, Petacchi will shout, 'Gruppetto!'

and anyone within earshot can halt their suffering momentarily and ride steadily up the mountains, safe in the knowledge they will have some company for the rest of the stage. The problem with Petacchi is that he can hang on until well up the climbs before he calls for the gruppetto. If you get dropped before him, tough shit, you're on your own.

As I put on my rain cape this morning, I was dreading the day ahead. Three mountain passes, 184km, and finishing on the wall-like Tre Cime di Lavaredo isn't exactly my idea of fun. That's why I put in a lot of early attacks this morning to try and make it in the lucky break that would see me over the first couple of climbs ahead of the peloton.

I got a bit too excited, though, and when I didn't make it across to the group of twenty that finally got away, I suddenly realized that I had wasted an awful lot of energy and may just have bought my ticket home!

I got halfway through the second climb with the main group before my legs screamed at me to let the wheel in front of me drift into the distance.

There were about a dozen guys around me. Petacchi had been long dropped, and my guys rode together until the end. On the last climb, we all just rode as best we could, and our aim was simply to survive the stage. The last 3km were a nightmare, and I finished thirty-six minutes behind the stage winner Riccardo Ricco.

Monday 28 May: Rest Day

No race today, but we still had to train for an hour and a half this morning. Usually, we have a bit of a laugh on the rest day, but things have been pretty sombre in the Crédit Agricole camp lately. We have only six guys left from nine starters and, with another tough stage tomorrow, nobody is in the mood for jokes.

Stage 16 – Tuesday 29 May: Agordo (Dolomiti Stars)–Lienz (Austria), 189km

It was a cold six degrees as we left the stage start this morning. Everyone put on an extra layer and expected it to warm up once we hit the climbs later on. But it didn't. Instead, it started snowing and, at the top of the first mountain, the temperature was down to zero. The stage was on the verge of being cancelled, but the organizers decided there wasn't enough snow, so we soldiered on. I had a pair of winter gloves in my back pocket, but my arms were frozen, so I couldn't reach for them to put them on. Somebody reached into Tinkoff rider Pavel Brutt's jersey pocket, took out a sandwich and proceeded to feed him as he rode along-side shivering. Pavel's hands were so cold he couldn't move his arms! I punctured on the descent, and the sweat I had expended on the way up turned to ice on the way down. I just regained contact with the back of the bunch when we went into a tunnel and everyone slammed on the brakes and stopped.

The conditions were so bad everyone had decided to stop and change into winter clothing. There was a rush for the team cars as everyone tried to get warm. Team mechanics had to strip and dress me, as my hands were numb. Others pissed on their hands to heat them. Ten minutes later, dressed in a new long-sleeved jersey, leg warmers, long-sleeved rain jacket and short-sleeved rain jacket, I set off again.

It didn't warm up until about 50km to go and, as we had some climbing to do, I took my jackets off. I had one leg warmer off when we turned on to the first climb and had to ride up it looking like a gobshite with one bare leg! The peloton was happy enough to ride the rest of the stage at a steady tempo, and we all finished eight minutes down on a non-threatening breakaway group.

Stage 17 – Wednesday 30 May: Lienz (Austria)–Monte Zoncolan, 142km

Today was one of the days I feared most on this Giro. We would finish atop what is regarded as the 'toughest climb in cycling', Monte Zoncolan. Most of the talk at the stage start centred on gear ratios and who was riding what. The fewer teeth on your front chainring and the more teeth a cog at the back has, the easier it is to spin. Normally, a lowest gear of 39 front and 23 back would see you over most climbs. Today I used a 'granny gear' of 34x27 on Zoncolan. If you tried to pedal that on a flat road, your legs would spin round as if your chain was off, and you wouldn't get too far.

I tried to slip away in a group early on, to get a head start on the mountain, but having attacked twice I didn't have the legs to get into the move that stayed. Straight away, the Liquigas and Saunier Duval squads set a hot tempo at the front of the peloton. On the climb before Zoncolan, they upped the pace again and the bunch fractured. I punctured on the descent and, as

I went down solo, I was worried about finishing inside the time limit, which would be 20 per cent of the winner's time. My manager reassured me as he drove past, but it still took me a while to get back into a group.

Monte Zoncolan was really steep. For the last 4km, the gradient was 18 per cent. No team cars were allowed up, for fear they might conk out in the middle of the riders. It's the kind of climb where you have to lean your whole body weight over the bike to try and keep moving. If, like me, you were unlucky enough to be climbing alongside an Italian, you hadn't much hope of a push, as the fans fell over themselves to push their compatriots.

I struggled upwards until, suddenly, an Irish fan came alongside and gave me a huge shove. He ran gasping beside me for five or ten yards: 'Well done, Rochey. You're having a great Giro. Keep it going! Good man! Keep it going!' It was nice to hear the encouragement. The other day, a few guys had a big tricolour on one of the mountains. You can always recognize the accent, even if you don't see them, and it's nice to have the support.

Zoncolan's gradient was so severe, no one had any choice but to ride it at their own pace. Still, once it was over, it didn't seem as bad as it was hyped up to be.

Stage 18 – Thursday 31 May:
Udine–Riese Pio X, 203km

With the race almost over, I've been feeling a bit more confident of finishing this Giro. The last few stages, I've tried to get away in a move, but I've been unlucky. I always seem to go too early or miss the one that gets away.

Today was pan flat, and triple stage winner Alessandro Petacchi and his four remaining Milram teammates were hoping for another bunch sprint. The problem with that was they weren't willing to give us Crédit Agricole riders any leeway at the start of the stage, because we had one of the only other sprinters left in the race in Julian Dean. If one of us got into the break, then that would be one less team to help Milram chase later on. I tried a few times to escape this morning, but was marked closely by Petacchi's men.

Ironically, I still got my best stage placing so far. Having helped reel in the break towards the end, I had been given orders to try and jump away with about 500m to go, as there were two corners before the finish. Two Ag2r guys had the same idea, but took the first corner too fast and hit the barriers. I was on the inside, out of the way, and although someone else fell near me, I continued sprinting and took my best Giro result, crossing the line thirteenth, behind stage winner Petacchi. I have been given a bit of freedom now, and hope to try and get up the road tomorrow, but it's just pot luck really.

Stage 19 – Friday 1 June: Treviso–Comano Terme, 179km

It pissed rain at the start this morning and, to add to my woes, the pace was absolutely frantic for a good hour and a half after the start. I was suffering like hell.

Every time we went around a corner I got dropped and had to fight to get back on.

As the break went clear, my team manager was shouting in my earpiece at me to attack. But I was still struggling down the back and was doing all I could just to stay in contact with the peloton. Some hard chasing took place, and after two hours we had done 90km and the race was all together again.

Over the next two first-category mountains, the race sorted itself out, and those who had the legs kept racing, while the rest of us, a big eighty-strong group, just paced ourselves to the finish, losing twenty-three minutes by the end.

Stage 20 – Saturday 2 June: Individual Time Trial, Bardolino–Verona, 43km

Even though I rode today's final time trial pretty hard, I still lost six minutes to the winner Paolo Savoldelli. Not that it really matters at this point, with only one day to go.

After the finish, I waited for my roommate Christophe Kern, and we rode back to the hotel together. On the way, we passed a McDonald's and decided to go in. We drew some strange looks as we parked our bikes outside and – in our full time-trial regalia – walked in and ordered a McFlurry each. With only the final stage to Milan ahead of us, we celebrated the end of the Giro by eating the ice cream outside on a bench.

Stage 21 – Sunday 3 June:
Vestone–Milan, 185km

Today, as the classification leaders in their pink, white and magenta jerseys drank champagne at the front of the peloton before the start, I just wanted them to hurry up and get it over with.

It took almost five and a half hours before we rolled over the finish line in Milan.

Straight after the finish, Dad rang and congratulated me on finishing my first Grand Tour and asked me how I felt. I finished 123rd, completing the three-week race three hours and eight minutes slower than winner Danilo di Luca. If you looked at my face ten minutes after the finish, you probably wouldn't notice much. On the outside, I look like I've spent a few days at the beach, but on the inside, I'm empty. While I'm not in any pain, I feel absolutely drained of all energy – hollow.

Looking back, I didn't know what to expect coming into this Giro, and I was unlucky enough to be part of the most aggressive Giro in years. Every attack I made was like buying a lottery ticket, and only a handful of riders were lucky enough to get into one of the three big moves that stayed away to the line.

I've learned a lot in this Giro. On the downside, my climbing is something I will have to work on, and my descending wasn't up to scratch either. As we hurtled down the mountains, I found myself focussing on all the wrong things, thinking I was going to hit the deck on almost every corner, especially if it rained. I crashed three times, all due to treacherous road conditions, and

I never hit the brakes for any of them. I crossed the line on my bum once for my second highest stage placing of the race. On the upside, I gained a lot of experience in how to set up the sprint for our galloping Norwegian Thor and Kiwi sprinter Julian, and maybe I can develop into a top lead-out man some day.

9

Florian

After the Giro, I went home to ride the national championships again. I won the time-trial title in Dungarvan ahead of renowned time triallists and former champions David McCann and David O'Loughlin and was over the moon.

I was really strong in the road race but totally miscalculated my effort in Waterford. One of the strongest in the race, not for the first time, I let my legs rule my head. Frustrated that the large front group I was in wasn't riding hard enough, I attacked them midway through the 170km race and went clear on my own. I opened a gap of two minutes on the rest of the break and stupidly spent 45km out in front riding into the wind, while the rest of the break shared the work behind me. Four of them – O'Loughlin, Mark Cassidy and Páidí O'Brien of Sean Kelly's Murphy & Gunn pro team, and local amateur Rory Wyley – finally caught me with about 40km to go. We continued to ride hard, and the title race came down to a sprint between the five of us. But as O'Loughlin sailed to his third championship, I paid for my earlier effort and finished fourth for the second consecutive year.

For the whole season, I had been riding very aggressively, attacking all the time and getting clear in breakaways, but it wasn't paying off. I knew I had to start wising up a bit if I was to win races.

After the national championships, I took three days off the bike. I'm always afraid to do this, because I'm afraid of losing whatever form I have, but this time I was very tired after the Giro and needed a break, probably mentally as much as physically. It was the first time I had taken two days off in a row since turning pro, but I told myself it would do me good.

My aim was to be in top form for the new professional Tour of Ireland at the end of August. Although my Crédit Agricole team wasn't going to be riding the race, I was released to ride on the Irish national team and I wanted to perform well in the five-day race. I was really excited about riding a top professional stage race in my own country, and I couldn't wait for it to start.

Unfortunately, though, things didn't go to plan. I picked up a bad saddle sore from the stitching in my team shorts at the Tour de l'Ain, but rather than treating it and resting for a day or two, I continued to train and did a few spins in the rain before the Tour of Ireland, which only aggravated it more. It got badly infected and was even worse when I arrived in Ireland.

Because I had never ridden the amateur Rás Tailteann, riding the Tour of Ireland was a big thing for me, and I tried everything to ride. If it had been any other race, I wouldn't even have gone to the start, but the Tour of Ireland was really important for me. I had been picked as leader for the Irish national team in my national tour. My dad and my brothers

Alexis and Florian had flown over to Ireland to watch me race. My cousin Dan was making his debut as a *stagiaire* in Ireland with Team Slipstream, and the rest of my dad's family and friends from Ireland were all there to cheer us on.

Although I had been off the bike for four days before the race itself, the saddle sore was living up to its name and I couldn't even train with it. I stayed in bed for two days in the hotel before the race, and the day of the race I just said I'd chance it. But at the start of the first stage, amidst all the glamour and colour of the race, I was worried. Instead of thinking about how I could win the stage, I was worried about just finishing.

Soon after the start, I actually got into a breakaway group with seven or eight riders. But once we got caught and I was back in the bunch again, I had nothing to distract me from the pain. I started thinking about it again and, in the end, it got too much and I abandoned the race after about 78km. I was gutted.

Despite leaving the tour, I stayed in Ireland for a few days, as Florian and Alexis were still on the race with my dad, and Christel, who was living in Dublin with my Nana, was there too. Florian wasn't feeling very well that week. He had a headache, a sore throat and had been coughing and complaining of being really, really tired. We thought he had a cold or the flu and just put it down to the travelling from France and then travelling with the race every day.

When we got back to Antibes, I went to the hospital and was treated for my saddle sore. It took two visits to have the wound cleaned up and, after about a week, the blood tests were coming back clear and I returned to training, if somewhat gingerly.

Meanwhile, though, Florian was still sick. My mother noticed how pale and skinny he looked and brought him to the doctor's. The pain in his head at first made her think he might have meningitis, but then he started vomiting every time he ate something. The doctor told her he had a fever and, if it continued, to come back the next day. Florian went home and vomited all night. The next morning Mum brought him back to the hospital and he got further exams done, and blood tests.

On 2 September 2007, I was on a boat off the coast of Nice with my dad and some friends. After a while, we noticed that we both had five or six missed calls from Mum. Dad phoned her back, and I saw the colour drain from his face as he spoke to her. I instinctively knew something was wrong.

Mum was crying hysterically into the phone. 'Florian has . . . got cancer . . . and he's . . . going to die.'

She was in shock and could hardly speak. Florian's blood tests at the hospital had come back, and the results were horrifying. He had been diagnosed with stage three leukaemia. His white blood cells were 98 per cent blast (immature cells found in bone marrow), a rate so high that his blood almost wasn't red any more. At just seven years of age, Florian was given a 20 per cent chance of surviving.

As Dad relayed the details to me while he ordered a taxi to the hospital, I felt as if I was having a heart attack. I didn't know what was going on. How could Florian have cancer? He was only seven. Surely they'd made a mistake? The next hour or so is still a bit of a blur, but I know that I drove to the hospital, where we all met up in the paediatrics department.

The first person we saw was Mum. Still in severe shock,

she was crying and wailing out loud, 'He's going to die, he's going to die.' While my mother was in tears and shaking, my dad and I had a different reaction. We were shocked into a sort of stunned silence. I didn't know what to feel. I was sort of emotionless. Numb. Florian was lying on a trolley as they were doing tests. He was very lethargic and pale. I'm not sure if he knew what was going on. He was probably scared to see everyone crying but, if he was, he didn't have the energy to do anything about it. At last the doctor came in and herded us into his office, trying to calm Mum down. He closed the door behind us and tried to explain what was happening. He told us Florian was going to be transferred by ambulance to a bigger hospital in Nice. Immediately, I wanted to know what we could do to make him live.

Mum would later be told that if she hadn't brought him to the hospital that weekend, Florian might not have made it to the Monday. As Dad now lived in Paris, I had bought an apartment down the road in Cannes and Christel was studying in Canada, Mum had just sold her house and moved into a new apartment in Antibes with Florian and Alexis. From that day on, though, she lived at the hospital. For eight months, she never left Florian's side. As my apartment wasn't ready, I moved into Mum's and looked after Alexis, who was nine at the time, while Mum stayed at the hospital.

Initially, Florian's treatment looked like it was working, but after a slight improvement his leukaemia was so out of control that the normal treatment just wasn't making any difference. The hospital in Nice contacted a cancer advisory board in Brussels and got approval for an experimental drug, if Mum and Dad agreed to it.

Luckily, the trial drug began to work and, alongside the

drug, the doctors started to speak about Florian getting a bone-marrow transplant. Christel, Alexis and I all got a blood test to see if our bone marrow matched Florian's, but the only one that did was Alexis's.

For weeks before the transplant, Mum stayed with Florian, night and day, while Dad moved back from Paris into the Roche Marina Hotel to be near everybody. Mum was the only one allowed in near Florian, though, and she had to go through a massive protocol of cleaning and scrubbing to be allowed in. When he was on the trial drugs, and the steroids to stop him vomiting afterwards, you could see his face transform from one week to the other, depending on the treatment. One day his face would be bloated and another day he would look like a skeleton. When his hair began to fall out, Mum simply told him he needed a haircut and shaved his head, telling him it suited him much better. Instead of putting him on a drip, she took it upon herself to hand-feed him, bit by bit, as if he was a baby bird.

While in hospital, Mum had become friendly with the mother of a little girl who was going through the same thing as Florian and was on his ward. She was a good few months ahead of Florian in her treatment and, as her family had already gone through a lot of what we were about to go through, the girl's mother would explain each step to Mum as she came to it. Her daughter had gone through a transplant herself six months earlier, so the mother was a great source of comfort and support to our mum at the time. Unfortunately, though, her transplant wasn't successful, and the girl died on the day Florian was due to have his operation. We were devastated.

A few days before Florian's transplant, Dad caught the flu

and wasn't allowed near Alexis for fear of passing on germs. On the day of the operation, I brought Alexis to the hospital. They took him down to the theatre, while I had to wait in another room. I'm not sure Alexis was aware of what was going on at the time. He was only nine, but he was braver than I'll ever be. He told me about it afterwards, and it must have been very traumatic for him. His hip was sore for two or three weeks afterwards. Beforehand, Florian had been forced to lie perfectly still while a laser painfully killed his own bone marrow during six hours of radiotherapy. After the transplant, he was at his lowest point. While we waited for Alexis's cells to show up in Florian, he suffered badly. The morphine dosage was upped to the maximum possible while his cheeks sank deeper and deeper into his skull and his body faded to nothing.

Even a long time after the transplant, when he eventually began to recover, we still weren't allowed into Florian's room at the hospital. The risk of infection was extremely high for six months afterwards. But Alexis was great with Florian. I'd pick him up every day after school and drive him to the hospital, and we'd look in at him through the big glass panel. Months later, when Florian began to recover, they'd play Nintendo DS games with the Bluetooth on, racing each other in *Mario Kart* or other games. I also bought a chalkboard, and we'd write a message on the board, and Florian would answer us from his bed.

Florian would still be in hospital seven months later, and by the time the 2008 season came round in February, Christel and Dad had taken over from me and looked after Alexis while I was away racing. Christel had taken an internship in a company beside the hospital and visited

Florian and Mum every day during her lunch break and after work.

At the beginning of March 2008, I was on the far side of the world, racing in Africa, of all places. Although it was now in its fourth season, the UCI ProTour was still having its troubles. The major race organizers, ASO, RCS and Unipublic, who organize the Tours of France, Italy and Spain respectively, along with a collection of the world's top one-day classics, were holding firm in their argument that they should be allowed to select whatever teams they wanted for their races rather than be forced to invite all the top ProTour teams.

In 2008, my Crédit Agricole team fell foul of this battle, with Italian organizers informing us that we wouldn't be invited to Milan–San Remo, Tirreno–Adriatico or the Giro d'Italia. I had based my whole winter training on getting into these races but now found myself on a dramatically different race programme.

Half our team was sent to Spain to race, while myself and the other young riders went off to Africa to ride the inaugural Tour of the Ivory Coast. After a six- or seven-hour flight into Africa, we had a police escort to the team hotel, which gave us the first indication that this was going to be a tough week.

The hotel was terrible. The place was filthy and squalid, and we only ate boiled rice for the week, as we were afraid to take a chance on anything else. When we arrived there was a scruffy local guy in the lift who was paid to press all the buttons. Most of the time, however, the lift stopped and the doors opened halfway between floors, which scared the life out of me. We'd be stuck there, and the guy would have the neck to ask for a tip just to press the buttons again.

On the day before the race started, my teammates and I took a cab into the centre of the former capital, Abidjan, just to have a look around. It was a pretty scary experience. We were the only non-Africans in the whole place. Unbeknown to us, a peace accord between the government and the rebel New Forces group had only been signed two days before the race started and, after years of political unrest and a civil war, a new prime minister had been sworn in. The former French colony was in the middle of a political upheaval, and there weren't many French residents left around, as it wasn't deemed safe.

Here we were, a gang of European cyclists walking around the streets, sticking out like a sore thumb. The price of food and fuel was well on its way to doubling in the Ivory Coast that month and a few weeks after we went home dozens of police and protestors were injured in food riots on those same streets. When the locals saw us, they didn't see cyclists or foreigners. They saw dollar signs. We went to cross the road, a busy dual carriageway, when suddenly this guy ran out in front of us and threw himself in front of two lanes of traffic. After half a dozen cars had screeched to a halt inches away from him, the guy got up and beckoned us across the road. When we got to the other side, he wouldn't let us go until we gave him a tip.

After some time, we found this European bar and went in and had a drink. We ordered a local beer, but it was probably the quickest drink we'd ever had, as we were dying to get out of the place after a couple of minutes. That was the only time we ventured out of our hotel that week.

The race itself was crazy too. The first day was an

elimination race. It was held on a short course in the middle of the town in daytime traffic, and the safety element left a lot to be desired. Every time we crossed the finish line, the last two or three riders were eliminated. This went on until there were only four of us left, and I got third on the stage behind two race cars, a Ferrari and a Maserati. Roberto Ferrari attacked from the start, and we never caught him again, while his LPR-Brakes teammate Alessandro Maserati just sat on the back of our group all day and then out-sprinted me for second.

After each stage, we had some mental transfers to the next day's stage start. We were herded into a mini-bus, and it would take us three or four hours to do 50km through the jungle to get to our next hotel. We saw extreme poverty in Africa. Every village we rode past had its own militia protect-ing it at the entrance and exit, which was a bit frightening. The potholes were unbelievable. You'd need a stepladder to get out of them. But the scenery in the jungle was spectacular, which was just as well, because one day we had a six-hour transfer through it in a mini-van after a stage. To this day, I don't know how the race was given a 2.1 status by the UCI.

On the fourth stage, I had got into an early twelve-man breakaway group and was still there in the final kilometres, by which time it had whittled down to just four of us: with me were Rony Martias of Bouygues Telecom, the Italian Walter Proch of LPR, and Austrian Stefan Rucker of the Elk Haus team.

Martias was going to take over the yellow jersey at the end of the stage and knew I wasn't a threat for the overall classification. As I was riding for a French team, I think he would have preferred to see me win the stage rather than either of the other two. He also knew that my Crédit Agricole team would make a better ally than the Italians if he needed help later on in the race, especially if he had helped one of us win a stage, so, when I attacked, he didn't chase me down straight away and I opened a good gap – good enough to win the stage.

That stage, however, was the first day we had been given a road book with a map of the finish on it, and then only the night before. Having looked at it, I knew we would be coming to a roundabout with 300m to go. The road book said we could go both ways round the roundabout, so I went left, as I had attacked on the left-hand side of the road and the wind was coming from the right. But before I even got halfway round it, the entire crowd was standing in the middle of the road, expecting the riders to come round the other way. I was coming round behind them, and they were completely blocking my way. I bunny-hopped my way back up on to the kerb and on to the finishing straight. By that time, however, the Italian had gone the other way round the roundabout and was now about to win the stage. I went mad, cursing everybody from a height. I sat up and Martias passed me, and I cursed him too as I crossed the line for third, completely pissed off at missing out on a certain stage win.

The following day, the finish was supposed to be in front of the United Nations barracks but, because of protests outside it during the stage, the organizers decided to move it, without bothering to tell anybody. I had the whole team leading me out, with about 5km to go. All the sprinters were getting ready for the gallop to the line as we went past the 1km-to-go banner. We kept riding hard for what seemed like ages, but there was no sign of a finish line in sight. Suddenly, we saw a guy up the road shouting at us to turn right, so everybody sprinted into the corner, thinking the line was going to be just around the bend. We turned out of the corner into a 3km straight, with no sign of the finish there either. Everybody was looking at each other, asking, 'Where's the line?' After a stall, a few riders jumped away and things got going again. The finish finally came about 2km further on and, in the end, my teammate Jimmy Engoulvent won the stage, and I got seventh.

The stage had finished in the military zone, in the middle of nowhere. There were no buildings near us, let alone showers, so we sat in the blazing African sun getting changed out of our sweaty gear and washing ourselves with whatever water we could find, before taking a massive UN Chinook troop-carrying helicopter for the next transfer.

On the second-last day, we had to ride 10–12km on a dirt track, full of clay, stones and gravel. By the end of it, there were about seven or eight of us left. I attacked and got away with Proch again. We just looked at each other and said, 'Let's go, let's go.' The race referee drove alongside us as we passed the 5km-to-go sign and told us we had thirty seconds. We put the hammer down, as we knew we would be contesting the stage between us. A few minutes later, the commissaire's car came up to us again, and he rolled down the window. 'They got the signs wrong. It's actually 10km to go.'

I went crazy again. 'What the fuck sort of a race is this? Yesterday they moved the finish. Now this? Every fucking day there's something wrong. This is a load of bollocks.' And I sat up.

On the final morning, we were met by a proper tropical storm. The rain was hopping off the road like bullets in front of us as we set off. When we got on to the finishing circuit in the town, the race organizers couldn't control the traffic on the circuit. There were cars coming from every direction and for our own safety the stage was cancelled. Upon hearing the news, we turned our bikes on the road and rode back to the airport for our flight home. I finished sixth overall in the week-long race, but was happier just to be getting out of there in one piece.

In Africa, it had been hard to find out how Florian was doing, as Mum had to keep her phone off in the hospital. After Florian had had the bone-marrow transplant from Alexis, for two or three weeks it was really as if he was dying. If it had been one or two days later, we could have lost him. But Florian's condition gradually improved and, finally, three weeks after I'd been to the Ivory Coast and almost eight months after he had been rushed to hospital in Nice, Florian came home to Antibes. Here, he would spend almost another year in bed in his room. Things were very dangerous for about six months, and he needed a lot of blood transfusions. Nobody was allowed in to see him for a very long time, while Mum and anybody else who entered the house had to wear surgical masks. The environment had to be sterile, and I was wary of passing germs on from racing in various countries.

I got my first win for Crédit Agricole at the GP Internacional Paredes Rota dos Móveis stage race in Portugal. On the first day, it was pissing rain, and coming towards the finish there were only about fifty riders left to contest the bunch sprint.

I was feeling good and riding alongside my British teammate, another sprinter, Jeremy Hunt. I asked Jez if he wanted me to attack. 'If you're one hundred per cent sure you're going to win, attack,' he said. 'If not, then lead me out for the sprint.' There were about 5km to go, so I told him I'd think about it.

We were riding on the wheels of the Italian Acqua e Sapone team. I was seventh or eighth wheel, and there were four or five Italians riding full gas on the front. We came to this little hill and, at the bottom, I decided to go. I jumped hard to the left, and one of the Acqua e Sapone guys came with me. Because of his presence up front, the peloton momentarily stalled as a new team took over the chase. It was long enough to give us a gap, and the two of us were heading for a two-man sprint to decide the stage. With the bunch organized again and now breathing down our necks, I attacked my breakaway partner about 300m from the line and, in the uphill sprint, won the stage. Jeremy led the bunch in for second place, just a bike length behind me.

I was made up, as my first win for Crédit Agricole had also given me the yellow jersey of race leader. The following day, I was tenth on the second stage and held on to the jersey. On the third of four stages, we had Eric Berthou in the front group, which meant that my Crédit Agricole team didn't have to chase the break. The Portuguese team LA Aluminios-MSS set the tempo all day, while, up front, one of their riders came up to Berthou and tried to persuade him to contribute to the breakaway.

'I'm not riding,' he answered. 'I have Roche back the road in the yellow jersey.'

The Portuguese rider looked at Berthou and smiled. 'Don't worry about Roche. With a finish like today, you're better off riding, because he's not going to be in yellow any more.'

The whole MSS team rode on the front of the peloton for the whole stage, and my Crédit Agricole teammates didn't have to ride one metre. The Portuguese train eventually caught Berthou and the rest of the breakaway group on the long climb to the finish, where the home riders just kept going, blowing the race to bits in the process. I lost my yellow jersey as they took first, second and fifth on the stage and took over the race lead. Not only that, but they also won the next stage and went home with the top three riders overall. Shortly afterwards, most of that team was arrested when the Portuguese National Anti-doping Council (CNAD) found a host of doping products at their team headquarters.

Shortly after Portugal, Roger Legeay, our team boss, hit us with the news that Crédit Agricole would not be continuing their sponsorship of the team for 2009. He told us he would continue to search for a new sponsor, but that we were free to look for another team. The news didn't unduly worry me, as I was confident Legeay would find another sponsor by the end of the year. I had planned to stay with Crédit Agricole for the following year, so decided to wait and see what happened.

Although I had not been considered for the Tour de France originally, my good early-season results threw me a chance of making my Tour debut that July. When I got back to my new apartment in Cannes, the team informed me of its plan for me to go to the Tour of Switzerland in June. Depending on my form there, I would either go to the Tour de France or stay at home in July, so I planned to do well in Switzerland to ensure selection.

Two days before the Tour of Switzerland, though, the

decision was taken out of my hands when I woke up in the middle of the night vomiting. I'd been having pains in my stomach for a few weeks, but was foolish enough not to go to the doctor straight away. That night, I convinced myself that I had picked up food poisoning or something. But, the next day, I continued throwing up. This time, there were traces of blood, I had a massive headache and there were strange lumps protruding from my stomach.

I went to the doctor then saw a specialist at a clinic, where I had a gastroscopy. The doctor turned to me and said, 'You had better phone your family to bring you some clothes, Mr Roche. You're going to be staying with us for a few days.'

I had ulcers in my stomach, one of which had started to bleed. Tests found no bacteria, and I was told that my ulcers were more than likely brought on by stress. While I'm on the bike, I have a great ability to block out absolutely everything else. Nothing else matters. I'd been so busy racing and travelling that I had put Florian and his illness to the back of my mind. Any emotions I had felt had been bottled up and stored for another day, but now that I was back in my apartment, on a short break from racing, it had hit me again. When I was at home, I worried. I hoped everything would be all right, that he wouldn't die, but even though Florian was home, the next six months or so were crucial. Now I'd had the worry of the last-minute search for a new employer on top of it. And I was adding to everybody else's worry by getting sick myself.

I ended up being in hospital for five days, and I had to ring the team to tell them I wouldn't be going to the Tour of Switzerland, which I knew also meant that I wouldn't be going to the Tour de France. I was so disappointed.

10

Beijing Bound

Shortly after being discharged from hospital, I was back training, although on my first few outings behind the motorbike, I felt as if I had a strap pulled across my chest. My disappointment at not being able to ride the Tour de France was, however, tempered a few weeks later by the news that I had been selected to ride the Olympic road race in Beijing alongside Philip Deignan.

I flew back to Dublin at the end of June, the week before the national championships. As has now become customary, everybody congregated in my Nana and Grandad Roche's house in Dundrum. Dan was in the middle of his first year as a professional with the Garmin team and had already got some pretty big results, winning the mountainous Route du Sud stage race in the Pyrenees just a few weeks before.

The week of the championships, we went training together in the Wicklow Mountains, and down to Eniskerry with Dan's brother Tom, his dad, Neil, and my uncles, Lawrence and Peter. Most of the Roche/Martin clan, including my Nana Roche, made the trip to Cork on the Saturday for the championships in Midleton.

Despite voicing his disappointment prior to the race at a course he deemed to be too short and relatively easy, Dan was in the thick of the action from the first lap and spent 90km out front in a little break, before a large chase group containing all the main contenders merged at the front on lap six.

Dan was the only one of the first move strong enough to go clear with the next breakaway. This time he had three others for company: reigning champion David O'Loughlin, amateur rider Brian Kenneally and the ever present Páidí O'Brien, now riding for An Post. O'Loughlin cramped up with 50km to go, before Dan dropped the other two on the penultimate lap and time-trialled to the finish. I finished fourth, for the third year in a row.

I was happy for Dan to have won the title, even if he had managed to do in his first year what I had failed to do in four attempts. The new Irish champion then spent three and a half hours riding a moped in front of me in the south of France the following week when I was preparing for Beijing.

I was as excited as a little kid about riding the Olympic road race. Before the event, myself and Philip Deignan attended an Irish Sports Council pre-Olympic training camp at Réallon ski station in the French Alps. We were really focussed and put in eight days of hard training in the mountains, with lots of specific, high-intensity work. After training, we'd have lunch, before trying to catch an hour's sleep. We'd then have a massage and lie in our beds watching a DVD, before dinner and an early night sleeping at altitude. It was just like riding a stage race.

During the camp, I got confirmation that Legeay hadn't found a replacement sponsor and my Crédit Agricole team would definitely be folding. Although I had a win and a couple of good results for the year, I wasn't confident in finding a team. There were a lot of teams in trouble. The French teams were bringing down their rosters from twenty-eight to twenty-three riders and, as I was happy where I was, I hadn't even begun to look for a new team.

Having ended the Tour of Wallonia in seventh overall, I took the eleven-hour flight to Beijing with just my bike and a small carry-on bag. I'd given my vanity case to Philip at training camp, and everything else would be waiting for me at the Irish camp in the village. The Olympic village was huge, with national flags draped from every balcony of the massive apartment blocks. I was expecting it to be noisy, with music playing from balconies and so on, but it was more like a military camp instead. There was a post office, a shopping area and a barber.

The athletes' rooms were a bit on the sparse side, with just two beds and two wardrobes in each. I was rooming with Philip, which was great, as we both go to sleep at the same time and there's no messing about watching television until all hours. The heat was unbelievable, though, and the rooms were so clammy we slept with the windows open rather than risk catching a cold by turning on the air conditioning.

After the long flight, I was itching to get out for a spin, but in China that proved pretty difficult. It was harder to get out of the Olympic village than it was to get into it. We had to go through security, like you do in an airport. Our bags and bikes would be scanned and checked before being loaded up in the team car. It took an hour of driving to get out of the city, and we'd drive past the city zoo, the Great Wall of China and Tiananmen Square to go training for three hours on a course that was every bit as tough as people said it would be. There were armed soldiers positioned all the way around the 24km lap, which had a 12km climb on it.

In Beijing, we kept up the routine of training, lunch, nap, massage, a DVD and dinner before bed. Dinner was the best part of the day in Beijing. Apart from seeing all the famous sports stars in the massive food court, the Irish cycling team table really had a good laugh. David O'Loughlin was riding on the track, and Robin Seymour was mountain biking. We had all known each other for years, and knew how to wind each other up every day. We also got on well with the Irish badminton team and, between us, we bought three bikes – one green, one white and one orange – to get around the village on.

One bad thing about having to race on the first day of the Olympics was not being able to attend the opening ceremony. Everybody dreams of walking out on to the Olympic track behind their national flag, proud to show everybody who you are and where you come from, but four hours standing in the centre of the track afterwards wouldn't have been a good idea the night before the road race.

With only two riders, our little Irish team was always going to be outnumbered, so we planned on riding off the back of the bigger countries. I didn't like the circuit, and it was really creepy having no crowd on the side of the road to cheer you on. Things went astray when I got excited too early and attacked three times. But the distance was a bit long for me, and my lack of steady racing soon told. When they put the hammer down at 30km to go, I had nothing left, finishing a disappointed sixty-fourth. Hopefully, I will get another chance to prove myself, in London in 2012.

* * *

For the last six months or so of the 2008 season, Crédit Agricole allowed me to ride for myself more. Before that, I would be told to go with the first group and see how it went. If the front group didn't make it to the end, I came back and got dropped. After a few good results in April, they told me to chill out and see how things panned out in races, try to follow the top riders as far as I could. Once the team's tactics changed, everything changed. I became more of a protected rider, and they had more confidence in me.

My first race back after the Olympics was the four-day Tour du Limousin stage race in France. Before the first stage, Ag2r showed an interest in signing me, which cheered me up a bit. On the 170km opening stage from Limoges to Guéret, I attacked on a climb after 50km. German rider Hannes Blank jumped across to me, as did my former Cofidis teammate and good friend Geoffroy Lequatre, who was now riding for a rival French team, Agritubel. The three of us worked hard together and built up a maximum lead of five minutes over the peloton with 80km to go. But 30km later, our advantage was down to three minutes.

With 10km remaining, the sprinters could smell victory and, with their teams massing at the front, we were dangling just half a minute up the road. I knew the final climb was 5km long and there was a 5km descent to the finish. Geoffroy told me he was on his last legs but rode really hard to the bottom of the hill for me to keep the gap open. I attacked my two breakaway partners on the last climb. I knew my effort would have to be flat out all the way over the top and down to the finish. When you have the whole peloton chasing you, it's very hard to stay away. But I was so

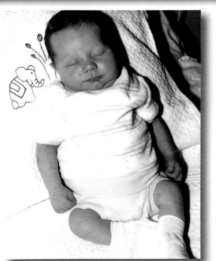

Left: Mum and Dad's wedding day in 1982. To the left, behind my dad, is Phil Anderson, the first Australian to wear the yellow jersey at the Tour de France.

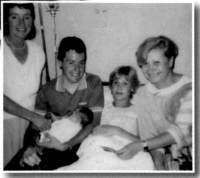

Above and left: A dream come true. Mum dreamt about a baby boy named Nicolas while on holiday in Spain and *voilà*, here I am.

Below: Dad meets the Pope after winning the Tour de France and Giro d'Italia in 1987. I'm holding his yellow jersey, while Christel wonders what the smell is.

Above: The Roche dynasty. Cycling began as a means of transport with my great-granddad Ned (*left*) who rode a bike up to his late 70s; my granddad Larry (*right*) met my Nana Roche on a spin.

Below: Racing on my mum's Gios bike. Fifteen years later, my brother Alexis used the same bike when he started cycling.

Above: Riding the Robinstown GP outside Navan on my new Stephen Roche bike. Notice the two different wheels; I must have punctured and been given one of Dad's good wheels.

Left: My first win came in an under-fourteen race in Dundalk on my mum's bike.

Left: Big brother is watching you. Me and Christel in 1986.

Below: We enjoy the sunshine in the back garden at Hereford Lane.

Bottom: We look the model brother and sister here but I always had a competitive streak and Christel bore the brunt of it when we were young!

Above: The gang's all here: (*clockwise*) myself, Christel, Alexis and Florian having a laugh.

Right: Florian was diagnosed with leukaemia in 2007, but the bone-marrow transplant from Alexis put him on the road to recovery. They are brave boys.

Below: Out for a meal with Christel in Dublin. It's always good to come home to Ireland.

Left: My first time riding for Ireland at the Manchester Youth Tour; I went on to win the race. Páidí O'Brien is on the left.

Below: Racing at the national championships is one of the highlights of my calendar; this was back in 2004, neck and neck with David McCann.

Bottom: I lined up alongside David and Philip Deignan here at my first ever world championships in 2006.

Left and below: My first win as a professional came in the Tour de l'Avenir in 2006 and gave me the coveted yellow jersey.

Bottom left: Cycling has taken me to some unexpected places, like Ivory Coast. We got changed in the open air in the middle of a UN base before boarding a Chinook helicopter for a stage transfer.

Below: I started racing with Crédit Agricole in 2007 and got in the team for the Giro d'Italia, my first Grand Tour. Dad came by to check on my progress.

Above:I got my first stage win for Crédit Agricole in the rain in Portugal in 2008, with my teammate Jeremy Hunt leading the bunch in for second place.

Right and below: You can see my delight on the podium, and I held on to the yellow jersey for the second stage of the race.

determined not to be caught that day. I put all my frustration, all my anger, into every pedal stroke. I threw myself down the descent and did the last 5km eyeballs-out with maybe twelve seconds' lead, so I must have been going really well. Losing, though, wasn't an option that day. I just had to win.

The peloton was really breathing down my neck in the final kilometre, and I dug so deep into my reserves that I was seeing stars. I managed to hold on by three seconds on the line to win the stage and also become the first race leader of the 2008 Tour du Limousin.

When I got off the bike, the tears came, and I could barely walk. All the stress of keeping everything bottled up inside me just came flooding out. I had used up every last bit of energy in trying to win the stage. I put absolutely everything I had into it. Crossing the line with my hands in the air was like opening a pressure valve, and it took me fifteen minutes to calm down and get my breath back.

I had just taken the biggest win of my career, and now led the race by eleven seconds. I also held the best-young-rider jersey and led the combination classification, but I knew it wasn't going to be an easy ride. I'd been away for 120km and was on my hands and knees at the end of it, so the first 30km of stage two were really hard, as I hadn't recovered properly and there were loads of attacks that we had to keep chasing to protect the yellow jersey. I began to come around a bit as the stage progressed and, at the finish, my teammate Sébastian Hinault led me out for the sprint. Séb is a really good sprinter and could have won the stage himself, but he did a fantastic job to get me in the right position for the uphill gallop. It looked as if I was set for my second stage win in a row, but I messed it up in the final metres, and Japan's Yukiya Arashiro of the Meitan Hompo team sneaked in under my arm on the line. I was really disappointed with second, because I knew Séb had sacrificed his own chances for me in the sprint. But at least I had held on to yellow and had even increased my lead by two seconds. Ag2r handed me a contract after the stage, and I signed with them for two years.

The following day, I was so nervous and worried about attacks that, instead of letting my teammates do their job, I chased time bonuses and tried to mark early attacks myself. In my eagerness to stay with the leaders, though, I had neglected to eat or drink anything, and shortly after the first climb of the day I simply ran out of fuel and almost came to a standstill. I could only watch as a twenty-eight-man group formed ahead of me and simply rode away. By the end I had lost twenty-nine minutes and my yellow jersey. But I had some consolation in the fact that Séb was in the lead group. Having sat at the back, in defence of my race lead, Séb had enough in reserve at the finish to win the stage, and also took enough time off everyone else to inherit my yellow jersey. It was now my turn to help him.

Séb went into the final day with just a single-second lead over Australian sprinter Allan Davis and Arashiro. There were attacks all day, but all Séb had to do was follow the Aussie. On the final climb, about 10km from the finish, I had to ride full gas all the way up, to discourage any attacks and keep the peloton together. After that, it was fingers crossed Séb could hold on for the overall win. He had done enough to win the race, and Crédit Agricole went away from the Tour du Limousin with two stage wins, overall victory and all four days in yellow. Séb also got a contract with Ag2r.

Although I'd been disappointed to miss the Tour de France in July, my form had earned me selection for the Tour of Spain in September. I didn't quite know what to expect at the 2008 Vuelta. I knew I was in pretty good shape going into it, and now had the experience of the previous year's Giro behind me, but it was a new race and it remained to be seen how I would handle it.

I'd had a couple of bad days on the 2007 Giro and realized that, if I was to aim for the overall classification in a major tour, I would have to be way more consistent, but I was only twenty-four years old and still learning how far I could push myself and what I was capable of. I didn't go into the Vuelta with ambitions for the overall. Instead, as Crédit Agricole's sprinter, my target was to try and take a stage win on one of the flatter days. As it turned out, the 2008 Vuelta changed the direction of my whole career.

I took eleventh on the opening road stage, and by the end of stage two I realized that I was really going well. World champion Paolo Bettini had attacked on the climb before the finish, and there were only about fifteen of us left in the front group at the top. After a regrouping on the descent, some of the sprinters came back. Gabriel Rasch worked really well for me, keeping me out of the wind and building up enough momentum in the final 2km to put me on Tom Boonen's wheel with 1km to go. I went a bit too early and had to settle for fifth in the gallop behind the Belgian sprinter. Ninth the following day gave me hope that a stage win at some point in the Vuelta was becoming a possibility. It was freezing cold for the longest stage. At the top of the finishing climb to Andorra, which we had to tackle twice on the stage, it had started snowing. I got really cold and had the hunger knock, running out of energy on the final ascent to the finish and losing over seven and a half minutes.

But it was on the next stage to Pla de Beret that I realized for the first time that I was capable of riding with the top guys on the big climbs in the big races. Now, on the twisting 20km ascent to the highest point in this year's Vuelta, I tried to hang in with the big guns as long as I could, as the Astana team of Alberto Contador wound up the pace. When Contador attacked halfway up, I lost contact but kept myself in a good rhythm. A few kilometres later, I caught Christophe Kern, who had been dropped from the break. He did a good job of pacing me until the last 2–3km, where I just rode as hard as I could to the line in the hope of getting a bit of time on those behind me. I finished the stage eighteenth.

As I was now in the top twenty overall, I had stopped contesting the sprints and concentrated on saving my legs for the overall battle. Our other sprinter, Sébastian Hinault, was feeling good heading towards the finish and had been giving me a hand on the mountainous days, so I tried to keep him sheltered from the strong headwind for the final sprint to Zaragoza. I brought him as near to the front as I could with a kilometre and a half to go.

Séb was sitting in fourth place coming into the final left-hand corner. With about 200m to go, he kicked hard down the right-hand side of the finishing straight in Zaragoza. He got about a length on the rest of the sprinters, and held on to take a fantastic stage win ahead of Lloyd Mondory of Ag2r.

It was great for everyone's morale as, with the team due to fold at the end of the 2008 season, we knew it was one of the last races we would be doing together. We celebrated with a glass of champagne at the dinner table.

The next big day in the mountains was to the top of the legendary Angliru. Angliru is one of the hardest climbs on the pro circuit, maybe even harder than Alpe d'Huez at the Tour, and a climb everybody feared, especially coming at the end of the 209km stage.

I held my position among the top-ten contenders until about halfway up, when I started to struggle. Cunego, Moncoutié and Rebellin went flying by first. When Levi Leipheimer attacked shortly after, it was every man for himself. The heat was unbelievable until we hit the cloud line, where it suddenly got cold and misty. I was alone for the rest of the climb but managed to limit my losses and finish fourteenth at the top. I had also moved back up to eighteenth overall. It was my first big performance with the top guys in the mountains, and I was really happy with my ride, as it further boosted my confidence in my own climbing ability.

I was going well, but I knew my days were running out to try and win a stage or gain time on the overall classification. I would have to try on the road to Las Rozas. This is my diary of that day:

Stage 18 – 18 September 2008:
Valladolid–Las Rozas, 167.4km

Before today I'd never heard of Imanol Erviti, but after today I will never forget him. It was probably the best and worst day of my career thus far, all rolled into one. I took my highest ever placing on a stage of a major tour when I finished second into Las Rozas, but I was so close to victory that I only lost out in a photo finish.

I knew that today was my last chance to try to take some time back on the overall classification. Everybody expected a break to stay clear today, so the stage got off to a pretty fast start, covering 49km in the first hour. When the elastic did snap to the peloton, I was the last man to get across to an eighteen-man move, which also included my teammate Cyril Lemoine. I made a really big effort to get across to them and was out of breath for a few minutes afterwards. Looking around the group, both the Spanish Euskaltel and the French Caisse d'Epargne teams also had two riders present, but the two biggest threats to a stage win for me were world champion Paolo Bettini of Quickstep and late-attack specialist Juan Antonio Flecha of Rabobank.

With all bar five teams on the race represented up front, the peloton was happy to let us go, as race leader Alberto Contador's Astana squad quietly controlled things at the front of the bunch. We soon opened a decent gap but, as our advantage increased to eight minutes and I began to take enough time back to threaten Oliver Zaugg and David Moncoutié's positions in the top ten, their respective Gerolsteiner and Cofidis teams began to chase.

With about 30km to go, we realized we wouldn't be caught and tried to figure out how to outfox each other and take the win. Cyril put in a lot of hard work for me, attacking so that I could have an easier ride, as the other teams were forced to chase him. He also chased any moves that went clear. García Acosta of Caisse d'Epargne, Flecha and the two Euskaltel riders all attacked before I managed to go clear with three others at the 2km mark. With me were Tinkoff's Vasily Kiryienka, Xacobeo's David Herrero and the other Caisse d'Epargne rider, Imanol Erviti, whom I'd never seen before.

Kiryienka lost contact as we began the slight incline to the finish, and I knew this would be my best chance of a stage win at this year's Vuelta. There was a sharp corner 500m from the line, and the others stalled for a moment after the corner and started looking at each other. I looked over my shoulder and saw that Bettini and Karsten Kroon were just a few seconds behind us and closing, so I panicked and opened up the sprint with 300m to go.

Erviti was firmly planted on my back wheel, though, and just as it looked as if I would win the stage, he came past me. I sprinted again to try to get back to him, and we were only separated by half a wheel on the line. Neither of us put our hands up because we were both afraid to lose the stage, but Erviti got the victory in a photo finish. It took a while to get the results and, while we shook hands after the line, I was really frustrated. I've already had enough second and third places that I could have turned into wins this year. After getting rid of Bettini and Flecha from the break, I'd been beaten by a guy nobody had ever heard of.

Looking back, I made two mistakes. I sprinted too early and, when I did go, I didn't kick hard enough to open a gap. Opportunities to win stages in a big race like the Vuelta don't come along too often. The Spaniard won fair and square, but it was very annoying.

Seven and a half minutes later, the Gerolsteiner team led the peloton in with the time gap we had opened meaning that I had leapfrogged up to thirteenth in the overall standings. If I could finish there, it would be the best result of my career.

I did end up finishing thirteenth overall, the highest placing by an Irish rider in a major tour since 1993. The Vuelta had shown I could finish in the top five in the mass bunch sprints with Petacchi and Zabel one day and then, the day after, in the mountains, I could stay with the leaders again.

On the stage to Angliru, which was the hardest stage you could imagine, I was with the top guys and finished in the top fifteen. I couldn't believe the difference climbing with the front group made. The crowd just carries you on. When you arrive half an hour later with the gruppetto, the crowd is almost as tired as you are. I showed that I could recover well too, because I was second three days from the end and then finished a good fourteenth in the final time trial, which was my favourite result of the season. I was already looking forward to 2009 with my new team.

11

Apprentice

I wasn't that impressed with the opening day of my first training camp with my new Ag2r La Mondiale team. While other teams went to the sun for warm-weather training, we stayed at home and trained in the rain. We were holed up in a local sports centre in the middle of France in December, and we didn't see the sun once in ten days.

Their timekeeping wasn't great either. With Crédit Agricole, if training was at 10 a.m., we would arrive at 9.45 a.m. and be ready for ten. With Ag2r, everybody arrived at ten, but then we'd spend twenty-five minutes freezing our arses off because somebody was fixing his bike or somebody else wasn't ready. At Crédit, if you weren't there, we were gone – see you later. I hoped it would be different at the races.

My first meeting with my new Ag2r team boss, Vincent Lavenu, however, changed my views of the team entirely. Lavenu sat me down and reminded me that I now had four years' experience as a pro, had ridden two Grand Tours and had a couple of victories under my belt. He told me it was time to work my way up the pecking order within the team and that in some of the races I would have to start taking on the role of team leader. It would be a kind of apprenticeship. I was to act like a leader in everything I did, from the way I rode, to the way I behaved at dinner. Although I was still only twenty-four, I was to be an example to the younger guys as well. It was a pretty motivating speech, to be honest.

He told me the team wanted me in full form for Paris–Nice in March, that it was the first big goal of the season. Paris–Nice was a race I'd always wanted to do, but I had never got the chance with Cofidis or Crédit Agricole. Now that Ag2r were giving me the opportunity, I wanted to take it. As my dad won the 'race to the sun' in his first year as a professional, it's one of his favourite races, and I've been brought up on it. The final stages were usually held in my home area, and I had spent hours upon hours training on the nearby climbs of the Col du Tanneron and Col d'Eze.

The Vuelta had given me an increased confidence in my ability. I worked hard to keep my weight down and my fitness up over the winter and I had a good start to the 2009 season. The year before, Ag2r had had a terrible start, so everyone on the team was told that we had to be present at the classics and be in form for Paris–Nice and then the Amstel Gold Race, La Flèche Wallonne and Liège–Bastogne–Liège. I also had other aims myself. I wanted to ride my first Tour de France and, if possible, to ride it in the Irish champion's jersey. I'd been waiting on that jersey for a long time. I'd finished third once and fourth three times in a row. I was sick of waiting.

Unfortunately, my Paris–Nice debut was far removed from my dad's storming win on his debut in 1981.

My cousin Dan finished two places higher than me, in

seventy-second place in the first stage time trial. Both of us covered the course forty-nine seconds slower than 2007 Tour de France winner Alberto Contador. The second stage came down to a bunch sprint. After losing concentration and getting caught out in an earlier split in strong crosswinds, I regained contact with the front portion of the peloton. I avoided a big crash with 2km to go and tried to give Séb Hinault a hand in the sprint. But I moved out into the wind too soon, and Séb took seventh. I was thirteenth on the stage. I lost time on stage three due to a problem with my gears in the crosswinds, then was caught by the peloton near the end of stage four after getting into a long breakaway. I had a really tough day the next day and couldn't do anything except try to recover from the previous day's efforts. It was not a debut to remember.

After riding my first Milan–San Remo classic in Italy, I took eleventh overall at the Critérium International two-day, three-stage race in France in April. I finished just thirty-eight seconds behind German winner Jens Voigt, who took his fifth victory in the race, and came agonizingly close to winning the white jersey of best young rider too, losing out by just fifteen seconds to Jérôme Coppel of Française des Jeux.

In May, I rode the week-long Tour of Catalonia and took fourth on stage two when Luxembourg champion Kim Kirchen attacked with 1km to go and I went with him on the hill. But when Kirchen sat up with 300m to the line, a lack of confidence meant that I hesitated and three sprinters came from behind me. I took ninth on the penultimate stage and eleventh on the last day to finish seventeenth overall. Dan was also riding for Garmin and was in flying form, eventually finishing second overall, just fifteen seconds behind world-number-one-ranked Alejandro Valverde, who was later given a two-year ban for his involvement in the Operación Puerto blood-doping affair.

The Ag2r La Mondiale team that rode that Tour of Catalonia was told that, without naming names, most of us had been selected for the Tour de France in July. My performance in Catalonia meant that I was quietly confident of being one of those selected. We were also told the team would have a pre-Tour training camp in the mountains just before the Dauphiné Libéré stage race in June. At the training camp, I really got stuck in and rode hard for the week in the mountains. I wanted to make sure I was considered for the Tour and applied myself to all the training full on.

Two days after the training camp, we began the week-long Dauphiné Libéré. An important preparation race for the Tour de France for all teams taking part, the Dauphiné Libéré is even more important for Ag2r, as its company has its headquarters in the area. The race began well for me, with sixth place on the opening stage behind my former team-mate Angelo Furlan. But from then on, things went downhill. At the Tour of Catalonia, I had been able to attack on the mountains but at the Dauphiné I felt as if I was glued to the road. Instead of progressing, I had fallen backwards. I went okay in the sprint stage but in the mountains I was hoping to get up there, to be able to hang in with the big guys and be in the thick of the action. But I wasn't good enough to be with the top guys on the climbs, so I was pretty disappointed afterwards.

The training camp in the mountains had taken a lot out of me and, in fact, out of the whole team. None of us performed in any way well, and after the race we were all told that the Tour team was now up in the air and wouldn't be selected until the evening after the various national championships the following Sunday.

After the Dauphiné, I lost a lot of confidence. I wanted to go to the Tour and was still hoping to get picked, but my performance in the mountains had thrown doubt into my mind. The only glimmer of hope I had was the fact that José Luis Arrieta, our Spanish veteran, had been the only Ag2r La Mondiale rider to perform well at the Dauphiné, and he was also the only one of the Dauphiné team to have missed the training camp. At the national championships, I would be one of five riders contesting four places on the team, and was in no way certain of my spot.

When I was living in Varese in Italy, I had two climbs where I gauged my fitness. Sacromonte is a 6km climb at 8 per cent gradient, just outside the city centre of Varese. The other one is Cuvignone and is 9km long at 8 per cent gradient. This second climb is also nicknamed 'Basso's Climb', because former Giro winner Ivan Basso also tests himself there before big races.

When I use Sacromonte, I usually ride around the lake in Varese for about an hour to warm up, and then time myself up the climb three times in a row before taking my average. The Cuvignone is a bit further away, so I use the forty-minute ride to the bottom as a warm-up, and then it takes about half an hour to get to the top. A few days before leaving for Ireland and the national championships, I beat my record by about twenty seconds, so it reinforced my belief that I had been fatigued from the training camp at the Dauphiné.

If there was one race, apart from a stage of the Tour de France, that I wanted to win in 2009 it was the Irish national road race championships. I've always put a lot of importance on the nationals. I've tried to come home every year for them since I was a kid, and to be able to wear the shamrock jersey in the pro peloton would be a dream come true for me. In 2009, I had even more reasons to want to win it. I had been chasing the national title since I was eleven and hadn't been out of the top four since turning senior. I needed to make the step up to the top of the podium. Also, I still hadn't won a race yet for that year, and it was as good an opportunity as any to claim my first victory for the 2009 season.

I was determined to prove to both the team and the Irish public that I was going well, and I knew that if I could win the Irish title, it would go a long way to earning a Tour place. A national champion always draws a little bit of extra media attention on the Tour and it would be in the sponsor's interest to have me on the team if I won. I didn't expect any of the others to win their championships but there was always the possibility that one of the guys could have pulled the French title out of the bag. A French champion was always going to get selected over an Irish champion for the Tour.

In line with all the other national championships in Europe, the Irish title race was to be held on Sunday 29 June, one week before the start of the 2009 Tour de France.

Once again, I stayed in Dundrum for the week before the race. Dan didn't make the trip with me this time round, as his excellent form had already earned him a place on Garmin's Tour de France team for the following week, and some pre-Tour team time-trial training and reconnaissance rides in Montpellier had been arranged in the lead-up to the race. His family still came over from England, however, to support me and Dan's younger brother, Thomas, while my uncle Lawrence acted as *directeur sportif* for me, driving behind me for the duration.

On the Wednesday evening before the championships, I rode the Stephen Roche Grand Prix, which also doubled as the national critérium championships in 2009. Although I was involved in plenty of moves throughout the hour-long race around the houses in Meadowmount, I had to make do with fifth place, as the now late Paul Healion went clear with Simon Williams and took a fine victory, with Martyn Irvine taking bronze. I only knew Paul from racing together once or twice a year, but he was friendly to talk to and always had a smile on his face. Paul was in the form of his life that season and, riding for the national team a few weeks earlier, had realized his dream of winning a stage of the FBD Ras after ten years of trying. Two months after becoming national critérium champion, Paul was tragically killed in a car accident. He was thirty-one.

Four days after the critérium championships, the road race title was to be held in the village of Dunboyne in County Meath. The race was held on a mainly flat 22km circuit, to be tackled eight times. There was only one drag on each circuit, coming about 6km from the line, and I knew it would be decisive at the end of the race, when everybody would be getting tired.

I wanted to prove to Ag2r that I was in good form by winning the title, but racing at home is always hard. All the foreign-based professional riders come home to try to win the title, and you also have the domestic guys who base their season on doing a good ride in the championships, and they can never be underestimated. Over the years, the standard of racing back in Ireland has risen considerably, and there are plenty of good youngsters at home who have the potential to be top professionals in the future. I knew that wearing a professional team jersey at the start of the championships would be akin to having a target on my back.

The fact that Dan was already in France getting ready for the Tour and Philip Deignan was out sick meant that, as the biggest 'name' there, that target would be even bigger. It can be frustrating at times being the pre-race favourite. Everybody knows who you are, and everybody is waiting for you to move, so they follow you in the hope of getting into the main move of the day. But I also knew that if I was an up-and-coming domestic rider then I'd be doing the same thing, so I couldn't really complain.

As is often the case in the championships, a large group went clear on the very first lap. Most of the strong riders in the race, including two of the Irish-registered An Post professional team, were in that group and, with no teammates to help me, I knew that if I didn't get across to them my race was over. I would be left to spend the day chasing on my own. I was the last one to get across to the move, with another An Post rider, three-time champion David O'Loughlin. And that was it. We were gone.

With everybody in the break keen to stay clear of the peloton behind, the pace was pretty fast for the first half of the race. This suited me down to the ground, as it meant that nobody would be able to attack and I could just roll through with the others instead of being forced to chase continuous attacks. The constant speed saw us gain four minutes after five laps and, while I was outnumbered for now, I knew the relentless pace, combined with the sheer distance of the race, would be likely to whittle the baker's dozen down to a more manageable number towards the end.

With teammates Páidí O'Brien and Ronan McLaughlin alongside O'Loughlin up front, the An Post team held numerical superiority in the break. Under the guidance of former world number one and team manager Sean Kelly, who was driving the team car behind them, An Post soon began to use that to its advantage. McLaughlin split the group with an attack on the sixth time up the hill, leaving myself and the three An Post boys up front alongside amateurs Robin Kelly, Martyn Irvine and youngster Sean Downey of Banbridge with two laps to go.

I knew I had to get rid of a few more, though, and the next time up the hill, I put in a dig. I turned round at the top, and my effort had dropped everyone apart from O'Brien and O'Loughlin. Although I still had two An Post riders for company, I knew that Páidí and David were good strong riders and that if we worked together over the final lap we would be sharing the medals amongst ourselves. Having raced with both guys over the years, I knew their strengths pretty well. If I let Davey get any kind of a gap, his strong time-trialling skills would make it extremely hard to catch him, whereas Páidí was one of the best sprinters in the country and if I left it to a sprint finish there was a good chance I would be beaten. I had to get rid of them.

As we neared the end of the final lap, each of them took turns to attack me. I knew I had to react straight away. Each time I caught one of them, I went straight to the front, keeping my speed up in order to make it harder for either of them to recover and launch another attack. Davey jumped clear on the final hill, and I swung across the road after him. I clawed my way back to him and, as we neared the crest of the hill, I jumped hard on the pedals. I knew this was my last chance to get away from the two, and I gave it everything as I went over the brow of the hill and headed into Dunboyne.

They were just a couple of metres behind me for what seemed like ages. I didn't look around, I just rode as hard as I could to try and open a decent gap and, for a minute or two, I didn't know if they were just hanging me out to dry, waiting to reel me in and attack me as soon as I tired. My heart was flying, half because of the effort I was making and half because I knew this was my chance to win the title. My legs were burning and I was gulping in air but, in a masochistic way, I felt good and was slowly opening a gap on the two chasers. My legs were on fire, but I knew that if I could ignore the burning sensation of the lactic acid filling my legs for another 3–4km, I would be champion.

I rounded the final left-handed bend, about 300m from the finish, to see my uncle Peter standing in the middle of the road, screaming like a maniac. He could see the empty road behind me and knew that I had a big enough gap to win the race, and was jumping up and down with excitement. He was almost in tears and looked even happier than I was, if that was possible. Even now, nearly three years later, that is the best memory I have from that day. By the time I entered the finishing straight in Dunboyne, I had enough time to look around me and savour the moment. I pedalled the last 200m with my hands off the bars, waving to the crowd. I finished about twenty seconds clear. I had become national road race champion of Ireland.

As I crossed the line, my overwhelming emotions were relief and satisfaction. Relief that I had finally become national champion and satisfaction that I had put myself squarely back in the frame for a place in the team for the Tour. I took a few minutes to ride up the road and catch my breath before returning to the finish line, where I was immediately mobbed by my family, friends and well-wishers. My Nana Roche told me later that she had been crying as I rode towards the line. As usual, she had a big kiss for me afterwards. My sister, Christel, my cousin Eric and the rest of my family were just as delighted. My uncle Neil couldn't have been happier if Dan had just won, and it seemed as if everybody at the finish wanted to shake my hand, pat my back or have a photograph taken with me.

Davey and Páidí were the first two riders to congratulate me, and they were followed by almost everyone else in the race as they crossed the line in dribs and drabs. That's the thing about Irish cycling. It's like a big, mobile family. Everybody knows everybody. When I was on the podium with Páidí, I realized it was fourteen years since I first raced with him. When you do well, especially abroad, everybody shares the glory. If people feel as if they know you personally, most of the time, it's because they do.

Everybody wanted to know if I'd be wearing the Irish champion's jersey at the Tour the following week but, honestly, I was in the same boat. The first thing I did after the presentation was to ring my *directeur sportif* Julien Jourdie and tell him I'd won. Ag2r's Tour team was supposed to be announced after all the European championships had been decided, but there was still no word. I was on tenterhooks. I needed to know if I was going to be riding the Tour de

France the following Saturday. Julien congratulated me and proceeded to tell me that the team had still not been decided but, in the middle of a conversation about wheels, he let slip that my good wheels were on my time-trial bike already. What would I need my time-trial bike for? It must be for the Tour surely? I tried to think of any other reason he would have mentioned it but couldn't come up with anything. I didn't push it, but my hopes of riding the world's biggest race had just been given a big boost.

My week in Ireland was now over and, after a bit of a family celebration in Dundrum, I flew back to Italy the next morning. I had left my mobile on all night but still hadn't heard anything about the Tour team. I switched it back on as soon as we landed in Milan airport, but there were no messages, no missed calls during the flight. As I went to grab my bags off the luggage carousel, however, my phone rang. My heart raced as I looked at the number and saw it was Vincent Lavenu, the Ag2r La Mondiale *directeur sportif.*

'*Bonjour*, Nico, we were thinking of you for the Tour from the start, but then you weren't going well at the Dauphiné. But winning your national championships proves you are in good form. Sorry for calling so late, but I had to phone the ones who didn't make the team first. Congratulations . . . you're riding the Tour.'

A Cheshire-cat grin spread across my face. I was going to the Tour de France. Not only that, but I would be riding it as Irish champion, in my new champion's jersey. Then it began to sink in. Today was Monday. The Tour de France began on Saturday. In just six days, I would be riding the biggest bike race in the world. That phone call sparked possibly the most hectic week of my life thus far.

After a quick spring clean of my apartment in Varese, I packed my bags and flew out to Marseille the next day. From there, I drove to Montpellier, where I met up with the rest of the team. We spent a couple of days on the team time-trial course, before driving to Monaco for the Grand Départ.

Our sponsor, a French private-pensions company, planned on using the 2009 Tour de France to re-brand itself and, while we got a whole suitcase of new Ag2r team clothing for the Tour, the new company colours didn't exactly make us the envy of the peloton. Instead of our previous colours of mainly white jersey with blue and yellow trim and blue shorts with white and yellow trim, the jersey, still basically white, now had blue and brown diamond shapes scattered around the Ag2r La Mondiale logo – not too bad – but the shorts . . .

They were a colour that could only be described as 'shitty' brown, with white writing down the leg. Each pair drew gasps from the riders as it was unveiled. As the guys pranced around their rooms in the new gear, I could afford to laugh at their predicament. After all, I was a national champion now and, in the professional peloton, that meant I would be wearing a newly designed team-issue jersey and shorts in the colours of my country. Being a national champion is, for a professional, like going on the cycling equivalent of *Pimp My Ride*. Soon I would also have my bike re-sprayed in the Irish colours and would get a new team helmet, glasses and anything else you could think of. However, it didn't take long for someone to remind me that, as I was the national road race champion, I was only entitled to wear the champion's kit in road races and would have to wear the new brown team gear in time trials, both individual and team, which soon wiped the smile off my face.

We'd been given a new team bike a week before the nationals, and another new one on the Tuesday before the Tour, but the bottom bracket – the centre axis where the cranks attach to the frame – had fallen out of mine twice already. I was stressed out enough about making my Tour debut without having to worry about whether my cranks were going to fall off halfway through the first stage. In an effort to fix the problem, the mechanics over-tightened mine and the next day I couldn't turn the pedals. They did find the problem, though, and I rode it on the prologue course the next day and it seemed fine.

We were up at 7 a.m. on the Thursday before the Grand Départ to get our blood taken for a UCI pre-Tour dope test. No matter how many times you have it done, nobody likes having a needle stuck in them. The guy has twenty-five minutes to do a team and if he's in a hurry you can be left with a huge bruise. After breakfast we had our bikes adjusted and checked, which took until lunchtime. Then we had a massage and went to the rider briefing. Here, we had to sit for about two hours listening to the rules and regulations of the race, before being shown highlights of the previous year's Tour. Watching it really made the hair stand on the back of my neck, and it really hit home that this was the biggest race in the world.

My new Ag2r national champion's jerseys arrived about half an hour before the team presentation that evening, but there were no shorts with them. I wouldn't be getting them, or my new champion's helmet, until some time in the second week, and the guys laughed as I too was forced to don the brown shorts for the pre-Tour spectacle, where each squad rolled up a ramp on to a stage to be introduced to the massive crowd. I was so nervous and stressed as we waited to go on that my stomach was doing somersaults. I was starting to think that the new brown shorts mightn't be such a bad idea after all.

While we waited our turn, an English journalist asked if I had any comments about my cousin not riding the Tour. I was shocked. 'What do you mean, Dan's not riding? Are you sure?' I asked.

'Yeah, he pulled out this morning. He's injured.'

By then, half the world knew that Dan had been forced to pull out of the Tour with a knee injury. I was in the same town as him, and hadn't a clue until six o'clock that evening. I had seen Dan the day before, training with his Garmin team. I noticed he was the only one without a time-trial bike, but didn't read anything into it. I found out later that he'd been suffering with tendonitis in his knee for a few days beforehand. Dan was in such good form that his Garmin team had taken a gamble that it might heal up before the start of the Tour and named him in the team anyway. It didn't, though, and they realized Dan could do serious damage if he rode three weeks on it, and pulled the plug.

For Dan to have made it all the way to Monaco, to see all the razzmatazz involved in the Tour before having to pull out two days before the race must have been terrible. My cousins Simon, Eric and Tom had come to Monaco on the Sunday evening, as had my mum, who burst into tears of pride when she was interviewed by Italian television before the stage. Unfortunately, Florian couldn't come with her. Just before the Tour, Florian had been allowed outside to go for a walk and get some fresh air, but he was still very weak, and a trip to Monaco would have been too much. It was the first time Mum had left his side in almost two years, and the fact that she was there was a sign to her that Florian was getting better. Florian and Alexis sent me a brilliant drawing of me on a bike with the Irish flag to show their support.

I didn't get back to the hotel until 8.15 p.m., just in time for dinner. Dan phoned me later on that night from Dad's hotel in Antibes. He hid his disappointment by eating a pizza into the phone and slagging me that I couldn't have any until the end of the season. But after almost making the Crédit Agricole team the year before, I knew how bad he must be feeling.

I tried to cheer him up by reminding him how, having skipped the 2008 Tour, I had gone on to ride a really strong Tour of Spain. We talked until about 10 p.m., and then I went to bed, jaded from the long day of pre-Tour activities and nerves. I couldn't wait to get on my bike and release some nervous energy.

I was going to be riding the Tour de France! This time round, I had agreed to write a diary for the *Irish Independent* during the race.

12

Tour Virgin

Stage 1 – Saturday 4 July: Individual Time Trial, Monaco, 15.5km

My dad called in to the team hotel last night and told me I needed to calm down. I was an absolute nervous wreck before the prologue. I always get nervous before a big race, but this was unbelievable. I was almost rattling. He advised me to take a breather and emphasized that, by being stressed, I was only wasting more energy. The short time trial almost went according to plan. I would have been inside a minute and ten seconds of the stage winner if Fabian Cancellara hadn't blitzed the rest of the field to take eighteen seconds out of second-placed Alberto Contador.

Stage 2 – Sunday 5 July: Monaco–Brignoles, 182km

I had a few butterflies rolling out of Monaco this morning but, as we got going, they slowly disappeared. Today was hectic, though, with a lot of argy-bargy in the final kilometres, and the butterflies came fluttering back any time I heard the noise of mangled metal scraping along the ground in one of the day's many crashes.

My Ag2r team plan today was to send someone up the road to try to take the mountains jersey. One of my team leaders, Cyril Dessel, got into a four-man break-away group and had a good chance of a stage win if this group stayed clear, but the Saxo Bank team of race leader Cancellara made sure they didn't get too much leeway.

When the Columbia HTC and Cervélo teams joined the chase for their sprinters Mark Cavendish and Thor Hushovd with 30km to go, we knew the game was up, and Cyril's group was reeled in with 9km to go.

Our team doesn't have one of the top sprinters in the race, a real fastman like Cavendish, Boonen or Hushovd. There's only really me and French sprinter Lloyd Mondory, so we both have to rely on our wits and pot luck to follow the best wheel in the final kilo-metres. I used to think it was all about having a strong team to lead you out, until I watched a programme about the Columbia team on Eurosport last night. Cavendish went into fine detail about his preparation for each sprint finish, and it blew me away. The amount of work each rider does to protect Cavendish, and the amount of background information they have about the finish, the last corner and the last kilometres is incredible. In a straight-out sprint, Cav would still destroy me, although I'd have a better chance if it was uphill.

Today I was constantly diving from one side of the

road to the other, trying to pick the fastest line to the finish. I was on Tom Boonen's wheel on the left side of the bunch with 3km to go, but quickly realized the former green-jersey winner wasn't going anywhere and moved to the right on the final corner. I almost hit a wall on the bend, but I knew I had made the right move when one of the Euskadi guys hit the deck on the other side of the road.

The crash left a big gap between me and Cavendish's train, which meant I was in the wind way too early. Hushovd and Bonnet came past me with 200m to go, and I got eighth on the stage. Eighth! On my first stage of the Tour de France! I was ecstatic.

Stage 3 – Monday 6 July:
Marseille–La Grande Motte, 196.5km

Today wasn't fun at all. We knew something was going to happen, but didn't know what, or when, which meant everybody was nervous. It was stop–go all day and, as usual, there were a lot of crashes.

The first thing you learn when you start cycling is that if you can stay out of the wind you can save a lot of energy. A headwind means you can simply position yourself directly behind the wheel in front of you, saving up to 20 per cent. A crosswind, though, needs a bit more effort.

If the wind is coming from the left, you position yourself to the right of the rider in front, about halfway down his bike, depending on the severity of the gusts. If the wind is coming from the right, you ride on the opposite side, always using someone else as a buffer. Sounds simple enough, doesn't it? The problems begin when the diagonal line, or echelon, stretches all the way across the road and the guys at the end are riding in the gutter to try to get shelter. Add a few parked cars or traffic islands that have to be flicked round, and you have a recipe for mayhem.

In a crosswind, a good team will ride just far enough across the road to give their riders shelter, leaving the rest of the peloton to scramble in the gutter behind or create another echelon. Today, the Columbia team put the hammer down just as we turned into a crosswind section with about 30km to go. They split the peloton in two and immediately opened a gap of about twenty seconds on the rest of the bunch.

I'm really annoyed with myself for missing the split, as I wasn't in too bad a position when we went round the corner where the wind changed. But Columbia made a brilliant effort to split the race, and it was panic stations in the bunch. I'd been expecting it for over an hour, but it was going and stopping all day. I was riding in the top thirty or so just before it happened. I thought that would be enough, but I missed it by two riders.

Cavendish took his second stage win in a row, as my group finished forty seconds down. Almost all the team leaders were caught behind. Cavendish had his whole team up front, as it was the driving force. Yellow jersey Cancellara also made the split. So too did Armstrong. It just goes to show how good Armstrong is at reading the race. He just doesn't make any mistakes and is now third overall.

Stage 4 – Tuesday 7 July: Team Time Trial, Montpellier, 39km

In a team time-trial, whole teams race against the clock, with both your individual time and the time of that of your teammates taken on the fifth rider across the line, provided you are with that fifth rider.

Although your team leader or someone else may be a better time triallist than you, they still have to cross the line with four others, so there is no point in them riding off on their own. Me, I am not a bad time trial-list. I was Irish national champion last year, and Rinaldo Nocentini and Christophe Riblon are also good against the clock, but we are not what you'd call specialists.

Some teams choose to deliberately burn up some of their weaker riders in the early part of the stage, but if you are left with only five men in the final kilometres you are taking a risk that nobody punctures or crashes. If that happens, then you lose time anyway, because you have to have five crossing the line.

At the team meeting, we decided to take it a bit easy on the corners. Team manager Vincent Lavenu reminded us not to sprint hard out of the corners, as the last man in line would not even be round the bend when the first one exited the corner. We decided to try to keep the team together. Some guys took a break from the front at the start, some in the middle, but we were one of the few teams to finish with nine men, and I think it showed we are a pretty evenly matched team.

I was feeling all right. I didn't skip any turns on the front, but usually I'm capable of taking a lot longer turns into the wind. We lost a bit of time in the last 10km because we didn't have the power, but I think everybody rode to their limit today, so the management was pretty happy with our ninth place, a minute and forty-eight seconds behind the Astana team. After the time trial, we rode the 10km back to the hotel at a snail's pace, had a shower, ate a light lunch and lay on the bed watching the rest of the teams on television.

It was impressive to watch those last few top teams go flat out on the same roads we had just covered. The speed they were doing was amazing. On Monday, when Armstrong got into that group and gained forty seconds, I thought, Wow, he could take the jersey in the team time-trial. Now, he's not far off it in joint first place, with most of his teammates in the top ten. Not bad for a guy who has hardly raced in four years.

Stage 5 – Wednesday 8 July: Le Cap d'Agde–Perpignan, 196.5km

Today's stage was hectic. It was so stressful that when I crossed the finish line I felt like I'd done 600km instead of 196km. I think the crosswinds two days ago, the team time-trial yesterday and then more crosswinds today made the last three days really exhausting.

Each morning at the team briefing we get an idea of where the wind will be coming from. Our team manager buys an oversized map of the local region and redraws the route of the day's stage on it so we can see where the dangerous corners are or where the wind will change direction, etc. Then, during the race, Vincent tells us on our earpieces, 'Okay, in 15km, you have a right-hand turn where the wind will be a three quarter tailwind, which will be very dangerous.'

You pay attention to the wind. You study it in the morning and watch out for flags or other signs of its strength or change in direction during the stage. Today, I knew that after the second climb we would be on the seafront and the wind would be very strong. This is the perfect scenario for the strong teams to try to split the peloton. I fought hard to stay near the front going up the climb and was in a perfect position on the descent. Then the bunch hesitated at the bottom and *phooom!*, loads of guys flew past and I went from the top twenty to around the top sixty.

Everybody was panicking as we got near the seafront, thinking, Where is it going to go? What's going to happen? There was a lot of pushing and shoving around to get up to the front and hold your position. If I'm not at the front, it's not from want of trying, it's just that sometimes the roads are so narrow, it's impossible to get near it.

The split went three guys in front of me. Denis Menchov and I were the first two guys to try to close the gap. I gave it everything, but I was going nowhere. Then, a few minutes later, I was struggling in that group to hang on. I couldn't get shelter, as I was caught at the back of the echelon. My head was rolling like Paula Radcliffe's as I fought with the bike to hold the wheel in front. I didn't get a breather until about 10km later, when we rejoined the front of the peloton and fanned out across the road.

After we had rejoined, I tried to go back to the car

for bottles, but our car wasn't there yet, as there were splits all over the road and it was caught behind the third group. For 40km, I kept coming back for bottles, but still no car. I was dying of thirst. When a big group behind caught us with about 15km to go, Arrieta handed me a bottle and saved my life. I got a bit of a breather, but I wasn't feeling the best for the sprint, so I just stayed in the middle of the bunch. With six guys up the road, I wasn't going to kill myself for seventh or eighth.

Stage 6 –Thursday 9 July: Girona–Barcelona, 181.5km

This morning, I woke up to the sound of my teammate Hubert Dupont whizzing in the bathroom of our hotel room. Hubert is riding his second Tour. As I try to focus my tired eyes, Hubert exits the bathroom, opens the bedroom door and walks out into the hallway. I turn and look at the clock. It's six o'clock and, because of another late team dinner, I've only had about seven and a half hours' sleep. That's not enough rest for anyone, never mind a Tour de France rider, but once I'm awake I can't go back to sleep again.

I shuffle out of bed and resign myself to an early start. At least I won't be on my own at breakfast. As I return to the room from my own call of nature, Hubert is weighing himself on the team scales left out in the hall every day to make sure we don't lose too many fluids during the race. He comes back in and promptly falls back into bed. He is asleep in a flash, and I am cursing him. I lie on the bed and try to delay things by reading another bit of J. R. R. Tolkien's *The Children of*

Húrin, a prequel to *Lord of the Rings*, but I'm still first at the breakfast table.

This morning's start to the stage was mental. I tried to get away a few times early on, and got into a few groups, but nothing would stick. Eventually, after about an hour of trying, and with only about sixty riders left in the bunch after the fast start, I gave up and drifted to the middle of the pack, only to watch Scottish rider David Millar and two others ride clear.

The peloton rode tempo most of the day and cranked it up a bit when we got into the last 50km. We had rain for the first time on this year's Tour, and the roads were really slippery. I made sure I was in the top ten as we descended the last of four climbs on today's stage, but the roads were like glass and one of the motorbikes crashed on the way down.

There were at least three more crashes on the run in to Barcelona, the combination of oil, diesel and petrol that you always get in a city centre making the road surface treacherous. I didn't see any of the crashes today, though, as my job was to help Nocentini in the final sprint. I didn't even know the bunch had split behind us. At least this time I didn't miss it.

We had Lloyd Mondory and José Luis Arrieta on the front with about 3km to go, and I stayed on the right, so Nocentini could see me and pick up my wheel, but he got boxed in on the left. Nocentini got eighth and I got twelfth; I was a bit disappointed with my own sprint. I was hoping to get a top ten. Twelfth isn't bad – it's the Tour de France, after all – but, psychologically, a top-ten placing is better.

I got a nice surprise last night. The guys from helmet manufacturers Spiuk called to the hotel and presented me with a new green, white and orange Irish national champion's helmet with my name on it. It goes nicely with my new Oakley glasses. I have two pairs now. One pair are mainly green, with an orange 'O' and white earpieces, while the other pair are the opposite way around. I had to take them off towards the end of today, though, as the oil stuck to the lenses and I couldn't see properly.

I'm still waiting on my national champion's shorts to be delivered, but I haven't heard anything about them yet, apart from the fact that they will be mainly white. It's probably just as well I didn't have them today, or they would have had to have been binned. The Barcelona roads also left my lovely new Irish jersey in a bad way. I only have two champion's jerseys, and I think I will have to give this one to the mechanics to power hose before it's put in the wash.

Hopefully, our first foray into the real mountains tomorrow will see our team leaders Vladimir Efimkin and Cyril Dessel live up to expectations and, hopefully, I will exceed the team's expectations. The team is not too confident about my climbing as we head to Andorra. For this Tour, Ag2r wanted me to work a bit in the sprints and hasn't considered me for the climbs, so I hope I can prove them wrong.

Stage 7 – Friday 10 July:
Barcelona–Andorra Arcalis, 224km

Climbs on the Tour de France are rated according to their severity and longevity, with a third-category ascent more difficult than a fourth-category one, and so on.

Those of you who enjoy skiing in the winter may have made the bus ride to the ski station at the top of Arcalis in Andorra. That's where we finished today. At 28km, the mountain is so long and steep it is classed as *hors catégorie* (out of category), with the maximum amount of King of the Mountains points available for first over the line. Coming at the end of the longest stage in this year's Tour, after a mammoth 224km and almost six and a half hours in the saddle, it was always going to be a savage climb. We then had to ride another 20km down the mountain after the stage to our hotel, but that's another story.

Ag2r started the day well, placing Nocentini and Christophe Riblon in a nine-man breakaway group that opened up a gap of over fourteen minutes on the peloton during the stage. But they would need all the advantage they could get to make it to the top of the final mountain ahead of the climbing specialists.

Christophe sprinted for all the King of the Mountains points at the top of each of the day's five climbs, except the last one, and by the end of the stage had moved into second in that competition.

Rinaldo was the highest placed rider overall in the break. He had started the day three minutes and twenty-seven seconds behind race leader Cancellara, and if he could finish even one more second ahead of the rest of the peloton he would become the new leader of the Tour. As Agritubel's Brice Feillu rode away from the lead group to win the stage and take the polka-dot jersey away from Christophe, he had a different jersey in mind. Christophe was more concerned about pacing Rinaldo up the final kilometres, and gave up his King of the Mountains aspirations to ensure that our Italian teammate would finish far enough ahead of the other contenders to take the yellow jersey.

As all this was going on, the peloton rode relentlessly skywards behind them, with me hanging on for dear life as the Astana team ate into the breakaway's advantage. On the mountain, I couldn't get my heart rate up to where it had been at last year's Tour of Spain. The most I could get up to was 175bpm, whereas at the Vuelta I could get up to 185 or 190 bpm. I don't know why this is, but when Cadel Evans attacked with about 3km to go, I was dropped and decided it would be better to ride steadily to the finish rather than try to ride flat out, possibly blowing up and losing way more time.

At the bottom of the climb, the guys were saying, 'Take it easy on the climb, tomorrow is a hard day.' But the guys don't have the motivation that I have. They just want to get in breakaways and don't give a damn about me being twentieth or thirtieth or whatever. Okay, if it's your tenth Tour, maybe you are better off conserving energy and trying to get in breaks some days. But this is my first, and I want to ride hard on the climbs to see what I can do. I don't want to drop off the pace, thinking of tomorrow. I need to go for it on the ascents to improve, so we have a difference of opinion there.

Now, we have the yellow jersey – the leader of the Tour on our team. Rinaldo took fourth on the stage, and leads the race by six seconds from Contador and eight seconds from Armstrong. We will try to defend the race lead but, with two first-category climbs along the road to Saint-Girons, it's not going to be easy.

Stage 8 – Saturday 11 July: Andorra–Saint-Girons, 176km

For a French team like my Ag2r La Mondiale team, having the yellow jersey at the Tour de France is a dream scenario. Live global and domestic television means that your product or company gets plenty of airtime and free advertising, so naturally our sponsors, who have been on the race this past week, want us to hold on to yellow for as long as we can.

Unfortunately for us, Rinaldo Nocentini's donning of the leader's jersey on Friday evening was followed by two very difficult mountain stages in the Pyrenees. Second and third overall, Contador and Armstrong were probably delighted to see a French team in yellow. They knew we would defend it 100 per cent, and they also knew their Astana team wouldn't have to do as much work if we had yellow. I'm sure they will take it when they want it.

Today began with plenty of attacks as we began the first climb of the day to Andorra immediately after the start. As we now lead the race, everybody looked at my Ag2r team to chase. I spent most of the 23km climb on the front of the bunch trying to reel in a large move that had gone clear and included dangerman Cadel Evans.

Evans was eventually persuaded to drop out of the

front group, as his colleagues knew his presence up front would hinder their progress and encourage other teams to chase. Even though we had Vladimir Efimkin up the road and had a valid reason not to chase, everybody kept attacking us in the valley.

I was told to ride hard at the front and keep chasing. After a long, hard pursuit into a serious headwind, at the bottom of the final climb, the Col d'Agnes, I just blew my lights and sat up and waited for the next group on the road. Rinaldo stayed in yellow, but I lost fourteen minutes on the stage and any real hope of a good overall placing in this Tour. Up front, Efimkin had been sitting on the break in defence of Nocentini's jersey, and he attacked with 5km to go and tried to win the stage but was caught 500m out and finished fourth.

Stage 9 – Sunday 12 July:
Saint-Gaudens–Tarbes, 160km

The Tour Village is where everybody congregates before each stage. A big outdoor square is usually taken over by race sponsors, staff, journalists and riders. Here, you can enjoy anything from a coffee and a continental breakfast to an English-language newspaper, a packet of sweets and a haircut. It's not, though, where you expect to get shot.

This morning, I was sitting talking to one of the main bosses of Ag2r, our sponsors, when a loud bang, like a gunshot, went off. Immediately, I felt a sting behind my left knee. I looked down to see blood pouring from my leg and a massive bruise appearing at the back of my knee around the tendon area. I had been shot!

The Tour security rushed to search the area as I clutched my leg in agony, but nothing was found. We looked on the ground for evidence of a pellet from a gun, or even a paintball or something, but found nothing. I still don't know what it was, but it frightened the life out of me and may have repercussions later in the race if my knee doesn't get better.

The adrenaline was still pumping through my body as we started the stage and, as is often the case after you get a fright, my legs were empty for about forty minutes. All I could think about was, What the hell just happened? It didn't help that I had a yellow jersey to defend or that the attacks went from the gun – pardon the pun.

Having the race leader on your team, everything else goes out the window, and Rinaldo is automatically protected by us. That means that he never has to ride in the wind. We always have to be in the top ten or fifteen in the bunch. One, two, or all of us surround him at all times and make sure he gets shelter. If he's thirsty, we go back and ride up through the peloton with bottles for him. If he punctures, a couple of us stop with him and pace him back to the bunch. If he needs to pee, the same thing happens, unless the bunch is travelling too fast to regain contact. Then, he simply relieves himself on the move, as one of us pushes him from the side. You're not long learning which side to push from either: the old saying 'pissing into the wind' comes to mind! If Rinaldo has a mechanical problem or wrecks his bike and the team car can't get to him quickly enough, one of us will give him ours. All this saves the race leader precious energy, but it soon saps the strength of the rest of the team.

The plan today was to let a group get up the road and we would ride tempo on the front of the bunch over climbs of the Col d'Aspen and the *hors catégorie* Col du Tourmalet. We wanted to ride steadily up the Tourmalet so there would still be a large number of riders in the peloton at the top. That way, we were likely to get more help from the sprinters' teams as they sniffed a possible stage win on the run in from the last mountain.

With 6km to go to the summit, I took over on the front of the peloton, and it was a fantastic feeling to be leading it up the mountain with the yellow jersey on my wheel, a great experience. I was disappointed with my sprint, even though I finished tenth on the stage. I was blocked in the middle of the group and world champion Alessandro Ballan and Sylvain Chavanel almost crashed in front of me. I slammed the brakes on before the final right-hander. I gave it all I could to get out and dived into the next corner, but my pedal hit the ground and I almost came down myself. People ask me why I take part in the sprints, but I love it. I love the thrill of people leaning on you, the pushing and elbowing, the split-second decisions that have to be made, but I never take any crazy risks.

Monday 13 July: Rest Day, Limoges

Who shot Nicolas Roche? It doesn't have quite the same ring to it, but I felt a bit like JR Ewing this morning. Loads of people asked me what happened after reading my diary entry. My dad even phoned me, because journalists were ringing him asking, 'Who shot Nicolas?' 'Is he okay?' 'What was it?' 'Will he be able to continue?' Although Tour security searched the area, they still have no idea what I was hit with.

Today went a lot quicker than I hoped it would. After the previous day's stage, we were loaded on to a bus at around 6 p.m., given a police escort to the airport and flew the forty minutes or so to Limoges and the first rest day of the Tour. Nobody likes transfers, but it could have been worse. The mechanics and soigneurs had a five-hour drive to get the team cars, bike van and team bus to the hotel.

Usually, in the mornings, I'm up at 7.30 a.m., full on and ready to go. Today, though, with no racing to be done, I woke up at around quarter past eight. I enjoyed my extra few minutes' sleep and, with no rush to carbo-load before the stage, I flicked on the telly and settled back in bed for a longer rest. Just when I was comfortable, there was a knock on the room door. It was the UCI anti-doping guys – the 'vampires'. They have earned this nickname in the peloton because they come in the night (or at least very early in the morning) and take your blood. I have no problem with the tests – in fact, I think they are essential – but I could have done with the lie-in.

Getting a needle stuck in your arm soon wakes you up, and at half eight I was ready for breakfast. After that, I cleaned my shoes and helmet, met the rest of the team for a coffee on the bus and headed out for a two-hour training ride. It's a good idea to keep the legs turning and go for a spin.

We did 60km and, as we were only taking it easy, our team manager came along for the ride too. The media asked Rinaldo to wear his yellow jersey on the spin, and we were followed by lots of press and TV motorbikes. Rinaldo is a 31-year-old Italian, and I have been friends with him since before joining this team. He's a funny guy. He has very curly hair, but always tries to keep it flat, which means he brings a hairdryer everywhere with him. He's always smiling, is game for a laugh and can give and take a slagging, which makes it easy to ride hard for him when you have to.

I had a nap for about an hour in the afternoon, before donning the compression therapy boots, or 'space legs', as we call them. These are a pair of over-sized inflatable boots, something like bouncy castles for your legs, which reach from your toes almost to your hip. They start to inflate at the toes and the pressure goes first to your ankle, then back to your toes, up to your calf, back to your toes, and then up your whole leg. It really squeezes you hard. The first time you put them on, you think your leg is going to break.

Myself and Vladimir Efimkin sat for half an hour in these inflatable boots, on the same double bed. I often wonder what an outsider would think if they walked into the room to see two grown men sitting in their boxers with space boots on, but they are supposed to be great for flushing the toxins out of tired muscles and are best followed up with a good massage. My leg seems to be getting a bit better now and, hopefully, it will be fine.

Stage 10 – Tuesday 14 July:
Limoges–Issoudun, 194.5km

Last night, I was rooming alone and this morning I had to be woken up at nine. I was knocked out. I fell asleep listening to James Blunt at about half ten and, despite not having raced the day before and having eleven hours' sleep, I didn't know where I was. I was really tired and was hoping for an easy day.

Every day, as well as the rest of my cycling kit, I place a tiny, flat radio in a pocket inside the back of my jersey. A cable runs up the inside of my jersey to a tiny microphone clipped on just under my collar and then to an earpiece. To stop the earpiece falling out and to make sure I can hear properly with the wind, it is held in by a strip of tape.

With this earpiece and microphone, I can talk to and hear all the other riders on my team, as well as my manager, Vincent Lavenu, in the team car. Vincent uses the radio to issue instructions about the route ahead, who the riders in the break are, what the gap to the leaders is, etc. We tell him if we have a puncture, or need bottles, and by the time we drift back to the car he has them ready for us. More importantly, though, he can warn us of dangerous corners, wet roads ahead, a crash or other critical safety information.

There was a bit of a war this morning between the teams and the race organizers at the start in Limoges. The Tour organization, ASO, had decided to ban team radios during the stage, with the penalty of being thrown off the race if anyone was caught using one. Three quarters of the teams were against the idea on safety grounds and wanted to neutralize the stage from the start.

At first, we had a laugh. Like big kids, every team had one or two riders who went back to the team car and said stuff like, 'What did you say? I couldn't hear you. I think my radio is broken.' Instead of telling your team-mate into the radio to slow down on the front, we rode up and grabbed their jersey for the laugh.

My role today was to take care of yellow jersey Nocentini and also to help our other leader, Efimkin. It may have looked easy on paper but, after the rest day on Monday, it was a hard enough day. I had to keep them both out of the wind, bring them up the bunch and stop with them if one of them had to pause for any reason. Efimkin had to stop twice today as his cranks came loose. I waited with him as the mechanic tightened them and then rode into the wind ahead of him as we chased through the team cars back up the peloton.

The roads today were really dead, like Irish roads, and I don't think there was a metre of flat all day. The radio ban actually helped today because if the racing had been flat out all day the bunch would have been split to bits.

In the final 25km, the speed really ramped up, and we went from 35kph to over 60kph in a flash. I was to help Lloyd Mondory in the sprint and brought him up to the front with 5km to go. I then went back for Nocentini and couldn't find Lloyd. I stayed in my position and just missed a Katusha rider, who fell in front of me on one of the last corners. It would have been a nice sprint for me today, but the team hasn't always been happy with me going for the sprints, so I just did what they asked me to do and didn't even think about sprinting. I crossed the line in seventeenth place.

I also found out this evening that there was a police investigation into the incident that left me with a massive bruise on my leg. The gendarmes found out that it was an exploding ice compressor. But just to keep the conspiracy theory going, my soigneur told me that as I lay on the ground clutching my leg he ran around the back of the lorries to find an old guy bent over laughing. When my soigneur confronted him, he said, 'Ah, they were only having a bit of fun,' which makes me think somebody did do it on purpose. Although it hurts when I walk or climb the stairs, it seems to be okay on the bike, so hopefully it will hold out until Paris on Sunday week.

Stage 11 – Wednesday 15 July: Vatan–Saint-Fargeau, 192km

Today was crazy at the start. It was very fast for the first 25km, with a 56kph average speed. My team didn't want to let a group go clear with more than four or five riders in it, because a larger group could build more time on the peloton and potentially take the yellow jersey from Nocentini. We were filtering everything that moved. If a break jumped clear, one of us hopped on the back of it, or if it was a big group, we all chased on the front of the peloton and brought it back straight away. The roads were really narrow and it was very windy, so the constant stop–start rhythm in the bunch was pretty dangerous.

Sure enough, after about 20km there was a massive crash in the peloton. About fifty or sixty riders came down, and there were bodies everywhere. Thankfully, I missed it, because I was at the front chasing down a move, but my team leader Vladimir Efimkin got really badly hurt. He went head first over the handlebars, and all of his face is cut, from his chin to his forehead.

Two breakaways went clear a split second before the collision and, because of the mayhem behind, they were soon forgotten about. Our team, along with Saxo Bank and Columbia, went to the front of the bunch and spread across the road to slow things down and allow the fallen riders to regain contact. Nocentini didn't come down, but he was held up by the crash, so I dropped back to wait for him and bring him back to the bunch. There was at least half an hour of chaos as teams went back for their teammates and guys picked themselves up and made their way back to the peloton, dripping in blood.

I went back to work on the front, but Efimkin went missing again, so I drifted back to look for him. He was down the back and looked pretty dejected. Apart from his face, his knees, arms and elbows were also cut and sore. I tried to cheer him up and persuaded him to drop back to the doctor. I waited with him twice and paced him back to the bunch. He went off with the race doctor after the stage, and it looks like he will need a good bit of treatment. Hopefully, he can continue because, realistically, he is our only hope of a high over-all placing on the Tour.

As I was busy going up and down the bunch all day getting bottles for the guys and bringing Efimkin to the doctor, we had two guys, Cyril Dessel and Stéphane Goubert, on the front, and the rest of the guys were keeping Nocentini out of the wind. It was a hard day but at the end of it we still had the race lead. During the stage, Mark Cavendish came up alongside and tapped me on the shoulder. 'Hey Nico, I think your dad doesn't like me,' he said.

I laughed. 'What do you mean he doesn't like you?' Cav was complaining that my dad had been a bit hard on him on Eurosport the day before for his celebrations upon crossing the line. Cav made a phone call gesture as he won the stage but explained that it was because his team had a new mobile phone manufacturer as a sponsor and he wanted to give them a plug.

I didn't see yesterday's programme, but I think my dad was saying that, some days, Cav says he wants to win the green jersey, other days he says he just wants to win stages. Whereas Thor Hushovd has to try to go in breaks and get mid-stage sprint points to get the green jersey, I think Cav doesn't have to try to win the green jersey – it will just come naturally to him. Some people think Cav is cocky. I've known him for about ten years, and he is the same with me now, after winning eight stages of the Tour and fifty professional races, as he was when he was a junior.

Cav just does what he does best, and he won his fourth stage, equalling the British record of eight stage wins, in just two years as a pro. You can't argue with that.

Stage 12 – Thursday 16 July:
Tonerre–Vittel, 211km

Today was very hard. We were so worried about Nocentini losing the yellow jersey on the stage that we were at the start way before any other team. The team plan was to let a small group go clear and keep them on a short leash until the sprinters' teams took over at the head of the peloton. If we could get a man into that small breakaway group, then all the better, because he could sit at the back in defence of Rinaldo's yellow jersey and possibly win the stage.

I was really active in the first part of the race. As the first of the day's six climbs came very early on, it was up to me to try to infiltrate any escape groups, as our sprinters didn't have the legs to be jumping around on the early climbs. We seem to be heavily marked by the Astana and Columbia teams at the start of each stage, even though our team manager assured them that we would still defend the yellow jersey if we had a man in the break. I guess they don't want to be forced into doing all the work either. I can't blame them, because the past week or so has really taken its toll on us. Normally, at the team meal in the evening, everyone is laughing and joking. Last night, there was silence as we munched our way through our pasta dish. You could see it in our faces. The previous six days had been so demanding we were too tired to laugh.

The speed this morning was unreal. The break didn't go clear until 100km into the stage, and we covered 95 of them in the first two hours. We kept the gap to the leaders down to just under four minutes in the hope that the sprinters' teams would come and give us a hand on the front of the peloton, but nobody came. We're all worried about tomorrow. It's a real mountain day. Normally, we should lose the jersey to a climber, but the team kind of hopes we can hang on to it for another day.

Our real overall hope, Vladimir Efimkin, is still pretty torn up after his crash on Wednesday. His face is full of open cuts and, in this heat, you can imagine how sore it must be to have salty sweat running into your wounds all day. His chest is also burnt from sliding along the road, and his legs are in ribbons.

I'm worried about the mountains coming up. I've given a lot in the past week in the defence of the yellow jersey, and I'm pretty wrecked. It's been a fantastic experience, but it's been extremely tiring. My team is not one of the super teams in cycling. We have had to defend yellow jerseys before. I've even had the yellow jersey on a five- or six-day race, but we've never had to contend with anything on the scale of the Tour.

I'm still a bit bitter about losing fourteen minutes on stage eight last Saturday, after chasing hard to keep Nocentini in contention in the valleys. But I see the Tour in a different light now. If I hadn't done that work, I would be in the top ten now, but maybe we wouldn't have had a week in yellow with Nocentini. Hopefully, in the last week, I will be active enough to get into a few breakaway groups and show off the Irish champion's jersey.

Stage 13 – Friday 17 July:
Vittel–Colmar, 200km

Only myself, Hubert Dupont, Vladimir Efimkin and Stéphane Goubert finished in the front group today, after a rain-sodden 200km stage over five mountain climbs.

As we wait for Nocentini to return from the podium, we eat a snack, some ham and potatoes. I am not tired yet, but I expect I soon will be. I'll turn on my iPod and drift off. At the moment, I'm too pissed off to be tired.

When I started today's stage, I didn't think we would still have the yellow jersey on our team. With five climbs, including one first-category mountain on the way to Colmar, we thought an attack from the likes of Contador, Armstrong or some of the other contenders would end Rinaldo's reign in yellow. As he only leads the race by six seconds, we didn't think he'd be able to hang on. But the attacks never came, and my Italian teammate is still race leader. Although it means we will have to defend the lead tomorrow, that's not why I'm pissed off.

I've been going okay on the climbs in this Tour. On the tough second-category climb of the Col de la Schlucht, after about 100km, we were attacked by a big group of fifteen. I went in the next counterattack, just to make sure we were represented in the front group. Cancellara was there, as was Sérgio Paulinho from Astana and King of the Mountains Egoi Martínez. This forced Armstrong's Astana team to chase, and we were all together again at the top.

On the main climb of the day, the Col du Platzerwasel, I punctured out of the first group about halfway up the mountain. The Mavic neutral service car gave me a new back wheel, but the gears weren't working properly so I had to stop again and wait for my Ag2r team car. I rode back up through the field to the second group and then got back on to the front group on the descent. There were only about thirty riders left in the front group, so I was happy enough.

Coming in to the finish, we were sprinting for fifth place and the last available UCI points. Nocentini was on my wheel, so I led him out with 400m to go, but when I turned round he hadn't followed me, so all I did was lead out the sprint for the other guys, and finished seventeenth myself.

Sometimes, I don't understand this team. Coming to the Tour, our priority was to score world-ranking UCI points. Even though the Tour is the biggest race in the world, you only get points for the first five each stage and, despite having the race lead for the past week, we haven't been scoring. With four riders up the road, there were still some points available on the line. Hubert had ridden pretty hard coming into the town, then Astana put Yaroslav Popovych on the front and he took over. In the last kilometres, I radioed to Vincent Lavenu and asked him if I could contest the sprint, but he said, 'No. No. No. Priority is to ride for the yellow jersey.'

I argued the case that Rinaldo's jersey was not in any danger, as his main rivals hadn't taken any time during the stage and were definitely not going to try in the final sprint, but the answer was the same.

Why couldn't I have a go? To some guys, fifth or sixth is nothing, whereas for me, I came here aiming for a top five on a stage and literally threw away the best chance I've had all race.

Of course I'm frustrated by it. On the other hand, the team gave me the chance to come and ride the Tour. In fairness, I was told that I was just here to work in the mountains. But the team does make some strange decisions. I'm asked to attack on a flat stage, when I should be kept for the mountain stages. I totally disagree with that. It's a pity for them and for me too.

Hopefully, we can keep yellow for another day tomorrow. It's not as hard as today. I know Rinaldo would love to wear it as the Tour enters Italy on Tuesday, but I can't see us keeping it in Verbiers on Sunday.

Stage 14 – Saturday 18 July: Colmar–Besançon, 199km

There was a lot of fighting in the crosswinds early on today. As usual, my team was trying to get somebody into any move that went clear. The benefit of having someone in the break when your team has the yellow jersey is twofold. Firstly, if we got a rider into the break, he could sit on the back in defence of Nocentini's yellow jersey, would not have to do any work in the break and could possibly win the stage if the group stayed clear. Secondly, once the gap was enough to allow one of the breakaways to take over the race lead, the rest of the team wouldn't have to drag the peloton along behind, because they would be chasing their own man down.

The guys were jumping on anything that moved and after about 20km I slotted on to the back of a big group. There were thirteen riders in it, with most of the teams represented. They drove along for about 50km to establish a gap, and then built up a lead of over seven minutes at one stage. My orders were to sit at the back of the group and not contribute to the workload.

Sitting on the back of a break all day means you can't win, even if you do cross the line first. If you win, everybody says you didn't ride all day. If you don't win, they ask, how could you not have won? Also, if you are riding through, you are sheltered all the time except when you are on the very front. Ironically, at the back, you have to switch wheels constantly, and you catch a lot of wind. Any time I went back to the team car today, the pace increased, making it more difficult to get back up to the break.

Up front, Italy's Daniel Bennati of Liquigas and his Belgian teammate Frederik Willems gave me tons of abuse, as did another Italian, Daniele Righi of Lampre. It was unbelievable. They called me every name under the sun because I didn't work in the break. The other ten guys, though, knew they would be doing the same in my position, and just got on with it. George Hincapie, who had the most to gain – a chance to take over in yellow if we got a big enough gap on the stage – didn't bat an eyelid. He'd won a mountain stage a few years previously by defending Lance Armstrong's yellow jersey in exactly the same way.

With 50km to go, Bennati came up to me and said, 'You're going to have to pay me a lot of money if you want to win this stage, or you will never win, because I will chase you down. There's no way you're going anywhere without me.'

When I attacked with 11km to go, I gave it everything into a headwind on the final hill of the stage. But the first one on my wheel was Bennati. When he came up to me, I swung across the road, only to see Russian champion Sergei Ivanov counterattack. Nobody moved. I knew it was game over. Two more went clear, and I thought, How am I going to get back up to salvage anything? With 2km left, I went absolutely flat out and caught the two chasers just before the finish. I decided to sprint straight past and if they got my wheel, they got my wheel, if they didn't, I would get second, which is what happened: second on a stage of the Tour. If I had been offered that at the start, I would have taken it with both hands, but after the stage there wasn't the pleasure that should have been there. Again, I was disappointed.

I found out later on that Bennati had gone on live TV and told the world that I was a small rider and that nobody should have any respect for me. In fact, the first two words out of his mouth when asked what he thought of the stage were, 'F**k Roche!' I twisted and turned a lot that night before I went to sleep.

Stage 15 – Sunday 19 July: Pontarlier–Verbiers, 207.5km

This morning before the start, I waited along with the

Italian media outside the Liquigas team bus. We were all waiting on one man, Daniel Bennati. While they wanted to grab him for a few words, I wanted to grab him by the throat, and that's exactly what I did, in front of the press.

I told him he needed to give me some respect. I told him that he would have done exactly the same thing as I had if he had been in my shoes. You do whatever your team manager tells you. If he tells you not to ride, you don't ride. If he tells you to go and get some UCI points at the end, you go and get some UCI points. If he didn't understand that our priority was the yellow jersey, then he didn't understand cycling.

In the end, Nocentini only held on to yellow by five seconds. If I had ridden even once, he could have lost those five seconds. I told Bennati that if he had a problem, he should have come to me after the stage, not go on live television and tell the world. I think he was surprised I had the balls to go and grab him in front of the Italian press, but the cheeky bastard said he did nothing wrong. He just played ignorant.

Today was miserable. I was hanging on the whole day. I think I was more mentally tired than anything. It was one of the worst days I've had on a bike in ages. I was going out the back almost from the start. Very few riders congratulated me on my second place, apart from a few friends. Righi even came back and had another go at me, calling me a bastard. My head was wrecked and my legs felt like I was riding into a brick wall.

I decided to ask Armstrong what he thought of the

whole situation. I speak with him most days, and he's sound enough. He'll come up and ask how the legs are, tell me to watch out for the next climb, that he did it a couple of months ago and it gets steep at the bottom – stuff like that. I told him what had happened. He basically said that it's just a bike race and each team has its own interest. There's no right, no wrong, only points of view, which made sense. I'd done what I had to do.

He told me that Hincapie was disappointed because my team was chasing behind and he lost his one chance of going into yellow. I explained that it was the riders and not the team manager who had decided to chase. They had worked hard for the previous eight days and wanted one last day in yellow. Today, they got it, and Rinaldo lost his yellow jersey to Armstrong's teammate Alberto Contador on the climb to Verbiers.

On the final climb, I brought Nocentini to the front just before the bottom. I got dropped when Contador attacked and totally sat up with about 5km to go, mentally drained.

Monday 20 July: Rest Day, Switzerland

My Ag2r team is staying in a nice Swiss hotel, perched on the side of a cliff and surrounded by vineyards. After 2,851km of racing and over sixty-three hours in the saddle, I was really looking forward to having a nice lie-in this morning. But, as anyone who has ever worked hard all week only to be woken by their kids jumping on the bed at six o'clock on a Saturday morning will testify, you never really get a rest when you need one.

On the first rest day, I had been woken from my race-induced coma at half seven by a knock on the door from the anti-doping controllers, and yesterday, at exactly the same time, I woke up to a helicopter hovering over my bed. At least, that's what it sounded like. I looked out of the hotel window to see a chopper watering the vineyards next door. Incredible.

After breakfast, we all met at the team bus and went for a training ride. The mechanics had put some green handlebar tape on my bike to match my Irish champion's jersey, which was cool. We rode for an hour and forty minutes today, climbing up the nearest mountain and back down the other side. It was a hell of a climb, and my legs were pretty tired.

My room mate, Hubert Dupont, stayed in bed today, as he has a contracted muscle in his calf and wanted a proper rest. Dessel has an inflamed Achilles tendon. Arrieta and Riblon only did forty minutes, while myself, Nocentini, Goubert and Mondory did the full spin. Goubert did an extra half an hour on his own. Masochist.

On the spin, I couldn't get my heart rate up. I've had a sinus infection and a bit of a chest infection for the past three days. I've had asthma since I was around nineteen. Because I'm a professional cyclist, I had to go through a massive protocol to prove I had asthma and to be allowed to use an inhaler. In the past, there has been a lot of abuse, with guys claiming they had asthma so they could use products to enable them to breathe better – although I've been told that inhalers do nothing unless you do actually have asthma. There are only certain laboratories approved by the three main anti-doping bodies, the UCI, the AFLD and WADA, who carry out the asthma test. They give you an inhaler that works the opposite way to Ventolin: it closes your lungs. They see how much your lungs close, open them again and work out some kind of percentage to see how many milligrams, or inhaler puffs, you are allowed to take. Take any more than you are supposed to, and you risk a doping violation.

The team doctor gave me antibiotics yesterday, which will probably make me feel even more tired than I am now. My coughing is slowly getting worse, waking me up in the night, but it's not going to stop me getting to Paris. It's not a good enough excuse. I don't think a broken leg would stop me now.

The incident with Daniel Bennati got a bit of attention in the Italian media yesterday. Surprisingly, though, they complimented me on my *palle* in confronting Bennati and even called him a chicken. He's not the best liked rider in the peloton and has had his fair share of run-ins with guys, most notably with Cavendish, who rubs his nose in it every time he beats him.

Stage 16 – Tuesday 21 July: Martigny–Bourg-Saint-Maurice, 159km

I'm so disappointed about today's stage. I finished fourth, but I think somebody must have put a curse on me for this Tour, some black magic or something.

The first climb was a bit of a mess. The *hors catégorie* Col du Grand-Saint-Bernard came after just 16km of racing, and there were large groups all over the place after only a few kilometres of climbing. My team had nobody in the twenty-five-man lead group, so there was massive panic in the team car. They were going crazy that there was no Ag2r rider in the front.

There were bodies everywhere, with Arrieta the first to try to get across the gap to one of the big groups. Then myself and Stéphane Goubert rode past him and got across to the second or third group. The pace accelerated continuously until there were only four of us left, and we continued to ride hard until we made it to the front of the race. The 28km of climbing, to over 2,500m, that followed, took me an hour and eight minutes to get to the top. When I crossed the summit, there were only two guys ahead, and I was with seventeen chasers, including my teammate Goubert.

We all rode pretty steadily until a few kilometres into the second climb of the day, the little sister of the first climb, the Col du Petit-Saint-Bernard. With the top of the climb just 30km from the finish, the attacks came left, right and centre on the way up, and it was really hard to hold the wheels. Goubert is pretty experienced and when I saw that he was just riding steadily, ignoring most of the attacks, and was still getting back up to groups, I followed suit. I rode steadily, in my lowest gear of 39x23, and for a long while I was last man in the group. I kept riding around guys that were getting dropped and, fifty minutes of climbing later, there were only four of us left.

On the descent, myself, Goubert and French riders Sandy Casar and Pierrick Fédrigo, who has already won a stage in this Tour, were chasing four others: Amaël Moinard from Cofidis, Jurgen van den Broeck from Silence Lotto, Mikel Astarloza from Euskaltel and King of the Mountains Franco Pellizotti from Liquigas. These four had gone clear towards the top of the mountain and crested the summit about a minute ahead. With the peloton over two minutes back, the stage victory was going to come down to a battle between our two groups, and we thundered down the rollercoaster, switchback-laden descent to try to close the gap.

I knew if we could catch the four guys in front, I had my best chance of getting a Tour de France stage win. We could see them ahead as the gap closed to twenty-five seconds, then they disappeared as we went through a forest. The gap came down slowly to twenty seconds, fifteen seconds. All four of us were riding flat out and, with Goubert in the move with me, I was feeling really confident of winning the stage. The kilometres ticked away agonizingly, and it seemed like it took us for ever to make contact, but we eventually reached the back wheel of the leaders with about a kilometre and a half to go.

Asterloza, knowing that there was no way he would win a sprint, had just jumped clear of the leaders before we made contact. With 1km left, Goubert went to the front and gave it everything for me to try to win the stage. At thirty-nine years of age, this is Stéphane's last Tour. In twelve seasons as a pro, he has never won a race, and this was probably his best chance of ever doing so.

Instead of thinking of himself, though, Stéphane went to the front of the group and drove it along behind Asterloza, sacrificing his dreams to give me the best chance of winning in the sprint. Stéphane's selflessness really motivated me. I was sitting waiting, ready to go.

I've been in this position three times at major tours now. I've been second twice, once at the Tour of Spain and once last week, and something has always gone wrong. Today, as I started my sprint with 300m to go, my chain came off, falling over the big chainring on to my pedal side. I was last man out of the last corner and finished fourth.

Stage 17 – Wednesday 22 July: Bourg-Saint-Maurice–Le Grand Bornand, 169.5km

Today was what's known in cycling terms as the 'Queen Stage' of the Tour de France. I don't know where the term originated, but it's usually given to the hardest day of the race and, with one second-category climb and four first-category mountains to be covered on the 170km through the Alps, today was never going to be easy.

The day didn't start too well for me when I crashed 2km into the first climb. A few guys slammed on in front of me, and I hit the pile of bodies on the ground and was buck-a-rooed sideways out of my saddle and landed on my arse on a grass verge.

I got up with a cut hip and a dead leg and remounted my bike. A few hundred metres later, though, I was standing at the side of the road again. My front derailleur was broken, and I had to wait for the team car to change bikes. Because everyone was attacking at the bottom of the climb, I was the last man on the road. Even the gruppetto, the group of sprinters and non-climbers who stick together and form a large bunch on the early climbs in an effort to beat the daily time limit, were ahead of me.

If I didn't want to end up in the gruppetto and lose forty minutes, there was only one thing for it, and that was to chase as hard as I could all the way up the mountain. When I realized this, I panicked a bit and took a fit of coughing until I settled down into a steady climbing rhythm. I caught the gruppetto after about 6–7km, but rode straight past because I had to keep going to try to regain contact with the main peloton. I rode the full 18km climb on my own, and with 300m to go to the top I made contact with the back of the bunch and then used the descent to move up the pack.

On this descent, I realized my spare bike was set up differently from my race bike, with clincher tyres, carbon rims and aluminium brakes. My other bike had tubular tyres, which grip the road differently, and both carbon rims and brakes, which give a short, sharp, braking action and can stop the bike pretty quickly. My spare bike took a lot longer to stop, as I found out on the first couple of bends, nearly giving myself a heart attack in the process.

At the bottom of the descent, we turned right and headed straight up the second climb, the 16km-long Col de Saisies. Saxo Bank started riding at the front of the peloton, and we went up it at a fair pace. After the descent, we went through the feed zone, and I had time to refuel and get a bit of a breather. The second-category Côte d'Araches was okay and, at the top, there were only about thirty-five of us left in the peloton, with Armstrong, Contador, the Schleck brothers and all the main contenders still there.

The penultimate climb, the Col de Romme, saw the Schleck brothers attack the rest of the race in an effort to gain some time before tomorrow's time trial. The peloton imploded, and the efforts of defending the yellow jersey for a week and being in two long breakaways, one only the day before, meant I wasn't feeling too hot, and I couldn't even try to follow the wheels. I tried to push a gear but hadn't the power and when I tried to spin a gear I couldn't spin it fast enough.

Hubert Dupont stayed with me at first in an effort to pace me back up, but he has a totally different style of climbing to mine. Where I like to sit down and ride steadily, Hubert is more of a specialist climber, and his in-and-out-of-the-saddle style and continuous change of pace soon cracked me. When I tried to give him a breather, I was too slow for him and, eventually, I told him to go ahead.

Stage 18 – Thursday 23 July: Individual Time Trial, Lake Annecy, 42.5km

Although I wasn't due to start today's individual time trial until 3.48 p.m., I was up at the usual time for breakfast before leaving the hotel to do a preview ride of the course with my dad, who had flown in the night before, and my teammates Stéphane Goubert and Rinaldo Nocentini. We talked about gear selection and measuring our effort on the 4km climb. I decided to use a 44-tooth inside chainring, a decision that would come back to haunt me later that day.

The race against the clock gave me two options. As I was never realistically going to challenge the time-trial specialists like Cancellara, Contador and Wiggins, I could either ride the time trial well within myself, not caring about my placing on the stage, or I could ride flat out and see how I got on.

For most people, the first option would be the easiest. A lot of guys simply try to work out how long the winner would take to cover the 25 or so miles. Then they add the percentage they have to stay within in order not to be eliminated under the time-limit ruling. Once they keep a few minutes inside of this time, just to be sure, they can ride well within themselves and save some energy for the following three days. In effect, if you do it right, riding a time trial when you're not a contender can be like having a virtual rest day.

I decided to ride hard. I started the day twenty-fourth overall and, even though it made no difference if I dropped to thirtieth or fortieth overall with a slow time, or even moved up a few places with a fast time, I wanted to test myself over the distance and see exactly how far off the top guys I would be after three weeks of racing. It's very important for me to work on my time trialling if I'm to make the next step up to be a big stage-race contender.

Today I wore my new brown and white Ag2r skinsuit

for only the third time in this race. As national road race champion, I can only wear the shamrock jersey on the road stages. As the stage would take me less than an hour – fifty-one minutes and forty-three seconds, to be exact – I just took one bottle. To gain every possible aerodynamic advantage, there are no pockets in a skin-suit, so I stuffed an energy gel up one leg of my shorts for easy reach.

Today, the Irish fans almost outnumbered the French – or maybe it just felt like that because they really make their presence felt, with big tricolours, body paint, Guinness hats, inflatable hammers: you name it. It's great to get the support and makes me really proud to be Irish. Today I saw a guy with a T-shirt saying 'Roche Rocks', which is a great play on words, as *roche* means rock in French.

I always try and wave, or at least nod or smile at them if I'm suffering too much to take my hands off the bars. Today, though, all I could manage was a half-grimace, half-smile, or a flick of my finger off the bars as I tried to keep my speed up on the 4km climb. My choice of inner chainring had proven to be too big as, after almost three weeks of racing, I didn't have the power I usually use to roll over that type of climb. Watching Armstrong and Contador on TV afterwards, I noticed they were using much smaller gears and could spin up the climb, whereas I was fighting with my bike all the way up.

I struggled to keep a good pace going, finishing three minutes and eleven seconds slower than yellow-jerseyed stage winner Alberto Contador for fiftieth place on the stage. I dropped one place on the overall to twenty-fifth but, like I said earlier, it doesn't really matter much. I'm also sixth in both the points competition and best-young-rider competition.

With three days left, I'm getting tired, as is everybody else. My two team leaders Vladimir Efimkin and Cyril Dessel have gone home. Efimkin was suffering from the after-effects of landing on his face a few days ago, and Dessel with an inflamed Achilles tendon. It takes longer to do everything now, because of fatigue. My reactions are that of a pensioner, and I feel like a car with a run-down battery. It might look good, but it's slow.

Stage 19 – Friday 24 July:
Bourgoin-Jallieu–Aubenas, 178 km

Looking back, I would have been better off sitting in the bunch all day today, conserving energy and sprinting at the end, but that's all well and good in hindsight. Instead, I went clear in a large breakaway group which could have taken twenty minutes and propelled me up the General Classification.

The attacks started almost as soon as we started climbing, within a couple of kilometres of the start. Ten guys went clear, including José Luis Arrieta. I got across to them in a group of five, before Christophe Riblon came up with three more, making it a nineteen-man lead group.

As both my Ag2r team and the Caisse d'Epargne team had three riders in the break, we rode hard at the front to try to establish a good gap. Both teams knew we could move up in the team classification if we took some time on the peloton. Some of the other riders weren't as committed, and sometimes it's harder to ride fast in a big group than it is with maybe seven or eight riders. My old friend Bennati also made the break. Although he contributed his fair share to the move, we just ignored each other for the most part.

The peloton, though, wasn't taking any chances and we never got more than just under three minutes. The Dutch Rabobank team had missed the move and were hoping their sprinter and three-time world champion Óscar Freire could hold on over the final climb and win the stage, so they led the chase.

Inexplicably, with the gap down to two minutes but the break moving smoothly, Arrieta jumped clear with Leonardo Duque from Cofidis. There was absolutely no point in this move, as all it did was break up the momentum of our group as everybody started attacking. When the team car came up to hand Christophe a bottle, he fired it on the ground in disgust. Normally, Arrieta is a clever rider, but this attack made no sense. It also meant that myself and Christophe had to keep chasing down any other counterattacks, and it was a total waste of energy. I'd already lost fourteen minutes with these kinds of tactics on the road to Andorra at the end of the first week, and both myself and Christophe had had enough. With the gap coming down steadily and with Arrieta representing our team in the front, we decided to wait for the bunch. Arrieta's group was caught 5km later.

The final climb of the second-category Col de

l'Escrinet was agony. It was only 16km to the finish after the summit, but the cumulative efforts of the past three weeks and having ridden hard in the break meant I was almost crying on the climb. The easy option would have been to give up and just ride into the finish, as a lot of guys did. Hubert passed me on the climb and pepped me up with a bit of encouragement. I knew that if I could hang in there, I would have a good chance of a top ten in the sprint, as most of the fast guys were dropped on the climb.

I was a little bit off the back on the descent, and it had started to rain. There were a couple of guys in front of me, between me and the back of the lead group, and I just closed my eyes to avoid the spray from their wheels in the wet and went past them.

In the last few kilometres I was fighting with Martijn Maaskant from Garmin for a good position in the sprint. He's around the same age as me, but the Dutchman is bigger and stronger, and he hit me with a few good shoulders, which forced me to ride in the wind for too long.

I eventually got a bit of shelter, but I was too far back. I lost the wheel in front of me in the final kilometre, which meant I had to sprint to catch up before the real sprint had even started. In the end, when I popped out to the left of the group, the lactic acid set my legs on fire and I was riding on empty. I crossed the line eighth, and wrecked.

Stage 20 – Saturday 25 July:
Montélimar–Mont Ventoux, 167km

Whoever thought of putting the toughest climb of this year's Tour at the very end of the second-last stage, after twenty days of racing, over 3,295km and eighty-two and a half hours in the saddle, is a very sadistic person.

For those of you who don't know the climb of Mont Ventoux, here's the rundown. At 1,192m high and 22km long, the Ventoux is rated an *hors catégorie* climb, which, on the Tour, means it's actually too hard to rate. The average gradient is 7.5 per cent, but the last 16km are actually 9 per cent, and its sun-scorched slopes claimed the life of British rider Tom Simpson in 1967.

Ventoux means 'windy', and the climb's wide-open, rock-strewn, lunar landscape sees gusting winds of around 100kph for much of the year, with the road to the top often closed because of this. If you're a good climber, it will take you at least an hour and a quarter to get to the summit.

Today saw the Saxo Bank, Garmin and Astana teams drive the front of the peloton along at a blistering pace. With around 30km to go, I was the only one of my team left in the front part of the splintered bunch, as the others – apart from Christophe, who was up the road in a breakaway group – had all been caught out in the crosswind.

At the bottom of the climb, the pace lifted again as the Schleck brothers tried to rid themselves of Contador and Armstrong to claim a place on the final podium in Paris. Everybody knew it was their last chance on this Tour to change the overall standings, and the pace was unbelievable on such a steep gradient. I lost contact with the front group, and Hubert caught me and helped to pace me until I could no longer keep up. I wanted badly to defend my top-twenty-five position in the overall, and I used every last ounce of energy to drag myself up the rest of the climb. There was a 40kph headwind towards the top, and my legs were screaming as I tried to keep a steady pace. I crossed the line, shattered, seven minutes behind the stage winner Manuel Gárate of Rabobank, and had held on to my twenty-third place overall by just fifteen seconds. I was so tired after the stage that I fell asleep in the team car for over an hour.

Stage 21 – Sunday 26 July: Montereau-Fault-Yonne–Paris Champs-Elysées, 164km

Today we had to get up early to get a TGV high-speed train transfer from the Alps to the start in the outskirts of Paris. The stage itself started pretty easy, with all the jersey winners parading in front of the photographers at the front of the peloton. As usual, though, the speed increased dramatically once we entered the Champs-Elysées circuit, and we were soon riding flat out. The fact that it was the last stage, combined with the huge crowd packing the circuit, gave everyone the incentive to use every last joule of energy as the laps counted down, and I rolled across the line in the middle of the bunch as Cav took his sixth stage win.

I've had a lot of tough days on this Tour. I don't think I realize yet how well I've done, finishing twenty-third overall, fifth in the young rider competition and sixth in the green jersey competition. My team Ag2r held the yellow jersey for seven days with Rinaldo Nocentini, and I took five top-ten placings on stages. I was so riled by the abuse I got from the Italian riders for following my team orders that I couldn't enjoy my second place, while the day I got fourth, my chain came off in the sprint.

My favourite souvenir of this Tour is a photo I've seen of me climbing the Tourmalet on the front of the peloton with Nocentini in yellow on my wheel and Contador and Armstrong behind him. It was always a dream to wear the national champion's jersey at the Tour de France, and it was a really thrilling experience for me, as the fans moved back to open the road ahead, to lead the bunch up the mountain, wearing the Irish champion's jersey, with all the top guys behind me. One of my goals on this Tour was to get the Irish jersey a lot of exposure. A fan came up to me the other day and told me I was doing a fantastic job for Irish cycling. I was delighted to hear that. I think Irish cycling deserves a bit of credit. We have Philip Deignan at Cervélo and my cousin Dan at Garmin, and these guys are really top riders too. But for Dan's injury and the fact that Philip had already ridden the Giro, both could have ridden this Tour.

13

Moving Up the Ladder

After my good Tour de France debut, Ag2r admitted they should have had more faith in me from the start. They told me I would be a protected rider in future Grand Tours, scrapped my previous two-year contract and offered me a year's extension until the end of 2011.

My 2010 season got off to a bad start, though, at the five-day Etoile de Bessèges stage race in France. The penultimate stage was spent spitting out the grime-and-grit toothpaste of the rain-lashed roads and, along with half the peloton, I caught a stomach bug and spent much of the night suffering from a bad headache and vomiting.

Next morning, I felt as if I was going to die and didn't start the last stage. Instead, I went home and stayed in bed for three days, before thinking I felt a bit better and stupidly deciding to ride the Tour of the Mediterranean on the Wednesday.

I couldn't eat for two days after Bessèges and spent the first two days of the Tour of the Med eating baby cereal as it was the only thing that stayed down. I felt really bad at one point on the opening stage and went back to the team car to give them my jacket, as I was really hot. While I was at the car, thirty guys got dropped in the crosswind and I spent the rest of the stage with them, losing over ten minutes.

I began to eat a little the next morning, but realized my mistake after a few minutes when I was last man in the bunch, spewing my breakfast on to the side of the road, while still trying to keep in contact with the peloton. Luckily, I hadn't eaten much so it didn't last long. Once my stomach had emptied again, I began to feel better, but could only eat bananas and sip water for the rest of the race and had no energy to do anything other than get to the finish.

There are only two things worse than being sick in a bike race. And one of them is having the shits in a bike race. Thankfully, it has never happened to me but in the Ivory Coast I saw guys who had obviously eaten more than boiled rice start stages with toilet roll replacing race food in the pockets of their jerseys. They even had the straps of their shorts undone to save time if they had to run for a field in the middle of a race. I've seen guys returning to the peloton minus their mitts, having forgotten loo roll. I've heard stories of guys' legs having to be sprayed with bottles of water by their teammates to clean them afterwards. But there's one thing even worse than being sick or having the shits on a race, and that's stopping or, in cycling lingo, 'packing'.

For whatever reason, packing is always the last resort. The sport is so hard that when you begin initially as a youngster, you have to fight tooth and nail just to be able to finish races. It can take weeks, maybe even seasons, before some riders can finish in the peloton. My dad has a saying: 'To finish first, first you must finish.' Finishing is engrained in a cyclist's psyche.

Nobody likes packing a race, even if they're sick or injured.

I've seen guys finish stages with broken fingers, wrists, collarbones, elbows. Cadel Evans rode most of the 2010 Tour with a broken elbow, but didn't tell anyone for a week. Sean Kelly broke his collarbone in the 1988 Tour. His immediate reaction was to get back on his bike and finish the stage. When it became apparent that he couldn't hold the bars and would have to abandon the Tour, he stopped on the side of the road and cried like a baby. King Kelly, hard man of the classics. He wasn't crying because of the pain. He was crying because he had to pack the Tour. Like I said, nobody likes stopping.

While I was down the back of the peloton puking off the side of my bike, my cousin Dan was very unlucky not to win the stage. Having spent 140km out front with two others, he attacked again in the final 20km and, despite being sent the wrong way in the last kilometre, was only caught with 400m to go. I was still feeling terrible at the start of stage three but when we got racing I was okay and managed to finish in the bunch, even picking up a point on the first of three climbs along the way. When my stomach problems eventually cleared up, I got sinusitis, but at least I could eat with that.

My tummy bug meant that I couldn't visit Florian, as he was still recovering from leukaemia, and his immune system was still very weak. In January, he had gone back to school, but it took so much out of him that he would be sick afterwards and could only go for one day a week for a long time. The plan was for him to come to the finish of the 2010 Tour if I was riding it and he was well enough. On one visit to the doctor during the 2009 Tour, Florian asked him if he could be a professional cyclist. The doctor told him that he didn't think he would be able to race but he could still cycle for fitness and exercise.

'But what about Armstrong?' Florian asked him. The doctor had to explain that Florian's cancer treatment was totally different and far more severe than Armstrong's. He was very disappointed with that news.

By the end of February, I was fully recovered and, after third place at the GP dell'Insubria, I took my first top five overall in a ProTour stage race at the Tour of Catalonia in April. Another thing I was happy about was the support I was getting from the team. Even though Catalonia was hard, I was enjoying being team leader, and the lads had ridden really well for me. Having been dropped by the leaders on the final descent on the Friday, my Ag2r teammates rode really hard to help me regain contact, and I just kept fighting to hold on to my fifth overall. I enjoyed the experience and showed I could handle responsibility by performing consistently well all week.

Disaster then struck at the Tour of Romandie in Switzerland. During the time trial, I was riding pretty strongly, until the final descent. Like my Junior Tour stage win in Waterford, it was one of those descents where you have to pedal a lot to keep your speed up and, suddenly, I felt a sharp twinge, like a cramp, in my left hamstring. With 3km to go and a chance of moving into the top ten overall, there was no way I was going to let a bit of cramp slow me down, and I kept riding as hard as I could, while trying to ignore the pain in my leg. There was a little ramp upwards with about 300m to go, and I sprinted up it. As soon as I got out of the saddle, it felt as if I'd been stabbed in the leg. When I got to the finish, I got off my bike and limped to the team bus.

Having lost a minute and fifty-five seconds to my rivals to finish forty-ninth, I was more disappointed with my time-trial performance than I was worried about my leg, and didn't pay it that much attention. I limped around the hotel all evening, but was convinced that I'd just gone too deep and therefore a sore leg was pretty normal after a hard time trial. The next morning, when I went down to breakfast, though, my leg was killing me. I had a massive bruise at the back of my thigh and the pain was too much to contemplate starting the stage. It felt like a pulled muscle or bad tendonitis, but I would have to get an MRI scan before deciding what kind of treatment I needed.

An MRI scan three days later revealed I had torn my left hamstring, and I was ordered off the bike for at least three weeks. All of a sudden, from having a great start to the season, I went to not being able to ride my bike. I immediately worried about missing the Tour de France.

After all the racing I'd done, a week or ten-day break would have been welcome, but three weeks was way too long. I spent the first five days in my dad's hotel in Nice with Australian rider Simon Clarke, who lived beside me in Varese. That was a nice bit of a break, but after that it got boring. I don't even take three weeks off the bike in the winter, so I didn't know what to do with myself now. I couldn't ride, but if I was hoping to make the Tour team I knew I had to work hard to stay fit. I couldn't do anything except swim. In Nice, I donned a wetsuit and swam in the sea with a triathlete friend of mine, and in Italy I swam endless lengths in the pool in Varese. I also ate as healthily as possible, watching my portions, and maintaining my weight while I was off the bike.

After two and a half weeks, I drove to Grenoble to see the Ag2r La Mondiale team doctors. I was pretty nervous, as the result of another MRI scan would either make or break my season. Although my leg hadn't completely healed, it was a lot better than everyone expected, and I was given the green light to go back to training. I was told I would possibly miss the rest of the season if I tore the hamstring again, so I took it easy for a few days, doing only an hour and a half to two hours before building up to bigger spins.

Having posted some good times on my training climb in Varese, my comeback race was in the one-day GP Canton d'Argovie in Switzerland. The race was really aggressive, with lots of attacks, but I was feeling good and managed to get into the winning break on the final climb. There were six of us away, and I took fourth in the sprint behind Kristof Vandewalle, Emanuele Sella and Heinrich Haussler. I was happy that my training had gone well, and even happier that I never felt a twinge out of my hamstring, even in the final sprint.

With only one race in my legs in the month prior to the Tour de Suisse, I didn't know how my form would hold up to a nine-day ProTour event and so decided to concentrate on riding just four stages of the race full on. I wanted to ride the prologue and time trial flat out, because I needed to concentrate on my time trialling. I knew I had to take the opportunity to try to learn from each time trial and improve. I wanted to give it a go on stage three because I felt the slight uphill finish was ideal for me, and there was a really tough stage in the mountains on the fifth day where I wanted to try to hang in with the big boys.

In the prologue, I was third quickest at the intermediate

time check, which came close to the top of a long hill, but I didn't take any risks on the wet descent and I lost a fair bit of time on the last three corners, which all came inside the final 2km. I knew if I fell that my hopes of riding the Tour were out the window, so I didn't want to chance crashing, and ended the stage in twenty-first place.

The second stage was held in showery conditions, and although I hadn't had so much as a twinge from my hamstring I was worried about putting it under too much pressure in the cold and wet, and finished twenty-second in the bunch sprint, moving to fifteenth overall.

I was in a good position coming into the final hill on stage three, and attacked with 2km to go, pulling clear of three riders, including Fränk Schleck and Lance Armstrong on the climb. In my eagerness to do well on the stage, though, I had gone way too early and, as Schleck rode past in the final kilometre to win the stage, my legs were gone. I was still missing that little bit of power on the climbs and, as others followed Schleck's lead, I had to be content with ninth. I was happy, though, that my hamstring had withstood its first real test and I'd also moved up another four places overall to eleventh, seventeen seconds off the race lead.

The next day, Mark Cavendish collided with Cervélo's Heinrich Haussler in the final metres and brought down most of the main contenders for the stage victory, including my teammates Lloyd Mondory and Séb Hinault. Cav's pedal caught in the wheel of Haussler, who was immediately upended in the process. I was unhurt in the sprint, having decided earlier in the stage not to contest the gallop to the line, as I was looking to do a good ride in the tough mountain stage the following day. There was a bit of a protest at

Cav's sprinting the next morning, and the stage was delayed as everyone sat around on the line for a few minutes, but in the end there were no changes overall and I finished in the peloton as a five-rider breakaway dominated another rain-soaked stage. Although I lost a minute or two on the next couple of mountain stages and didn't have the power to do a good final time trial, I finished nineteenth overall, and my performance was good enough to earn me pre-selection for the 2010 Tour team.

I was happy with this, as I felt I'd done enough all year to deserve my place and it proved to me that the team trusted me and knew I would do my best. I had proved that even though I was injured I could stay focussed and fit, and if I said I would be good for the Tour, they now expected me to be good.

14

Team Leader

I was much more confident going into the 2010 Tour de France than I had been the previous year, although the fact that this would be my first time riding a three-week tour as team leader meant that my nerves steadily increased as the days counted down to the prologue time trial in Rotterdam.

It might have been only my second Tour, but a lot was expected of me this time round. As team leader, I had more responsibility and more pressure to get results. I always like to have a challenge but, in a way, I felt that I could only disappoint people from here on.

For the first time in a major tour, the team would be relying on me to aim for the overall classification, with Nocentini to back me up. Both of us were coming back from injury, though. Nocentini had a great start to the 2010 season, winning the Tour of the Med and the one-day Tour du Haut Var. But a crash in the GP dell'Insubria in February, where he slid through a left-hand bend, hit some hay bales and flipped over a guard rail, saw him break his leg in two places and some bones in his foot. For me, the hamstring tear I suffered at the Tour of Romandie was gone, completely healed. But that didn't stop me worrying about it. On every training spin or every race leading up to the Tour, I was thinking, Will it be okay today? Will it hold up? It had stopped physically bothering me but, in the back of my head, it was still niggling me.

On my Tour debut in 2009, I got into a lot of trouble within the team because rather than helping our nominated sprinter at the finishes on the flatter stages, I knew I was sprinting faster than him in the first week and was eager to get results. Now, I had a different role to play. I planned to ride conservatively in the first week and let new Swiss champion Martin Elmiger and Lloyd Mondory do their thing if it came down to a bunch gallop. I knew I would need to save as much energy as I could until we got to the high mountains, where I would try to follow the top guys when the big battle began. The dreaded Belgian cobbles and the little climbs on the first two road stages, combined with the nervous nature of the first week of every Tour, meant I would have to try to stay around the front of the peloton just to keep out of danger, but tempting as it might be I wouldn't be rubbing elbows with Cavendish, Hushovd or any of those guys in the sprints this year.

Expectations came not only from within the team, but from family, friends and an ever-growing band of Irish fans who had watched me steadily edge nearer a big victory and yearned for the first Irish stage win at the Tour since my dad's on stage sixteen of the 1992 edition. A lot of people just laughed when I first said I wanted to have a great Tour. They put it down to talk. But my early-season results had shown that I was capable of doing it. I was really motivated and focussed. I had trained hard, dieted and rested well, had done everything right. For the first time, I had the team really behind me too, and I didn't want to disappoint them or anybody else.

Weighing heavier than any of that, though, was the pressure I put on myself. I badly wanted to progress. I knew I had to keep moving up a step each year and, while I had finished twenty-third overall on my debut, I knew that I had clawed back almost ten minutes on stage fourteen on the day I finished second, which propelled me up the rankings. In my second Tour I wanted to be able to ride consistently with the top guys and had earmarked a place in the top fifteen overall as my goal. I was very conscious that this was going to be a hard task, but I always like to give myself a high target. Inside, I knew that if I won a stage and was nowhere near that placing overall, I would probably be even happier. I knew that to achieve a top fifteen, though, I would have to sacrifice my chances of a stage victory. If I did manage to remain close to the overall contenders, nobody would be willing to let me slip into a breakaway group, so unless I lost a lot of time and was out of contention for the overall, taking a stage win would prove to be very difficult.

I also knew that I could take it easy for a few days, lose loads of time and be given a bit of freedom to chase stage wins, but I was at the stage in my career where I needed to know how far I could go in the challenge for the overall race. I love the thrill and excitement of riding for GC. People say I could be a green jersey contender if I concentrated on that, but going for the green jersey would mean having to go for every sprint, every day, and forgetting about the overall. It could be something I'd like to do in a few years, if I see that I'm not going to be a realistic overall contender. Also, I think

I could challenge for the Mountains jersey in the future, if one day I decided to go for it. I may not be a super-climber, but I am capable of being in four or five breakaways in a week if necessary, and taking points on the major climbs. But I wanted to see how far I could get in the GC if I pushed myself. I reckoned there would be plenty more years to try to win stages. As long as I was developing and learning about myself as a rider, I wanted to keep pushing my limits. If I blew up after ten days or two weeks, then I would try to slip up the road in a break and snatch that elusive stage win.

Dad told me to stop chasing futile breakaways, asking me how I could compare myself to the top riders if the only time I tried to stay with them was when they all rode past me after I'd spent 180km in the break. 'Okay, it's great, you get good publicity, and people say, "Great ride, but pity you got caught in the end." We know you can do that now,' he said. 'But you can never go to the next level by doing really long break-aways and going nowhere. It's not four unknown riders in a breakaway that will bring you forward. If you can hang on to Contador and Schleck on the climbs, they'll bring you forward. They will bring you up to the next level, if you have it. Bite the bullet, stay in the bunch and try to calculate, and watch and learn from these guys.'

Ag2r La Mondiale began the 2010 Tour with a very different team from the previous year. Only myself, Christophe, Lloyd and Rinaldo survived from the previous edition. While myself and Nocentini would ride for the over-all, the other guys were to try to chase stage wins. Lloyd and Martin Elmiger would contest the sprints. We only really had Christophe and John Gadret to support us in the mountains, while youngsters David Le Lay, Maxime Bouet and Dimitri

Champion would aim for breakaways and stage wins, which would keep our sponsors happy.

For the first time in a year, I would be leaving my Irish champion's kit at home, having been beaten by Matt Brammeier to the title the week before in Sligo. After having the national champion's jersey in 2009, it was a comedown to have to revert to the usual team kit, especially those brown Ag2r shorts. The previous year, it had been so easy to pick me out in the bunch, for commentators and for fans. So many people recognized me and came up and told me I was doing a good job. It wasn't just that I was wearing the jersey of Irish champion. I felt that I was an ambassador for Irish cycling, flying the flag in the top races. I was going to miss it.

As a small compensation, shoe manufacturer Specialized gave me a new set of shoes for the Tour on the Wednesday before. Mainly white, they had my name and a big Irish tricolour along the side. Once again, I had agreed to write a tour diary for the *Irish Independent* back home. My daily reports from the 2009 race had proven to be very popular with the Irish public and, thanks to the internet, had also gained followers from all over the world.

Saturday 3 July: Prologue Time Trial, Rotterdam, 8.9km

Although the prologue time trial is always the shortest stage of the Tour, Saturday felt like one of the longest days of my life.

I wasn't due to roll off the start ramp until 7.24 p.m., but I'm an early riser and was up twelve hours before-hand. After breakfast, we went for a two-hour training spin and then had lunch. So much of the day was spent waiting, lying on the bed. I even managed a short nap before we headed to the start at 4.30 p.m. Here, I spent fifty minutes warming up on a home trainer, and then went into the start house. I was hoping for a top-twenty placing on the stage, but the wet roads made the course a totally different prospect from our previous day's reconnaissance. Although it didn't rain for my ride, the white road markings and some of the corners were pretty slippery, and I didn't want to come down in the last shower. I ended up in forty-seventh place. Not great, but not terrible.

I'd like to have shaved another ten seconds off my time, but was happy to be a few seconds faster than Basso, Gesink, Sastre and Fränk Schleck. I expect all of them to be up there in three weeks' time. If I'm still worrying about seconds at that stage, I'll have ridden a great Tour.

Stage 1 – Sunday 4 July: Rotterdam–Brussels, 223km

Maybe the Tour organizers should ask somebody like the makers of Valium to sponsor the opening road stage every year. My nerves are nearly gone! Today's opening stage was really dangerous. Although it looked like nothing happened in the bunch for ages, everyone was on tenterhooks.

Everyone was expecting one of the big teams to put the hammer down and try to split the race at any minute. Nobody wanted to be left behind. This caused violent waves of acceleration and deceleration in the bunch, and wasn't great for the nerves.

The Dutch spectators were unbelievable, coming out in their droves, but instead of staying on the footpath, they caused a lot of tension in the bunch as they stood out halfway in the road, right in our faces, only jumping back at the last minute.

That's okay on a mountain stage, where we are riding slowly by, but today we were travelling at over 50kph for most of the stage. There were a few near-misses, until my luck ran out with about 120km to go and I joined a pile of riders on the deck. I was moving up the right-hand side of the peloton when everybody just fell in front of me. From what I heard from other riders, a dog walked into the middle of the peloton. Again, the crowd was at fault. Somebody owned the dog, and you can't tell a dog to jump back at the last minute.

There's nothing you can do in a situation like that, except hope for a soft landing. Unfortunately, I didn't get one. It took me a bit of time to get up off the ground. My chain came off too. As I was putting it back on, Maxime Bouet turned round on the road and came back to pace me up into the bunch. Radioshack had three riders, including Lance Armstrong, in the crash, so we got back on with them.

I rode up to the doctor's car, and she treated me on the move. I had a bad cut on my finger where I landed on the chainring, and she cleaned my knee with antiseptic, taking a few bits of gravel as a souvenir.

Coming into the finish, Mark Cavendish took a few guys out on a bend with about 3km to go. I wasn't going to be contesting the sprint, so I was far enough back to avoid that.

With 1km left there was a lot of nervous switching and moving up front, but I was well out of the danger zone – or so I thought. Going under the red kite, signalling the final kilometre of racing, the whole bunch collapsed in front of me. I slammed on the brakes. My front wheel locked and turned sideways, catching the steel feet of the nearest crowd-control barrier. The sudden stop catapulted me on to it, and it fell down, taking a few spectators with it. I rolled back on to the road and joined the rest of the race in a stack of broken bikes and battered bodies which literally took over the whole finishing straight.

Up front, Lloyd was still in contention. He'd been keyed up for this stage for ages, had managed to stay upright, and was one of a small group about to contest the sprint for stage glory. Until about 300m to go, that is. Here, a Lotto rider came up his inside and tried to squeeze through a gap that wasn't there. To avoid hitting the barrier, he pushed Lloyd out of his way and on to the ground. It was a disgrace. It's the second time in a big race that something like that has happened to Lloyd when he was in a good position for the sprint. He ended up carrying his battered bike over the line as riders from the pile-up behind streamed past him.

There are always bound to be crashes on the first day of the Tour, but I was hoping I'd stay away from them. I haven't lost any time overall, as a UCI ruling gives crash victims the same time as the group they were in if the crash happens in the last 3km. Ironically, that rule was brought in to stop people fighting for minor placings and possibly causing crashes in the process!

Stage 2 – Monday 5 July: Brussels–Spa, 201km

The one sound every racing cyclist dreads is the un-mistakable scraping of metal along the ground. It's usually pre-empted by the screech of brakes and the smell of burning rubber.

If the sound is coming from anywhere other than behind you, then you're in trouble. You'd better hope your reflexes are sharp, or you're going down. Sometimes you can react quickly enough to bunny-hop an outstretched leg or swerve *Matrix*-like around a set of handlebars or wheels that are coming in your direction. Other times, although it seems like it's happening in slow motion at the time, you're on the ground before you know who or what has hit you.

Already stiff and sore from two crashes on the open-ing day, today, I got lucky. I survived another day of carnage on the Tour. It was a ridiculously dangerous day, with riders falling left, right and centre. The first big crash came on a descent after about 60–70km. I heard the scraping noise behind me. I was on the out-side of the bend, and a few guys tried to move up the inside. Somebody's front wheel skidded out from under him, and they just wiped out everybody behind me.

We were doing at least 70kph at the time. Mickaël Delage was badly injured in the crash and had to abandon the race. On the climb up the Col du Stockeu, which we also race over in the Liège–Bastogne–Liège classic, Sylvain Chavanel of Quickstep was fifty-nine seconds clear with Maxime Monfort of Lotto. With 35km to go, it started to rain. I was sitting in about fortieth position in the bunch and was hoping they would be reeled in and the front group would thin out a bit on the final climb so that I could have a go in the sprint.

The descent was really slippery, and on the way down into Stavelot it was as if someone had thrown a hand grenade into the peloton. There were bodies everywhere. I think a couple of motorbikes fell too. I took a little trip on to the grass but managed to pull my feet out of the pedals and regain my composure in time. I actually stood there at the side of the road for a minute, taking a breather as riders emerged from the ditch on both sides of the road. It was chaos.

About twenty guys, including race leader Cancellara and second overall Tony Martin, stayed upright and rode on in the front group. When I remounted, I was in a second group with Armstrong and others, about a minute back, while pre-race favourite Andy Schleck was about four minutes down and the rest of the race was in smithereens.

My group rode up to the front group, and immediately noticed it was not riding hard. Instead, it was waiting for the Schleck group to regain contact. This meant that, up front, Chavanel, who had dropped Monfort, was now well on his way to building up a three-minute lead and taking over in yellow.

Despite the fact that he was about to lose his yellow jersey to the Frenchman, Cancellara helped organize a go-slow in the peloton after everybody had regained contact. He was more worried about his Saxo Bank team leaders Andy and Fränk Schleck losing time than losing his race lead.

I agree on the principle of making some kind of gesture about the dangerous route for the opening stages, but the way it was done today wasn't right. If we have to wait and have a protest every time a couple of team leaders crash, then we'd never race.

Some guys think they're the big boss, they open their mouth and you obey them. Nobody waited for me the other day when I crashed, and nobody will next time, so what's the big deal about waiting for the Schleck brothers and the other leaders? Okay, I want to beat these guys and if we hadn't waited today I could have taken some time on some guys who will probably finish higher than me on GC. That's not the ideal way to do it, but crashes happen every day in cycling. It's part of the race.

I don't know why Cancellara and the others wouldn't let anyone sprint at the finish. Maxime Bouet told them, 'Okay, you can protest, but I'm going to get second,' and he edged ahead on the line. He got a lot of stick off Cancellara and Bernhard Eisel of the Columbia team, but he will wear the white jersey of best young rider on stage three because of that placing.

Last night, I used one of the two ice baths that we have built into the team truck to try to help me recover from my altercations with the road. We have to sit in them, up to the bellybutton, for eight minutes. I think I'll give it a miss this evening. I've had enough cold water to do me for a long time.

Stage 3 – Tuesday 6 July: Wanze–Arenberg Porte du Hainaut, 213km

For weeks before this Tour, everybody had been talking about the seven sections of cobbles that we would have to negotiate as the race left Belgium and entered France via the farm roads normally reserved for tractors and also used in the 'Hell of the North', the Paris–Roubaix classic.

I was really nervous about today, as it was important for me to show that I was capable of riding in the front with the big guys – for my status in the team and in the peloton, as much as for my own morale. It's a way of saying, 'Look, you can trust me. I told you I would take risks to be in the front and be there when you need me.'

I was pretty stressed out this morning, as I don't have much experience of racing over cobbles. The guys on the team knew I wasn't my usual self and had to keep telling me to calm down.

Riding over cobbles is a bit like trying to pedal a bike with two pneumatic drills for wheels. The vibrations shake and rattle your body as you bounce your way across each section of what the French call *pavé*. There are things you can do to try to limit the shock. Some riders use two layers of handlebar tape for extra cushion. Years ago, riders used to strap their wrists for the Paris–Roubaix classic and, in the eighties, suspension forks were once in vogue.

I decided to use my normal Reynolds carbon wheels today. The only difference was that my tyres were a bit wider and I put less pressure in them, in the hope that I would be a bit more comfortable. I used a 24mm tubular tyre instead of the usual 20mm, and only put 6.5 bar in my wheels, instead of the usual 8.

Once I hit the cobbles, I just concentrated on the wheel in front and rode as hard as I could. To be honest, once we hit the first section, the cobbles just flew by. You can't control your bike very well on *pavé*, because you have to keep a loose grip. The vibrations are incredible. I was hopping all over the place. If you grip the bars too tight, you don't absorb the shock and you can also get blisters on your hands.

To avoid bouncing around too much, you have to stay in the saddle. Some people say it's easier to ride as hard and fast as you can across the cobbles in a big gear. For me, I was just concentrating on trying to stay with the leaders. Because you can't change gears with all the bouncing, whatever gear I went into the section on, it had to ride until I got back on the smooth road afterwards.

The whole team worked really well for me today. Lloyd was fifteenth in Paris–Roubaix this year and has great experience of racing over the cobbles. He did great work for me until the peloton split.

There were plenty of accidents again today, but luckily I steered clear of them. My teammate David Le Lay broke his elbow and his collarbone before we even got to the cobbles. Nocentini and Max Bouet crashed as well, so now, with just three road stages gone, everybody on my Ag2r La Mondiale team has crashed in this Tour. I was caught behind a big pile-up that saw Fränk Schleck abandon the Tour on the second section. That's how I didn't make it into the front group of six riders.

With 12km to go, the Lotto rider directly behind me overshot a corner and came off. If I had been behind him, I would have been gone too. That's how close it is every day.

I ended up in a seven-man chase group with some pretty good riders. Last year's winner Alberto Contador was there with his Astana teammate Alexandre Vinokourov, last year's Giro winner Denis Menchov (Rabobank) as well as Bradley Wiggins (Sky), Johan van Sumeren (Garmin) and Jurgen van den Broeck (Lotto).

I took twelfth place on the stage. It wasn't a bad result, but I didn't know there were only six riders ahead of us coming into the finish, or I would have sprinted. The guys in the team car kept telling me in my earpiece, 'Six in front,' and with all the clattering and the noise of spectators, I didn't understand what they meant. I just thought we were closing in on a group of six riders. I didn't know they were the only six riders ahead of us. When I got on to the team bus afterwards, I saw the result on the TV screen. Van Sumeren led in our group for seventh on the stage. That's my only disappointment. Otherwise, I was very, very happy with my ride.

We're not the strongest team in the Tour. We're just a bunch of riders who get on well together and are focussed on what we do. We don't have a superstar in the team. I'm not Schleck, Hushovd or Cancellara, but we just try to do our best. We have reasonable goals that we want to achieve in these three weeks. I'm up to eleventh overall, which I am very happy about, but the hardest part, the mountains, is still to come. Okay, I've put forty or fifty seconds into Basso and Armstrong today, but I know it won't count for anything if they put twenty minutes into me on the first mountain.

Stage 4 – Wednesday 7 July: Cambrai–Reims, 153.5km

Dimitri Champion is one of the quietest, most focussed guys on my Ag2r team. Last year, he won three races and lived up to his name when he won the French national road race title just before the Tour. Usually keen to get into breakaway moves, Dimitri has had a very quiet first three days of this Tour. He has tried to get into a few moves, but nothing has worked for him. Today, the warm sunshine, combined with a flat stage ahead, saw him eager to get up the road and get some publicity for the team. He jumped clear after about 2km and sparked off the main break of the day.

Sometimes when a break goes clear, the peloton takes it easy for a couple of hours, lets them get maybe ten minutes and then has to ride hell for leather to bring them back before the finish. Today, the peloton was taking no chances. The maximum advantage Dimitri and his three breakaway partners got was around two minutes, and everybody knew we would be seeing them again before the end of the stage. Of course, the guys up front always hold a little bit back for when the backlash comes from the bunch, and they spill their last ounce of energy trying to hold on to a crumbling lead in the final kilometres.

It didn't work out for Dimitri and the breakaway

group today, though. They were caught with 3km to go. But it's good for the morale of the team to have a guy in the break, and it's one of the team's policies to get as much air time and publicity as it can during the Tour. There's no better way of doing this than spending all day out front.

Our sponsors Ag2r and La Mondiale were even happier when Dimitri went up on the podium after the stage to be awarded the most combative rider of the stage. Tomorrow, he will wear a red number to indicate this.

For the first time since the Tour started, I felt safe in the peloton today. The route of today's stage took us mainly on big, wide roads, with better surfaces than on the previous days and it wasn't nearly as dangerous.

Sometimes it's hard not to get sucked into going for the sprint. Already this year a lot of top sprinters have crashed out, aren't in top form or are riding with injuries. With maybe 10km to go, I did get a bit excited thinking about it. If you're riding for the sprint, you keep on pushing up, bit by bit, taking the odd risk, jumping into little gaps and bumping shoulders with guys to hold your position. I had to calm myself down and put it in the back of my head. I didn't even want to think about it.

For the first time, I've made a conscious decision to stick to my plan of conserving energy and riding for the GC for the first two weeks. I tried to hover around the top thirty or forty riders instead – far enough away from the back to be out of danger and near enough to the front to be able to see what's going on.

At the moment, my race plan is going fine. I'm just concentrating on keeping close to the leaders and being discreet. I'm eleventh overall, but nobody over here even notices. In France, all they talk about is the top ten. All the public sees on the results on TV are the top ten after each stage. I'm on the same time as the top ten. I'm eleventh, but there's not a word about me.

After three nights of sleeping on my own, tonight I'm rooming with Dimitri. In a single room, I'd got used to having my own routine, reading my book and falling asleep, but when David Le Lay crashed out yesterday, the team cancelled a room, so now I'm sharing. It can be hard sharing with a different guy every night for three weeks. Everybody has their own habits and different times for going to bed and getting up. I've never roomed with Dimitri before, but I know he gets up early like me, because we are always first down for breakfast. Hopefully, he will be tired after his 150km off the front today and he'll sleep tonight.

Stage 5 – Thursday 8 July:
Épernay–Montargis, 187.5km

Because of the heat of Wednesday's stage, I drank loads afterwards to rehydrate, and again before going to bed. I woke up at least four times last night to go to the loo. Myself and my new room mate Dimitri got on all right. We went asleep at about 11.15 p.m. and both got up around 8 a.m. for breakfast. We'll be sharing for the next few days so I'd better curb my late-night visits to the loo so as not to disturb him.

Today's stage went pretty well for me. A three-man

break went clear early on, but the peloton rode pretty swiftly behind them all day and brought them back in the last 3km. In the run in to the finish, I was just trying to stay near the front, because there was a really sharp right-hand corner before the finish. We were told in our earpieces that the tarmac had melted on the bend because of the sun, and I wanted to stay as close as possible to the sprinters, without actually getting involved, just in case there was a split in the peloton after the corner.

It's easy to lose time in a bunch sprint if you're not alert. Everybody usually gets the same time crossing the line, unless there's a gap of one whole second between riders. Then, even though you finished in the top half of the bunch, you could lose half a minute, because the time is taken from the first rider to cross the line to wherever the gap in the bunch is. The further back you are when this happens, the bigger the time gap. It would have been stupid for me to lose the forty or fifty seconds I earned on the cobbles by not being alert in a bunch sprint today, so I stayed close enough and finished fourteenth on the stage, with our sprinter Lloyd Mondory a few places ahead of me in ninth.

The team was brilliant again today. Everybody apart from myself, Lloyd and Christophe Riblon took it in turns to go back for bottles for the rest of the team.

It's a tough job. I know, because I did it often enough myself. You wait for a decrease in pace in the peloton before drifting back to the team car behind the bunch. Here, you load up with as many bottles as you can. You can fit two in your bottle cages, three in your pockets, and after that it's time to stuff them down the front and back of your jersey. Now, laden down with the extra weight of maybe a dozen or more full 500ml bottles, you have to ride up through the team cars, catch back up to the peloton and hand them out to your team-mates.

It's more difficult if your team is the one doing the driving on the front of the race, as you have to make it all the way to the top of the peloton before you can distribute your liquid luggage. It's harder still if the road or the pace suddenly goes upwards. I drank around ten bottles with the heat today, and the peloton was really moving all day so the guys were like yo-yos.

My dad called me last night from London, where he is doing analysis for Eurosport. He reminded me to stay focussed and concentrated, and to try not to waste any energy as we were approaching a couple of tough days on Saturday and Sunday. He told me to believe in myself, that I was well on the way to having a good Tour and to try to rest and recover as much as possible after each stage. Although he mostly leaves me to make my own mistakes and learn from them, sometimes it's not bad having a former Tour de France winner as a dad.

The sprint finish today saw Mark Cavendish back to his best. A lot of people wrote him off this year, but he is still one of the fastest guys in the world. I have known Cav since we were under-fourteens, and I have always got on well with him. He gets a bit of stick for some of the things he does, like giving the fingers when he won the stage in Switzerland or whatever, but Cav is very emotional. He wears his heart on his sleeve. To be a sprinter like that, you need a bit of an ego. Once in a while, he goes a bit overboard, but that's normal. He said today that he was on a cloud last year, and he fell off it this year. He even cried on the podium, which is not like Cav. I don't see anything wrong with crying on the podium, by the way. If I ever get to win a stage, watch out for the tears. I'll flood the place.

Stage 6 – Friday 9 July: Montargis–Gueugnon, 227.5km

I woke up this morning to thunder and lightning and, for the first half an hour or so of racing, it looked like it was going to be an epic day of suffering in the rain. Today was the longest stage of this year's Tour, a mammoth 227.5km, so the last thing we needed was to be told we had an extra neutralized section of 7km to ride before the race even began. In old money, we had to ride 145 miles in total today, and would spend almost six hours in the saddle.

The break went almost from the gun today, so the peloton settled down into a nice rhythm early on. The roads were wet for about 100km, and then the sun came out and we started cooking again. I stayed as near the front as possible all day, with my new minder Maxime Bouet at my side to keep me out of danger. At twenty-three, Maxime's riding his second Tour, having ridden it with Agritubel last year. His job is to keep me sheltered from the wind all day. If we have a crosswind, he rides on whatever side the wind is coming from, and I ride on the opposite. If I need to move up the peloton, he brings me up in his slipstream, and if I need to stop for any reason, he stops with me and helps me back to the peloton, all the time wasting his energy so I can save mine. To be honest, I didn't expect him to be so good at his job. He crashed earlier in the week and has bandages everywhere. His hip, shoulders and back are all cut up. One of his legs is wrapped up like a mummy, but he is so focussed, and he's always there beside me.

Yesterday, I had been eating some of the energy sweets the team use when Lance Armstrong came up alongside me for a chat. We talked for a few minutes as we rolled along and ate, and he asked me how I liked the sweets. I told him they weren't great, but were a change from the muesli bars we usually get. Today, midway through the stage, I got a tap on the back. I turned round, and it was Lance with a handful of Honey Stinger organic energy sweets. 'Here you go, Nic, try these. They're the best around. Let me know what you think.'

Even in full flight, during a stage of the Tour, Lance is a good businessman. He recently bought into the Colorado-based company that makes the Honey Stinger sweets, energy bars and gels – and who better to have as a mobile sales rep in the middle of the peloton? He was right, by the way, they were really nice.

As today's stage came to a close, the long breakaway ahead was coming back, and Dimitri Champion rode alongside and asked if he should have a go on the final hill with about 20km left. We were expecting a strong tailwind finish, so I told him to give it a go. He rode across the gap to the three leaders with Anthony Charteau of Bouygues Telecom, and we were hoping his group would get forty or fifty seconds, which, in a tailwind, would be very hard to bring back.

But we turned into a crosswind, and the breakaways were reeled in 10km later. I finished forty-second on the stage, in the middle of the bunch, and held on to eleventh overall.

Stage 7 – Saturday 10 July:
Tournus–Les Rousses Ski Station, 166km

The weather on this year's Tour has been strange. It's been really hot and humid for most of the stages – the past two days we've ridden in over 35-degree heat – but in the evenings there have been torrential rain showers and thunderstorms.

Last night, there was no air conditioning in our hotel room, so myself and Dimitri decided to leave the windows open for a bit of fresh air. After putting in my earplugs to drown out the noise of a Tour party in the village beside us, I eventually fell asleep but for the second night in a row we were jolted awake in the middle of the night by a thunderstorm. As the sky cracked and rumbled overhead, the hailstones hopped off the open panes and into our bedroom, and we had to jump up and shut the windows. Even with earplugs in, the rattling of the windows made it hard to sleep, and we prayed the storm would blow out before this morning's rendezvous with the first mountains of the Tour.

We had six mountains today, with three

second-category climbs coming in the latter part of the stage. The final one took us to the finish line at the top of the Les Rousses ski station. I went over all the climbs in the top thirty riders or so, and had a couple of team-mates around me all day, giving me drinks and looking after me. The second-last climb was hard. There were a lot of attacks, and Nocentini went clear, with the notion of getting up the road in order to help me when we caught his group on the final climb, but he blew his lights, and that didn't work out as planned.

The last climb was even harder, because it went up in fits and starts. Guys were going full pelt on the flatter bits and then completely blowing the next time the road went up again. Our climber, Christophe Riblon, was disappointed today that he didn't have the legs to stay in the front group and give me a hand, but that happens. Everybody can have a bad day. Although I had no teammates left on the last climb, they had done their job and my legs were good.

I would have liked to have been in the top ten on the stage but, in trying to save my sprint until the very last moment, I left it too late. I finished eleventh today and moved up to eighth overall. At the moment, I am only two seconds behind last year's winner, Alberto Contador, after a week of racing. If somebody had offered me that at any time during the Tour, I would have taken it. Although we have a week done, the tough bit of the Tour has only started.

Stage 8 – Sunday 11 July: Les Rousses Ski Station–Morzine Avoriaz, 189km

The sun was back out this morning for the first real test of this year's Tour. When you start at one ski station and finish at another, you know there are going to be plenty of climbs along the way. Today, we had five mountains to tackle, but two of them – the climb of the Col de la Ramaz and the climb to the finish in Avoriaz – were first category and would be really hard.

Before the start, I gave everyone on the team a specific job. Dimitri looked after the water in the early part of the stage, instead of having lots of guys going back to the car all day. I told him I didn't care what he did for the rest of the stage once he got the water. Martin Elmiger, Rinaldo and Lloyd stayed with me in the valleys and made sure I was sheltered from the wind and near the front of the group.

Maxime did the water when we hit the hills, and John Gadret helped me on the climbs. Christophe was a bit pissed off with his bad day in the mountains yesterday, and he wanted to try to get away in a move so that, even if they got caught, he would be there at the end to help me on the last climbs.

Thanks to the efforts of the team, I got over the first four mountains pretty comfortably, but the big test would be the final climb to the finish. I was in a group that had basically been whittled down to all the top guys on the Tour: Sastre, Contador, Schleck, Basso, Evans, Gesink, Kreuziger and Menchov.

I didn't feel as comfortable on this climb, though, and with around 6km to go, I started to feel like I was getting the bonk. For those of you who have never heard of 'the bonk', it's also known as the 'hunger knock', or simply 'the knock'. It's when you haven't eaten or drunk enough during the day to replenish your energy stores, and suddenly you've nothing left in the tank. If it gets bad enough, sometimes it's hard to see straight, never mind ride a bike up a mountain. When the pace increased shortly afterwards, I couldn't follow the wheels and got dropped.

I had simply dug too deep on the last climb and, like a car that was running out of petrol, I began to splutter about 5km from the summit finish. I eased off the throttle a little bit and could only watch as the Tour favourites rode away from me. I knew there was a little group of four or five that had been dropped just before me, and I eased up slightly to try to recover and tag on to them when they caught me. I hung on to this group until about 2km to go to the summit, but then I chugged again. I couldn't follow the wheels, and they pulled away into the distance. I kept grinding forward and upward, just hoping I would get across the line before I ran out of fuel altogether.

When I saw that I was losing a lot of time for the overall classification, I started to have a bit of a panic attack and began to hyperventilate. I just wanted to get to the line as quickly as possible. John Gadret had been dropped earlier but caught me in the final kilometre and paced me, acting as tow truck, encouraging me and setting the pace to the finish, where I made it about 100m past the line and then fell on to the grass, dehydrated and completely wrecked.

The race doctors came over straight away. One of them held my head and poured cold water on me, while the other held my legs in the air. They handed me a can of Coke to drink and in a few minutes I recovered. Since the Tour began, I've been really strict with myself at meal times. For dinner, I've eaten just plain pasta with no sauce, maybe some cheese and a drop of olive oil. From now on, I will just eat normally and not worry about eating too much. You use up almost 10,000 calories on a hard mountain stage, so a bit of pasta sauce isn't going to go astray.

I crossed the line in twenty-third place on the stage, losing two minutes and eighteen seconds to stage winner Andy Schleck. I dropped from eighth overall to sixteenth, and am now three minutes and eleven seconds behind new race leader Cadel Evans. I was very angry with myself afterwards, and disappointed to have lost time on some of the favourites. But this is a three-week race, and anything can happen. I realize I've had a good Tour so far. This time last year, I was twenty minutes down after the first week, so it's not the end of the world.

Monday 12 July: Rest Day, Morzine

My grandad Arnaud was a bit worried when he read about my collapse at the finish yesterday in one of the papers over here, and texted to see if I was okay this morning. I phoned him to reassure him I was fine. Although I recovered pretty quickly afterwards, I opted to take the team bus down the descent, rather than join some of the guys who rode back down.

As today is the first rest day of this year's Tour, all of the Ag2r riders' wives, girlfriends and kids spent last night in Morzine. My girlfriend, Chiara, came to visit me at the end of yesterday's stage. The sight of me lying flat on my back on the edge of the road with my legs in the air and a couple of doctors around me probably wasn't how she expected to find me.

Although there is no problem with wives or girlfriends visiting the riders for the rest day, none of them stayed in the team hotel, and they are not allowed to eat dinner with us. I booked an apartment for Chiara in the hotel grounds, while Dimitri's wife and baby stayed down the road a little bit.

After breakfast, I changed the cleats in my shoes, because they were damaged from one of the crashes I had in the first couple of days. The team was due to go out for an hour and a half's training at 10.30, but I didn't think this was enough, so I did an hour after breakfast on my own and then rode back to the hotel and went out with them. The trouble with staying in this area is that you can only go up or down a mountain. There are no flat roads, so we did a couple of climbs before heading back to the hotel for a coffee. I also did five twenty-second sprints to get my heart rate up and to remind my body to stay alert, that the race wasn't over yet.

For lunch we took the ski lift back up to the top of yesterday's climb and ate in a restaurant at the top. Although there was no snow on the mountains, the scenery was beautiful, and it was a nice change of environment and took our mind off the race for a few hours. In the cable car, which was basically a creaky old bus on cables, we had a good laugh at Nocentini's friend Luca, who has a fear of heights. As little old ladies marvelled at the views below, and we laughed like schoolkids, poor Luca almost had a heart attack.

Today, I bought a couple of bottles of nice Italian wine for the team staff and organized a little gathering for them in the hotel without the riders. The mechanics, soigneurs, managers, osteopaths and drivers are normally so busy they don't get time to just sit down and have a drink and a chat, so this evening they had a little bit of time out, which is important for everyone.

At around 4 p.m., I went up and chilled out on the bed. I didn't really want to fall asleep, in case I had trouble going asleep again later that night, so I just relaxed and listened to music on the new iPod speakers I had treated myself to for my birthday. I then went downstairs and had a coffee with the Astruc family from Paris. They were fans of my dad years ago, and now they follow me in the big races and were on the climb yesterday with a big flag for me. When you see a French flag or a Spanish flag or whatever, you always wonder who it's for. When I see an Irish flag, it gives me chills, because there is no other Irish rider in the race, I know it's for me, and it really motivates me to do well.

Stage 9 – Tuesday 13 July: Morzine Avoriaz–Saint-Jean-de-Maurienne, 204.5km

With five mountains, including the first-category ascents of the Col de la Colombière and the Col de Saisies to climb, today was going to be one of the hardest stages of this year's Tour.

Although we had two first-category ascents to tackle beforehand, the Col de la Madeleine was always going to be where the race could be won or lost. The top of the Madeleine can be seen pointing 2km up into the sky as you approach it. The road to the summit goes up in gradients of between 6.5 and 9.5 per cent, and drags on for an incessant 25km of torture.

The mountains of the Tour, as in any bike race, are ranked according to their difficulty. The smaller climbs are category four, with the hardest mountains ranked as first category. The Col de la Madeleine is *hors catégorie*. It's way harder than any of the climbs we've done so far, and the King of the Mountains points awarded for the first rider over the top are way higher than for any other climb.

We reached the foot of the Madeleine after 145km of racing. By then, a group of eight riders, including Rinaldo, had a six-minute advantage on the rest of us in the peloton. Although most of the breakaway riders were no real threat to the overall contenders, Spaniard Luis León Sánchez of Caisse d'Epargne had begun the day just five minutes down, and was now virtual leader of the Tour on the road. He had teammates Christophe Moreau and Spanish champion José Iván Gutiérrez in the move, and they were driving the break along in an attempt to gain as much time as possible on the favourites behind.

I was riding very close to the limit for most of the way up. Behind me, a lot of the team leaders, including Bradley Wiggins of Sky, Mick Rogers of HTC Columbia, 2008 Tour winner Carlos Sastre from

Cervélo and Ryder Hesjedal of Garmin all went out the back door. Even yellow jersey Cadel Evans began to suffer and got dropped out of the group.

I was still there, still suffering. Still counting down the kilometres to the top: 12, 11, 10 . . . I was on the limit and hoping this would be as hard and fast as it got. With Evans gone, though, Andy Schleck knew he would take over in yellow if he put enough time into him. Alberto Contador had other ideas. He knew he could take it himself if he could get rid of Schleck, so he ordered his men to the front in an effort to drop the Luxembourg champion. Contador's right-hand man, Daniel Navarro, hit the front 9km from the top and blew the group apart, pulling Schleck and Contador clear as I was ejected out the back.

I was in bits. I seemed to go from being reasonably comfortable to losing it in seconds. There was no in-between. I can ride at a certain tempo just under my limit for a long time, but the top guys like Contador and Schleck still have a couple of notches to go up.

About a kilometre and a half from the top, I blew my lights again and got dropped. I was so disappointed, but I just couldn't hold the wheel in front of me. There were still 34km to go to the finish, and another team-mate, Christophe, caught me after a couple of corners on the way down. We knew we would lose time hand over fist to a larger group if we couldn't get back on, so we did a crazy descent, throwing ourselves into corners, to get back on to the group ahead and drove our group to the finish in Saint-Jean-de-Maurienne. I dropped one place to sixteenth overall, and am now seven minutes and forty-four seconds behind new race leader Schleck.

My tiredness after the stage was soon swamped by a feeling of disappointment. I seemed to be going backwards but, afterwards, when I looked at the guys who were in my group, I realized it could have been much worse. Sastre, Wiggins and Rogers all lost the same time as me. Evans lost over eight minutes, and his yellow jersey.

Apart from Schleck and Contador, almost everybody else seems to be good one day, bad the next, and fighting for places. Maybe now that I have lost a bit of time, I will be given a bit more leeway to get into breakaway groups, although I'm not convinced. Either way, I haven't given up fighting yet.

Stage 10 – Wednesday 14 July: Chambéry–Gap, 179km

Bastille Day is always crazy on the Tour. The French national holiday means that the roads are lined with fans, and more people watch the stage live on TV because they are off work. Because of this, every French rider and every French team wants to win the stage or, at the very least, be in the winning breakaway. This, combined with the fact that the only real chance the sprinters had of gaining points for the green jersey on an otherwise mountainous stage came after just 20km, meant that we were set to have a really fast start to today's stage.

For my Ag2r team, having somebody in the break today was even more important, as the team is based in the start town of Chambéry, and we had hundreds of supporters out to watch us. Almost everybody on the team had a go, but all the early attacks were chased down relentlessly as the teams of green jersey Thor Hushovd and other sprinters tried to keep their men in contention to take the maximum points available.

After Alessandro Petacchi outsprinted Hushovd for the points in La Buissière, the attacks just kept going, which meant that the peloton was screaming through the early stage towns and villages. After four riders went clear about 35km in, yellow jersey Andy Schleck called for a truce, as he wanted to stop for a wee. He tried to encourage others to stop with him but, seconds later, there was another attack, and it was mental again for another 7–8km. Maxime got across to the main move of the day after a hard 30km chase as the peloton wore itself out and began to ride at a more manageable tempo.

Last night, Vincent Lavenu talked with me about trying to get into the early breakaway and regaining five or six minutes on the GC. He said the Saxo Bank team of the yellow jersey would probably not chase me because it wouldn't see me as a threat as I was almost eight minutes down.

I was a bit worried that a move like that could back-fire. In 40-degree heat, 180km of hard riding over some really tough terrain, including three more mountains, would be really tough going. We also had a strong headwind to contend with. I might gain six or seven minutes, but my efforts in doing so could see me lose twenty in the days afterwards.

So we came to a compromise. We knew there was a tough little climb about 20km from the finish, with a tricky descent into Gap – the same one that saw Lance Armstrong cut through a field in order to avoid crashing into Joseba Beloki when he broke his collarbone on a hairpin a few years ago. I knew everybody would be trying to keep safe on the descent, so I said I'd have a go on the way up, about 5km from the summit. Maybe on such a hot day, Andy Schleck and Contador would not be too worried about chasing me, and I might get a minute or two if I stayed away. I know I'm going to lose time on the hills again and also in the time trial, so every minute counts. This is the Tour de France, the biggest race in the world, and if that was a way to get a minute back, then why not try it?

I spoke to my dad on the phone this morning, and he agreed there was no guarantee that the leaders wouldn't go after me if I did get into a long breakaway, and all could be for nothing anyway. This was the best solution. I talked about it with the team and we decided to go for it on the last climb.

With 20km to go, the peloton was about fourteen minutes behind the break as we started up the tough little final climb. With 15km left, Martin Elmiger came up to me and said, 'Nico, do you still want to do your move?' I had almost forgotten about it. I thought about it for a minute, as we had Maxime up front, but I knew I wasn't going to catch him anyway and if I wanted to stay in the running for the overall then I had to try something. I said, 'Yeah, why not?' Lloyd Mondory brought me to the front of the bunch and opened a gap for me, and I just went for it.

It was a big ring climb, but there was a strong head-wind. When I went, I didn't worry about whether they would chase me or not. After opening a gap on the way up, I knew I had to go full pelt down the other side to pull out any sort of decent advantage. I'm an average descender in the dry but in the wet I'm terrible. The tarmac had been melted by the sun on some of the corners, and as I tried to cut one of the chicanes as tightly as possible, my wheel hit a pothole and jumped across the road. For a split second, I had visions of the peloton laughing as it passed me crawling out of the ditch on the way down, but I made it round the corner. The last 3km to the line were flat and I went full gas into the headwind to try to gain as much time as possible. I took back a minute and twenty seconds and moved up three places to thirteenth overall.

I really enjoyed those last 15km. I like to attack, and I was missing the thrill of going for a stage placing, so seventh on the stage kind of made up for that a bit.

As soon as I crossed the line, a UCI chaperone grabbed me by the arm and brought me to anti-doping control. Inside the anti-doping room, I had to sit and wait for about half an hour, as there were a few guys ahead of me. When it was my turn, I had to enter a glass cubicle, a bit like a shower but with a toilet in it, to give my urine sample. To avoid any chance of concealment or cheating the test, you have to drop your shorts around your ankles and lift your jersey up. As I did this, one of the anti-doping officers stood directly behind me, while another one sat outside and watched as I peed. Sometimes you can't go and you have to wait for ages. Luckily, I was ready to go, and was in and out in a few minutes.

While I was busy peeing, my bike was also brought for a dope test. Seriously! A guy put a red sticker on the crossbar, and my mechanic went with my bike to have it scanned for an illegal motor by a race official. Recently, there have been allegations and investigations into the possible use of motorized bikes in the professional peloton, sparked by a YouTube video. Although nobody has ever been found using one, according to former pro-turned-journalist Davide Cassani, a silent motor can be placed inside the frame and switched on when needed by a button under the brake lever. I had never heard of it until a few weeks ago, and don't know if it actually exists. After all the rumours, though, I think the UCI was right to bring in the scans anyway. If people were doing it, or even thinking about doing it, they can't now, which is a good thing. It's hard enough keeping up when the riders are pedalling.

Stage 11 – Thursday 15 July: Sisteron–Bourg-lès-Valence, 184.5km

My bedroom last night, which I was again sharing with Dimitri, was so narrow and cluttered with furniture that I had to put my suitcase in the bathroom. When we went to bed, I had to make sure I zipped it up and put it in the bath in case one of us fell over it if we went to the loo in the middle of the night. Imagine the headlines: 'Roche's Tour hopes down the pan, as he falls in bathroom.'

My Ag2r team didn't really have a plan of attack for today's stage. Although we had one third-category climb along the way, today's stage was always going to be one for the sprinters. We decided not to waste our energy trying to go with early moves, unless there were seven or eight riders in it. We knew that a break of three or four riders would easily be brought back when the sprinters' teams gathered at the front in the latter part of the stage. The team is more competitive on medium to hard stages, so we knew we were better off saving our energy.

Today, we went through the feed zone after 100km. This is where all the team soigneurs hand us up cloth bags called musettes filled with food and drink for the remainder of the stage. We grab the musette with one hand as we ride past, throw it over our head and, as it dangles in front of us, pick out whatever's inside. Stuff like energy bars, bananas, maybe a bit of fruit cake or a sandwich are stored in our back pockets as fuel for later in the stage as we replace the empty bottles on our bikes with fresh ones. Every day, lots of fans go to the end of the feed zones and pick up the discarded bottles and empty musettes as souvenirs. Most of the teams now use biodegradable bottles and bags to try to be as eco-friendly as possible.

As we entered the feed zone, I was riding down the back of the peloton having a chat. The pace was really slow, as everyone was grabbing their musettes, when I looked up and saw Lloyd falling off his bike halfway up the peloton. Lloyd is renowned for crashing on our team, partly because he is a sprinter and is always involved in the high-risk gallops at the end of stages, and partly because he just seems to have bad luck. We joke that he needs to get a personal sponsor for the amount of shorts he goes through in a season. He usually crashes around fifteen times a year. He has already had three falls since we left Rotterdam on stage one. Today, however, he seemed to bounce back up and before I even reached him he was already standing up holding his broken wheel in the air, looking for a new one.

At the time, I had a bit of a laugh, because it was a sight I have got used to seeing. When he came back up the bunch, I rode up alongside and started slagging him: 'Another crash, Lloyd – how many is that now? Are you going for the record?' He just shrugged it off, as usual. A few minutes later, though, I went around the other side and saw his shorts were ripped and there was blood pouring down his leg from a wound on his arse. I didn't realize he had been hurt, and I felt really bad and apologized.

The last 25km flew in and, as I kept near the front for safety's sake, I finished seventeenth on the stage without contesting the sprint. Lloyd managed a credible eighth place despite his war wounds, as my mate Cav took his hat-trick of stage wins.

Everything is going well within the team. All that's missing is a few results. We've had a few sixth, seventh or eighth places, but no top fives and, although nobody has said anything, we can feel the pressure building. My job is to try to stick with the plan to go for the General Classification and get as many UCI points as possible for the team. I'd like to get into a move like I did last year, where I got clear on a tough mountain stage, but I will probably have to wait until nearer the end of the Tour. If I get a chance to do something like that, I'd love to do it. I can't see myself doing nothing for another ten days and then getting my arse kicked on the climbs, so at some point or other I will try something on one of the mountain stages. I don't know which one, but if I see an opening or if I feel that I have to go one day, I'll go for it.

Stage 12 – Friday 16 July:
Bourg-de-Péage–Mende, 210.5km

Today's stage was without a doubt one of the hardest days on this year's Tour. On paper, it was a medium-difficulty mountain stage, with five climbs, although three of them were third category and would be slightly easier than the other two second-category mountains. The one everybody feared, however, was the final climb to the finish after 210km.

I know the ascent to Mende from previous editions of Paris–Nice and, although it's only 4km long, the gradients are back-breaking, ranging from 10 to 15 per cent in steepness. Everybody knew it would be a perfect springboard for Contador or any of the other climbers to attack the yellow jersey of Andy Schleck and, as it flattens out in the last 700m or so, everybody would have to keep enough in reserve to be able to push a big gear at the top to limit any losses.

The first hour of racing today was unbelievably fast. As the early attacks tested the elastic of the peloton, a visibly tiring Dimitri was dropped after only 6km but somehow managed to get back on during a very brief lull. He was lucky he did, because the next 100km felt as if we were on a rollercoaster.

As well as the race for the yellow jersey, things are pretty tight between a few guys for the green jersey of points leader and the polka dot jersey of King of the Mountains. Anthony Charteau of Bbox and Jérôme Pineau of Quickstep have fought each other for the mountains jersey for the past two weeks and started out this morning with only a few points separating them. This battle ensured that we ripped up the first three climbs of the day. Thor Hushovd wanted to take the green jersey back off overnight leader Alessandro Petacchi, and had infiltrated an eighteen-man break that went clear on the second climb, so the pace kept going in the valley as Petacchi's Lampre team tried to reel him in before he got to the only two intermediate sprints of the day after 75km and 133km.

The plan for Ag2r had been for one of the guys to get into the early breakaway if there were sufficient numbers there to see it stay away to the finish, but everyone missed the move. I had a really, really uncomfortable first hour and a half of racing. I wasn't able to spin a big gear, and both the heat and the fast start had me gasping for air. I felt like I had nothing in my legs and only started to come around later on.

Although most of the eighteen guys in the break were well down on GC, four of them could be considered dangermen to the overall leaders. Ryder Hesjedal started the day in twelfth place overall,

Alexandre Vinokourov began the stage one place behind me in fourteenth, while Andreas Klöden had previously finished on the podium at the Tour and was also considered a threat.

The presence of these three in the break meant that Andy Schleck's Saxo Bank team had to ride hard at the front of the peloton to keep the gap down, and they never got more than three and a half minutes. With teammate Vinokourov up front, Contador was content to let Schleck's team chase and, like a cat waiting to pounce, just sat and watched the mice play at the front. Normally, on a stage like this, there is some respite but today the pace was hectic all day. I didn't even have time to stop for a pee.

As we got nearer to the foot of the final climb, more and more teams were fighting for a spot at the front of the peloton. I looked at my bike computer and saw the speed rising from 80kph to 100kph. Everybody wanted to be well positioned for the final climb and, thanks to Martin Elmiger and John Gadret, I went into the hill in the top twenty-five riders.

John had a go at the bottom and went clear but was brought back by Joaquim Rodríguez, who eventually won the stage. I was climbing behind Bradley Wiggins of Sky and his teammate Thomas Löfqvist. Although they were drifting slightly off the pace as Contador attacked 2km from the summit and split the peloton, I just stayed on Löfqvist's wheel, as he was riding a perfect tempo for me. I knew there was no point in trying to jump around them, because I would probably blow up further up the climb. I knew I needed all my strength and power for the last kilometre, where it flattened out a bit, so I didn't panic. Once I saw that Rogers, Wiggo, Hesjedal (who had been dropped from the break and caught), Basso, Sastre and Evans were all going at the same speed as me, I decided to pace myself and stay with them to the top.

On the final corner, with 450 metres to go, Evans jumped up the inside and went for the sprint from our group. I tried to follow him to contest it, but blew up, letting the wheel go in front of me. Sastre overtook me. He gave me a shove and cursed at me because he was worried he would lose a few seconds on the line. I held on to the back of the group and crossed the line in twentieth place, tapping the Spaniard on the back to apologize as we crossed the line. I explained that I thought I had more power in my legs than I actually had, but I don't know whether he believed me or not.

Everybody is getting tired now, and there is still a long way to go. I seem to be climbing in the top twenty riders, but I know that if I do that every day, I will slowly but surely drift down the overall classification. Last year, I thought I had pressure, but now I realize most of it came from myself. This Tour seems to be harder and I have set my goals higher, but I don't want to let the team or anybody else down.

Stage 13 – Saturday 17 July: Rodez–Revel, 196km

Once again we had a really fast start today, and I was struggling. I wasn't feeling right at all. I was in bits. Every time I got out of the saddle, it felt like someone was pulling my brakes. I was on the limit and hanging on to the back of the peloton. I was having a really hard time mentally, as I didn't know if there was something wrong with my legs or my bike. Either way, there was nothing I could do. The pace was too fast to stop and change bikes. And if it was my legs, then the way I was feeling I'd never get back on, new bike or not. I had to suffer across the first two mountains of the day and, finally, after the intermediate sprint after 50km, I got a new bike off the team car. I started feeling a lot better immediately and rode straight back into the bunch – it was a problem with the bike, and not me.

Sometimes the power hose the mechanics use to wash our bikes each evening can wash the grease out of the bottom bracket, making it torture to turn the cranks. Maybe a brake block was rubbing or I'd been given an older back wheel that was faulty or needed to be greased. Tonight I'll have a chat with the mechanics and see if they found anything.

The plan for me today was to stay quiet and try to conserve energy for the next three stages, which are very tough. But the final climb, 8km from the finish, was short and sharp – the type of climb I like. With the sprinters' teams suffering, I thought I could have a go for the stage win there. I jumped clear on the way up, and Carlos Barredo of Quickstep came with me. But the Spaniard spent more time looking behind him than riding.

After a lot of messing around, another little group came across, including Alexandre Vinokourov of Astana and Luis León Sánchez of Caisse d'Epargne.

When Vinokourov went to the front, Barredo let the wheel go, and once Vino saw he had a couple of metres, he put the hammer down. I tried to chase him just as we crested the climb, but Sánchez and Barredo chased me down and then sat up. Everybody, apart from Vino, was more interested in looking round than riding to the finish. We all ended up going back to the bunch, while Vino soloed away from us to take the stage victory.

After the stage, I was really pissed off. When I crossed the line, I was interviewed by French TV and was so angry that I had to ask the journalist a few minutes later, when I had calmed down a little, not to air it. I wouldn't have come across very well. I was angry with myself and with the other guys in the break, who seemed obsessed with what was happening behind them rather than trying to go clear. To me, when you attack 5km away from the finish, you don't look back. You ride flat out to the finish. It didn't work out today, but it could have been a great move. Maybe I should have been more patient. I am now annoyed that perhaps the energy I used to attack today will have adverse consequences on the tough mountain stage tomorrow.

Stage 14 – Sunday 18 July:
Revel–Aix-3 Domaines, 184.5km

This morning I solved the mystery of my terrible start to yesterday's stage. The mechanics told me the ball bearings were gone in my rear wheel axle and had been grinding instead of spinning freely. Although they fixed my bike overnight, I reverted to my Irish champion's bike for today's stage and felt a lot better.

Yesterday, Christophe Riblon was depressed. He came into this Tour off the back of a good performance at the Dauphiné Libéré, where he finished seventh overall. A good climber, Christophe had GC ambitions when the Tour started two weeks ago, but began to suffer almost straight away, losing time every day.

I have known Christophe since we were amateurs, and raced against him in the amateur classics. When I turned professional with Cofidis, Christophe signed for Ag2r and has been there ever since. We get on well together, because we have similar views about how the job should be done, although I can't share a room with him because he stays up too late and then gets up late in the morning. Like me, he gives out a lot if he thinks things aren't right. He's a great motivator and does a lot of work for the team rather than riding for himself. The other day, on the Col de la Madeleine, when he knew we had dropped Rogers and Sastre, Christophe just got to the front and didn't think about himself. He wanted to get me up the road as far as possible to gain time on them.

The plan for the team today was to try to get either Christophe or our other climber, John Gadret, into the break. After a lot of hard riding, Christophe got clear in a move with eight others after 25km, and they built up a maximum lead of over ten minutes on the peloton. They knew they would need all the time they could get before they hit the last two mountains.

I was dying with thirst on the way up the first climb, the *hors catégorie* Port de Pailhères, which was 15km long with gradients of between 6 and 10.5 per cent.

But, unless you're Andy Schleck, you don't even contemplate dropping back to the team car to get a bottle and riding back up the group on a mountain that tough. Luckily enough, Marc Madiot, the team manager of Française des Jeux, was on the side of the road as we passed one of his riders that had been dropped from Christophe's breakaway group. I asked him for a bottle and, even though we are on different teams, he gave me one and I gulped it down.

A few kilometres later on the climb, Martin Elmiger sprinted up alongside me, red faced and gasping. He handed me a fresh bottle and, with his job done for the day, promptly blew his lights and almost came to a standstill on the side of the mountain. As it's so hard to get drinks on the ascent, we had a team helper on the summit, also handing out bottles to our riders. But he had taped an energy gel to the lid of the bottle, and when I went to grab the gel it just exploded all over my hands, face, shoes, bike, everywhere. Not a good idea.

Meanwhile, up front, Christophe had dropped the rest of the breakaway group and was on his own, two minutes and fifty-two seconds ahead of us as we got to the bottom of the final climb. The pace of Alexandre Vinokourov as we hit the slopes split the peloton almost immediately, though, and there was a good chance Christophe would be caught by Contador, Schleck or one of the other favourites before the summit.

As the group split, I found myself with the usual suspects: Basso, Klöden, Horner and a few others. Gadret was also there and, knowing that we had already dropped Evans, Wiggins and Rogers – three top time triallists that could overtake me in the final time trial – he set a good tempo to put some time into them. I was pretty pleased when we also dropped Basso near the top, but then frustrated to learn that he had closed the gap to three seconds on the line.

As we approached the finish, I didn't know how Christophe had got on up front. I had a different fight going on, a fight to stay in the top fifteen overall. In an effort to concentrate on my own climbing, I had taken my earpiece out on the final mountain. Just before the line, though, I could hear his name being called by the commentator, and then I looked across at the big screen and saw a replay of Christophe crossing the line with his hands in the air. I threw my fist in the air and shouted with delight. He had achieved his dream of taking a stage win at the Tour de France, and I was so happy for him.

Setting out on this Tour, my Ag2r La Mondiale team had two objectives. One was a stage win, and the other was to get me into the top fifteen overall in Paris. We have achieved our first objective, thanks to a great ride by Christophe today, but it doesn't take the pressure off me at all. I'm fourteenth overall at the moment, but there's still a week to go and a lot of mountains to be climbed yet.

My Tour diary had been going well and had gained a good following in the *Irish Independent*, but the next day's entry would take on a whole life of its own.

15

United We Fall

Stage 15 – Monday 19 July:
Pamiers–Bagnères-de-Luchon, 187.5km

If John Gadret is found dead in his hotel room in the morning, I will probably be the primary suspect. The 31-year-old French climber has been a teammate of mine at Ag2r for the past two years. Although we never had more than what you could call a workman-like relationship, we never had any reason to fall out or take a disliking to each other over the past two seasons. But after today's stage, if he had sat beside me on the team bus I would have had great difficulty not putting his head through the nearest window.

Today was yet another really tough stage, with the summit of the massive 25km-long *hors catégorie* Port de Balès mountain coming just 20km from the finish. If anyone was going to attack the leaders today, this was where it would be.

As usual, the Saxo Bank team of yellow jersey Andy Schleck set a fast tempo on the climb and the peloton began to lose riders out the back door. I knew that if I could hang on going over the top, I could take a lot of time out of some of the guys in front of me on the overall classification and move up a few places from my overnight position of fourteenth overall.

Halfway up the climb, I was riding pretty comfortably in the Contador and Schleck group, and some of the guys ahead of me like Basso and Klöden were beginning to struggle. As most of the other team leaders were left on their own, I still had Gadret with me for support, and I was looking to move into the top ten. Or so I thought.

Seven kilometres from the top of the climb, just as the pace began to increase at the front, I punctured a front wheel. I pulled over to the right-hand side of the road but our team car was number eleven in the cavalcade and it would take a lot of time for them to get to me through the streams of dropped riders. Gadret was riding behind me, so I asked him for his wheel as he rode up. This is a perfectly normal request, and if the team car is not around, to save time a teammate will often give his team leader his wheel or even his bike if necessary. I have done it plenty of times over the years, as have most cyclists, amateur or professional, at some stage in their careers.

So I asked Gadret, and I couldn't believe what happened next. The baldy little bollocks just shook his head and said, '*Non.*' At first I thought he was joking, but soon realized he wasn't when he rode past me. As Vincent Lavenu, in the car behind, shouted into Gadret's earpiece to wait, I took my wheel out and waited for a new one. The whole time, the group –

including Gadret – was riding up the mountain, away from me.

I eventually got a front wheel off the yellow Mavic neutral service car. Because it has to service any rider that needs a wheel or is in mechanical difficulty when their team car can't get to them, it doesn't have wheels set up to fit everybody's frames instantly. My front-wheel change took way longer than normal as the mechanic unscrewed the wheel's skewer to fit my front fork. At this stage, I was like a bull. I hopped back on my bike, only to discover that my new wheel had been put in at an angle and was rubbing off the brake blocks. I leaned down and opened my front brake and, fuelled by rage, started passing groups on the climb.

All I could think of was getting to the finish as quickly as possible. Rage alone, though, wasn't going to get me back up to the front of the race. Unbelievably, Gadret had attacked Schleck and Contador near the top, even though there was a group five minutes up the road and he had absolutely no chance of winning the stage. Vincent was still screaming in our earpieces, calling Gadret every name under the sun and telling him to wait for me on the descent and help me claw back some time on the long run in to the finish. Gadret just ignored him and kept riding.

There were loads of Irish flags on the climb, and the encouragement from the fans, some of whom were wearing GAA (Gaelic Athletic Association) jerseys, spurred me on even more. I flew up the last kilometre and, having passed lots of riders on the way up, I found myself on my own on the descent. I nearly killed myself on the first two corners because in my state of rage and frustration I had forgotten that my front brake was still open. I had to tighten it as I was descending, which slowed me down again. I spent the rest of the stage on my own, chasing like a madman. I didn't know who I had passed or who was in front of me. I could see world champion Cadel Evans up the road and was fixated on catching him next, but the line came too quickly.

I had finished almost eight minutes behind stage winner Thomas Voeckler but, more importantly, I lost between three and five minutes to some of the guys that I should have put time into and lost my top-fifteen placing, dropping three places to seventeenth. Lloyd had been in the early break and did a fantastic job to get fourth on the stage. Lloyd is a sprinter, and this wasn't his type of stage at all, so to get fourth was a brilliant ride and I was really happy for him.

After the stage, I reminded Vincent that Gadret was on the team for another two years, and that I hoped he never asked me for anything again, because I would not forget today for a long time. Gadret finished three minutes ahead of me and now lies just two places and two minutes behind me. He is the first French rider overall. Maybe he just wants to be the first Ag2r rider too – who knows?

By the time I got on to the team bus, Vincent was already in the middle of a blazing row with Gadret. Although I wanted to smash his head in, and had visions of a baldy French climber exiting through the windscreen, I let Vincent do his job as team manager and said nothing. I got off the bus as quickly as possible and travelled to the hotel in the team car. I couldn't stand to be near him. I will have to keep my hands in my pockets at the dinner table.

Stage 16 – Tuesday 20 July: Bagnères de Luchon–Pau, 199.5km

I was really angry and very frustrated after yesterday's stage. Last night, we had a team debriefing after the stage and myself and Gadret both had a chance to explain what happened on the road earlier. I gave my piece: that I was team leader, lying fourteenth overall, with a good chance to go into the top ten and a) Gadret refused to give me his wheel when I punctured, b) he attacked the front group while I was trying to get back on, and c) he had ignored team orders to wait and help me back up to the group in front.

Contrary to some reports, Gadret didn't say that he hadn't got his earpiece in or didn't hear instructions over the team radio. His explanation was that he was defending his position overall. He also said he was defending the team's position. We began the stage fourth overall in the team category, eighteen minutes and fifteen seconds behind leaders Caisse d'Epargne, and were highly unlikely to catch them.

Instead of jumping into the top ten, I had dropped three places, and the team had lost another three minutes to the leading team. It just didn't make sense. It didn't then, and it doesn't now. Gadret wasn't budging, though, and Vincent Lavenu wasn't happy with the bad publicity.

Ag2r had spent a fortune on TV ads prior to the

Tour. Built on the word 'unity', it showed the whole team doing everything together. One ad featured an Ag2r rider being chased by a dog while out training. The next clip saw the dog being chased by the whole team. Another had an Ag2r rider waiting on the podium to be kissed by the podium girl. When she kissed him, she turned round to see the rest of the team waiting their turn: 'Ag2r: We Stand United.' Yeah, right.

Speaking to friends and family on the phone calmed me down a bit, but my diary entry had gone worldwide and I had to turn my phone off afterwards because journalists kept ringing me left, right and centre and I didn't want to talk to any of them.

This morning, everybody acted as if nothing had happened. I decided it would be better to turn the page and forget about it. I'm not going to be going for a beer or on holidays with him, but I didn't want to undo all the good work the team has done for me since this Tour started. Besides, we have to ride on the same team for another year, so I have to be mature about the situation and move on. I have the support of the team, but Gadret can do his own thing.

Today, we spoke normally. Gadret gave me bottles during the stage. We even stopped for a piss together as we went over the top of the last climb, although the question of who would lead who back to the peloton never came up, as he took longer than me and we made our own way back.

Today was probably the hardest mountain stage of this year's Tour. As soon as we started we had to climb the first-category Col du Peyresourde, the top coming just 11km into the 200km stage. After that, we went down the far side and straight up another first-category climb, the Col d'Aspin, before tackling the monster that is the Col du Tourmalet and then another *hors catégorie* mountain, the 25km-long Col d'Aubisque.

Having lost so much time yesterday, I knew the only way I was going to get it back was to get into a long breakaway and hopefully stay away until the finish. When I saw Armstrong attacking on the first climb just after the start, I knew it was time to go. Lance doesn't waste energy going eight or nine times. When Lance goes, he goes once, and he doesn't come back.

A group of twelve went clear, including myself, Armstrong, Bradley Wiggins of Sky and Roman Kreuziger of Liquigas. Kreuziger's teammate Sylvester Smyd, a really strong climber, was also there and, knowing we could potentially claw back ten minutes and Kreuziger would shoot up the GC, he set a ferocious pace on the front as we climbed. Soon I was in trouble, though. My legs were burning and I couldn't hold the wheel in front. Near the top, the pace was way too fast for me and I could only watch in frustration as the eleven others rode away.

Behind us, the Astana team of the yellow jersey Contador was ripping the peloton to shreds in an effort to catch the break. Astana soon caught me and, still suffering with the pace, I drifted to the back of what was maybe a twenty-five-man group. A kilometre from the summit, I was in real trouble and got dropped. I had only covered 11km and had 180km to go.

Christophe and Martin waited for me at the top, and we chased back on the descent. With such a big group up front, the favourites were not too keen on letting them go and were riding full pelt to try and catch them, with us doing the same.

We went down the descent and began to climb the Col d'Aspin. Ahead of us, the race was in smithereens – the eyeballs-out start to the stage saw riders getting shelled out everywhere. Christophe set a steady tempo on the mountain and, slowly but surely, we caught and passed individual riders. By the top, we were in the third group on the road, behind the Armstrong break and the yellow jersey group. I knew if I didn't get across the gap to the second group, I could kiss any hope I had of finishing in the top twenty, let alone the top fifteen in the Tour, goodbye. If the pace stayed this fast, I could lose twenty minutes on the stage.

Thanks to Christophe and Martin, my group made contact with the back of the yellow jersey group at the bottom of the Tourmalet, but immediately we were faced with another 18km of climbing to the highest point in the race. One of my favourite memories from last year's Tour is of leading the peloton over the Tourmalet, a legendary Tour climb, with the yellow jersey of my teammate Nocentini behind me, followed by Contador and Armstrong.

This time round, I was suffering, but the Irish fans, who were on every climb today with their tricolours, made the pain bearable. Thankfully, the favourites seemed to have worn themselves out and, having caught dangerman Kreuziger, took it a bit easier on this climb as the break gathered momentum and built up a huge lead.

As we hit the slopes of the final mountain, we had 30km to climb before a 20km-long descent, and another 40km to go to the finish. The break that I had been in was now almost ten minutes up the road and would finish with almost seven minutes' advantage, enough to see me jump up to seventh overall if I had been able to hang on to them. Instead, I crossed the line in thirteenth place on the stage and dropped a place to eighteenth overall.

I'm pissed off today because the group I had been in stayed away until the finish. I'm frustrated because after tomorrow's rest day there is only one real chance to take back any time, and I know I will not take back seven or eight minutes. I also know there are a lot of guys who will be faster than me in the time trial on the penultimate day. I came here wanting to finish in the top fifteen – if the truth be told, probably nearer to the top ten. I know that with a little luck I could have finished higher and, to me, eighteenth place isn't good enough.

At this stage, everybody is tired. You could see it today from the gaps in the bunch. It's been a very demanding Tour, and there are riders all over the place. Now, I've had enough. It's been three weeks of suffering, tiredness and stress. I just want to get to Paris, and would prefer to race tomorrow and get there a day earlier.

Wednesday 21 July: Rest Day, Pau

Sometimes a 'day off' can be busier than a normal day on the Tour. There are always interviews to be done, friends and family to talk to, sponsors to meet, autographs to sign for fans waiting in the hotel and, if you're one of the top guys, you can throw in a press conference or maybe even contract negotiations on top of that. You quickly learn to filter out what's not important because, if you're not careful, you can end up spending all day on your feet and have no legs when the racing resumes the next day.

This morning, I got up at seven. I could have stayed in bed for another hour or two, but I couldn't sleep. I went down for breakfast, then got ready for training. Everybody knows Thursday's stage to the top of the Tourmalet is going to be the last chance for a lot of people, including me, to move up on the GC, and nobody wants to wake up in the morning with stiff legs. After breakfast, I rode for an hour with one of the team managers, Julien Jourdie, and then we went back to the hotel and did another hour and a half with the rest of the team, throwing in a few sprints to get the heart rate up.

The Irish contingent's numbers were swelled today in Pau with the arrival of two of my uncles, Peter Fitzhugh and Jude Roche, and my Nana Roche from Dundrum. Peter had come over a few days ago with a group of friends, and they had ridden the Etape du Tour, a cycling event where anybody can come over and test themselves on one of the mountain stages of the Tour a couple of days before we do.

Jude came over with my Nana Roche, who mixed a trip to Lourdes with a trip to the Tour. She is mad into cycling and brought a huge Irish flag with her. This morning she went around the shops looking for a flag pole so that she could fly the tricolour high on the top of the Tourmalet tomorrow. The guy behind the counter noticed she was Irish and, being a cycling fan himself, jokingly said he would only serve her if she knew Stephen Roche. You can imagine the look on his face when she told him that she was his mother.

Thursday will be the second time we have climbed the Tourmalet on this Tour. It is a very long climb, around 35km to the summit, with some really steep sections, so it will take well over an hour. I have decided to ride up the mountain concentrating on my own performance rather than anyone else's. I will see where I stand at the top. I hope my Nana said a few prayers in Lourdes.

Stage 17 – Thursday 22 July: Pau–Col du Tourmalet, 174km

With three seriously tough climbs on today's stage and a mountain-top finish on the highest peak of the Tour, the Col du Tourmalet, today was D-Day for anybody who wanted to move up the general classification, me included. The rain that greeted us at the start in Pau was just going to make it harder.

Going over the top of the first-category Col du Marie Blanc after 56km, I pulled my rain jacket out of my back pocket and, with it, my small race radio. For some reason, the radio pocket in the inside of our shorts this year is in the middle rather than to one side. The few times I kept the radio there, the constant rubbing and chafing of the plastic on my spine left me with a sore back, so lately I have been keeping it in my back pocket – old school. Now, though, it's lying in bits on the side of a mountain somewhere. I think they cost a grand each.

After I had pulled on my rain cape to protect me from wind chill on the way down, I almost got dropped on the descent. I don't know if it was because I wasn't concentrating properly, if I was already thinking about the Tourmalet. Maybe it's because I was the only rider on my Ag2r La Mondiale team using tubular tyres today. All the other guys went with clinchers, as they have a lot more grip in the wet. Me, I made my decision based on weight rather than safety. The wheels we use with the tubs are a lot lighter than the clincher wheels. I knew I had to get up the Tourmalet as well as possible if I wanted to move up the GC. So, I took the risk and chose the lighter wheels.

I started at the front of the peloton but at the bottom of the meandering descent found myself in the last fifteen riders. The bunch split shortly after that, and I found myself in the wrong end of the split. Even though he was feeling terrible today, I had to ask Dimitri to help me get back on. I felt sorry for him, because his legs were almost gone. He went to the front, though, and rode as hard as he could until we made contact. I apologized for making him suffer any more than he already was, and Dimitri drifted to the back to suffer in silence.

The next climb, the 25km-long first-category Col du Soulor, was ridden at a steady tempo, and I was feeling good. As we began to rise above the cloud line and into the mist, a handful of sheep ran across the middle of the peloton. For a minute, I thought I was on the Sally Gap. Going across the top of the Soulor, a team masseur handed me a musette with two bottles of warm tea and a plastic bag in it. I had handed my rain cape back to the team car on the way up, so I shoved the plastic bag up my jersey to ward off the cold on my chest and sipped the tea on the way down. With the mist, I couldn't see ten yards in front of me on the way down, and in a few kilometres I was freezing, but at least the climb had thinned the bunch of kamikaze sprinters, so the descent was safer, even though we were doing 100kph on the straights.

The sprinters are normally better bike handlers than the climbers and have no fear. They throw themselves up the inside and outside of the bunch going into corners, and it's chaos. The climbers don't take risks. You just follow the guy in front of you.

In the valley after the Soulor, Martin handed me a sleeveless jacket, and I pulled it on as Saxo Bank began to string the bunch into one long line in an effort to shed as many riders as possible before the Tourmalet.

Cancellara, Sorensen and then Fuglsang all burnt themselves out in the first few kilometres of the mountain but had succeeded in their team leader Andy Schleck's quest to leave yellow jersey Contador with no teammates. I was climbing well, and as the group whittled down to around fifteen riders I was still hanging on. When Schleck attacked with 9.5km to go, though, the increase in pace saw me drift off the back.

I kept focussed, concentrated on my breathing and rode at my own pace. Ryder Hesjedal came by me, but he was going too fast. Then Roman Kreuziger came past, and I hopped on his wheel. His tempo took me back to the group ahead and I stayed there with Menchov, Sánchez, Gesink, Hesjedal, Rodríguez, Van den Broeck and Horner until 5km to go.

This is when Gesink started to accelerate. He was going fast, slow, fast, slow, and I began to crack. I prefer a steady rhythm on a climb, and soon Gesink's slow was even too fast for me and I lost contact. I rode on my own for a kilometre and a half before Damiano Cunego of Lampre caught me. I stayed with him until he increased the pace again a kilometre from the summit. I fought my bike, pulling the bars in an effort to get to the top. I changed from a 39x23 gear ratio to my 'granny' gear of 39x26 to try and spin my legs, because I knew that if I went for power I'd probably come to a standstill on the slopes. The last few corners were really steep and I was pulling faces when I crossed the line for twelfth place on the stage, three minutes and twenty-six seconds behind stage winner Schleck.

I had taken time out of Vinokourov, Sastre and Löfqvist though, and moved back up three places to fifteenth overall. For the first time in three weeks, today I'm happy. Happy to be back in the top fifteen, happy with my ride today and happy the mountains are over.

Stage 18 – Friday 23 July:
Salies-de-Béarn–Bordeaux, 198km

With the mountains behind us, today's flat stage was always going to be a day for the sprinters. The battle for the green jersey is far from over and, with two intermediate sprints offering points along the way and with another thirty-five points on offer for the stage win in Bordeaux, Norwegian champion Thor Hushovd would have his work cut out to defend a slim four-point lead.

Today, the break went very early, just 12km into the 198km stage. They were gone for the day, or at least until the sprinters wanted them back.

People often wonder how the peloton can seemingly chase a breakaway group all day and then suddenly reel it in with just a few kilometres left and end the stage with a bunch sprint. The truth is, those four guys probably knew they hadn't a chance today, and all they could hope for was some publicity for their sponsors.

The rule of thumb in cycling is that a breakaway needs a minute for every 10km left in the stage if it wants to stay away, even more on a mountain stage. The more riders there are in the breakaway group the better: the more work they can share at the front, and the harder it will be to bring them back. The trick is to leave them dangling. If you bring a group back with, say, 25km to go, then you will have to chase again, as others see their opportunity to counterattack. If you leave it until the last few kilometres, however, and really turn the speed up so nobody can attack, then most guys resign themselves to a bunch sprint finish.

Today, as the four leaders soldiered on into the wind,

I sat in the bunch protected by my Ag2r team. Today wasn't a day for heroics. With a 52km time trial looming on Saturday, I had to save as much energy as possible to try to hold my top-fifteen place overall. The rest of the GC contenders were in exactly the same position, each one hoping they could leapfrog the guy in front of them in the penultimate stage's 'race against the clock', and praying that the guy behind wouldn't overtake them on the leader board.

It was a pretty calm day for me. In fact, it was a bit boring. I passed the day chatting to teammates and friends in the bunch, and made sure I ate and drank enough during the stage. I spoke with Christophe Le Mével of Française des Jeux for a while. He lives in Italy now, like me, and we laughed and chatted about cars, women, houses and Italian culture. Like two oul' ones in Moore Street.

Tonight, Dimitri is a bit down. He's had problems with a bursitis (an inflammation of the fluid-filled sac between a tendon and the skin) on his foot since the start of the Tour, and each stage has made it worse. The heat and the tightness from his racing shoes have left him in agony over the past few days, and he will have an operation the week after the Tour. It's been a hard Tour for Dimitri, but he's been a great teammate and we've got along well in our three-week stint as 'roomies'.

My dad phoned me yesterday to ask if he could come over for the time trial. Aware that a former Tour winner's presence will draw attention to both of us, he didn't want to be putting extra pressure on me. I told him I wanted him to be there. It's been a long three weeks, and I haven't seen him in almost a month and a half, so on Saturday he will be following me in the Ag2r team car for the full 52km.

I am not bad against the clock. I won the Irish national time-trial championships a few years ago. But I'm not up there with the top guys, and need to improve. My dad loves time trials – they are his thing. By coming in the team car, and following behind me, he will be able to keep a good eye on me, see where I need to improve, and we can work on that in the winter. I hope I can hold on tomorrow.

Stage 19 – Saturday 24 July: Individual Time Trial, Bordeaux–Pauillac, 52km

In a time trial, there is no peloton to hide in, no team-mates to bring you bottles or shelter you from the wind. There is no drafting. Each rider starts a couple of minutes apart, and their efforts are timed over a set distance. It's just you against the stopwatch. Whoever covers the distance in the fastest time wins. It's that simple. It's why the French call the time trial 'the race of truth'.

Today, on the 52km ride from Bordeaux to Pauillac, Alberto Contador and Andy Schleck would find out which one was telling the truth when they both said they could win this year's Tour. Me, I would find out if I could hold on to that fifteenth place overall that I targeted on the first day of this diary over three weeks ago.

This morning at 7.30 I was woken by a knock on the

door by the UCI 'vampires'. They had selected myself and teammate Christophe Riblon for our third random anti-doping test of this year's race. Half awake, we were individually brought to a room where we had to give blood and urine samples. I have absolutely no qualms about the tests and believe they are a good thing. I have lost count of the number of times I've been tested since taking up cycling as an amateur, but I'm still afraid of needles. Dope tests cost money, and some anti-doping bodies buy cheaper needles to save money. With needles, it seems the cheaper they are, the bigger they are.

Maybe the sight of a massive needle about to be stuck into your vein would be less horrific if it was a beautiful young girl in a nurse's uniform who carried out the tests, but no, it's usually some old guy who doesn't look like he knows what he's doing. Mark Cavendish recently recalled a dope test where the independent dope test guy for the Columbia team stuck a massive needle in one side of a rider's arm and out the other. I tried not to think about that as the guy flicked the syringe with his finger and aimed it in my direction. As usual, I just looked away and pretended nothing was happening.

In cycling there is an old superstition that you never shave the night before a time trial or a hard day. The 'logic' behind it is that the energy used to grow back your stubble could be better used in the race. If I had gone unshaven before every hard day on this Tour, I'd look like Grizzly Adams now. But, this morning, I arrived down for my breakfast of pasta and omelette with a bit of fluff on my chin. I was leaving nothing to chance.

Afterwards, I went for an hour's training with Christophe and John Gadret. We rode our time-trial bikes for an hour and a quarter just to get the feel of the new, more aerodynamic position and get used to the tri-bars and different set-up of the bikes.

After training, I had a coffee with my dad. We had a chat about the stage, and he told me to stay focussed, to ignore all the media and cameras and, once I got on the bike for my warm-up, to just concentrate on my job and try to ride the best time trial possible.

In the start area, I hopped on my time-trial bike again, which was set up on a home trainer beside the team bus. For forty minutes, I warmed up, ignoring everything around me and just staring at my handle-bars as the house music pumped in my ears. I progressively began to raise my heart rate to 130bpm for a few minutes, then 140bpm. I did about fifteen minutes at that, and then did one or two sprints to get the heart up again. I slowly went up to 150bpm, then 160bpm for another while and did a few sprints to get up to 170bpm. Today was a really long time trial, and it would be spent riding at threshold, just under the point where my body begins to produce lactic acid.

A couple of minutes before I was due to start, I took off my glasses, which were covered in sweat, and put on my spare ones. To eliminate the risk of a puncture on the gravel-strewn car park, I hopped on my road bike to ride across to the start house as my mechanic ran beside me, carrying my bike.

There was no time for nerves in the start house. I knew what I had to do. I could not lose any more time than a minute and fifty-six seconds to Astana's Alexandre Vinokourov if I wanted to keep my place overall. I took a few deep breaths and really concentrated hard as the timekeeper counted down. *Cinq . . . Quatre . . . Trois . . . Deux . . . Un . . .* Go!

In the first few kilometres, my dad and Vincent in the team car behind were a bit worried. I had started off more slowly than usual but once I got out of the city I picked up speed and put the hammer down. Vincent spoke to me through my earpiece and sometimes over the megaphone attached to the roof of the car. My dad had told me they weren't going to lie to me during the stage. They would give me all the time gaps of the guys near my position overall, especially Vinokourov's, and if I was doing badly, it would be up to me to ride harder, if I could.

The wind had really picked up for the later riders, and all the GC contenders were at least four minutes slower than the earlier starters. At the first time check, I had lost thirty-eight seconds to Vino. I knew I was still on target, but I couldn't afford to crack towards the end or I would lose my placing. I didn't look at my speedometer once. I picked a point, focussed on it and kept on doing it until I got to the finish. For some reason, Vino's second time check never came over the radio. My dad's nerves got the better of him, and he actually rang the race director Jean-François Pescheux and asked him for the time gap. With 20km to go, I had only lost fifty-eight seconds, so I knew I was capable of holding on to the finish. In the end, I held on to my overall position by forty-seven seconds, and I was coming close to fourteenth overall, as I was riding faster than Radioshack's Andreas Klöden, just missing out by twenty-three seconds. It was probably the best time trial I have done in my career thus far.

Stage 20 – Sunday 25 July: Longjumeau–Paris, 102.5km

I was up at 7.30 this morning for the drive to Bordeaux train station. Here, the whole of the Tour boarded the TGV for the three-hour transfer to this morning's start in Longjumeau.

The fight for overall positions was over, and all that was left was a stage victory for one of the sprinters and the battle for the green jersey. After a couple of break-away attempts were reeled in, Mark Cavendish once again showed he is the fastest sprinter in the world and took his fifth stage win of this year's Tour, as Alberto Contador crossed the line with his hands in the air to take his third Tour de France win. I crossed the line tired, but happy to retain my fifteenth place overall.

My team had two targets coming into this Tour. We achieved both but, financially, we will not be much better off than we were three weeks ago. As usual with every race, our prize money from the Tour will be divided among all the riders on the Ag2r La Mondiale squad. It will be split in twenty-eight parts. Our biggest payday on this Tour was when Christophe took €8,000 for his mountain stage win, so we didn't exactly go home with a wad of cash in each of our pockets. I earned €2,000 for fifteenth place. Divide that by twenty-eight, and you'll see why professional cyclists don't exactly make Premiership footballers envious.

To mark my first Tour as a team leader and to thank all of the riders on the team, Maxime, Christophe, Rinaldo, David, Martin, Lloyd, Dimitri and even Gadret for their help over the past three weeks, I decided to buy them a gift. As a souvenir of this year's Tour, I bought the riders and my manager Vincent a Festina Tour edition watch. I realize that all the guys put their personal goals to one side for three weeks to try to help me do the best I could, and it was just a small gesture to show that I really appreciated all they had done for me. Riding the Tour can sometimes feel like you're living in the *Big Brother* house for three weeks. Everybody has their arguments, but nobody ever wins anything in cycling on their own, and each of those guys really helped me during the Tour.

My mother and my two biggest fans, my younger brothers, Florian and Alexis, also came from Nice to see me finish in Paris today. It was Florian's first trip away from home in two years. They both know I love cooking, so they bought me a present of a cookery book, and we had a laugh at the start and finish today. It was really great to see them. My sister Christel also flew over from Dublin and, although she had to catch another flight back pretty soon after the stage, I was really pleased she could be there.

What I didn't know at the time was how courageous Florian was being. Mum told me later just how tired he was and how sore his legs were. He didn't complain, though. They came by train to the start of the stage and then drove to Paris for the finish.

16

La Vuelta 2010

After the Tour de France, I could have ridden some smaller stage races and some big one-day races, but I wanted to do something different, and opted to ride 'La Vuelta' again for some more experience, so I spent a week or so recovering, and the rest of the time preparing for the tour of Spain. It would be the first time I had ridden two three-week Tours in the same year, and it was going to be a bit of an experiment for me.

A week or so after the Tour, I missed my cousin Dan Martin's great win at Tre Valli Varesine, because I got stuck in traffic. Having gone for a long, hard spin that morning, I decided to go and watch the finish of the Italian one-day race that afternoon, as it wasn't too far from my old apartment in Varese. Because it was a beautiful, sunny day, I went to the lake for a coffee first. I was yapping away, when I realized the race would be on its way to the finish. On the motorway, we got stuck in traffic, and I missed the finish, where Dan soloed in ahead of all the stars for a great victory. I spoke to him on the phone afterwards, but he was so busy with media interviews that I didn't see him until the following night, when we had a glass of wine to celebrate his latest win, and also his twenty-fourth birthday.

The weather in Italy was pretty miserable up until a week before the Vuelta, with rain every day. I had trouble with my sinuses from training in it, but it cleared up just before the start. With no racing in my legs, I had to do a lot of long rides at home in Varese, with sessions behind a motorbike to try to bring my speed up. For a fortnight or so, I rode out to Chiara's uncle's house, which is about an hour away from my apartment. I'd meet Fabrizio there, and he would motor pace me on a 75km loop for another hour and twenty minutes or so. After that, I'd ride home the long way for another hour and a half's training.

I missed two days' training in a row on the Thursday and Friday, two weeks before the Vuelta. Okay, the first one was actually a planned rest day, but the second one was my own fault. My apartment in Varese was on the top floor. I had a garage downstairs, but I rarely used it for my bike. Instead, I had a little bike shed on my terrace where I usually kept my trusty steed. When fully kitted out for training – getting ready is always the hardest part of the day – I grabbed my bike off the balcony and brought it down in the lift. Before the Vuelta, however, I decided to redecorate my apartment again, and left the bike in the garage. When I went to get it out the next morning, I couldn't find the key. I was standing outside in my Ag2r gear, with enough food and drink for a five-hour spin, but with no bike. I called the local locksmith but, because it was a public holiday in Italy, he wasn't available and couldn't come out until 5 p.m. The whole day was wasted. To add insult to injury, he charged me €150 for two minutes' work, and I gave him an earful.

I also broke my diet for a pizza. Seeing how angry I was at missing training, Chiara bought me one to cheer me up, so I sort of had to eat it. I enjoyed it, but had to do two very long, very hard training rides on the Saturday and Sunday to pay for it.

I was a bit worried going into the Vuelta, because I hadn't raced in a month and didn't really know how my form would be. At my pre-race medical, I was actually lighter and had less body fat than I had at the Tour, which was good, but being skinny doesn't mean you're going to be fast – although knocking another few seconds off my test climb ride beforehand meant I was going pretty well.

I was starting the Vuelta with the aim of trying to ride for the General Classification again, but if I didn't think I had the form to do that then I'd try to go for a stage win. In the Tour, I wanted to see how far I could go if I just stuck with the big guys for as long as I could. In the Vuelta, I had more options. I wanted to attack more. Okay, I was trying to ride for GC, but I wanted to enjoy a bit of racing as well, and didn't want just to follow wheels for three more weeks. The Vuelta is renowned for its aggressive stages, and I wanted to do a bit of attacking and try to get into moves and go for stage wins. I have always been an aggressive rider, and attacking is what I like to do. It's what gives me a thrill.

A pretty good Ag2r La Mondiale team assembled in Seville for the Vuelta. The team was based pretty much on the Tour, with me as sole leader and the other riders going for stage wins. I had Rinaldo and our stage winner Christophe with me from the Tour team. Then there was the very experienced José Luis Arrieta, our local Spanish rider, who was retiring after the 2010 Vuelta. We had a couple of young riders, Guillaume Bonnafond, who crashed out of the Giro this year, and Blel Kadri, and climbers Hubert Dupont and Ludovic Turpin. Sébastian Hinault's yellow shoes were also sure to be a feature in the bunch sprints.

I reckoned I would know whether I could ride for the GC or not after the first couple of days, as there were a few tough climbs on the opening stages. If I lost too much time there, I'd have to change the plan.

The weather had been incredibly hot in Spain that week. We arrived to 45-degree heat on the Wednesday before the race start. It was so hot, we couldn't go out training until 7 p.m. The race was due to start with a team time-trial in Seville. At 10 p.m.! How did the race organizers get away with that? Having a stage so late at night, under the street lights of Seville, might be good for the TV cameras, but it was going to be chaotic for us. We would only get on to the turbo trainers at around 9.30 p.m., warm up and then ride the time trial together. It was only 16km but, in a team time-trial, you have to go full gas for the whole distance. Anybody who does any type of sport knows it takes a while to get rid of the adrenaline and excitement afterwards. We probably wouldn't be able to sleep until 2 a.m. Once again, I kept a diary in the *Irish Independent*.

Stage 1 – Saturday 28 August: Team Time Trial, Seville, 16km

I think I ate something that didn't agree with me on the first night we arrived in Seville, because I have been spewing my guts up until this morning. I haven't eaten properly in two days and although I felt a lot better today I decided to skip lunch just in case. We were second team off tonight and, with such a late start, we had dinner at six before we went for a couple of practice laps of the course an hour later.

I suppose it's not often you read about me enjoying a stage, but I did tonight, despite a lot of bad luck. Disaster struck after just 1km, when Nocentini punctured on the cobbled section just after the start. Guillaume Bonnafond, José Luis Arrieta and Sébastian Hinault were caught behind him and, as the rest of us didn't know Rinaldo had punctured, they had to ride round him and fight hard to get back on, as we were still riding flat out.

The trio regained contact on a very twisty section after a few kilometres of chasing, but the massive effort took its toll soon after and, all of a sudden, we were down to the bare minimum of five riders. I was pretty strong during the stage, and Christophe and Blel Kadri were going very well too, with climbers Hubert Dupont and Ludovic Turpin giving their best too. Towards the end, Hubert couldn't ride through in the line any more and had to sit at the back. We knew we couldn't afford to drop him, though, because his front wheel would be the one that stopped the clock.

Even though we finished seventeenth out of twenty teams, I was happy that I felt good during the race. To add to his woes, Nocentini had a dope test after the stage and didn't get back to the hotel until 1.30 in the morning.

Stage 2 – Sunday 29 August:
Alcalá de Guadaíra–Marbella, 173km

This morning I felt a lot better than the past couple of days, so I had a good breakfast, with some rice.

I didn't enjoy today's stage at all, though, and was happy to see the finish in Marbella. On the route map, we had one third-category climb after 75km, the 630m-high Alto de Pruna, to contest today. But, after that, if you looked at the profile of the stage, you'd see a much higher and longer climb of about 40km winding its way up towards the popular tourist village of Ronda that wasn't even given any mountain points on the stage.

I started to suffer from the heat after about 90km and, coincidentally, it lasted for the next 40km or so and I was in pain on the long climb. Normally, I love racing in the heat but today's 45-degree scorcher was too much. I really suffered like never before. I had goosebumps and a headache for a good hour and a half, and I reckon I had a hunger flat a couple of times today from not eating properly the past few days.

Luckily, the guys rallied around me and kept my morale up. In the blazing sun, they had to go back to the car for cold drinks every twenty minutes or so. I had a few mini cans of Coke to try and settle my stomach, and probably used at least twelve bottles of water today. Sometimes I just threw out a quarter-full bottle when a new, cold one arrived from the little cool box in the car. Some of them I just poured over my head. Even though I ate plenty of food and drank loads of bottles, it took a long time to come around.

Stage 3 – Monday 30 August:
Marbella–Malaga, 157km

Last night my Ag2r La Mondiale team stayed in a massive hotel in the centre of Marbella. Our hotel had over five hundred bedrooms, and it felt pretty weird to be standing in the foyer sweating in our cycling gear as people were walking around the place in swimming togs and flip-flops. It's frustrating to see everybody on holidays, looking forward to the sun, when you're silently hoping it might rain, or at least cool down a bit.

As is usually the case on a day when you get a hunger flat, I was starving after Sunday's stage and had a massive bowl of pasta for dinner. I was pretty tired too, and was in bed by 10.30. Last night I had a room with a pool view, which meant that I had to put in earplugs to drown out the sound of the guy playing the piano outside for the holidaymakers.

On one of the early descents today, Hubert and seven or eight other guys overshot a corner and went straight into the ditch at about 70kph. I'm not sure how it happened, but I think somebody just cornered too fast and their front wheel slipped. The heat is also making the descents pretty dangerous with the tarmac melting on the road, so that could have been the cause. Hubert is pretty cut up on his legs, back, hip, everywhere. He'll have a sleepless night tonight.

I made sure to stay near the front on the final descent, which was really quick. Then we hit the last 2km climb to the finish, which was really steep and difficult. It was way harder than it looked on the race manual. I had looked at the graphic this morning, and it looked like the climb started 2km from the finish and flattened out with 500m to go, but once we went round the corner with 2km left there was no flat. We just kept climbing to the line, and it was tougher than I expected.

We sprinted into the first corner, everybody vying for the best position. Guillaume, Ludovic and Blel came up to me on the climb and kept the wind off me for as long as they could, which was a great help. From about a kilometre and a half out, I was at, or very near to, my limit. I knew this type of finish would suit the likes of Philippe Gilbert and Joaquim Rodríguez – two punchy little climbers who can sprint well on a short, sharp hill like today's. When Gilbert went on the corner, I was on his wheel, marking him, but he was way too quick for me. There was nothing I could do. Whereas Gilbert had a little bit extra in the tank, I was already at full gas and just kept going as hard as I could until the finish line. I think I passed two guys on the way up and another passed me before the line, and I ended up sixth on the stage.

I'm a bit sick of sixth places now. At least if you get fifth, you get a few UCI points and a top-five placing. Sixth is just classed as 'another top ten'. I've had enough of those this year, but it was important for the team that I got some sort of result to keep everybody's morale up.

Stage 4 – Tuesday 31 August:
Malaga–Valdepeñas de Jaén, 183km
I had a hard start to the stage this morning, as my legs were still a bit tired after yesterday's uphill finish, but as

the race went on I felt better and better, and ended the stage pretty strongly to take eighth place.

Sometimes, the first hour of racing is the most difficult, as breaks continuously try to get established but are often reeled in if they include any riders deemed to be a threat. On a stage race, you can be a threat to numerous people for numerous reasons. If you're high on the GC, then you're obviously going to be a threat to the race leader and other overall contenders, and will rarely be allowed to go anywhere. If you are up in the King of the Mountains classification on a hilly stage, then the Mountains leader's team is going to try to take you back so that he can earn maximum points over the climbs. On a flat stage, the sprinters' teams calculate how many riders and which ones they can afford to let open a gap before they methodically reel them in towards the end of the stage.

Today, though, the early break went after just 25km and, because they went before the first climb, the Omega Pharma Lotto team of race leader Philippe Gilbert started riding straight away at the front of the peloton and kept the pace pretty steady.

It's important for our team to try to have someone in the break each day, because there's always the little chance that they could stay away until the finish. The day that you have nobody from your team in the move is usually the day that the break gets ten minutes and contests the stage win. If that happened and we had nobody in it, then we would be kicking ourselves.

We had Guillaume in the four-man break today. The quartet up front built up a maximum lead of almost six minutes, but with Guillaume having started the day just two minutes and fifty-nine seconds down on Gilbert overall, the Lotto squad knew that if it didn't rein him in a bit he would take over the red leader's jersey at the end of the stage. He managed to stay away until 3km from the top of the final mountain.

Ag2r had a team car parked near the top, and the mechanic handed me a welcome cold bottle on another scorcher of a day. Today was a different type of heat, though. Although it was 'only' 38 degrees, it was a lot more humid, with little or no air, and the sweat was dripping off me for most of the stage. But like I said yesterday, when you're in the thick of the action, you forget about all that, and as we approached the short, steep final climb to the finish I was feeling pretty good and took eighth.

Immediately after the line, I rode straight across to the barrier on the left-hand side of the road and grabbed it to stop me keeling over on the steep hill. The road ahead was blocked with photographers, police, fans and team officials, and there was no way I was going to try to ride through all those people in that heat. I could hardly breathe as it was. I waited there for the team soigneur to come down to me. The first thing he did when he saw me was pour water on me to cool me down and hand me a towel to dry off.

After the stage, I had yet another cold shower in the team bus, and then ate some mashed potato and chicken before heading for the team car and a 110km transfer to tomorrow's start town.

Although it was still way up in the thirties outside,

we didn't put the air conditioning on in the team car, or even open the windows. I don't know where it came from, but most professional cyclists believe that if you put on the air conditioning after a hot stage, you are more likely to catch a cold, so we all just sat there sweating and had to have another shower when we arrived at our hotel.

Stage 5 – Wednesday 1 September: Guadix–Lorca, 198km

Although most of the guys on the team are winding down their season with this Vuelta, I'm aiming at a good overall position at the end of the three weeks, so I have to be serious about my job. When we finish dinner at around 10.30, I can't join them for a coffee and a chat afterwards, because I have to go to bed to try to be in the best possible shape for the next stage. So, last night, I bought a good bottle of wine for the dinner table as a small way of saying thanks to the guys for their hard work on the early stages so far.

I'm rooming on my own at the Vuelta for the early stages, and my room last night wasn't too bad. But for the first ten minutes or so I thought I was in the opening scenes of *Once Upon a Time in the West*. If you haven't seen it, look it up on YouTube. My room must have been over the air-conditioning system for the whole motel, because all I could hear was a creak that reminded me of Sergio Leone's three cowboys waiting on a train, as a windmill or something squeaks in the background. Last night, I was that cowboy . . . until I put my earplugs in and fell asleep.

Today was a long and boring day on the Vuelta. For most of the 198km, there were four guys up the road who were always going to be caught, and we knew it would end in a bunch sprint. I spent most of the stage sitting in the peloton chatting with Philip Deignan from Letterkenny. Although we've never ridden on the same professional team, Philip was with Ag2r for four years and left just before I joined. Philip is a class act when he's on form, and won a stage and finished ninth overall in last year's Vuelta. We get on really well and are always slagging each other about something.

Just before the Vuelta, Philip and his teammates on the Cervélo Test Team were told that the squad would no longer exist next year and he would be out of a job. Even though he has one year left with Cervélo, it doesn't look like Philip's contract will be honoured, and he has to go looking for a new team for 2011. To make it even harder for him, he was laid low with a virus for most of this season and hasn't had many results.

That's all the ammunition I needed for today. Most of the stage was spent sadistically asking him if he was looking for a team next year and if he had tried contacting Ag2r. I told him I knew the Ag2r team leader and that he was sound. Philip said he heard he was a bit of a bollocks from Dundrum. I said I could put a word in for him for next year if he liked, but that I didn't know if Philip was any good. I asked him if he had any results lately. He laughed and replied that he had exactly the same amount of wins as me this year. None.

Philip then jokingly said he had applied for

university and would be leaving for Trinity College on the first rest day of the Vuelta. I told him it was a pity he wasn't a good cyclist or he could have applied for a sports scholarship.

The slagging went back and forth like this for the day, and we had a good laugh. It was either that or spend the day gawping at the barren, desert-like scenery as we rolled along, waiting for the inevitable bunch sprint. Philip deserves a place on any ProTour team and, personally, I'd love to have him as a team-mate next season, but I think he is in the process of sorting a team out himself for 2011.

Stage 6 – Thursday 2 September: Caravaca de la Cruz–Murcia, 151km

The Atkins diet. The bikini diet. The cabbage-soup diet. Forget them all. Get yourself a bike, ride a three-week tour and you can eat what you like. Former Irish champion Mark Scanlon famously lost five kilos while riding for Ag2r in a mountain time trial up Alpe d'Huez during the 2005 Tour de France. How long did it take him? Forty-five minutes.

Cyclists have a David Blaine-like capacity to make food disappear at a dinner table. An average male needs around 2,000 calories a day to maintain his weight. A Tour de France rider can eat almost 10,000 calories a day during the Tour and won't put on any weight. Six or seven hours in the saddle will see to that.

Before and after each stage, our Ag2r team doctor weighs us to see if we have lost any weight during the stage. We then have to make sure we rehydrate properly and put it back on. A few days before the Vuelta, we all had our body fat measured. Your average, healthy Joe Bloggs has around 15–20 per cent body fat, with an athlete's percentage ranging from 12 to 15 per cent. Stage racing cyclists are notoriously lower than that. Mine is around 6 per cent. Skinny.

At twenty-three years of age, Blel Kadri is five foot nine and a half and weighs just 10 stone, or 165 kilos. He is a rake-thin French climber and won a stage of the Route du Sud earlier in the year. Of the whole Ag2r La Mondiale team, Blel had the highest body-fat percentage.

At only 8 per cent body fat, Blel is by no means over-weight. In fact, if you saw him walk past, you'd probably say he needed a good feed. But to a fellow cyclist, he might as well be morbidly obese, and we have been calling him 'Chubby' since the race began.

The food on the race hasn't been anything to write home about. Last night we were at another roadside motel and, as we sat down to yet another self-service buffet, Blel walked over to the table with a big grin on his face. He had helped himself to a greasy pile of chicken and some tasty-looking Spanish tortillas full of cheese and sauces. Just as he sat down and was preparing to tuck into his dinner, the team doctor walked over, whipped Blel's plate from under him and said, 'Forget about it. Get something else.' Cue even more slagging for poor Blel.

Today's stage was pretty mundane until about 15km from the bottom of the only climb of the day, the second-category Alto de la Cresta del Gallo. Everybody knew the climb was an ideal place to attack. The top was only 18km from the finish in Murcia, and the descent was brutal, with a really bad road surface and dangerous corners. If you were in a little group going over the top, you could maybe stay away and win the stage, or take some time out of your rivals for the overall. Everybody had the same idea as we approached the bottom of the climb – get to the front at all costs. The whole team gave me a hand to stay there. They had their work cut out for them, though, because the constant surges and waves in the peloton meant that I spent about 10km going like a yo-yo from the front to the middle of the bunch in the lead-up to the climb. Each time, the guys had to ride out in the wind and bring me up the outside of the bunch into a better position.

I was comfortable enough on the climb itself, going over the top in about eighth or ninth place. On the way down, however, I lost two or three places, because Rabobank leader and two-time Vuelta winner Denis Menchov and a couple of other guys were pushing to pass me any time I braked. It didn't seem to me that the group was going to split on the descent, so I just let them by. I preferred to let them pass than take the risk of someone cutting me up on one of the corners and maybe crashing.

There was a long flat bit after the descent, and I had Ludovic and Rinaldo with me heading for the finish. Rinaldo wanted to try to have a go in the sprint, as he hasn't been back to his best since breaking his leg earlier in the season. I told him to try his luck, and we both agreed to do our own sprint in the final gallop.

The finish was too flat and too fast for me, with a big tailwind, and suited a bigger, more powerful rider. It was no surprise that Thor Hushovd took the stage. Sprinting is all about positioning in the final kilometre or so, and I ended the sprint where I started it, in tenth place.

I'm still eleventh overall but psychologically it's better to be tenth, because you're on the first page of the results on TV, which is the only page they show after the stage.

Stage 7 – Friday 3 September:
Murcia–Orihuela, 187km

As team leader, I had given out to Guillaume two days ago for being in the final selection coming into the finish and not helping me in the sprint. This morning, my manager gave out to me for letting Rinaldo ride his own sprint yesterday. He pointed out that, as team leader, I should have made Rinaldo lead me out and maybe got a higher placing than tenth. His point was that I might have made the top five and earned valuable UCI points for the team. It shows how things have come full circle from last year's Tour de France, where, even though I was faster than our official sprinter at the time, I was told not to sprint, as I would need my energy to help the others later in the race. Now that I'm leader, though, I'm still making mistakes, still being given out to, and still learning.

Today had a touch of déjà vu about it, as the stage consisted of about five different loops of varying lengths. As the loops were criss-crossing each other several times, you were constantly riding past places you'd been in maybe a half-hour before, but this time going in the opposite direction. I stayed pretty near the front until about a kilometre to go, but the finish was very narrow and twisty, and there was a lot of pushing and shoving going on in the bunch. I was expecting a crash on one of the narrow chicanes in the sprint, but couldn't afford to drift back too far in case there was a split in the bunch.

As it happened, there was a split in the peloton in the final kilometres, and Xavier Tondo was caught in the second part. Although he only finished a handful of seconds behind me on the road, the time is taken from the first rider on the stage to the first rider in the split, which means the more the peloton is strung out, the bigger the gap to the split. Tondo lost eighteen seconds to stage winner Petacchi, and I moved up to tenth overall. I said in yesterday's diary that I'd prefer to be in the top ten overall. Maybe today I should say that I'd like to win the stage tomorrow.

Today is Blel Kadri's birthday. He's twenty-four. As ever, we have been slagging him about his weight all week, but we'll have a birthday cake and a glass of wine for him tonight to make up for it. Fat boy will like that.

Stage 8 – Saturday 4 September:
Villena–Xorret del Cati, 190km

Today's stage was always going to see the first real shake-up on the overall classification, with the ultra-steep climb of the Alto del Xorret del Cati coming just 3km from the end of the stage.

Things began with a bang, as race leader Philippe Gilbert, among others, crashed shortly after the start. We went from doing about 60kph on a big, five-lane motorway to slowing right down as we changed on to a single-lane road. I slammed on the brakes and didn't crash, but I was held up for a little while as guys picked themselves up off the road in front of me.

On the first climb of the day, the third-category Puerto de Onil after 24km, last year's King of the Mountains David Moncoutié dragged a group including my Ag2r teammate José Luis Arrieta clear over the top, and it spent the rest of the stage out front. With 40km to go, the group had over five and a half minutes' lead on us, but then Philip Deignan went to the front of the bunch on the penultimate climb for his Cervélo team leader Carlos Sastre and single-handedly brought the gap down to three minutes forty-eight in 12km.

Coming into the foot of the final climb, there was the usual jostling for position, as we all knew this would be the make-or-break climb of the day. Blel Kadri's birthday cake last night must have worked wonders, because he did a great job for me today. He led me into the bottom of the final climb, riding 4 or 5km out in the wind, so that I could get shelter behind him and save my energy for the final assault.

Although the break was still clear, we were just concerned about the whittled-down group of overall contenders around us as we hit the climb. Four or five Liquigas guys rode really hard on the first half of the 4km ascent, trying to get rid of some of their rivals for their Italian leader Vincenzo Nibali. Then Sastre attacked, but didn't get too much of a gap. I was in a fairly good position with about a kilometre to go on the climb. I was riding behind Spanish duo Igor Antón and Joaquim Rodríguez, who began the day joined on time for the overall lead. Also there were Nibali and Xavier Tondo of Cervélo. When we caught Sastre a few hundred metres later, Rodríguez attacked, and I went out the back door.

I maintained my rhythm, however, and latched on to the back of the group again shortly afterwards. I had just made contact with them when Antón attacked the group, and the change of pace saw me dropped again. Guys like Rodríguez and Antón are 10–15 kilos lighter than me and are very explosive on steep climbs like today. When I have to go a second or third time, it's just physics that's holding me back. I would have a lot more power than them but am heavier, so I prefer a long, steady climb.

Only Rodríguez and Nibali could follow, and the rest of us were left up to our own devices. I crossed the line fifteenth on the stage. I moved up to eighth overall and am only nine seconds off fifth, but tomorrow is another hard day in the mountains.

Stage 9 – Sunday 5 September: Calpe–Alcoy, 187.7km

I found out this morning that the race organizers made a mistake in the General Classification after yesterday's stage. The Italian Marzio Bruseghin had finished with me on the stage, but they had given him the same time as the group in front of us, which took twelve seconds off his overall classification. They changed it this morning, so I officially began the stage in seventh place overall, my highest ever position on a Grand Tour.

With seven mountains to be climbed on another blistering day, and plenty of little hills that weren't even on the map, today was one of the toughest days of the Vuelta so far. Thankfully, it wasn't as hard as it could have been because when the break went the peloton didn't really attack each other until the very end of the stage.

The Euskaltel team of race leader Igor Antón have a very strong team and played their cards well today, letting a fourteen-man break open a big gap during the stage. It worked out well for them, even though at one point it looked like Antón would lose his red jersey to Frenchman Jean-Christophe Péraud of Omega Pharma Lotto.

With Péraud in this fourteen-man group was Blel Kadri. Even though he is a first-year professional and is riding his first ever Grand Tour, Blel has been doing great work for me on this Vuelta. The plan today was to send someone from the team up the road in a move so that if the peloton split on the final climb and got across to them, I would have somebody strong already up there to help me. If we didn't catch them, we would have somebody in a position to go for the stage win.

The breakaways stayed away until the finish, and Blel took fifth on the stage and a couple of valuable UCI points for the team. I am really happy for him, and he is delighted with his first big result.

Although Péraud didn't get the seven-minute advantage that he needed to go into the race lead, he did get enough time to leapfrog me in the General Classification, so my seventh place didn't last long, and I'm now eighth overall. I know I could move up a little when Péraud drops back down the GC, but I also have guys like Schleck, Menchov and Sastre behind me, so it will be hard to stay up there. It will be a good challenge. I think Schleck will come right in the final week. He is just back after breaking his collarbone at the Tour, and I reckon he will get better as the Vuelta goes on.

Monday 6 September: Rest Day, Tarragona

After yesterday's stage, we had a 400km transfer and didn't arrive at our hotel until 10.30 p.m. Once again, we had no air conditioning on in the team car, for fear of catching a cold, and spent the whole journey dripping in sweat.

To pass the time on the trip, myself and team manager Julien Jourdie decided to wind up the other *directeur sportif* Didier Jannel. Didier is in his first year as manager of the team and has only directed a few races so far. The Vuelta is his first Grand Tour.

On the Vuelta, as in all pro races, each team has two cars on the race. One drives behind the peloton all day and the other goes up the road and looks after our riders if they make it into the breakaway of the day. Didier's job has been to drive behind the breakaway groups, and he has been pretty busy, as Ag2r have had a rider in the break on most days. Didier had just driven behind Blel, who was part of a fourteen-man break and had finished fifth on the stage.

On the way to the hotel, Julien took a phone call and, when he finished speaking, he winked at me and put on a depressed voice. Julien told Didier that Blel had been disqualified after the stage. Julien told him that the race commissaires had penalized Blel a minute and a half and he had been fined 300 Swiss francs, which is the international currency of cycling.

Didier took the bait immediately and got angrier and angrier, as he had been there right behind him all day, and demanded to know why Blel had been penalized. Julien told him that the race referees said that Didier had spent too much time talking to Blel during the stage, and that he had given him shelter from the wind. As Didier grew more and more apoplectic, Julien added that Blel had received a lot of 'sticky bottles' during the stage, and it was lucky that both he and Didier weren't thrown off the race.

A 'sticky bottle' is the term used for a bottle that is held on to for a few seconds too long as it is handed to a rider from a team car. A tired rider will sometimes try to get a few metres of a tow from it. There is no real benefit in doing this, though, because if you go back for bottles, you usually have to take five or six on board and then ride back up to the bunch with them anyway and, as long as the rider doesn't hang on for more than three or four seconds, the commissaires usually turn a blind eye.

Didier was outraged. He hadn't given Blel any sticky bottles, or spent too long talking to him during the stage. He wanted to ring the race organization and appeal the decision. He probably would have too, if we hadn't told him we were only joking.

Although we had no stage today, I went training for two hours this morning at ten o'clock with most of the team. All of the guys came on the spin except Nocentini and Arrieta, who both decided to have a lie in instead. They went out later in the day. Midway through the spin, we all stopped at a beachfront café and had a coffee and a chat in the warm sunshine. It's probably the first time on this Vuelta that we actually enjoyed the sunshine. For the past ten days we have been praying for cooler weather.

Stage 10 – Tuesday 7 September: Tarragona–Vilanova i la Geltrú, 175.7km

Today's stage was really fast. We started on a motorway and went up one side, before turning round and coming back down the other side and into Tarragona again.

Joaquim Rodríguez had started this morning in second place overall, equal on time with race leader and compatriot Igor Antón. Rodríguez knew there was a time bonus sprint after 42km and that if he could place himself in the top three in the gallop to the line, he would take a few seconds off his overall time and become the new leader of the Vuelta.

With points as well as time bonuses of six, four and two seconds on offer for the first three over the line in the village of Valls, points competition leader Mark Cavendish also wanted to try to distance himself from American sprinter Tyler Farrar, who began the day just three points behind Cav. So there was plenty at stake.

The pace was frantic for the first hour, and we covered 51km in that time, catching one last group just a kilometre before the first bonus sprint.

As I had started the day just one second off seventh place and just three seconds off sixth, I too wanted to contest the sprint in the hope of nabbing a few bonus seconds. I spent the final kilometres leading up to the sprint shouting into the microphone of my team radio asking for one of the guys to give me a hand in the sprint. I started to get angry when nobody responded, but found out later that my radio wasn't working.

The sprint line itself was in a really dangerous place. I saw Rodríguez setting up for the sprint as we descended full gas off the big motorway. Suddenly there was a tiny roundabout at the end of the motor-way and the bonus sprint was just 100m after it. I went into the roundabout at the same time as Vincenzo Nibali, the Italian leader of the Liquigas team. Nibali started the day in third place overall, so he knew if he won the sprint and got the six-second bonus, he could take over the lead of the Vuelta. As we leaned into the corner, we collided accidentally and were both lucky to stay upright. There was a bit of shouting between us afterwards as Nibali wanted to know why I was going for the time bonus. I told him I could move up to sixth, the same way he could move up to first if he won it. The argument didn't last too long, though, and I think both of us got more of a fright than anything else, and we both apologized a few metres later.

Cavendish won the sprint from Farrar, with

Rodríguez taking back two seconds for third, making him the virtual leader of the Vuelta.

Today we had the first-category climb of the Alto del Rat Penat to tackle, with the summit coming just 30km from the finish. The climb was hectic. The Xacobeo team set a ferocious pace on the early kilometres, and then Liquigas took over. My Ag2r team had looked up the climb on Google maps the night before and we knew that parts of it were 18 per cent gradient. I decided to keep my 'granny gear' of 39x28 on for the stage and was happy that I did. I got over the ascent in the top twenty riders or so, but could feel my legs were a little sluggish after the rest day the day before.

The descent was really rough, full of potholes, cracked tarmac, storm drains and even lumps of clay. My girlfriend, Chiara, travelled in the team car today, and she nearly had a heart attack on the way down the mountain. Drivers in the cavalcade all have their own little signals and know what to look out for on the way down a mountain, but Chiara was both shocked and amazed at the speed and skill of drivers and riders alike on the narrow road, as the guys who were dropped on the way up flew past her window at 80–90kph in an effort to regain contact on the way down.

The last 15km were really fast, as Liquigas piled on the pressure in the hope that their sprinter, my old 'friend' Daniel Bennati, could win the stage. They left it too late, though, and my old nemesis, Imanol Erviti, soloed clear of the front group and won the stage. It was his second ever Vuelta stage win, having beaten me in a photo finish at the end of stage eighteen in 2008.

Maybe if I concentrated on going for stage wins instead of the overall, I would have more big stage victories now, but I need to know how far I can go in these big tours. When you are close to the race lead, you are never going to be allowed to slip away in a break and contest a stage win. At the moment I'm still learning and gaining experience. When I find my limit, then I will maybe change my tactics.

Stage 11 – Wednesday 8 September: Vilanova i la Geltrú–Andorra, 208km

Today's start was incredibly fast and for the first hour or so the peloton was really strung out in one long line. It took a long time for the main break of the day to go clear. Big groups of fifteen to twenty riders were constantly attacking and being brought back. Former race leader Philippe Gilbert was really active again today and won the first intermediate sprint after 45km, moving him up to second in the points competition for the green jersey.

Soon after the sprint, two riders, Mikaël Cherel of Française des Jeux and Johann Tschopp of Bouygues Telecom, rode away and, happy that they were no major threat to proceedings, the peloton eased up.

My Ag2r La Mondiale team was great again today, looking after me all day with bottles and riding alongside me to keep me out of the wind and conserve my energy before the final mountain to the ski station at Andorra. I ate and drank and relaxed a little bit as the two leaders worked hard up front to open up a good lead on the slumbering peloton.

While the bunch eased up, I took the opportunity to stop for a wee and, while I was down the back of the bunch, I spent a bit of time talking to Philip Deignan again. His team had told him that while he had started the Vuelta sick, he might actually get better after a few days of racing, which is something I don't understand. Maybe if Philip only had a head cold or something he might have got better, but he has been out for a lot of the season with a virus and has never reached his usual good form this year. We were speaking for a few minutes about this and that was when he told me he was going to quit the Vuelta at the feed zone, halfway through the stage. I thought he was messing, but it turned out he was serious. I told him that I'd see him around during the winter. He was pretty disappointed at having to abandon the race and plans to have a few more medical tests to check out what is wrong with him. Philip is a great friend of mine and we get on really well, so it's disappointing to see him having to stop. Hopefully, he will get whatever is making him sick sorted out and be back to top form pretty soon.

Once the two escapees had built up a lead of over fifteen minutes, the Rabobank team of Denis Menchov suddenly decided it was time to give chase, and the hammer went down in the peloton. The speed went up dramatically straight away. We spent around 100km in one long line, and Blel Kadri, Christophe Riblon, Sébastian Hinault and José Luis Arrieta did all the hard work keeping me out of the wind as we snaked along the valley before reaching the long climb up to Andorra. On the route map, the mountain is categorized as only being 10km long, but we were climbing for about the final 25km today.

Hubert Dupont rode alongside me until around 6km to go, as we continuously changed from the big ring to smaller gears and back as the gradient increased and decreased. I was feeling really good for most of the climb and, as race leader Joaquim Rodríguez rode away with Vincenzo Nibali and Ezequiel Mosquera, I was comfortable in the second group of maybe a dozen guys. Igor Antón and Fränk Schleck tried to get across to the trio, and it was every man for himself after that. Some of the guys who had gone clear on the mountain blew their lights and came back to our group, but when Xavier Tondo attacked us about 2–3km from the summit, I cracked. I didn't even try to go with him and just rode at my own tempo, losing forty seconds to Tondo by the top. There were only eight or nine of us left at that stage, and I finished last of the group, thirteenth on the stage.

I'm a bit disappointed, because I was hoping I could stay where I was overall. I only dropped one place to ninth, but my nearest rivals gained time on me today. I also let Schleck and 2008 Tour de France winner Carlos Sastre come back to me. Sastre will probably get another fifteen or twenty seconds on the climbs every day. I'm sure Schleck, a solid climber, will finish ahead of me too. The way he was climbing today, he was flying.

When we arrived in Andorra, my teammates were looking forward to picking up some gifts for their families. As the stage starts a little bit later on Thursday and shouldn't be as hard as the past couple of days, they planned to have a short walk around the shops and buy some gifts for their wives and kids. But after we eventually found our way to our hotel, we found out that today is a bank holiday in Andorra and all the shops were closed. If you think I was disappointed after the stage, you should have seen their faces.

Stage 12 – Thursday 9 September: Andorra la Vella–Lieda, 172.5km

Today's stage had an unusually late start of 1.15, but I got up at the normal time of eight o'clock. Some of the guys took advantage of the late start to buy gifts. As team leader, though, I have to try to conserve as much energy as possible for the tough stages ahead, and wasting energy by walking around was out of the question for me. Instead, I had another coffee with some of the mechanics on the team bus, had a bit of a lie down and got my stuff ready for the stage start.

One of our young riders, Guillaume Bonnafond, has complained of being very tired the past couple of days, so I had told him to take it easy and not to worry about his team duties, just focus on recovering for the hard days ahead. At breakfast this morning, he said he was still tired and was feeling pretty fragile, but he somehow mustered up enough energy to go shopping with the other guys. I gave out to him before the stage and told him that it didn't make sense to be complaining about being tired and then to be seen walking around the streets when he could be resting in bed instead.

The plan today was to try to get somebody in the break if it contained more than five or six riders. If it came down to a sprint finish, the guys were to give a hand to our sprinter Sébastian Hinault in the closing kilometres.

Once again, Blel made it into the breakaway, his third of the week. This time he had eight others for company, but as one of them, Spaniard David García, was only five minutes down on leader Igor Antón, they were never allowed to gain more than three minutes or so and were fighting a losing battle into the strong headwind.

Blel has been in three breakaways so far and finished fifth on stage nine into Alcoy last Sunday. He is pretty excited about being so active in his first Vuelta, but if he continues like this I don't think he will get to Madrid on Sunday week. He's a good, powerful rider and is still very young. It's all good experience for him, and he has shown he's not afraid to have a go, that's for sure. He was pretty chirpy after today's stage, when we were getting changed on the team bus, until Christophe reminded him that he'd been in three breakaways so far but had managed to get dropped out of the only one that stayed away until the finish.

Even though we had a strong headwind for most of the stage, the average speed for the day was 44kph, and that included a 12km climb. It was pretty much full gas all the way. I just sat in the middle of the bunch all day and tried to recover from the efforts made on the two previous mountain stages. Christophe stayed with me for most of the stage. The headwind in the final hour or so meant that there were constant streams of tired riders coming back down both sides of the bunch, so it was imperative to stay alert in order not to drift back too far.

In the last kilometre and a half we had a couple of bad corners and twists, and Séb was left to his own devices. Mark Cavendish pulled another sprint victory out of the bag, thanks to a great manoeuvre by his lead-out man Matt Goss in the final corner. Without braking at all, Gossy lashed into the corner first, with Cavendish on his wheel, and the two of them came out of the bend a few metres ahead of the rest of the sprinters. As they had a big enough gap, Cav tried to give Gossy the win, but the Australian had automatically sat up, stopped pedalling and started celebrating another Cav victory.

I seem to be going through phases of feeling good and bad during this Vuelta. A lot of it is in my head. Like today, when the break went clear, I knew I didn't have to be 100 per cent focussed and began to think about things. I was thinking to myself, I'm sore here, I'm sore there. I'm hungry. I feel tired. I'm not in the humour to eat anything. I'm fed up. Being a professional cyclist is a lot like working in an office or doing any other job. Sometimes you get fed up and start thinking of things you don't like about the job. This usually happens when the pace slows down and you have time to think. Once the speed goes up again, you start to concentrate and then you realize, Actually, I'm not going too bad.

Stage 13 – Friday 10 September:
Rincón de Soto–Burgos, 196km

Today was one of those days that never seems to end. It wasn't really a recovery day at all. I was feeling okay on the two third-category climbs, but I know that today's hills were nothing like the mountains we will face in the next three days. The first and last hours were flat out and then the three hours in the middle were spent quietly sitting behind the wheel in front of me. After two weeks of racing, nobody is in the humour to chat any more, so we just rode along for the most part in one long, silent line. People often say it must be great to see all the beautiful scenery in all the different countries as we ride along, but the last two countries I've been in just looked like a cyclist's arse to me.

All the GC guys were nervous coming into the finish and were fighting to make sure they didn't lose any time if the bunch split in the sprint, but I crossed the line in thirty-fourth place and kept out of danger. There is a lot of pressure on the team to get a stage win now. My job is to try to get a good placing on the GC, and the other guys are trying to help me but are also trying to get a stage win.

You can see the tiredness creeping in after each stage, the bags appearing under the eyes at the break-fast table. We still have a bit of a laugh at stupid stuff like somebody spilling their yoghurt drink all over themselves when the team bus hits a bump, but guys are more interested in sleeping on the bus now instead of chatting and slagging each other. The bus driver is a great guy and always has everything spotless and ready for us, but he's pretty grumpy and is prone to a bit of road rage. He's always blowing the horn, which pisses off anyone who's asleep. We used to laugh at it, but now people are too tired to see the funny side. We've got lost three times on the way to various hotels so far on this Vuelta. The first week was funny. Now it's just a nuisance. Last night, it took us forty-five minutes to do nine kilometres on the bus, and the driver got dog's abuse from the guys as we flew past our hotel on the other side of the motorway. But it's just tiredness, everybody wanting to get inside, lie down and rest.

I'm still rooming on my own, which suits everyone, because I go to bed earlier than the other guys and get up earlier too. They watch TV after dinner, while I go straight to sleep. We are in the wine-producing area of Spain tonight. José Luis Arrieta is from around here, and his wife and kids are visiting him, so I'll have a half-glass to be sociable, but no more than that.

Stage 14 – Saturday 11 September: Burgos–Peña Cabarga, 178km

For the past two days on the bike, I have been doing as little as possible, hiding in the bunch, saving energy for this third week of racing. For the past two weeks, off the bike, I have been doing even less. I've been adhering to the cyclist's motto of 'Never stand up when you can sit down and never sit down when you can lie down,' all to arrive in this final week of the Vuelta in the best possible position.

After two relatively flat days, today was the first of three very hard days in the high mountains. I began today's stage in ninth place overall and knew that if wanted to stay there I would have to fight tooth and nail on these climbs. Today we had four mountains to tackle, but by far the most important would be the 6km climb to the finish at Peña Cabarga. I had to be well positioned going into it and then hang on for as long as I could on the way to the summit.

Because it's so important for the overall contenders to be one of the top-ten riders into the bottom of the climb, you have ten teams trying to position their team leader in the best place possible at the foot of the mountain. It's the same if we have to negotiate a dangerous section of cobbles, like the one in the first week of the Tour de France. You have ten team managers, in ten cars, telling all their riders to get to the front at the exact same time. This results in a mêlée in the bunch as everybody tries to fit into the same space. Ironically, instead of making it safer, most of the time it makes it more dangerous and can cause crashes.

As we approached the bottom of the climb of Peña Cabarga, we were doing 75kph as each team tried to overtake the others on the main road to get their leader into the best position. I was a bit far back in maybe twenty-fifth position, but I had Rinaldo and Blel with me to bring me nearer to the front. Knowing that the slightest touch of wheels can bring the whole lot down like a house of cards, I told the guys to bring me up on the right-hand side of the peloton because I didn't want to ride in the centre. I was hoping that by being on the edge I could run up on the grass and ride round anybody if they fell in front of me.

Simply riding in somebody else's slipstream uses 20–25 per cent less energy than if you have to ride out in the wind, and Rinaldo and Blel did a superb job for me again today, thundering along on the edge of the peloton, cutting into the wind for me. Suddenly, there was a bang and the sound of bike metal scraping off the road. Somebody had crashed. I glanced across to see race leader Igor Antón in his red jersey fly over his handlebars at about 75kph. There was a big wave in the peloton as his bike jagged across the road and cut down more riders, who, in turn, created a domino effect behind them.

I found out later that Antón had hit a piece of wood in the middle of the road. Just because you crash, it doesn't mean the race waits for you, so he tried to get back on his bike, which is always your first reaction. If it's at a slow part of the race, there's a good chance you will be able to catch up with the bunch. You hop on your bike, chase hard and regain contact with the peloton. Only then do you start looking at your wounds, and the race doctor can treat you on the move so you don't lose time.

Antón crashed at the fastest point of today's stage, a crucial point. Even if he had had superficial injuries he would have had trouble getting back into contention and probably would have lost his race lead, but by finishing the stage, he could have fought another day. Blood streamed down his arms and legs. He looked like something you'd see in a butcher's window as he picked himself up off the ground. His shorts were torn and his race leader's jersey was in shreds. Still he wanted to carry on. As soon as he threw his leg over the saddle, though, the Spaniard realized something was wrong. As well as having a few serious-looking lacerations on his legs and arms, his elbow was broken. His Vuelta, a race that he looked capable of winning, was over.

Hubert was caught up in the crash too and, after the stage, he told us there was a big line on the road where Antón's pedal had scraped the tarmac as he slid along the ground.

As soon as I heard the clatter, I shouted into my microphone to Blel to ride as hard as he could to get us out of the danger zone. Not caring about his own prospects for the stage, Blel suffered into the wind for the next 2km as the final mountain approached. He did a great job, delivering me to the foot of the climb in sixth place.

Roman Kreuziger led his Liquigas leader Vincenzo Nibali on to the climb first. With Antón gone, Nibali knew he would become race leader if he didn't lose time to the rest of us on the mountain. I was riding at the back of our little group, which also contained Rodríguez, Schleck, Tondo, Velits, Danielson, King of the Mountains David Moncoutié and the two Xacobeo guys, Mosquera and García.

García attacked on a really steep hairpin with maybe 2km to go, and the group slowed down. I remembered how they had cut their pace and then kicked again on the climb to Andorra and didn't want to lose time like I had there, so I immediately went to the front and led the group at my pace. I didn't care when, one by one, Rodríguez, then Nibali, Mosquera, Schleck and Tondo attacked me. I just wanted to keep my rhythm going to the line. Although the others stayed away, myself and Moncoutié eventually caught Schleck and Tondo again and, as we came to the line, I put in a dig to try to gain a few seconds. I finished fifth on the stage and clawed back one second on Schleck.

Italian Marzio Bruseghin and Spaniards Rigoberto Urán and Rubén Plaza all lost time today and, with Antón having left the race, I jumped up four places to fifth overall, behind new leader Nibali, Rodríguez, Mosquera and Tondo. Fifth overall is the highest place I've ever been in on a Grand Tour, and to be in it with just a week to go is great. I'm my own worst critic, but I'd have to be stupid if I wasn't pleased with today.

Stage 15 – Sunday 12 September: Solares–Lagos de Covadonga, 187.3km

My fifth place yesterday certainly got the attention of people at home. I had more texts after the stage than I've ever had before, even after winning races. My dad was delighted with my performance, and my little brothers were over the moon, as were the rest of my family. Even this morning at the pre-stage team meeting, my teammates and managers expressed how happy they were with my performance and were talking about what a good experience we were going through, fighting for the overall classification at this Vuelta.

Today we only had one mountain to climb, but it came right at the end of the stage and happened to be one of the toughest on the race. The ascent to Lagos de

Covadonga is one of the legendary climbs of the Vuelta and is the Spanish equivalent of Alpe d'Huez in France. I'd never ridden up it before, so I was a bit nervous beforehand.

The first 80km were hectic, as breaks tried to go clear. Having seen how hard it was to get two seconds on Schleck or Tondo on the climbs the day before, I figured I'd try to take a few seconds whenever I could from now on and had it in my mind to go for one of the early bonus sprints if I got the chance. As luck would have it, I latched on to the back of a little five-man group just before the second sprint of the day. We went through a tight chicane, and I got a bit of a surprise as the sprint was straight after it. Matt Goss went to get the points on offer and stop anybody else gaining too many on his teammate Mark Cavendish, the points competition leader, and I got second. I had planned to surprise Gossy before he started sprinting, but I wasn't going to beat one of the fastest lead-out men in the world in a straight sprint. He took the six-seconds bonus, and I got four.

My Ag2r La Mondiale team has been riding well for me since the start of this Vuelta and today did another fantastic job leading into the climb. As the rain started to come down for the first time in two weeks of racing, I had the whole team around me and everyone was psyched to try to get me into the best position at the bottom of the ascent. In fact, I had to tell Guillaume to calm down a bit, as he was getting carried away driving on the front of the bunch.

As usual, the Liquigas team of new race leader

Vincenzo Nibali did a great job, leading him on to the climb at a fast pace. The climb itself started off okay but got steeper and more irregular as we went up through the trees. Spanish climber Ezequiel Mosquera was on his favourite territory now and, in an effort to take over the race lead, he attacked us with 5km to go.

Mosquera's change of pace put a strain on our group, and only a handful of guys remained. Surprisingly, one of my direct rivals, Xavier Tondo of Cervélo, went out the back door. I knew if I could open a big enough gap on him, I could move into fourth overall, but I'd need a minute and twenty-one seconds on him by the top.

Tondo went out of my head, though, when Nibali put the pressure on 2km later. What annoys me, looking back, is that it wasn't even on the steep part of the climb. Nibali just rode really hard on a slight downhill section and nearly killed himself as he slid into a gutter on a corner in the rain. When he managed to straighten himself up again, he had dragged second-placed Joaquim Rodríguez, Peter Velits and American Tom Danielson with him. I had let the wheel go and lost a huge amount of energy trying to chase them on the little descent, and when the road started to head skywards once more, the quartet just disappeared into the mist.

Velits had begun the day just seventeen seconds behind me, and I knew he still had about 3km left to eat into my advantage. As they rode clear, I was left with Fränk Schleck, who started the day just a second behind me, and Carlos Sastre. We knew Sastre wasn't going to help us, as we were riding away from his Cervélo teammate Tondo. Fränk just nodded to me and said, 'Come on, Nico,' and we knew it was to our mutual benefit to ride together to the top. There was no point in attacking each other and losing more time to the guys up ahead, so Fränk rode hard on the steep bits and I took over on the flatter sections.

At the top, I finished twelfth on the stage. I had dropped one place to sixth overall, but I can't be too disappointed. I'm always hard on myself, but it would be unfair to be disappointed today. Velits had a better day than me today, but I had a better day than Tondo. I am only eighteen seconds off fourth place now. Behind me, Schleck is still a danger, even though I took those four bonus seconds out of him today, while Danielson is just a minute back.

Today I lost teammate José Luis Arrieta to tendonitis. The Spanish veteran had been suffering the past few days but struggled on until midway through the stage. He is due to retire at the end of the season and this is his last Vuelta, so he was pretty disappointed on the bus afterwards to be leaving his home race in this way.

Stage 16 – Monday 13 September: Gijon–Cotobello, 181.4km

With four climbs, three of them in the most difficult first category, and the third summit finish in as many days, today was the Queen Stage of this year's Vuelta.

It was one of those days where the pace never slowed down. There was never a moment when everybody decided to let a group go. There were attacks in the mountains, in the valleys, on the descents. There were no rules today, as everybody wanted to do something before the rest day on Tuesday. The start was so vicious that my Ag2r La Mondiale team lost three riders on the third-category climb after just 40km and, like many others, they never got back on.

The first big mountain, the Puerto de San Lorenzo, was officially 10km long, but we were climbing towards it for 50km. It was ridden at about three-quarter pace, and I was riding near the front. Although I didn't have any problems on the climb, it was fast enough. At the top, there were a lot of guys left in the front group, so I didn't know if it had been as hard as I thought it was and wondered if maybe I was on a bad day. We had covered 88km in the first two hours, and I knew I needed to be on a good day today or I was going to be in trouble.

After a long descent, we had another first-category climb, the Alto de la Cobertoria. At 8km long, the gradual incline wouldn't have been too bad on its own. But with the Liquigas team of race leader Vincenzo Nibali and the Saxo Bank squad of Fränk Schleck gradually winding the speed up at the front, it was pretty tough. Here, though, I realized I was going pretty well. Don't get me wrong, I was suffering like everyone else, but more and more guys were getting shelled out the back as we rode towards the summit and, by the top, there were only about eight of us left.

Although there was a breakaway group already up the road, Schleck had attacked us near the top. But, with 39km to go, I wasn't too worried. Riders like Schleck have a kind of cruise control on the climbs. They can ride faster than the bunch, but just under their own limit, for a long time. The mountains are his playground, but I knew there was a strong headwind waiting for us in the valley, leading up to the final climb. With nobody to share the workload with, it would have been suicide for him to continue and, after a few kilometres, he came back to us and the pace settled down a little.

Going over the top, I wanted a bottle from our team car. The proper way to take a bottle is to go to the back of the group, put your hand in the air and wait until the commissaire signals for your team car to come up and give you a drink. But because all the team leaders were in my group, nobody was obeying the rules. There were cars blocking the road everywhere. Alexandr Kolobnev was taking about five bottles on board to bring up to his Katusha team leader Joaquim Rodríguez, who started the day just four seconds adrift of Nibali.

He was taking ages, though, and I was getting pissed off waiting, as each time he'd hang on to each bottle for a few seconds longer than he should have and was blocking my Ag2r team car from coming through. Some guys try to take advantage on a climb, by hanging on to the bottle as the car is moving. When he had at last finished, I said, 'Hey, Kolobnev, five seconds not twenty on each bottle.' He came up to me later and apologized, saying he had to get five or six bottles for his teammates at the front, but I had no problem with him really, I was just thirsty.

On the descent, Blel and Rinaldo, who had been dropped on the climb, regained contact with my group, as did about twenty others. Blel loves his new role of riding for an overall contender and was really motivated again today. He's been very dedicated and has done some awesome work for me these past two weeks. He also knows that I will do the same when it's my turn to ride. There hasn't been one day where I haven't finished on my knees, and the guys appreciate that I'm doing my best and giving everything to repay them for their faith in me and their work on this race.

In the valley after the penultimate climb, Blel came up and said he wanted to chase the front group down because he thought I could maybe get a top five on the stage. I didn't want all the climbers to arrive at the bottom of the final mountain fresh, so I agreed, and told him to get to the front and ride hard. Even though I was suffering, I was hoping that the smaller, lighter, less powerful climbers would suffer even more on the flat if Blel could set a fast tempo. The Liquigas guys were already riding tempo on the front, and when Blel arrived they started giving out to him because he started to push the speed up even more. They asked him what he was doing. He said he was 'riding for Roche' and they just let him at it, giving him a hand every now and then.

Having one of our little Ag2r team on the front is probably a strange occurrence for a lot of the other teams. After a while, one of the Garmin Transitions guys rode up alongside Blel and complained that he was going too fast. Blel just repeated his 'I'm riding for

Roche' mantra and kept drilling at the front. Garmin leader Christian Vande Velde then rode alongside me and said, 'Hey Nico, do you know your rider is riding for you?'

Of course I knew. Garmin was a bit pissed off about it, because they had a rider in the break and his chances of staying away were getting slimmer with every turn of Blel's pedals. Vande Velde tried to persuade me to get him to stop, but in a friendly way. 'Hey Roche, why's he riding so fast? Are you that motivated?'

Yep. I'm that motivated.

Once we got to the foot of the final mountain, Roman Kreuziger took over. It's incredible how steady and fast Kreuziger can ride on a mountain. He's an unbelievably classy rider, really smooth on the bike. The speedometer doesn't move an inch when he climbs, and he can spend ages on the front, which suits me down to the ground.

When Schleck and Tom Danielson of Garmin attacked 8km from the summit, I was worried because they were two of my direct opponents, and if they got too much of an advantage on the climb they would leapfrog me in the overall standings. Then when I saw Sastre go, I thought, Uh oh, there's another one. But the idea was to stay as long as I could in the group I was in and not get over-excited. The two guys just ahead of me on GC, Peter Velits and Xavier Tondo, were still there, so I couldn't lose time to them either. When Tondo got dropped with 5km left, I started feeling a bit better, then a kilometre later, Velits got dropped. But I didn't want to try anything, in case

I blew up and went backwards in the final 3km or so.

With 2km to go, my manager told me in my earpiece that Velits had already lost forty seconds and Tondo was at one minute. I had begun the day just fifteen seconds behind them and was moving up the overall standings. I wasn't worried about Nibali, Rodríguez and Mosquera, as they were already in front of me on GC. All I wanted to do was try not to lose too much time to Schleck, who was still dangling up the road, and try to get back on to Danielson and Sastre. I made the decision to attack.

I said at the start of this diary that I wanted to try to be a bit more aggressive than at the Tour this year, so I had nothing to lose. If I blew up, I would probably stay in sixth place. If I didn't blow, then I could move up a place. When I kicked with 1.5km to go, Nibali was in trouble straight away, but all I cared about were the three guys up the road. My personal race was to catch those three before the line and maybe get a bit of a cushion on Velits and Tondo. Once I caught Sastre and Danielson, then I didn't care if I blew up.

My manager heard on the race radio that I had attacked, and was shouting encouragement into my earpiece as I put myself into time-trial mode. I picked a point on the road ahead, rode flat out to there and then picked another one and did the same. There was no thinking about tomorrow or the rest of the race, everything was for now. I was counting down the metre board: 500m, 300m, 200m, 150m. When Rodríguez came by at 600m, and then Mosquera and García a few hundred metres later, I didn't even try to stay with them. I knew there was no point. I was already on my limit. My legs were burning, my breathing was getting heavier and my heart rate was very close to my maximum of 196bpm. When I crossed the line, I was in bits, totally wrecked, and had to sit on the roadside for a few minutes to catch my breath.

I'm very happy with my performance again today. Okay, I lost a little bit of time to Schleck, but I moved up a position to fifth overall and now have a minute and twenty-six seconds' cushion to Velits, in sixth. I'm feeling great.

Tuesday 14 September: Rest Day

After Sunday's mountain stage, we had a three and a half hour transfer to our next hotel. As I sat in the front of the team bus, with my legs stretched across the seats opposite, my dad called from Paris and we had a chat about today's rest day.

Normally I do an hour and a half ride in the morning with the guys, but today I also wanted to ride Wednesday's time-trial course in the afternoon on my own. Dad didn't agree with me. He said there was no point in having to go out twice on a rest day and I should just ride the time-trial course. In the end, I agreed with him.

After breakfast, I hopped in the team car for a fifty-minute drive to the course. It was 46km long, on big, wide, main roads, with long straights and only five corners on the whole lap. I did a lap on my road bike first, then another, faster lap on my time-trial bike, to get used to the stretched-out, more aerodynamic position. Then I put in two hard 10km sessions tucked in behind the car, which made my legs hurt. The morning flew by. By the time I was ready for lunch, it was 3 p.m.

Although it's late in the evening here now, I haven't seen any of the guys on the team today. I got up earlier than them and by the time I came back from training they were already back in their rooms. Some of them never left, except to go down for food. Even though we're in bedrooms beside each other, we're so tired now that we couldn't be bothered walking around. Instead, we just lie on our beds all day, reading, watching TV, surfing the internet or listening to music. We'll see each other at dinner tonight. I spent this afternoon sitting on the floor, sorting out my suitcase for the time trial. I have four distinct piles of clothes for Wednesday alone, one for the morning, one for the warm-up, another for the time trial itself, and yet another for after the stage.

Wednesday is going to be a pressure day for me, but I have to admit that most of the pressure is my own fault. I came into this Vuelta aiming to take a top-fifteen placing overall, possibly a top ten. Last week, I thought that I would be fighting for somewhere between ninth and eleventh place in this time trial. Now, I'm fighting to stay in fifth place, another big step up.

Now that I'm there, though, I'm not thinking that if I drop a few places I'll still finish in the top ten. Hell, no! I've spent two and a half weeks fighting like a dog through all the mountains to get here, and I'm keeping this spot.

Stage 17 – Wednesday 15 September:
Individual Time Trial, Penafiel, 46km

Last night during dinner, the drug testers called me for my fourth anti-doping test of this year's Vuelta. At least they let me finish my pasta before they brought me off for my urine test. I didn't sleep much afterwards. There were two main reasons behind that. One was today's looming time trial, and the other was the simple reason that, because we hadn't raced on Monday, I just wasn't physically tired. I tried to watch TV, but my mind was wandering all over the place.

This morning, I was up at eight and, after breakfast, I went out training at 9.30. My legs felt okay on my hour and a half spin, but I wasn't going hard, it was just a muscular wake-up for the effort ahead. I rode back to the hotel, shaved my legs and went downstairs for an omelette and a bit of pasta for lunch. We left the hotel in the team bus for the fifty-minute drive to the time-trial course at around 12.30, and I watched a bit of Sunday's stage on Eurosport before my warm-up began.

As usual, I did about half an hour in front of the bus with my bike going nowhere on the stationary rollers as my heart rate gradually increased to 175 then 180bpm without putting too much stress on the legs.

A time trial is all about rhythm, about pacing yourself over the distance. You need to keep a good average speed and hold it until the end of the race, then finish with nothing, knowing that you've left everything out on the road and that you couldn't have taken another second on your rivals even if you wanted to. I knew that if I started out too fast in today's 46km test, I could blow up in the last few kilometres. I also knew that if I started out too slow, I would never regain the time lost in the early kilometres.

I've been nervous about this time trial since yesterday. Sometimes, nerves can work to your advantage. Not today. I didn't have my heart rate monitor on for the stage, so I was trying to keep my speed as close to 50kph as possible. I rolled down the start ramp and went off thinking I was going okay. At the first intermediate check point, after 15km, I had gained around thirty seconds on Fränk Schleck, meaning the Luxembourg champion was only fifteen seconds ahead of me in fourth place overall.

Soon, though, I couldn't keep my rhythm steady at all and felt terrible on the bike. My speed kept dropping to 48kph, then 45kph, and I kind of panicked a little bit. At the halfway point the team manager relayed the information into my earpiece that I had twenty-five seconds on Schleck. I needed forty-five to move into fourth overall. On the way back, I had a very slight tailwind and tried to keep my speed up around 55kph. Once in a while, the display on my bike computer would shoot up to around 58kph, and I tried to really accelerate for the last 20km. I was keeping a nice 56–7kph average for a long time, but then, with 3km to go, I wasn't able to hold 52kph and faded terribly for thirty-eighth place on the stage, while Schleck finished twenty-six seconds slower than me.

The surprise of the day was Peter Velits of HTC Columbia. The Slovakian had begun the day in sixth place overall, a minute and twenty-six seconds behind me. I was told beforehand that he was a good time-triallist and had been Slovakian national time-trial champion twice as an under-twenty-three rider, so I was prepared to lose my fifth place to him today. Velits, though, pulled a storming ride out of the bag to win the stage, and not only leapfrogged me, but also Schleck and overnight leader Joaquim Rodríguez to jump up to third overall. Velits blitzed the rest of us to win the stage in a time of fifty-two minutes and forty-three seconds. He was a full three minutes and twenty-nine seconds quicker than me and even beat the world time-trial champion Fabian Cancellara by thirty-seven seconds.

Although I was prepared to lose one place to Velits today, I wasn't ready to lose three places, which is what happened when Xavier Tondo and Tom Danielson recorded better times than me to claw their way over me on the leader board, and I dropped to eighth place overall.

When you get a taste of being in the top five, you want to stay there. I don't think I did a terrible time trial. To lose less than three minutes to Cancellara is not disgraceful, but I just didn't do as good a ride as I hoped for. To have fought so hard for the past three weeks and to have only lost seconds on the mountain stages and then to have given away time on a stage like today makes me angry.

I'm really pissed off now and, after the stage, I sat on my own at the front of the bus, with just a banana, a bottle of sparkling water and sore arse muscles for company. I've already given out to anyone I've met so far, for nothing, and the constant streams of well-meaning texts from friends in Ireland and France just make me annoyed. Christophe and the team managers know to ignore me as I pull my baseball hat down, turn up the volume on my iPod and sulk in the corner. They also know I'm not going to be in a good mood until Saturday evening – at the earliest – and that's only if I do well on the climb. I've heard the weather is going to be terrible for the next three days, so I hope it stays dry on Saturday. Everybody has a bad day on a Grand Tour. Hopefully, mine was today. I can't afford another one.

Stage 18 – Thursday 16 September: Vallodolid– Salamanca, 148km

It took a long time to come around after my disappointing time trial but, once I had mumbled and grumbled to everyone and anyone about it for a while, I calmed down a bit and by dinner time I was almost back to normal, whatever that is.

Before dinner we had a debriefing and I also spoke to my dad on the phone. We looked at my performance and worked things out scientifically. We reasoned that while I didn't do a great time trial I didn't do a bad one either. Some other guys just did a better one than me. My dad told me to keep focussed and also reminded me that I don't have a time-trial bike at home and therefore don't get time to train on it and get used to churning the bigger gears in the more aerodynamic position. The team agreed that it's an elementary mistake for someone at my level not to be able to train on the time-trial bike, and the pain in my arse muscles since I got out of bed this morning makes me think they are right.

I felt a bit better mentally this morning but was still hoping for an easy day. The team plan was pretty simple: 'Stick with Nico.' Normally, on stages like this, we try to put a man into the early breakaway group in case it stays away to the finish. Today, though, everybody was told to just look after me. Keep me sheltered from the wind. Keep me fed and watered. There was no discussion about anybody going up the road or trying to get in a break. Our team plans for a stage win have been left by the roadside in an effort to see me take as high a position on the overall classification as I can. All our eggs are in one basket, and everybody is hoping the basket won't break.

The strong three-quarter head-crosswind meant that my Ag2r La Mondiale team couldn't be caught down the back even for a few minutes today. If we were down the back and a team went to the front and split the peloton, I could lose a lot of time. At one point, Caisse d'Epargne tried it, but the wind just wasn't strong enough at the time. Every team knows a split can occur any time the wind picks up or changes direction, and they all ride in a sort of mobile huddle, with their respective leaders tucked in out of the gale. It's a war of nerves as everybody looks at each other any time the wind picks up. My Ag2r guys are mainly light-weight climbers, so it's harder for them on these types of stages, but once again they did a great job today.

There's been a lot of effort put in to get me to the

mountains in the best position and possible shape on Saturday. They know I have a lot of responsibility, and also that I can have a bad day or a good day, but they trust me to do the best I can. Sometimes cycling is described as 'poker on wheels'. Well, I'm the only card left, and we're going all in.

Today's stage went by really quickly. We were done in three and a half hours. The last 20km was mental, really stressful. They brought us to within one roundabout of the finish in Salamanca and then we did a loop through the small, tight streets of the town. Maybe it was good for the crowds, some of whom got to see us twice, but with lots of roundabouts, traffic islands and even little speed ramps to be bunny-hopped over, all at around 60kph, it wasn't great for my nerves. I was left on my own for the last few kilometres as the guys tired and Blel tried to give our sprinter Séb a hand in the gallop to the line.

I learned afterwards that there were a couple of splits in the bunch in the final kilometre. Xavier Tondo, Tom Danielson, Joaquim Rodríguez and even race leader Vincenzo Nibali lost nine seconds to stage winner Mark Cavendish, so I gained four seconds on all of them. I'm now just four seconds off seventh, fourteen seconds off fifth and nineteen seconds off fourth. The GC has been chaotic every day on this race. The top ten hasn't changed, but we've all been hopping up and down the *classement*, leapfrogging over each other most days. Every Grand Tour I ride, I try to stay as close to the front as possible in the sprints, in case a split occurs. I've been fighting and using energy to stay up there every day but now I've been proven right to have done so, even if it is only four seconds. I was trying to stay near the front today, but in all the twisting and turning and pushing and shoving, all I was thinking was, Don't crash, don't crash, and wasn't as near the front as I wanted to be.

Guillaume is very sick now. He has the flu and it's getting worse. Because I was cleaning my shoes on the bus after the stage, and was a few minutes later into the hotel than the others, all the guys had picked their rooms, emptied their suitcases on their beds, and settled in. The only bed left was with Guillaume in his room. The staff decided it wasn't a good idea for me to be rooming with somebody who has the flu, and two of them roomed together and gave me a single room.

I feel drained tonight, probably more mentally than physically. Today was a nerve-racking day in the saddle, and maybe the pressure of it all is getting to me. It's been three and a half weeks since I left my home in Varese and I've been through a lot of stress, some really good moments and some bad ones. Somebody asked me today if I use a sports psychologist. We have one on the team, but I only see him two or three times a year. What do I need a sports psychologist for when I can tell you guys my problems?

Stage 19 – Friday 17 September: Piedrahita–Toledo, 231km

Today was the longest stage of the whole three weeks of racing. A 231km stage, preceded by 13km of neutralized riding to get to the start proper, made a total of nearly 250km, or more than 150 miles in old money. On top of that, the race organizers put an 8km second-category mountain – which turned out to have an 8 per cent gradient and was one of the hardest climbs of the whole Vuelta so far – at the very start of today's stage. On the third-last day of racing? That's ridiculous.

Luckily enough, plenty of other riders were very tired and very pissed off at such a hard start, and had decided among themselves to neutralize the mountain. Everybody spread out across the road and rode a steady tempo up the Puerto de la Chia. At one point on the climb, somebody tried to get through a gap and attack. I couldn't see who it was, but he was met with shouts of derision from the rest of the riders, his jersey was grabbed and he soon got the message that he was going nowhere.

If we had gone to war on that climb, fifty riders would have gone home tonight. The non-climbers, the Grand Tour virgins, the sick, the injured and the guys who have been suffering through this Vuelta, working for their team leaders for the past three weeks, would have lost contact and finished outside the time limit if we had raced flat out the whole way to Toledo.

I wanted to ride aggressively and went into the stage with the mindset of being able to do something at the finish. During the stage, I radioed the guys in the team car to give me a good idea of what the finish was like. I knew there was a hill in the final 4km of racing and it would be a good place to attack and maybe try to win the stage. I didn't know how tough the last 2km were, though, so I asked the guys to find out and let me know.

The tactic for me was that if one of the big guys attacked on the climb I was to follow and then we'd have only a 2km descent and a little drag to the finish. When Spaniard Luis León Sánchez attacked with 4km to go, I knew he was a really good descender and decided he would be a good wheel to follow, so I jumped out of the peloton and headed after him.

The problem was that I never actually made contact with Sanchez's back wheel. Instead I sat in the wind, maybe 5 metres behind him, as both of us rode flat out in an effort to go clear. The hill wasn't hard enough to get a big gap and we both got caught 2km later, but to my surprise the drag to the line afterwards was way harder than anyone had envisaged.

The climb to the finish was so difficult I was hyper-ventilating at the top. I had already made my effort just a few kilometres before and wasn't expecting to have to make another one just to stay in contact on the rise to the line. I was prepared for the first climb, then a 1.5km descent followed by a 1.5km drag. It ended up being very different from what I expected. We hit an uphill cobbled section, turned a sharp left-hander and went on to a really steep 400m section, before another 200m rise to the line. The second hill caused a lot of splits in the peloton as the end of three weeks' racing and the accumulative tiredness saw the bunch disintegrate in the last 500m.

Even though I was riding at my limit on the hill, I lost nine seconds to stage winner Philippe Gilbert, eight seconds to the next nine riders on the stage and two seconds to the next group of five riders. I fought to hang on to a little group of five riders, though, finished sixteenth on the stage and actually took time out of everyone else behind me. Sastre lost four seconds on me while my nearest rivals Schleck, Tondo and Danielson lost six seconds each, and I leapfrogged Danielson into seventh overall.

When I got to the team bus, I was going mental. I was screaming with frustration. I suppose it's my way of letting go of the pressure and stress of three weeks of racing. I was giving out that we should have had more information about the final climb. In the road book that we get with all the info about each stage on it, the final climb looked like a slight drag, but it was way more than a drag. The book said the hill was around 4 per cent but it turned out to be 10 per cent at some points. Having a 400m section with a 10 per cent slope on it is a lot different from being told 'there's a bit of a drag' to the line. 'You can't expect me to attack and then be there at the finish as well,' I shouted. *Directeur sportif* Julien Jourdie got the full brunt of it. He was the first one I saw, but it could have been anybody. He was as stressed as I was. 'Look at the fucking book,' he yelled. 'It says a 4 per cent drag. It's not my fault if they can't get the book right.'

We also had a soigneur at the line, who had driven up the climb to the finish a couple of hours before we got there. When relaying back the info to the team car earlier, his interpretation of the climb was: 'It kicks up a bit.' I asked him, 'What the fuck does that mean?'

Séb, who had finished fourth on the stage, tried to calm me down a bit. He is a punchy little guy and is good on these types of finishes. He rightly said that maybe I got over-excited when Sánchez attacked and I shouldn't have moved until somebody like Gilbert or one of the bigger guys went. I was actually waiting for the Belgian, a specialist at this sort of finish, to attack on the climb and was wondering why he didn't. Obviously, Gilbert had better information than I had and knew about the second hill.

In the end we agreed that it was nobody's fault in particular and I was as much to blame as everybody else but, in the heat of the moment, I just let fly. Shoot first, ask questions later.

I'm up to seventh overall with two days left. I'm sixteen seconds off fourth but eighteen seconds away from tenth. We all know that tomorrow's mountain-top finish will decide the race. I've ridden the climb once before but tomorrow they are adding an extra bit, a minor road to a telecommunications mast. It's supposed to be really steep, 19 per cent, and rises 300m in 3km. On a gradient like that, you can lose everything in a few hundred metres.

I'm nervous. Everybody in the top ten is. Even though we are direct rivals, we have a chat during the stages. Fränk Schleck, Xavier Tondo, Tom Danielson – we all get on and have good fun when we can. We have a quick chat about how hard the previous day was or how good or bad we are going during each stage, and we all know that we can finish fourth or eleventh overall at the top of that climb.

Stage 20 – Saturday 18 September: San Martin de Valdeiglesias–Bola del Mundo, 172km

When I got up this morning I knew today's stage would decide this Tour of Spain. Everybody did. The last mountain of the race, the savagely steep, 22km-long Bola del Mundo, loomed at the end of the stage and we all knew it would be the last place where any of us could open a big enough time gap on our nearest rivals to make a difference in the overall standings. For me, 'the globe of the world' would be the place where, if I had a bad day, I could possibly lose my top-ten place, or if a couple of others had a bad day, I could move into the top five.

The start was really fast and there were attacks on all three of the first mountains. Katusha and Caisse d'Epargne were fighting for the team prize, and were trying to get men up the road and chasing each other down all day.

Once again, my Ag2r La Mondiale team did a great job for me, and I had them all around me as we approached the final climb. Guillaume gave me one last bottle at the bottom and, suffering from his effort, started to drift down the back on the lower slopes of the climb. But I called him back up on the team radio. I told him it was the last hard day and I needed him to ride in front of me until he couldn't ride any more. In fairness to him, Guillaume came back up and rode as hard as he could. When he couldn't go any more, he just blew up and drifted back to suffer his way to the top.

At the beginning of this Vuelta, Guillaume had it in

the back of his mind that he could get a top-thirty or forty placing overall. He wasn't fully committed to riding for me and was trying to save a little bit for himself every day. The team director had a chat with him and explained that fortieth was not the goal of the team. The aim was to get me into the highest possible position overall. It took him a while to cop on to that but, every day since, he has done more and more, and today he was fantastic again.

In that respect, this race has been completely different from the Tour. Everybody put their own ambitions to one side. For example, Sébastian Hinault, our sprinter, worked for me every day on the flat sections into the wind. In the mountains, Séb did everything he could. He carried my rain jacket. He grabbed my food bag every day at the feed zone, where it's so dangerous that I don't even try to grab the musette from the team soigneurs as we whizz by. Because he's a sprinter, Séb's also great at accelerating into the bottom of the climbs to get me in a good position. He even manages to calm me down sometimes when I lose the plot.

With 5km to go, the pace went down slightly and, knowing that I wanted to keep it steady, Hubert turned to me and said, 'Nico, I'm on my last legs, I can't ride for much longer, but if you want me to ride, I can give you one last hand.'

Just as we were talking, though, Schleck put in a little dig at the front that whittled the group down to just the top seven riders on GC. The increase in pace saw Danielson dropped, so that was one less to worry about.

Schleck jumped again with 4.5km to go, and a few metres later Mosquera attacked Nibali and was soon trying to gain the fifty seconds he needed to win the Vuelta, with the Italian in hot pursuit. Tondo had been dropped with the acceleration of Mosquera, and I knew if got eight seconds' advantage on him, I'd move up to sixth overall. Schleck accelerated again, though, and I was struggling. Tondo caught me and I sat on his wheel for a few minutes before jumping again and regaining contact with Schleck, Rodríguez and Velits.

I was still ahead of Tondo but was suffering alongside the other three on the steep slopes. We turned off the main road with 3km left and hit a tarmac road with a 20 per cent slope that went all the way up to a communications mast at the top of the mountain. The surface was brutal, with holes, cracks and gravel everywhere. It was ridiculously hard.

As people dangled over our heads in ski lifts, I knew that at some stage the three guys that I was left with would attack me and I could completely crack. I knew there was a time bonus for the first three riders on the stage, but even I'm not that ambitious. Today was one of those days where everybody was flat out. There was no chance of surprising any of the better climbers to get third. I was hoping that when the little Spaniard Rodríguez attacked, I could just stay with Schleck and maybe drop Velits.

That's what happened, and I would have been happy with that, except Tondo managed to claw his way back to me with 200m to go and then attacked me. The Cervélo rider had ridden strongly on the climb, just letting me dangle ahead of him, and came back at the top. He took fifth place on the stage but, more importantly, gained three more seconds on the line.

I was so out of breath from the effort and the altitude that when I rode across the finish line our soigneur Yo-Yo had to grab me to stop me keeling over. I was totally exhausted, and it took me a good while to recover. Yo-Yo pushed me up the road a few metres and into the tent which the race organization had arranged for us to get changed in before we rode back down the mountain to our team buses.

In the tent where we got changed afterwards, Hubert came over and gave me a pat on the back and congratulated me. I shook hands with Tondo, Velits and Schleck, and we had a few words for each other before riding back down.

His work done earlier on, Guillaume was still climbing the mountain as I descended afterwards, and he shouted at me to find out how I'd done. We high-fived each other in the middle of the road as we met.

Today, I'm happy with the stage result but a little bit disappointed that I didn't overtake Tondo and move up to sixth. I tried attacking him coming to the finish to take a few seconds, but it didn't work out, so I have no regrets.

For me, the race for the overall is finished today. I'm not going to go for sprint bonuses tomorrow. Unless I won the stage, I'd never take back eleven seconds on Tondo, but I'll still have to be in the front and make sure there are no splits in the finish.

Stage 21 – Sunday 19 September:
San Sebastián de los Reyes–Madrid, 85km

Last night we had a special dinner with all the team staff to celebrate my teammate José Luis Arrieta's career. Instead of my usual bowl of plain pasta with olive oil – which I've had every single day for the past three weeks – I had a lovely steak dinner. Knowing that the stage didn't start until three o'clock the next afternoon, we all had a glass of wine and relaxed as José reminisced about his career. We laughed as we realized he had begun with five-time Tour de France winner Miguel Indurain as his team leader and ended up with me.

I didn't get much of a lie-in this morning, as I was woken up early by a knock on the door from the anti-doping officers for my fifth dope test of this year's race. At 11.30, we went down for lunch of pasta and rice, but the hotel had nothing arranged for us, so we had to have more bowls of cereal to stock up for the stage ahead. On the start line, they passed around trays of miniature cakes to everyone in the peloton, which helped fill the gap.

Although the stage started off slow enough, it just got faster and faster as the finish approached. Still close enough on time to overtake each other if we got a few seconds, myself, Fränk Schleck, Xavier Tondo and Joaquim Rodríguez couldn't relax until it was over.

I finished seventh overall, but was so close to fourth that I can't help being a bit pissed off. Looking back, fourth place was within my capabilities. The way I've been climbing on this Vuelta, I feel like I deserved it, but the two time trials let me down. Being so good on the mountains and so desperately bad in the time trial still gets to me. I lost three and a half minutes in the 46km time trial. If I could have been just one minute faster, I'd be fourth overall now.

It's about time that all the climbing work I have been doing all year has paid off, though. All I've done all year is train in the mountains. I've even lost weight to help me get up them quicker. Maybe that's why I haven't been so strong in the time trial and why my sprinting is not as good as it used to be either.

Overall, I'm happy. There are not too many guys who rode two Grand Tours for the GC this year, so I'm pretty satisfied. It's also the first time that I rode as a team leader with the full support of my team. At the Tour, I got help from some guys, not so much help from others and some just couldn't help me, so I was a bit limited in the mountains. This time, I had a real team backing me up. As I finally flake out on the bus, everybody is happy. The soigneurs, the mechanics and the rest of the guys are chirpy and smiling. I did my job, they did their job, and we're all relaxed now. Next stop Australia and the world championships but, first, I can't wait for my own bed tonight.

After the Vuelta, I was selected on a three-man Irish team for the worlds in Melbourne alongside David McCann and national champion Matt Brammeier. Most teams travelled to Australia around ten days before the worlds to get used to the time difference and get the long-haul flight out of their legs but, after being away from home for three weeks at the Tour and then another three weeks at the Vuelta, I just wanted to be able to relax in my own house and sleep in my own bed for a few days before making the long trip Down Under.

I was pretty tired after the Vuelta and spent the first week recovering, going out on my bike for easy spins and eating and sleeping. Even though the worlds would be 262km long, I found it hard to train for more than three and a half hours, and I wasn't really sure how my form was going into the race.

Australia is a long way to go for a one-day race, and the worlds is always a bit of a lottery. You have to have good legs on the day, make the right move, at the right time. I've never really had a good world championship since turning pro, but I only get one chance every year to ride for Ireland and I'd been in good form all season, so I was hoping I could keep it up for one more race.

With only three riders in the race, our little Irish team had to try and ride together and do as well as we could. The plan was to send Matt Brammeier up the road at the start. We knew there was an 83km section along the coast to Geelong before we hit the 16km circuit for the first of eleven laps. We figured that nobody would bother with chasing such an early break and, if Matt could get in a little group and ride hard, they might be able to get a lap in before the bunch even got on to the circuit and the race would be as good as over.

We nearly pulled it off. Matt was first one to jump clear straight after the start, was joined by three others and they came to within thirty seconds of lapping the field, which would have meant that if they stayed in contact with the peloton for the rest of the race, one of them would be world champion. I was okay for about 200km. I was in the right moves and riding well. Then my legs started to go about 20km later. I don't think it was from jet lag or anything, just from having a hard season. I didn't have much left in the tank after doing two big Tours for the first time, and it was time for a rest.

17

Dangerous Game

Buoyed by my seventh place at the Vuelta, I began 2011 with lofty ambitions, including a top ten overall at the Tour and a top five at the Vuelta, but my winter training didn't exactly go as planned.

To give myself a bit of a break from cycling, I had started running in November. I began with twenty minutes' jogging and built up each day until I could run comfortably for about fifty minutes after a couple of weeks. I ran on the street, in the parks and in the woods with friends until one day I had to stop at a traffic light with a pain in my right knee. I had to be picked up and driven home. A strained knee ligament kept me on my couch for the next two weeks.

With a week's training under my belt, including my first crash when my back wheel slipped on an icy patch of road, I headed to a ten-day pre-season training camp with Ag2r La Mondiale in Calpe, Spain, before Christmas and was obviously way behind the rest of the guys as regards fitness.

In January 2011, it was time for another training camp, this time in the Haut Var region in Aups. With one of the first goals of my season, Paris–Nice, just two months away and just over a fortnight's training in my legs, I was keen to make up for lost ground and did an hour more than everybody else most days, sometimes behind a motorbike. One day, I did two training spins with the team before a threshold test in the evening. It wasn't long until my body said 'no', and I spent the last day or so watching the others go training while I nursed a sore knee again. This time I had torn a muscle, in the same knee, and spent a frustrating seventeen more days off the bike.

An MRI scan finally pronounced me fit to train again in February, which meant that I'd only been back on the bike ten days before beginning my season at the Tour of Algarve in Portugal. Although I was under no pressure to do anything other than ride my own race without thinking about getting results, racing it was a mistake. I would have been better off staying at home, training and getting massage on my knee instead.

Next up were two one-day races in Switzerland, where I was feeling a lot better. After the GP Insubria on the Saturday, I did an extra 30km with Max Bouet to push me over the 200km mark for the day. I rode for the team the next day at the GP Lugano on the last climb, getting dropped before rejoining the front group with 300m to go to finish seventh.

I'd originally aimed for a top ten overall in Paris–Nice in March but, after my injuries, new signing Jean-Christophe Péraud was the official team leader. A silver medallist as a mountain-biker at the 2008 Olympics, he turned pro on the road in 2010 with Lotto and was ninth in Paris–Nice. Having joined us in the winter, Péraud quickly showed himself to be a good rider in the one-week stage races, with second overall at the Tour of the Mediterranean.

I was there to back him up and went into the race in the hope that I could ride myself in, not lose much time in the first three days and see how I got on in the first mountain stage on the Tuesday. I'd been doing a lot of time-trial work since I came back from my injury, and was hoping to do well in the 28km test on the Friday. If not, then I would simply change tactics and go for a stage win on the last two days.

The opening stage in Houdan felt like a Belgian classic, with most of it held on narrow, twisting roads with no hedges or ditches to give shelter from the wind. With no prologue time trial, and therefore no leader's jersey on the start line, everything was up for grabs from the off. Most of us expected a bunch sprint finish, but there was always the chance that a breakaway would stay away until the finish, which meant there were plenty of early attacks.

Whenever we entered a town or village during the stage, you had to have your wits about you to avoid the various bits of street furniture that littered the course. The streets were so narrow that guys were jumping up on kerbs and bunny-hopping roundabouts just to move up five or six places in the bunch. Although I saw a couple of my best friends and former teammates, Amaël Moinard and Geoffroy Lequatre, for the first time that season, there was no time for talking during the stage. Concentrating on the task in hand, we could only manage a quick 'hello' as we passed each other in the heaving peloton.

As usual, there were a few crashes. With 50km to go,

Sébastien Minard's chain jumped on a corner and his bike fishtailed, throwing him sideways on to the ground, while Peter Velits of HTC Highroad also fell. Séb was pretty cut up all along the right side of his leg. Days later, he was still suffering; his thigh was covered in road rash and every day he had to scrub his wounds to try and keep them clean. It wasn't until after the stage that I noticed that Hubert Dupont was limping around the hotel. He'd fallen during the stage and a few guys had ridden into him.

It was a long and stressful opener, and I just stayed in the wheels most of the time. The plan was to try to get our sprinter, Anthony Ravard, up at the finish and keep Péraud out of trouble. Ravard was in fine form, having won the season-opening Etoile de Bessèges stage race in France. I was riding close to him coming towards the finish, but he punctured with 2km to go. UCI regulations mean that anyone who punctures or crashes within the final 3km doesn't lose any time, so there was no need to stop with him. He would have to fight another day for his stage win.

We have nicknamed Ravard 'the pit bull', because he's small and aggressive and never gives up. He's never violent, but in the opening stage he had a bit of a bump off Jeremy Hunt with 15km to go and wanted to start a fight until I let a shout at him to concentrate on what he was doing. The next day, he also had a bit of an argument with one of the French guys on the Bretagne Schuller team, who nailed him to the barrier in the last 200m of the sprint, and after the line they traded slaps like oul' ones. It was funny to watch. Ravard is one of those guys who is hyper all day long. He never stops talking or fidgeting, and I told him he'd be better off saving his energy for the next day.

My legs weren't that great. They felt a bit heavy, as if I was in the middle of a stage race rather than just beginning one, maybe as a result of training too hard after my knee injury. I put a bit of pressure on myself to get back to full fitness as quickly as possible, doing between 800km and 1,000km per week for the month before Paris–Nice, so maybe that's why I felt a bit tired and sluggish.

After a good ten hours' sleep I still woke up with a sore back and neck. The root cause of my new affliction was my decision to wear a cap underneath my helmet. With the peak down over my eyes, I had to crane my neck a little bit more than usual and my slightly higher position on the bars meant that my neck muscles were killing me.

During the second stage, it was a case of 'train stops play' for the leaders, including Max, who had attacked from the gun, as a railroad level-crossing barrier came down in front of them. As they waited for the train, the rest of us soon pulled up behind them at the barriers.

In a situation like that, the rules are that the two leaders are allowed to start again when the train passes while the peloton is held back until the breakaways build up the advantage they'd held before the barriers went down. That's all well and good in theory, but once the leaders set off again there was chaos behind them. Although the commissaires had stopped their cars ahead of the bunch, they hadn't blocked off the entire road and were soon swamped by riders seizing their chance to edge up the outside of the peloton and move towards the front. As soon as the barriers rose, it was like a farmer opening a gate and a herd of sheep running loose. There was no need for the panic that ensued. It wasn't as if the finish line was only around the corner. We still had

40km to go, and there should have been a bit more respect shown for the commissaires and race organizers.

If the narrow roads and strong winds had made it difficult for riders to get to the front, you can imagine the pandemonium when the commissaires tried to drive through the middle of the peloton. Nobody wanted to leave their spot, as they had been fighting all day for it. As the cars finally came through the bunch there was another fight going on to tailgate their back bumper. Riders were stuck to the rear of the car, knowing that as the cars carved their way through the bunch, they would have an easy ride to the front in their slipstream. Nine kilometres later, Max and his break-away partner were reeled in and the stage was set for a bunch sprint finish.

Jean-Christophe also broke a spoke in his front wheel. Although he was our team leader for this race and is four or five years older than me, he is still trying to adapt to certain things on the road. When he stopped, he didn't say anything to anybody, just pulled in at the side of the road. None of us knew there was anything wrong with him, not even the team car. I noticed him stopping and asked him what was wrong. I radioed back to the team car and then radioed two of the guys to stop with him and help him back up to the peloton, when he got everything sorted. What did he think he was going to do, take out a spanner and fix it himself?

Max was pretty pissed off after the stage. He got caught up in the second half of the bunch when it split with about 8km to go and lost a minute. If he'd stayed with us, he would be ninth overall. He was also pissed off that Brice Feillu of Vaconsoleil had taken time out of him. Feillu goes out with Max's sister, so now the guys slag him that he's not even the best rider in his family any more, which probably doesn't help.

There was more mayhem in the third stage. The final few kilometres were pretty hectic, with lots of speed bumps, chicanes and traffic-calming bollards in the last two towns. You can't see these bollards if you're riding in the bunch, as they are only about knee high, but if you hit one of them you'll know all about it. It also makes it harder to ride back up in the cavalcade after a puncture or a crash. At the finish, I noticed the Bretagne Schuller team car had a broken rear windscreen. I later learned that French rider Mikaël Buffaz went head first through it during the stage while trying to get back on.

In the final sprint, I came around the last corner to see Peter Sagan of Liquigas tumbling sideways as his bike flew through the air and brought down three or four riders. Ravard was right behind Sagan when he fell but miraculously weaved his way around him to finish seventh on the stage, while I crossed the line in twenty-eighth and moved up to twenty-first overall.

On the team bus the next morning there was talk of me going up the road in an early move and gambling on trying for a stage win. But after a bit of discussion, team managers Vincent Lavenu and Julien Jourdie agreed that the peloton wasn't likely to let me go clear and, even if it did, it would keep me on a short leash and reel me in at the end anyway. I gave my opinion that a break of four or five riders would go clear at the start but the stage wouldn't be hard enough and HTC would be able to defend its yellow jersey and catch them again. I was right about the four or five riders, but when they went we never saw them again.

I started the stage in the middle of the bunch, and the first 5km climb was a real stinger because we rode up it flat out as French champion Thomas Voeckler went to the front and strung us out into one long line. Voeckler was pretty impressive on the next climb too, which came straight after the descent off the first. He continued to try to get clear and eventually succeeded in dragging four others away with him after about 25km of hard-core racing. Voeckler is one of the smartest riders in the bunch and a real winner. When he has the opportunity to win, he almost always manages to produce the goods. Even though he was gritting his teeth as Belgian rider Thomas de Gendt pulled the break along in the final kilometres in the knowledge that he would regain the race lead if they stayed away, Voeckler was canny enough to win the gallop for stage victory.

As the peloton approached the finish thirteen seconds later, my teammate Blel Kadri came up to me and said, 'Come on, let's try for the sprint for fifth.' The finish itself was great – a good, long, straight with no mad bends in the final metres or anything. Eager to please as usual, Blel started his sprint with 600m to go, but the headwind was a lot stronger than he anticipated. I shouted at him to keep going, but he ran out of steam and died about 300m out. I came around him and sprinted all out but ran out of legs and came up about 100m short, which is a lot in a sprint. But at least we got some good practice in for the future. I hadn't been in that position for a couple of months, and after the line I turned back to Blel and thanked him for his efforts. I promised him that when I was in top form I'd repay him with a win this year.

Blel is a 24-year-old Frenchman of Algerian descent.

Because he is a Muslim, there are certain foods he cannot eat, one of which is pork. Every single day, at every single hotel, we have ham in some shape or form, either for starters or for breakfast, and it got to be a long-running joke on the team. Most mornings, if Blel was not at the table in time, somebody would order a plain omelette and put it at his placing for breakfast. Just as he was about to tuck in, we told him it's ham and egg. Blel is by now well accustomed to this juvenile behaviour. But the look on his face on the rare time somebody does catch him out means it will probably go on for ever, although he knows we would never intentionally let him eat pork.

Blel is in his third year as a professional and had already proven himself to be a strong and loyal teammate, relishing the role of riding for a leader. I get on really well with Blel. He calls me 'Capo', which means boss.

I had moved up four places to seventeenth overall, but I would need Blel again on the fifth stage, which was billed as the hardest stage of this year's Paris–Nice. And rightly so.

At the foot of the final mountain, the first-category Col de la Mûre, there was a lot of attacking and it was pretty tough going on the way up. I'm not a rider who gets sore legs often. When I blow, it's usually because I'm out of breath or I just can't go any faster. When I'm in top form, I can be in pain on a climb but I can always dig that little bit deeper. The more you are trained, the more you can suffer. That day I couldn't suffer. Instead of asking for more, my legs gave in to the pain and I got dropped.

There was only 13km to the finish and I rode to the top alongside my former training partner Amaël Moinard of BMC at a steady pace. Blel and a few others caught us on the way down and he rode with me to the finish. Blel is always willing to help whenever he can, so he went to the front of our group and set a good tempo. I came around him once to give him a hand. I was trying to show him that his team leader was still going all right, but my legs were screaming at me to slow down so I just sat in his slipstream for the last 4km. Our six-strong group crossed the line two minutes and fifty seconds down on stage winner and new race leader Andreas Klöden of Radioshack, and my hopes of repeating my top-ten placing of the previous year were well gone.

After the line I put my arm around Blel and told him that if he stayed focussed in the next couple of years, he could be a top-class rider in the future. Blel just turned to me and said, 'Never mind the future, Capo. Let's think about this year. I'm here to give you a hand, and we're going to win a few races.'

His enthusiasm is infectious, but Paris–Nice is a big race and there was a definite gap between me and the top guys. Jean-Christophe Péraud was still in contention, though, and in the individual time trial he recorded an excellent time to finish fifth on the stage and move into the same position overall.

The penultimate stage finished in Biot, a few kilometres from where my family lives, in Antibes. The team wanted me to go up the road, and it would have been nice to get in the break as they would be at the finish. As it turned out, I watched the finish on TV, lying in the team bus. Already showered and changed into my tracksuit, my Paris–Nice was over for another year.

That morning there was no indication I would be in that position – sprawled out on the bus, yawning as the rain

Above: Team Ireland. Philip Deignan and me with Frank Campbell at the Olympics. Frankie did a lot for me when he was national team director.

Below: Suited and booted in Beijing. Our designer John Rocha had us looking dapper.

Above: So close... Imanol Erviti beat me in a photo finish at Las Rozas in the Vuelta a España in 2008.

Left and below: After joining Ag2r, my first training camp came with the obligatory shots for publicity. It was time for me to act as a leader.

Left: 29 June 2009. I'd been chasing the Irish national road race title since I was eleven, and my dream finally came true in Dunboyne in County Meath.

Below: A happy man. On the podium with Páidí O'Brien and Davey O'Loughlin.

Bottom: My family, including my Nana Roche, were there to celebrate the moment.

Left: Christel comes to visit at the Tour of Britain.

Below: I got to wear the Irish national champion's jersey for my first Tour de France in 2009, but still had to don Ag2r's new brown shorts for the first week.

Bottom: Rinaldo Nocentini took the yellow jersey after the seventh stage up to Andorra. Here I celebrate the team's success.

Above: Dad is often on hand to give me some advice during the Tour.

Below: The 2010 Tour was marked from the very first day with crashes. You can spot my arse in the brown shorts on the right as I just about manage to stay upright.

Catching up with Philip Deignan at the Vuelta in 2010. We are always slagging each other about something.

I was at my peak in the race though, and determined not to be dropped in the mountain stages.

Suffering, but still on Frank Schleck's wheel. My seventh-place finish in the Vuelta was my best in a Grand Tour so far.

Above: Sometimes you just have to push yourself to the limit – and then beyond.

Left and below: Disaster struck in the Critérium du Dauphiné, just three weeks before the 2011 Tour de France, when I hit a pothole. I was raw from my ankle to my chin.

Left: With Chiara in Dublin this summer. You have to appreciate every minute of your time off the bike.

Right: My 2011 Tour ended in disappointment, but I did everything I could at the front of the stages in the Alps.

Below: The brothers Roche. Alexis (*back*) and Florian (*middle*) came to visit for a rest day.

lashed off the windows outside. On the contrary, I was really motivated.

On each stage race, we have two team cars supporting us. One of them drives ahead of the race and slots in behind the breakaway if any of our riders gets into the move, while the other one follows the peloton all day. That morning, for the first time in the week, I put my rain bag into the breakaway car. If it started raining, I wanted easy access to my gloves, cape and other paraphernalia if things went according to plan and I got into the day's main move.

The stage started really fast and immediately I was jumping across to attacks, trying to get into the right move. I got up the road a few times but was brought back almost immediately each time. After a while, I started to struggle and drifted down the back of the bunch. Soon I was last wheel and felt like I had ridden 300km instead of just 60km.

I was feeling terrible. My legs were empty, my head was light and even my arms were weak. Exhausted, I just let the wheel in front of me go and had to chase for a bit. There was a group of eight or ten riders behind me and I stayed with them for a while, but even then I was suffering.

Dropped by the stragglers after about 80km, Julien Jourdie stayed with me in the team car for a while. He was hoping that the group in front of me would slow down and I'd get back on and recover again and be able to survive to the finish. But I couldn't see myself going another minute on the bike. When he realized how bad I was, Julien stopped the car and I abandoned. There was no big scene, no commissaire stripping me of my race numbers, no television crews in my face or anything like that. I climbed off my bike, got into the car and put my head in my hands. There was no big sobbing session, but a couple of tears of frustration betrayed me and sneakily rolled down my cheeks.

Having to abandon a race is really frustrating, especially after all the work I'd put in after my knee injury in January. It was the first stage race I'd abandoned in about three years where I hadn't crashed or been injured, and I tried to figure out what had gone wrong. Maybe I came back and did too much too soon. Injuries and illness are part of every sport. Sometimes it's harder to keep focussed when you're out of action than it is when you are racing. But I really paid attention to my diet when I was injured and started training hard straight away when I came back. Sometimes you think it should pay off immediately, but it doesn't work like that. I suppose it would have been too easy to have had two weeks off the bike and then have been able to come back and compete with the top guys in the world. If it was that easy, I'd take two weeks off every month. I was probably expecting too much too soon. It was back to reality.

When I tore my hamstring at the 2010 Tour of Romandie, I had three weeks off and then four weeks' training before I raced again. This time I came back straight away. I didn't have the foundation done, but I kept building and building anyway and eventually it all collapsed, leaving me with nothing but a massive headache and a DNF (Did Not Finish) behind my name.

After I abandoned, the roads became treacherous as the rain lashed down and lots of riders crashed, so at least I avoided some of that. Paris–Nice is nicknamed 'the race to the sun', but the weather had been terrible for the past two days. Martijn Maaskant of Garmin-Cervélo broke seven ribs, while Robert Kiserlovsky of Astana ended up under a parked truck. At the finish, Jean-Christophe Péraud held on to his fifth place overall, and had a great ride again on the final day. He got dropped on the Col d'Eze, but Blel got him back on the descent and the whole team was around him for most of the stage. Spaniard Sammy Sánchez did sneak a few seconds at the finish, and Jean-Christophe dropped one place, but sixth overall in Paris–Nice was a great achievement and the team could be happy with his and their performance.

It was weird and frustrating being at the final stage but not racing. Looking back, I probably didn't eat enough and got the hunger 'knock' the day I abandoned. The team doctor asked me what I had had for breakfast and I told him I hadn't been feeling hungry, so I just had an omelette. He berated me, and he was probably right. Trying to get back to form, I'd been very cautious about what I ate, and maybe that had something to do with my bad ride too.

I had two days off at my mum's in Antibes and stayed completely off the bike before a few easy spins during the week. Ten days later I arrived in Lloret de Mar, Spain, for the Volta a Catalunya, or Tour of Catalonia. Always top-heavy with mountains, the hundredth edition of the race had dropped its usual time-trial stage in favour of an extra day of climbing, which meant we would tackle sixteen climbs over the course of seven days, including the tough mountain-top finish to the ski station in Andorra on the Wednesday.

I was to be one of two protected riders for the week, along with Blel. It was his first role as a protected rider, but when I spoke to him on the team bus on the way from the airport he didn't seem too excited by the prospect. Blel had been progressing with every race and deserved his chance at being leader. But he said he'd rather try and get up the road a few times and go for a stage win than try to ride consistently all week and fight for fifth or tenth place overall.

In previous years, I'd gone into Catalunya knowing I'd be up the front every day. This time around though, I was very unsure of my condition and struggling to find form. I wasn't progressing as much as I wanted to, which left me feeling a combination of embarrassment and frustration. On the bike, my head was telling me that I was the boss and I should be riding strong and hard, but my legs weren't listening and I found myself having to drop down a gear instead of shifting up.

I wanted to finish close to the top fifteen overall, which I realized was very optimistic for somebody who had abandoned Paris–Nice and now faced the likes of Contador, Evans and Basso in one of the toughest stage races in Europe. I wanted to at least stay in contention for a good overall placing until Andorra, just for my head, if nothing else. With two first-category climbs on day one, I wouldn't be long finding out how I was going.

All the teams stayed in the same hotel on the first night, which meant I was able to have a good chat with my cousin Dan Martin after dinner. Riding for the Garmin-Cervélo team, Dan has been based in Girona for the past three years. Catalunga is his 'home' race now. He trains on those climbs all the time and was really looking forward to the week ahead. I also had a bit of a catch-up with Philip Deignan in the morning after breakfast.

On the ascent of the first-category Alt de Sant Grau, I had Séb Minard alongside me and we were in a good position near the front. Over the top, David Moncoutié of Cofidis attacked. The Frenchman was quickly joined by Contador, whose presence up front put most of the top riders on red alert and saw the likes of Scarponi, Evans, Basso and Dan all jump across the gap. Dan looked to be flying. He closed the gap pretty quick and seemed to be in top form.

I was near the front when Contador jumped, but the guy in front of me didn't go so I stalled a bit and then hadn't the legs to close the gap. I was pretty busy just trying to hang on. I seemed to be able to ride at about 80 per cent but couldn't get that little bit extra that just comes with good form. Blel made the move, but the group only got a handful of seconds and we caught them on the descent to the finish.

My teammate Ben Gasteur from Luxembourg had gone clear early in the day, with HTC Highroad's Latvian pro Gatus Smukulis, and with 6km to go, Ben and Smukulis were still hanging on out front with just 50 seconds' lead. Lampre led the chase for their sprinter Alessandro Petacchi as Séb kept me near the front of the bunch.

In the final kilometre, a fatigued Ben was dropped by his Latvian breakaway partner and we could see both of them dangling ahead of us. Séb had brought me to the front, but I didn't want to lead the sprint out and be the first one to come by Ben, so I told him to hold his sprint for another few metres, which was a mistake. Ben was going to be caught a few seconds later by somebody else anyway, and soon we were swamped by a host of sprinters from behind. I got boxed in and drifted back to fifteenth or twentieth, but Séb thought I was still on his wheel and stayed fourth or fifth in line.

As we had a strong tailwind, I should have just told Séb to put the hammer down and he could have easily led me out for a long time. We passed Ben with 500m to go. Going into the final roundabout, Max flew by on the inside of the bunch as everybody braked. I don't know how he got around it, but he led me out again before someone barged me off his wheel with 300m to go. Max kept sprinting, thinking I was still behind him, and got sixth on the stage. Sébastian was twelfth and I finished eighteenth, four places behind Dan.

I had told the team that morning that I was motivated, that I was going to do the sprint, and to stay with me at the finish. I had great support from the guys in the finale, so I was really disappointed afterwards not to have made the most of it. I just didn't have the confidence. Sometimes I make the mistake of going too early, but that day I left it way too late. The guys in the team car didn't know Ben had been caught until I radioed to the rest of the lads to say sorry for my bad sprint. I didn't hang around too long on the bus after the stage. Like a stroppy teenager, I just grabbed a bottle of water, a banana and my suitcase and dragged it into my room and had a shower and an autopsy into my missed opportunity.

The next day's stage got off to a bad start too. Actually, it very nearly didn't get off to any kind of start.

It had started to rain just before we were due to begin, in Santa Coloma de Farners, so I opted to stay on the bus until the last minute. Zipping up my rain cape, I exited as normal, grabbed my bike and began to pedal leisurely through the slowly moving race cavalcade that always lines up behind the bunch. There was no real hurry, as we weren't due to start for another five minutes at least. Guys were getting rain capes from their team cars, and four of the Spanish Movistar team were chatting at the side of the pavement, checking their tyre pressure and looking over their bikes, much the same as every other day.

I'd read in the race manual that we would have five minutes of neutralized riding before the actual racing began, but the cars were now moving a bit faster than usual. There were a couple of riders in the cavalcade in front of me and lots more behind me, so I didn't put any heed on it until I heard over the radio: 'Good luck for the day. Kilometre zero. Racing is on.' The stage started early.

I spent the next 4km jumping from car boot to car boot, through the fifty or so cars, all the way up to the first car, and eventually into the tail end of the peloton. I found out later that about twenty guys missed the start, including team leaders Levi Leipheimer (Radioshack), David Moncoutié (Cofidis) and Denis Menchov (Rabobank). I was the first one to get back on. As I rode sheepishly into the peloton after 4km of racing, I could hear my *directeur sportif* laughing over the radio: 'Four Movistar riders missed the start and are a long way back in the cars.' He obviously hadn't noticed that I missed it too. I wasn't the only Ag2r rider either. Blel and Christophe Riblon only got on a few kilometres later, while it took the Movistar guys about 15km to catch up.

As things settled into a steady rhythm, I had a good chat with Philip Deignan. If there's one guy in the peloton who understood how long it took to come back from injury, I figured it was him. We compared notes on how hard it was to get back to top form when you take time off. Then we moved on to more interesting stuff: cars and motorbikes. Philip told me he'd met Irish superbike rider Eugene Laverty a few weeks before on a trip to a physio up the north. I'd met Eugene at a radio station back in December and we spent a good few kilometres talking about his chances with the Factory Yamaha team in the World Superbike series.

As we entered the 9km finishing circuit, the breakaway had been reeled in to a manageable distance and no longer posed a threat to the sprinters' teams. There were a few attacks on the finishing circuit, which we had to cover four times, but Lampre and Movistar forced the pace at the front and held the bunch together until the final gallop.

Sébastien Minard did a massive load of work for me again but, in the sprint, Blel wanted to lead me out. I told him that I had Séb to do that and that he should either do his own sprint or conserve energy for the next day. Although Blel was co-leader, old habits die hard. Séb was with me until the second-last corner, about a kilometre and a half from the finish. There was a slight drag on the narrow run to the line. I got boxed in on the right-hand side, but the sprint started on the left and, as Petacchi galloped off to take his stage win, I couldn't get out.

I was angry with myself again. I felt like the rhythm was coming back but I just didn't seem to have the sprinter's reflex yet. If I went right, the sprint went left. If I went left, the sprint went right. I crossed the line in twentieth place and moved up to twelfth overall.

We had ridden at about 75 per cent all day. It was hard enough to give you sore legs but not hard enough to find out if everybody else was feeling better or worse than I was. The next day was a completely different story. With three first-category climbs coming before the final *hors catégorie* ascent to the stage finish in Andorra, it was always going to be an uphill battle.

We started right at the bottom of a 7km climb and it was

pretty hard all the way up as the early break fought for freedom from the peloton. Eventually, a group went clear over the top and we had Séb Minard in the move. I got over the second climb in the front group and there was a pretty quick tempo after that for the rest of the stage. Christophe literally put me on Contador's wheel at the bottom of the penultimate mountain, the first-category Alt de la Comella, with 30km to go. Under the pressure of his Saxo Bank team, we soon caught Séb and his breakaway partners and they went straight out the back door as we flew past them. I stayed near the front until the attacks came a couple of kilometres from the top, where I drifted back but regained contact on the descent after a hard chase, just in time for the summit finish.

I was okay for the first 3 or 4km of the finishing climb, but with about 5km to go I blew and just rode to the line on my own. I wasn't going well enough to stay with the top guys, but I continued riding as hard as I could to the summit, as I wanted to get the most out of myself on the climb. You can't replicate those kinds of efforts in training at home, so it was important for me to dig in.

I thought I'd finish in the top twenty-five or thirty riders, but after the stage I found out that I finished fortieth and lost three minutes twenty-nine seconds to stage winner Contador. I knew I had lost time but didn't think it was as much as that, so I wasn't very happy with my result. I'd been pretty much at my limit the whole way up, but at least I was feeling better than at Paris–Nice. Blel was eleventh on the stage. He had a great climb, and I was really happy for him.

I'd been talking to my cousin Dan earlier on in the day, and he was feeling really comfy on the climbs, so it was no surprise to see him take fourth on the stage. It's great to see Dan challenge for these big races. That night, my Ag2r La Mondiale team was staying in the same hotel as the Radioshack team and, after dinner, I had a good chat with Philip Deignan over a decaf. Our main point of conversation was how well Dan looked to be going and how great it would be if he could finish on the podium. It's great to have two other Irish riders in the peloton, even if all we do is slag each other.

The next stage was so fast and so blustery that most of the day was spent staying out of the wind and protecting Blel. In the final sprint, the guys looked after him while I did my own thing in the gallop. The last couple of kilometres were pretty hectic. With Petacchi having abandoned during the stage, the Garmin-Cervélo, Movistar and Sky teams saw their opportunity to provide the day's stage winner and all contributed to the pace setting at the front.

There was a lot of pushing and shoving, but I found a little opening with a kilometre to go and moved a bit nearer the top ten in the line. Then we dipped under a narrow bridge and the road went from two lanes into one and everybody stayed in whatever position they were in to the finish.

I didn't make the top ten, taking eleventh on the stage, but at least I felt as if I was in the sprint rather than just looking at it. Dan finished one place in front of me. He's not even a sprinter and was just trying to stay out of trouble! The next day, I found myself alongside Dan and his Garmin-Cervélo teammate Christian Vande Velde. Naturally, Vande Velde felt obliged to give me some stick about Dan finishing one place ahead of me the previous day.

'Hey, Nico, your cousin beat you in a sprint yesterday, haw?' laughed the American.

'Yeah, sure, even Petacchi abandoned when he heard Dan was going for the gallop,' I replied.

The start of the final stage was horrendous. It was raining, and the combination of tight corners and diesel on the roads from the city-centre traffic meant that it was pretty hard just to stay upright. A massive crash split the bunch in three after about 15km.

Blel was in the front group, where Dan's Garmin-Cervélo team was pulling really hard, as a lot of the team leaders were caught in the second group with me. After a hard chase, we all regrouped and it stayed together for another 35km or so before people started attacking again.

After 53km, I got away with Thomas Rohregger of Leopard Trek and Eugeni Petrov of Astana. A few minutes later, Zavier Xandio of Sky, Ivan Rovny (Radioshack), and Andalucia's Adrian Palomares came across to make six of us up front.

Just after we went clear, I could hear in my earpiece that the team was having a bit of a panic at the back of the race. Blel had stopped for a call of nature and, upon remounting his bike, noticed his stem had broken. The problem was that the cars had all gone by and he had to wait on the second team car, which was at the very back of the cavalcade. He was way behind. Even though all the guys waited for him, Blel panicked about losing his twelfth place overall. His new bike had different tyres on it so he was sliding all over the place on the corners and was so anxious to get back to the peloton that he almost dropped the rest of the team.

In the break, we rode pretty well together but the Lampre team rode tempo behind and kept us on a tight leash, never giving us much more than a minute and a half. Although the peloton was playing cat and mouse with us, I was with some really strong riders and we were going full gas in the hope of staying away to the finish.

We had thirty seconds going on to the finishing circuit and I attacked the break with 3km to go. My fellow escapees chased hard and recaptured me just 2km from the line. With their prey caught and the bunch now hovering just fifteen seconds behind us and closing, the lead group stalled momentarily . . . so I attacked them again. The last 2km were pretty slippery and I took a few risks on some of the corners in the hope that I would be able to get around them more quickly than a big bunch.

As the peloton swallowed up my breakaway partners, I had about ten seconds' lead and was riding flat out towards the finish, with just the adrenaline of a possible stage win to keep me going. I got to within 300m of the line before the sprinters stormed past and stole the stage. My legs empty, I sat up and coasted to the finish, exhausted.

I ended the race in thirty-third place overall, still three minutes twenty-nine seconds down on overall winner Contador. Levi Leipheimer didn't take to the start the final morning, as he had been sick overnight, which meant that Dan got his podium place, finishing third overall. He really deserved it. He even went for the sprints during the week in case his final position would be decided on countback. A pure climber, Dan's fourth place in the bunch gallop on Saturday had impressed me.

I was hoping to be climbing a bit better at Catalunga, but took some comfort from the fact that I was a lot more competitive and was going a lot better than I had been at

Paris–Nice. I'd ridden the final day really hard and the fact that I was able to attack towards the end gave me a bit of confidence and was good for my morale.

After Catalunya, I spent a week training in the sunshine of Mallorca. I did a lot of motor-paced training and felt my condition was improving. I then rode Paris–Camembert, the fourth round of the French Cup series. I went clear with three others on the third-last climb, the Côte de la Huniere, with 25km to go, but we were caught 5km later on the descent and a large group went clear.

I kept attacking on the final two climbs and got across to the new leaders, but five riders had already escaped to form a new breakaway group. Séb Minard rode flat out for the final 3km for me and we were closing on them fast, but I didn't have the legs after all the attacking and blew up in the last 50m, finishing tenth, just four seconds behind winner Sandy Casar of Française des Jeux. Afterwards, I was satisfied with my day. I'd been pretty active during the whole race and was able to attack a few times near the end. My legs actually felt pretty good and I was hopeful of a good result soon afterwards.

But again, fate was to intervene. A couple of weeks later, I crashed at the Amstel Gold Race when two guys in front of me locked handlebars. I was right behind them and couldn't avoid falling. Although it messed up my race, there were no major injuries, just the usual cuts and bruises. Three days later, at Flèche-Wallonne, I fell again. This time I was out of the saddle when my chain slipped on the rear sprocket. As all of my weight was on the front of the bike, I flew over the handlebars and hurt myself pretty badly.

I was carted off in a neck brace and ended up at the same hospital as Dan, who was behind me and fell in the resulting mêlée. Sitting in A&E waiting for doctors, scans and X-rays, we realized it was the longest time we'd spent together in months.

The crash at Flèche was frustrating because I felt I was finally coming into good condition. I'd been doing loads of training, working hard and doing everything right, but wasn't getting any payback for it. Now I'd need a few days' rest again to let my wounds heal a bit. I wasn't sure about riding Liège–Bastogne–Liège four days later but, once again, was over eager to get back fitness before the Tour. I suffered, though, and abandoned at the second feed zone after 170km along with my teammates Christophe Riblon, Mikaël Cherel, Guillaume Bonnaford and David Le Lay.

The team figured that because I started my season a bit later, it would be a pity to stop racing after the classics, so they entered me for the Tour of Romandie stage race in Switzerland. Looking back, I was still pretty sore from the crash in Flèche and probably shouldn't have ridden but, like the gambler chasing the next 'sure thing', I was chasing form and hoping for miracles.

I was twenty-eighth in the opening prologue, eight seconds slower than surprise winner Jonathan Castroviejo of the Euskaltel team. Still in pain after two crashes in a week, my legs weren't great at all. The rain the next day didn't help either, as I was very wary of crashing for the third time. Although my road rash was stinging in the rain, it was the mental scars that caused me most trouble.

Negotiating a very tricky descent in the wet, I was really nervous after my recent falls and eventually just cracked.

Fear got the better of me and I had to sit up and let the wheels in front of me drift away into the distance. I was really panicking on the corners. Once again, I was glad my Ag2r shorts were brown. I lost five and a half minutes, dropping down to seventy-ninth in the overall standings.

Stage two was another wet one, and I finished a minute and forty-two seconds behind stage winner Damiano Cunego. My teammate Mikaël Cherel took second on stage three behind Alexandre Vinokourov with Max eleventh and me fourteenth. I wanted to do well in the time trial but had no legs and finished over two minutes down in seventy-ninth place.

I felt a bit better on the final stage and was in the front group of about thirty riders after the last little climb. Mikaël was leading me out but I lost his wheel on the corner to take eighth place on the stage, won in a mass bunch gallop by British sprinter Ben Swift of Team Sky. As Cadel Evans (BMC) showed signs of things to come with overall victory, I knew I was nowhere near top form. The one thing I had in my favour, though, was the fact that I'd been in a much worse position in 2010, when I tore my hamstring before the Tour and couldn't do anything but swim. At least this time I was on my bike.

After Romandie, Ag2r's Tour squad spent two weeks reconnoitring some of the Alpine stages at a training camp in Montgenèvre while another nine-man team tackled the Giro d'Italia. Every afternoon, as soon as we got back to our hotel room after training, our first reaction was to switch on the TV to see how our teammates were getting on.

On the Tuesday, we had a longer spin than usual, taking in

the climbs of the Col d'Agnel and the Col d'Izoard, and so arrived back a bit later than usual and missed the end of the stage. Eager to find out the results, somebody switched on the internet while the rest of us grabbed a shower. A few seconds later, results seemed so very unimportant.

The tragic news of the death of Belgian rider Wouter Weylandt on the descent of the Passo del Bocca, 25km from the end of the day's stage, hit us like a ton of bricks. In disbelief, we all watched rerun after rerun of the news. Stunned, we sat in silence watching aerial shots of the medical crew trying to revive him. Thankfully, we had missed the actual crash footage because I heard it was pretty gruesome.

We were in total shock. It was really traumatizing for us, and we weren't even at the Giro. We could only imagine how his teammates, friends and family felt. Wouter's girlfriend was five months pregnant at the time and my heart went out to her.

As professional cyclists, we see crashes every day of the week. Sometimes there is a very fine line between a crash that can leave you with a few scrapes and bruises and one that ends your season, your career or, in Wouter's case, your life. A pedal here, a handlebar there, a pothole, a stray dog is all it takes. Sometimes crashes happen as if they are in slow motion. Even though you are travelling at 70kph, you can see the bike sliding across the road in front of you, the riders falling to your left. Somehow, you avoid it, weaving matrix-like around an outstretched leg or spinning wheel. Other times, though, you are on the deck before you know what hit you.

From the first day that you learn to cycle, falling off is inevitable, whether you race or just use your bike to go to the shops. In the professional peloton, some riders tend to crash more often than others. People often say that sprinters have the best bike-handling ability in the peloton, yet they crash more times than anybody else. There is no safety net.

Sprinters take risks, diving through gaps, rubbing shoulders and elbows with other sprinters at over 60kph. You don't win sprints by being shy or hesitant. How many times have the top sprinters crashed because they tried to get through a gap when there was none? In saying that, I've often gone through gaps in sprints and afterwards asked myself, How the hell did I get through there? A bit like driving a car, most of the accidents in cycling occur because guys over-estimate their own ability and push themselves to the limit to get to the front, but you also have innocuous little falls that can do as much damage.

The scars on my hips, knees and elbows are constant reminders of previous altercations with the road, but there are mental scars too. You can go through most of a season never thinking about crashing but, as soon as you do, that becomes all you think about for a few races, and it can take a while to get your confidence back, as I found out on that rainy descent at Romandie.

After Wouter Weylandt's death, we were training around Alpe d'Huez and the Col du Lauteret. At one point there was a 300m drop at the side of the road. Even though Christophe Riblon won a stage at the Tour de France in 2010, the roads were pretty narrow and he just didn't feel safe all day. I'm always 'Paddy Last' on the descents in training nowadays. Some of the guys take more risks. They enjoy riding hard on the downhill but, even though they take reasonable pre-caution, the roads are not closed and it's still pretty dangerous.

What struck me about Wouter Weylandt's crash, though, was that it could have happened to anyone, at any time. It's not as if he hit a car or fell over the edge of a cliff. An excellent bike handler, he'd already got through the switchbacks and tight turns, and his fall came on a fairly straight part of the descent. One of the Radioshack guys who was riding behind him later said that it happened when he turned to look at a group coming up behind him and his pedal hit a small wall, hurtling the 26-year-old Belgian across the road and head first into another wall. He was doing around 80kph with nothing but lycra and a Styrofoam helmet for protection. A post mortem later revealed that he died instantly.

I only knew Wouter Weylandt to say hello to. I never had a full-blown conversation with him, but he was the type of rider who always said hello and had a smile. From others, I know that he was a nice guy, an honest and friendly rider and a gentleman.

Just a few weeks later, Xavier Tondo of the Movistar team died when he was crushed between his car and a garage door on his way to training. I'd spent much of the previous Vuelta in direct competition with Tondo for sixth place overall, and we got to know each other pretty well. One day he would drop me; the next I would drop him. After the final mountain stage we gave each other a pat on the back and said, 'Well done.' Tondo was a really nice guy. He was thirty-two.

In June, his Colombian teammate Mauricio Soler won stage two of the Tour of Switzerland and dedicated it to Tondo. Four days later, Soler fell, just 6km into stage six, broke his ankle and fractured his skull. As I write this two months later, he is still in hospital with severe head injuries and is learning to talk all over again.

When I'm training, safety is something I always have in mind. I wear a helmet on every spin. But you never think about it in a race. You have to put it out of your mind. Once you're in a race, it's the type of thing you try to forget. It's too late for me now, at twenty-seven, to say I want to stop, that I don't want to crash any more. Cycling is what I do. It's my job. It's my life. It's what I love. Wouter Weylandt and Xavier Tondo loved it too. May they rest in peace.

After training camp, the team wanted me to ride the Bayern Rundfahrt stage race in Germany, but I asked to do an extra week of training in the mountains and went to another camp with the team in La Tousuirre instead. I thought I needed more training rather than more racing and was happy that the whole team was behind me and trusted me. Although I was now putting all my eggs into one basket – the eight-day Critérium du Dauphiné, which ended just three weeks before the Tour de France – I was pretty confident I would be okay.

Although I hadn't got as many results as the previous year, I felt more confident than ever going into the Dauphiné. Despite my lack of racing, I had trained hard and could feel my form finally returning. I began the race as team leader and, with five mountain-top finishes, was hoping I would have good enough condition to be competitive.

Having finished nineteen seconds behind winner Lars Boom in the opening prologue, my first big rendezvous with the mountains came the next day, on the opening road stage. Belgian Jurgen van den Broeck won at the top of the 7km finishing climb, having gone clear with just 2.5km left to the summit of Saint-Pierre-de-Chartreuse with former Spanish champion Joaquim Rodriguez second, six seconds back. Just one second behind Rodriguez was a little group containing Cadel Evans (BCM), Alexandre Vinokourov (Astana), Edvald Boasson Hagen and me.

Afterwards, I knew I'd passed Vino with about 300m to go but was so wrecked from giving it everything in the last kilometre that I didn't realize that he passed me again before the line for fourth. I was so convinced I got fourth that I even told the guys to double-check the results afterwards.

Fifth on the stage, my 'comeback' was heralded in the French press, but I knew that I hadn't gone anywhere. I'd just had bad luck. It was a ride I was expecting to do but wasn't fully convinced I could do. I knew how hard I had trained since Romandie and had pretty high expectations for the rest of the week.

I finished ninth on the second stage as HTC sprinter John Degenkolb claimed victory in Lyon. I was now up to fifth overall, just seventeen seconds off race leader Alexandre Vinokourov, going into the 42km individual time trial, which would be held on the same course as the penultimate stage of the 2011 Tour de France. Happy enough with my form so far, I was still taking every day as it came, but I knew the time trial would be the big test.

Disappointingly, I had one of my bad time-trial days again and was caught by Aussie specialist Cadel Evans, who started three minutes behind me. I lost three and a half minutes by the end of the stage, dropping down to sixteenth overall, three minutes twenty-six seconds behind new race leader Bradley Wiggins. I seem always to have a few minutes of a dip in my time trials, and if I knew what caused it I'd be world champion by now. I knew it wasn't my legs because I finished strong. I started off okay and finished great, but there were 7 or 8km in the middle where I don't know if I lost concentration or morale or what, but I was going nowhere.

When Evans caught me, though, I held him at the same distance for the rest of the stage. My ego kicked in and I just thought, No, no, no, I'm not losing any more time, which makes me think it's more of a concentration problem than anything.

I didn't really contest the sprint finish into Mâcon. As Degenkolb claimed his second victory, I had big hopes for the following three days in the mountains. I wanted to make it back into the top ten overall and needed to focus my energy on doing that.

Although I was still sixteenth overall, I was only half a minute or so outside the top ten, and stage five was my first big chance to move back up. But then disaster struck.

I remember I was descending on Séb Minard's wheel. He was bringing me up through the bunch. We didn't want to go right to the front, as the final climb to Les Gets was still a few kilometres away. I had my hands on the top of the bars beside the brake hoods and was tucked into an aero position. The road looked brand new and I wasn't expecting any holes. My front wheel found one, though, and suddenly bounced up in the air. Covered in sweat, my right hand lost its grip and slipped off the bars. I tried to grab them again but there was too much vibration and I just flew off the bike.

I hit the deck along with Quickstep rider Andy Cappelle and whacked my head off a concrete road divider. As I sat slumped sideways against the slab of concrete, Séb and another teammate, Mathieu Perget, waited anxiously to pace me back to the bunch on the climb.

I had hit my head pretty hard and didn't really know what was going on. I just sat there stunned. I was completely disorientated but kind of remember being on the ground and the doctor asking me, 'Are you okay, are you okay?' The next thing I knew, Vincent Lavenu had jumped out of the team car and began to heave me off the ground, saying, 'Get on the bike, it's important you finish today.' So I got on the bike.

That last climb was pure pain. I'd opened all my old wounds from the previous two crashes just as they'd healed, and I also added some new ones. I could feel a burning pain all down my right side. It was as if I had been dragged naked across a carpet. My shorts were almost ripped off me. Battered and bruised, I was raw from my ankle to my chin. All up my shin, my ribs, chest, even under my armpit was cut, all the way to my fingertips on one side.

Although I didn't really know what I was doing and was most likely concussed, I just went into autopilot and kept pedalling until someone told me to stop. Séb, Mathieu and Vincent in the car kept talking to me, keeping me alert. I finished the stage fourth last of 166 riders, twenty-five minutes behind the group of leaders I had been with at the bottom of the mountain.

Afterwards, I needed an operation to fix a hole in my elbow and got two stitches in my chin. I went back to the hotel first, though, because I wanted to clean my wounds myself. Normally, when you arrive in the hospital after a crash, the nurses just throw antiseptic on you to clean the wounds and it stings like hell. Even though I avoided that by taking my time in the bath and doing it gently, to be honest, I'd never been in that much pain in my life.

As well as missing the last two mountain stages of the Dauphiné, where I was really hoping to test myself properly and get some quality racing in, I knew my injuries were going to set me back even more in my preparation for the Tour. I'd no idea what was going on for about two days after the fall and don't even remember the team doctor taking pictures of my scars. I was so cut up, I couldn't walk for five days afterwards, but knew I had the Irish national championships to contest just two weeks later and had to get back on my bike.

After hobbling around the house for two days, I packed my bags and headed to one last pre-Tour camp in the Pyrenees, but I was so stiff after travelling to the team hotel that I had to sit out the first two days of training. On the third day, my swollen and bruised legs looked more like those of a rugby player as I gingerly pedalled out from the hotel. Carried away by the sunshine and scenery of the Hourquette, Tourmalet and Luz-Ardiden, I overdid it again with a five-hour spin.

The next day, it was raining and, paying for the previous day's efforts, I climbed into the car halfway up the Plateau de Beille and needed another day off when I went home to recover.

After such a disrupted season, I could have changed tack going into the Tour and concentrated on stage wins, or maybe the green or polka-dot jerseys, rather than focus on overall glory at the Tour. But I chose to continue aiming for a top place on GC, knowing I could end up having ridden three Tours and not having won a stage. When I'm older, I will try for stage wins. Okay, I could end up never winning a stage at the Tour in my whole career, but it's a question of choice. You can't do everything. I'm not strong enough, like Contador, to do everything. It's my choice to save my energy for the GC. That was the way I wanted to ride the Tour and that was the way I was going to ride it.

18

Un Tour Sans

The week before the Tour de France seems to get more hectic and stressful every year, with barely a minute to relax. Sometimes it was hard to remember what day it was, never mind what country I was in. This year, I found myself in three different countries in thirty-six hours.

The chaos started the weekend before the tour, when I left Varese for a trip home to Ireland for the national championships. Coinciding with one of the busiest holiday weekends in Italy, the week got off to a bad start when my girlfriend Chiara and I got stuck in traffic on the motorway on the way to Bergamo airport. We were so late when we got there that while I dragged my bike and bags to the check-in, Chiara rushed to park the car. The airport car park was full, so she had to drive back out of the airport to the long-term car park, but that was full too. With only about half an hour to boarding, Chiara ended up just abandoning the car at the back of the airport and walking for fifteen minutes back to me. One of the last couples onto the plane, we only made it to Dublin because our flight was delayed, and it was near midnight when we arrived. But at least we weren't as late as my cousin Dan. His flight from Girona was delayed too, and he didn't arrive until about 1.30 a.m.

As usual, my nana's house in Dundrum was full to the rafters, and Dan's mam and dad took up their by now familiar position on the couch in the sitting room. When I get back to Dublin, it's great to see everyone again and it makes you realize you have a lot of support at home and a lot of people willing you to do well.

After a short spin with my cousin Eric, Uncle Peter and my dad's former masseur Paul Tansey the next morning, I spent a couple of hours around Avoca and Powerscourt Gardens on the Saturday afternoon. Having lunch with my Aunt Pamela, Uncle Declan, Christel and Chiara, just relaxing and enjoying the surroundings on a beautiful sunny day, reminded me why it's my favourite place to go when I get home. Chiara and I hardly got ten minutes together for the three days I was home, so this was my favourite part of the trip.

One of my spokes had been broken on the flight over and as it was a special carbon-fibre blade, all I could do was tape it back together with insulating tape and hope I didn't hit any potholes during the championships. The title race didn't exactly go to plan for myself or Dan. We both made it into the race-winning breakaway group of nine but I ended up fourth while Dan was only beaten in a photo finish by defending champion Matt Brammeier of HTC Highroad.

When Dan went clear the last time up Slieve Beagh, I was missing a bit of race rhythm. As he was followed by Matt Brammeier, being seventh wheel out of seven when they jumped wasn't going to make it any easier on me. Although I was closing the gap on them by the top of the climb, I had three An Post guys on my wheel waiting to pounce. Not wanting to drag them across to Dan, I sat up and told them to ride. They tried to bring them back, but as soon as they ran out of steam David McCann attacked and stayed clear for bronze.

I remember former pro Mark Scanlon saying that winning the nationals and getting to wear the shamrock jersey for a year was like having a target on your back in the pro races. It's probably true, but I think it's important for the Irish jersey to be seen in the big pro races and was disappointed not to be able to wear it in this year's Tour. The nationals, though, were a perfect exercise to finish off my pre-Tour preparation, even if I was still very sore from the Dauphiné crash.

With photo shoots, interviews and meetings arranged, my three days at home wasn't just hectic for me but for everybody around me too. My nana's house was overrun with bikes and paraphernalia, and everyone was busy ferrying me around all weekend. My sister Christel had recently bought an apartment in Dublin, but I was so busy I didn't even have time to go and look at it. I felt like I spent the whole weekend running around. I even managed to do a quick interview in between mouthfuls of chicken salad at McDonald's in Dublin Airport on the way home.

I got back to Varese about 10 p.m. on the Tuesday and had just about enough time to go for a nice meal with Chiara in our local restaurant. Our birthdays were both on the next week after the nationals, but I wouldn't see her until the Tour's first rest day on 11 July, so this was our joint birthday party. Afterwards, I went home, gave myself a quick pre-Tour haircut, unpacked my stuff from Ireland and repacked my cases for the Tour.

The next morning I was up at 7 a.m. so that I could fit in a two-hour spin before catching a flight to Nantes and the Grand Départ of the Tour de France, but when I got to the airport my flight was cancelled. Myself, Ivan Basso and a few of the local Liquigas guys ended up having to get a flight to Paris instead of going direct to Nantes, which meant that we didn't arrive at the team hotel until 10.30 p.m.

There was no lie-in on Thursday morning, as I was woken at seven for the team's pre-Tour anti-doping test. In the morning we did a couple of laps of the team time-trial course, testing out some new Reynolds wheels. After lunch, it was into some new kit and on to the bus for the team presentation, which was very long, eventually getting back to the hotel for dinner at around 6 p.m.

The next day we did three hours, including the last 50km of the opening stage. I was pretty surprised by the final 2km climb and wasn't expecting it to be as hard. I thought the Mûr de Bretagne on Tuesday would be the first big hill, but the very first stage had a really tough uphill finish, suitable for Philippe Gilbert or even someone like Alexandre Vinokourov, Sammy Sánchez or Thor Hushovd. I'd better be up there too, I thought.

My plan would be to ride up the front and stay as close as possible to the leaders in order not to lose time. The previous year, I didn't contest the early bunch sprints, trying to save my energy for the overall battle and the high mountains later on. But this year, everyone would have to be focussed and stay alert on the early stages, as I could lose a lot of time on those little uphill finishes if the bunch splits on the early stages.

With Blel Kadri, Sébastien Minard, Jean-Christophe

Péraud, Hubert Dupont, John Gadret, Christophe Riblon, and Maxime Bouet we had a great team for this Tour, designed mainly to help me in the mountains. In fact we only had Séb Hinault for the sprints. They would be very hard to win, as we didn't have someone who could beat the likes of Cavendish, Hushovd or Petacchi in the big gallops, but the team was pretty strong and we were also keen to get in breakaways.

Blel was riding his first Tour, and was really excited and was happily taking in every little detail of the race. The first thing he noticed was my haircut. In my rush to get ready, I'd missed a spot at the back and left a big tuft of hair sticking out. He opted not to mention it until I was out in public and then made a show of me, taunting me that people were gawping at me everywhere I went. He cut it off before the team presentation, though.

With much of my early season blighted by crashes, I had only one UCI point to my name going into the tour, from my fifth place on the opening stage of the Dauphiné. That was 115 points fewer than John Gadret and 70 fewer than Jean-Christophe Péraud, but the team had faith in me as leader for this Tour and I felt the guys were really behind me, which was great motivation.

In the days before the Grand Départ, the main topic of the media conversation was the presence of defending champion Alberto Contador in the line up. Not because he was the undisputed favourite for the race, but because he had failed a drugs test for clenbuterol during the 2010 Tour yet still hadn't been sanctioned and was free to ride.

The levels of clenbuterol in his system were so low that if they had been tested in almost any other lab in Europe they wouldn't even have been detected, but the fact remained that the drug was detected and, as there is no lower limit on the amount of clenbuterol allowed in cycling, he tested positive. Contador and his lawyers argued that he had consumed contaminated meat during the second rest day of the 2010 Tour and ingested the drug unknowingly. After much deliberation, the Spanish federation agreed with him and let him continue racing.

The UCI and the World Anti-Doping Authority then challenged his acquittal and brought a case to the Court of Arbitration for Sport (CAS). Originally due to be heard on 6 June 2011, the case was delayed until the week after the Tour ended, so technically Contador was free to ride, which meant that he could possibly win the Tour only for victory to be taken off him a week later.

If the CAS then suspended Contador, the previous Tour would also be taken off him, as would the 2011 Giro d'Italia and a few other races he had won while the investigation was ongoing. This made his presence at the Tour a strange decision for me.

While on the legal side he was okay to ride the Tour, the bigger issue was the fact that he had failed a test and was under investigation. I'm not a scientist. I just go on what I read in the papers but I totally agreed with what British rider Bradley Wiggins said in an interview with *L'Equipe* before the Tour that someone who had failed four tests in a row couldn't be a mistake.

Other riders had been given two-year bans for the same offence and I was of the opinion that if he was guilty, he was guilty, and if he wasn't, then let him ride but don't drag it on for over a year without a decision either way.

If a guy is tested positive and banned, then he's a cheat, and I've no worries about saying that. If you use a doping product you should get a sentence, regardless of the damage done to the sport. I think two years is not enough and agree with UCI president Pat McQuaid that four-year sentences should be introduced, maybe even life bans.

The case was ultimately put back again until the end of the 2011 season and it was February 2012 before it was resolved, which was a ridiculous situation. Contador was eventually found guilty and I think it's going to damage the image of the sport. Not because it's one guy testing positive, but because he was found to have cheated the system and to have taken us all for eejits and continued winning races for over a year afterwards.

To me, doping is cheating. It takes a different mentality altogether. If I was to look back at races where I lost places, or like the one in Portugal, where I lost a yellow jersey to riders who later tested positive, then I'd probably crack up. But I can't think of that. All I can do is my best and if that's not good enough and I never win a stage of the Tour or even another bike race, I'll just keep racing as long as I enjoy it and as long as I have a contract.

I want to know how far I can go under my own steam. If that's not good enough then I'll just go do something else.

Although my season had been disrupted a lot, I still hoped for a top ten overall. But it was the Tour de France and everybody was ready for it. There were fifty guys who wanted to be top ten. I just hoped . . . not for good luck, but just for no more bad luck so that my legs could come back and I could show everyone I was still progressing. I wanted to get back to the top level and hopefully give a bit of satisfaction to all my fans and everybody that had supported me over the years. Once again, I kept a diary in the *Irish Independent*.

Stage 1 – Saturday 2 July: Passage du Gois–Mont des Alouettes, 191km

As usual, today's opening stage was littered with crashes. I don't know why it happens, but every year is the same. If you don't fall off or get held up by someone else falling off in the first week of the Tour, then you should offer your services as a route planner in a minefield.

There were so many collisions today that I didn't see a third of them until I watched the highlights on TV afterwards. Eager to get his altercation with the road out of the way early, German sprinter André Greipel was on his arse before we even hit the official start line.

It wasn't even 40km into the race when I fell, hitting the deck for a record fifth time this year. As the guys ahead of me slammed on the brakes and ploughed into each other, I wasn't unduly worried, as I saw it coming and had time to stop without doing any damage. But then some guy from Katusha, who was obviously looking elsewhere, smashed me in the back.

I fell on my chainring and it dug into my shin, so I have another open wound on my leg to add to the collection of cuts and abrasions from my Dauphiné crash. The only good thing about today's fall was, because the teeth of the chainring are sharp, at least the cut is clean. Although it was very painful at the time, it didn't bleed much, and a bandage should sort it out for tomorrow. As the race went on I forgot about my leg but noticed my wrist was getting a bit sore.

When I picked myself up, I was a bit anxious about my gears and, having been hit from behind, didn't know if my rear wheel was buckled. John Gadret was at the very back of the bunch and when he saw me fall, turned around on the road and came back to see how I was. As I remounted and made my way back to the peloton, I also had Séb Minard, Christophe and Hubert wait for me to pace me back up.

Upon making contact with the back of the peloton, I was all set to grab a couple of quiet minutes to feel sorry for myself and catch my breath again when Séb let fly at me. 'You can't just stay here, Nico. We have to get to the front. Follow me.' With that, he made his way up the left-hand side of the peloton with me in his slipstream.

Being at the front, however, doesn't mean you're immune to crashes, as Jurgen van de Walle found out later on. Riding in second place in the line, the Belgian was waving his hand in the air to warn those behind him of an upcoming traffic island when he hit a speed bump and was thrown to the ground, bringing down a half-dozen riders in his wake.

After a bit of a chase and with his jersey in tatters, Van de Walle returned to the front of the bunch in an effort to keep things together for his team leader Philippe Gilbert, who was favourite to take the stage on the short uphill finish.

It's only the first day of the Tour but already our

whole team has either crashed or lost time because they got caught up in a crash. As we started the little climb to the finish, only Séb Hinault was left with me in the front group, which had been whittled down to around seventy riders by the incessant carnage.

With nine roundabouts in the last 6km, the finale was hectic. With 2km to go, Séb disappeared into another pile-up and I was left alone in the front group. I didn't even notice until French champion Sylvain Chavanel came up alongside me and asked me where everybody had gone. I looked around, and there were only about twenty-five of us left.

The climb to the finish was pretty hard and I was just hanging on, trying to stay in contact with the leaders. Gilbert repaid Van de Walle and the rest of his Omega Pharma Lotto team's faith in him and proved he is the best in the world at these types of finishes to win the stage pretty comfortably. I crossed the line six seconds later for nineteenth after my biggest effort in three weeks.

Today's finishing climb was the type I really love, but I'm still not at 100 per cent so I'm pretty satisfied to have stayed with the top guys and not lost time. The big pity about today was that the rest of the guys lost a fair bit on the stage due to bad luck. One of the goals for the team was to get top three in the team classification in Paris, but losing twenty minutes or more on a stage where we should have only lost a handful of seconds is obviously a big hit, and we will probably lose more in the team time-trial. Hopefully the guys will not be too sore tomorrow and can keep me up there with a good time.

Stage 2 – Sunday 3 July:
Team Time Trial, Les Essarts, 23km

The thing I'm a bit angry about today is that after yesterday's stage they put all the guys involved in the second crash on the same time as me. I finished the stage completely knackered having tried to put time into some of those guys. Okay, there was a crash with a kilometre to go, but there were only a few guys down, not seventy.

In the first group, we'd all fought for time all the way to the line, only for the guys who lost twenty or thirty seconds behind us to be given the same time as us. I could have done with the extra few seconds' cushion for the team time-trial today.

This morning, our team must have looked like extras for *The Mummy Returns*, as we mounted our bikes for an hour-and-a-half training spin before our afternoon race against the clock. I have a new bandage on my shin to go with the one on my elbow from the Dauphiné crash. Séb Hinault began today's stage with three stitches in his calf. Sébastien Minard has a bandage on his right knee and one on his calf. Max has cuts on his left thigh and knee. Jean-Christophe has bandages on both legs and Hubert has a few scrapes too. Blel and John are the only two unscathed so far.

Even so, the team did a great job in the team time-trial. I went a bit too hard on the early part of the stage and suffered on the last drag with 2km to go but then Christophe and Jean-Christophe took over and were really strong. John was struggling a bit in the tailwind section but he rode really hard in the headwind and did the last kilometre flat out.

We had said this morning that between tenth and fifteenth on the stage, losing no more than a minute, would be good for us. We finished thirteenth on the stage and lost fifty-three seconds behind the winners, Garmin-Cervélo, so we were pretty much on target. Everybody is pretty satisfied with today's performance. We rode a good time trial, but the others were quicker: simple as that.

As today is my twenty-seventh birthday, the team will have a celebratory glass of champagne at the dinner table tonight and a slice of cake. There are only two times we are allowed to have champagne on the Tour; either you win a stage, or you celebrate a birthday. For the moment, I'll have to go with the easy option.

Stage 3 – Monday 4 July:
Olonne-sur-Mer–Redon, 198km

Some nights on the Tour, you're so wrecked that you fall asleep on the bus before you even get to the hotel. Other nights, you replay the stage over and over in your head or think about other stuff and just can't get to sleep.

Last night I went to bed around 10 p.m., and, having flicked through the available channels in the hotel bedroom, I opted for *Finding Nemo* over various French talk shows. I thought, This will help me sleep. It's nice and quiet and relaxing. But once I switched it off, Robbie Williams decided to continue singing the theme song of the movie, only this time my head was the auditorium: 'Somewhe-r-e beyond the sea ... somewhere waiting for me-e-e . . .'

We've been in the same hotel for five nights now and I've grown accustomed to my new bed, so that wasn't the reason I had trouble sleeping. I had no snoring teammate to blame, as there was nobody else in the room – well, except for Robbie, who was still giving it socks an hour later: 'My lover stands on golden sa-a-ands . . . and watches the ships that go sa-i-ling.'

The more I thought, I need to go asleep, the harder it was to nod off. Robbie, however, was still fresh as a daisy at midnight: 'She's there watching for me. If I could fly, like birds on hi-i-igh, then straight to her arms I'd go sailing . . .'

Half an hour later, I'd finally begun to drift off when I heard a commotion outside. The Saxo Bank team kitchen truck was parked right outside my bedroom window. I don't know if they were cleaning up after dinner or what, but I had to get up and knock on the window to tell them to shut the hell up. I think Robbie got the message too, and he finally left me alone in the land of nod.

Today the plan was to stay out of trouble and, thankfully, that's what I did. The break went very early today, right from the gun in fact. I was halfway down the bunch as we left the first town and heard on the radio that two guys were already up the road, a Euskaltel rider and a Française des Jeux rider. Then, two seconds later, there were three more guys chasing, including Max. It wasn't part of the team plan before the stage. That was Max doing some improvisation.

After just 3km, the lead quintet had forty-five seconds and they eventually got a maximum of seven minutes over the peloton. We knew it was a bit of a suicide move, though, as today was one of the only true flat stages in the first week where the sprinters would get the chance to fight it out for stage victory.

There has been a change in the scoring in the points classification this year, with a new system introduced where more points are up for grabs in the intermediate sprint during each stage, and this has changed the race slightly. In the 5km before the intermediate sprint each day, the bunch really speeds up as the sprinters try to claim enough points to take over the green jersey. In those 5km the breakaway's advantage melts. On Saturday, the break lost three minutes in 10km, and today they lost another two minutes in just 5km. I think the new system is a killer for the breakaways and don't think it's a good idea. They say it was to make the battle for the green jersey more interesting, but I think the competition for the green jersey over the last three or four years was always very good anyway. Maybe they're looking for non-sprinters to get involved in the competition.

I think someone like Philippe Gilbert could do well this year if he keeps going for the intermediate sprints. He can win stages and get in breakaways in the mountains, and if he continues to pick up ten points here and twenty points there, he could end up in green in Paris.

In other years there were more possibilities that the break would go to the end, but now I think everybody is fighting for the intermediate points and it almost neutralizes everything midway through the stage. Once the guys went hard in the bunch today, Max and his group lost time pretty quickly and only had a couple of minutes going on to the only climb of the day, which was actually a suspension bridge. Whoever won the sprint at the top would be King of the Mountains of the Tour de France at the end of the stage.

Before the bridge, we swung into a crosswind and it got a bit hectic as everybody was afraid a split would go in the gusts and gaps would open. The final 50km were a bit hairy too, as the sprinters jockeyed for position, and Max's group was eventually caught with around 25km of the stage left.

It was pretty nervous in the bunch again today. I had Blel and Séb Minard with me for most of the day, keeping me out of the wind and out of trouble. In the final sprint, I just tried to stay far enough away from the front to avoid danger but near enough not to lose any time. I rounded the final corner to see Cofidis sprinter Sammy Dumoulin tumble head over heels to my right, but luckily nobody else fell and I lost no time, and actually moved up one place to fortieth overall, fifty-three seconds down on the yellow jersey.

Séb Hinault put in a great finishing sprint to take fourth on the stage behind Tyler Farrar, Romain Feillu and José Rojas Gil. The team is happy with that and Séb was delighted to get a top five in his native Brittany. A punchy little rider, Séb has spent a lot of time on the

Tour working for other sprinters, including yellow jersey Thor Hushovd when they were at Credit Agricole together. Today he got a clear run for himself and got a great result despite having three stitches in his calf from the day before.

On the team bus afterwards, we felt sorry for Max, having spent most of the day out front only to be caught in the end, but it didn't stop the guys from slagging him. 'Did you get the mountains jersey, Max?' '*Non*.' 'Did you get the sprints jersey?' '*Non*.' 'Did you get the most aggressive rider then?' '*Non*.' 'Ah well, at least you'll be able to buy us a drink tonight with the money they must have paid you to let them win the sprints in the break!' '*Non, non*, I just misjudged the sprint,' Max started. 'I didn't see the line . . .' But everyone burst out laughing and told him not to worry about it, that we were only joking. 'Bastards.'

I've roomed with Max for a lot of the early season and we get on really well. At twenty-four, he is riding his second Tour de France and said at the start of this year that he wanted to go in a few breakaways and try and win the most aggressive rider prize overall. He's probably going to pay for today's efforts on the next couple of stages but hopefully he will recover and be able to have another go later on.

Stage 4 – Tuesday 5 July: Lorient–Mûr de Bretagne, 172.5km

Yesterday, the team doctor showed me a little trick he said would help boost my recovery. On his instructions, I asked one of the mechanics, Yoan le

Foulgoc, who was already pretty overworked, to cut me a piece of wood two inches by one into six strips of equal length.

The idea is that you put the wood under the foot of your bed at night so that you sleep with your legs slightly elevated, which is supposed to improve your circulation and aid recovery. Putting a plank of wood underneath the bed didn't seem to be the most scientific recovery programme in the world, but I thought it was worth a try. My dad's former teammate, Scottish pro Robert Millar, used to carry two ashtrays in his bag in the eighties so he could put them under the foot of his bed after each stage, so maybe there is something in it.

While I was at the dinner table with the guys, Yoan handed me the six strips of wood, wrapped up in black masking tape. When the meal was over, though, I couldn't find them anywhere. Thinking that maybe the waiter took it and disposed of it, I asked all of the restaurant staff, but nobody seemed to have seen it.

This morning, Yoan wasn't too pleased when I told him I'd lost them and then asked him to cut me another six pieces. 'But that took me ages, Nico,' he said as he poured himself a coffee on the team bus. 'Where did you put them?'

'I left them on the table, Yo-yo. I've no idea where they went.'

As we were speaking, Max, who'd overheard the conversation, piped up. 'Oh, the thing with the black tape on it . . . the wood?'

'Yeah, did you see it?'

'Yeah ... sorry. I left mine in the last hotel and I didn't know whose they were so I just took them.'

Having been in the break all day on Monday, Max was probably suffering but he promised to give them to me after today's stage. Yoan just threw his eyes to the sky, because he knew he'd still have to cut new ones for Max.

Today is my girlfriend Chiara's birthday. I won't see her until the first rest day of the Tour next Monday, so on the way to the start in the team bus I rang my local florist and got them to deliver a bunch of flowers to her in work.

As the rain lashed down outside, there wasn't much talking on the bus on the short drive to the centre of Lorient. It's always hard to get motivated to ride in the rain and, unlike Sean Kelly and some of the tougher Irish riders, I'm always complaining about it. The guys on the team can't understand it. 'But you're Irish,' they always say. 'You should be used to the rain.' I always tell them that in Ireland we were smart enough to invent pubs so that we could stay out of the rain.

On a wet day, there isn't much chatter in the bunch. Everybody is concentrating more because the rain and grit, mixed with diesel and oil from the traffic, make the roads like a skating rink sometimes and nobody wants to come down in the last shower.

At the team meeting this morning we decided that we should try and have somebody in the early break today, and Blel went clear with four others after just 2km of racing. Although there was a pretty good chance it would all come back together before the short, sharp climb to the line atop the Mûr de Bretagne, anything could have happened in the wet and they could have stayed away.

Unfortunately, though, they were reeled in with around 7km remaining as the rest of us bumped and grinded our way into position for the finishing hill, which was really hard. An attack by Alberto Contador with 1.5km to go started the disintegration of the peloton, and when Rigoberto Urán of Sky and Jurgen van den Broeck of Omega Pharma Lotto countered, the rest of us were left gritting our teeth to hang on.

As ten guys dragged themselves clear with about 900m to go, I was struggling to hang on to the second thirty-strong group of Bradley Wiggins and some of the other favourites. I had been in front of this group but my legs were fading and guys were starting to zip past me. With 600m to go, I was dropped, but Séb Hinault caught me and rode full gas to the line. He was hoping I'd be able to sprint across the small gap to the back of Wiggo's group and not get the time split, but I had completely blown and was already on my limit.

We crossed the line just a couple of seconds behind them, but as the time is taken from the front of the group, I lost nineteen seconds on the stage instead of just five. I finished completely wrecked. I'm a bit disappointed but, on the other hand, that's what I was really expecting. I was expecting to lose fifteen or twenty seconds but hoping I wouldn't. I knew I didn't have the best legs today and that it was going to be a tough one. It wouldn't have taken much for me to hang on to the second group but, while the last 500m was a bit flatter, there was a lot of wind on the top of the climb and I just couldn't do it.

I'm missing the rhythm and the ability to go deep, which is a pity, but I'm still hoping that this week will bring me on a bit and I'll be able to climb next week. I've been positive about it since my crash at the Dauphiné three weeks ago, telling everyone my legs will come back, but what happens if they don't? I'm trying to keep my head focussed and keep my confidence up, telling myself, Okay, I've had a hard time but I was flying a month ago and hopefully my legs are going to come back after a few days. I'm usually pretty strong mentally, but I'm starting to worry a little bit now.

I think if I had a break for two or three days and was able to recover, I would have no problem. But this is the hardest race in the world, and if somebody's not at 100 per cent you can see it straight away. You don't get a break at the Tour, so I just have to bite the bullet and hope for the best. Unfortunately, there will be no aggressive riding for me this week. I'm just trying to survive and recover in time for the mountains. Now where's Max and those bits of wood?

Stage 5 – Wednesday 6 July: Carhaix–Cap Fréhel, 164.5km

It's been really crazy trying to get to and from hotels on this Tour. Every single night so far, we've had an hour and a half to two hours' drive to our hotel. After a stage, all you want to do is get to your room and lie on the bed and relax but it seems that everybody else is given priority over the riders in the traffic. We're not foot-ballers or movie stars, so we have no police escorts, but the Tour guests and VIPs always seem to be waved through traffic while we're stuck in the middle of the jam with the fans and spectators.

Today we had a later start than usual but, as we had a journey of two and a half hours to the start, we were still up at seven anyway. Then we had to sit on the team bus and watch the Tour publicity caravan go by for forty minutes before we were allowed to move. Mad.

It was another hectic day in the peloton, with plenty of crashes. Although, thankfully, I missed them all, some of them only by inches, I saw quite a few. British champion Bradley Wiggins crashed when some Lampre guy got his rain jacket caught in his back wheel and caused a spill. Wiggo fell just in front of me, but I got around him and then had teammates Sébastien Minard and Blel Kadri with me to take me back to the bunch.

We rode full gas to get back to the peloton, and just as we were about to make contact we came into a small town. There was a sharp left turn and as we rounded it Andreas Klöden and Alberto Contador were picking themselves up off the ground on the right-hand side of the road.

Riding past the mêlée, we made our way back through the bunch and into a position of safety near the front. Then, about 3km later, there was another big smash involving Robert Gesink of Rabobank and Janez Brajkoviç from Radioshack. I didn't find out until later that Brajkoviç, one of the pre-race favourites, was carted off to hospital in an ambulance and had to quit the Tour.

A few kilometres later I heard another smash over to my right. What happened next was unbelievable. One of the camera motorbikes drove up the outside of the bunch with somebody's bike stuck to the back of it. I just looked over and thought to myself, What the fuck is going on?

The guy on the motorbike had tried to pass the riders on the right but in his haste had hooked Nicki Sorenson's bike with his pannier. The Danish champion did a quick impression of a rodeo rider being dragged on his back by a bull before finally being tossed into the middle of a family picnic on the grass verge.

Although he was relatively unscathed, Sorenson had no bike, as it was still attached to the back of the motorbike. In the peloton, everybody was shouting at the guy on the motorbike who, unaware of the carnage behind, had continued driving along in the middle of the bunch with a smile on him like he was king of the road. Meanwhile, Sorenson's bike was scraping along behind him and was in danger of coming loose and bringing down more riders.

The driver eventually copped on and stopped, while Sorenson got a new bike from his Saxo Bank team car and made his way back to the peloton with a good dinner-table story about 9km later. It could have been a lot worse if Sorenson's feet hadn't clicked out of his pedals so quickly. He could have been dragged down the road too, and it showed once again how dangerous this sport can be.

There were too many crashes today. Although I rode pretty near the front for most of the day with both Sébastiens, Hinault and Minard, the rest of the team had troubles of their own. John Gadret broke the hub in his rear wheel. It happened to me last year and I thought I was just having a really bad day until I changed bikes and realized the wheel had been grinding all day. But it was the first time for John, so he didn't know what was going on. He thought the frame was broken and wanted to change his bike. Christophe was at the back, trying to help him, but everybody was panicking.

Up the front, we could hear them in our earpieces: 'Hang in there, there's a group just up the road,' then, 'Keep going, another group just ahead.' Apparently, the back of the bunch was mayhem, with loads of splits after the crashes. Christophe had a hard day at the back of the peloton. He was just getting back on after a crash when Péraud stopped for a pee. Then Gadret had his wheel problem so he went back for him. Séb stopped, so Christophe went back with Séb. Then Gadret had another problem so Christophe stopped with him again, and spent the whole day in the cars bringing guys back up. He was no good to me today, but at least he was doing his job.

For the first time on this Tour, I thought some of the guys didn't pull their weight today, and I had a bit of a row with Max after the stage. It's hard to say something to him because we're good friends and have known each other for years. So when I told him, 'Hey, Max, today you were useless,' it might not have been the best approach. I told him I never saw him all day. Max said that he'd been on the front but I told him that was no good if he was on the left and I was on the right. He justified himself by saying he was working for Péraud, but I still wasn't happy.

I don't like going off to the *directeur sportif* and saying, 'He's not doing this, or that.' I'm big enough and bold enough to be able to tell somebody myself if I think they're not doing their job properly, so I said it to Max when we were alone on the bus. He was a bit upset after it and, in fairness, I probably would be too. He didn't come up to me the day before and say, 'Hey, Roche, you were useless today. You're supposed to be going for a top ten in the Tour and you get dropped on the first climb.'

I only saw Blel a couple of times with bottles today, but I was hoping he'd stay a bit nearer the front too. When I look at it now, both Max and Blel were in long breakaways the two previous days, so they were probably tired. We haven't fallen out over it, but I just reminded them to be alert for the rest of the race. In fairness, the team has been great all week, so maybe I'm just being grumpy because I'm not going as well as I'd hoped.

In the early kilometres today I was asking Mark Cavendish how he felt about the new points system for the intermediate sprints. Cav said it was very hard on his HTC team, having to try to lead him out twice during each stage rather than just at the finish. Riding along, we had a bit of a chat about how there are no more pure flat sprinter's stages. At the Giro, there were maybe two of them, and if you look at the Vuelta, there might be one or two this year, but now at the Tour all the finishes have been mostly uphill. Cav was saying that they're making it really hard for guys like him to win stages any more, but I saw the video of the finish on the bus after the stage and, despite being out of contention with 200m to go, he still pulled it off. Fair play to him to be able to win today, because there was some kick-up to the finish.

I finished safely in the bunch and moved up to twenty-fourth overall but I was so out of breath after the stage that I rode past the bus and needed a few minutes to cool down. Today was a day where I was hoping I wouldn't crash or lose time, so I was happy enough with it.

I'm writing this on the bus after the stage. There is only one road out of the car park, and it's complete chaos again. The gendarmes are giving the VIPs priority over us. We're here forty-five minutes and we haven't budged an inch. The VIP cars are barging their way out on the footpaths while we have to sit here and wait. Nobody thinks about the riders after the race, that we need to shower, eat, get a massage and sleep. We're just the show, and when the show is over, we're nothing again.

Stage 6 – Thursday 7 July:
Dinan–Lisieux, 226.5km

Last year, we used ice baths on the Tour as a recovery tool after the stages. This year, thanks to a new sponsor, Tec4H, we have gone one step further and introduced cryotherapy. According to the team doctor, it's good for inflamed muscles and tendons and stimulates the production of hormones which help recovery.

Every morning and evening I strip down to my boxers, socks and a pair of gloves and step into the portable chamber for three minutes. It's just a bit tingly to begin with, but with the temperature inside set at −150°C the teeth soon start to chatter and the shivers kick in. By the time it's over, it's bloody freezing. Sean Kelly had a go in one of the chambers before the Tour, but he's so hard he didn't even bother with gloves! He was like John Spartan in *Demolition Man*.

Last night, French TV decided to follow me as I took my turn in the chamber. After about forty seconds, however, the fuse blew and I had to start all over again. Sometimes I can't handle the full three minutes, especially in the mornings, but I couldn't back out in front of the TV cameras, so I had to stand there rattling and smiling as they asked me questions about it. This morning I only did two minutes, as it's hard to get motivated for a cryotherapy session when it's already raining and freezing outside.

At 226km, today's stage is the longest of this year's Tour. I haven't ridden over 200km since the Dauphiné, so I was a bit apprehensive before the start, especially when we saw the miserable conditions we'd be riding in.

Although the guy who dragged Nicki Sorenson's bike through the bunch on his motorbike yesterday was thrown off the race last night, there were lots of crashes again today. We had torrential rain and thunderstorms in the last 50km, which made the peloton very nervous, and the roads were like glass in the final 20km.

With 4km to go, my teammate Séb Hinault almost crashed. Going around a roundabout, his rear wheel skidded and his bike jack-knifed. I was just a couple of places behind him and could only watch in amazement as his back wheel slid at a 90-degree angle up alongside his front wheel before Séb managed to flick his way out of the skid. I don't know how he stayed up.

There was a lot of pushing and shoving for position as we entered the penultimate climb with about 3km to go. I had no choice but to be up there today. The final climb was so steep that if you weren't well placed you could easily lose time if somebody in front of you let a wheel go. Having taken fourth and seventh on previous stages, Séb naturally wanted to go for the sprint, so Jean-Christophe gave me a hand to stay near the front.

On the climb, I was maybe riding in about twenty-fifth place. Contador tried to go clear at the bottom but went the long way around the roundabout, which killed his effort. Former French champion Thomas Voeckler put in a solid attack in the final kilometre and the pace just flew up. After he'd been caught, though, with around 500m to go, there was a little stall in the group and, as I had empty road in front of me, I quickly moved up the inside along the barriers. I shot up to about five from the front with last year's Tour runner-up Andy Schleck and Alexandre Vinokourov of Astana just in front of me.

As I still had space in front of me, there was no need to slow down, so I decided to have a go for the stage win. I had nothing to lose. The sprint hadn't really started, and I knew that even if I jumped clear and got caught, I wasn't going to lose any time. Having nipped in between Andy and the barriers, I was about to go past Vino when the road curved into a left-hand bend and he just shut the door between me and the barriers, which meant I had to brake hard in the wet.

Once you have to brake in a sprint, you can forget about it. I sat for maybe 200m with my front wheel sandwiched between Vino and another rider's back wheel. I had no room to get out and could only watch while everybody else, including stage winner Edvald Boasson Hagen, jumped on the right. That was enough to see me drift back to twenty-first place by the time the line approached.

Somebody like Cavendish would probably have made it his business to squeeze through the gap. Once those guys decide to go, they go. They can get through the eye of a needle. Me? If the gap isn't there, I don't go looking for it. I didn't want to risk ending up on the ground so I didn't chance it. Séb took fourteenth on the stage and is going really well, and it's a pity he has been left to do his own thing every day in the finale.

I moved up one place to twenty-third overall today, and am now a minute and twelve seconds behind Norwegian race leader Thor Hushovd. Jean-Christophe is next placed of my Ag2r La Mondiale team, three minutes and seven seconds down in fifty-second place.

I was feeling a bit better today. I'm happy that I was able to stay at the front on the last climb. There's a lot of pressure on me to be near the front every single day. If I'm seen near the back, even for five minutes, I'm told to get back up the front.

Christophe and Blel are a bit disappointed with their form so far, while John and Hubert are finding it really hard to recover after the Giro and are struggling at the back of the bunch most of the day. Max was a lot better, and Séb Minard is very strong and is always there to give myself and Jean-Christophe a hand to stay near the front.

Through crashes, hold-ups and sheer fatigue, the rest of the guys on the team have already lost too much time to be considered for the General Classification, so we don't have a back-up plan, unless Jean-Christophe pulls out an amazing ride next week. All we can do now is try to stay safe and wait for the mountains, where hopefully we can stay in contention for another couple of weeks.

Stage 7 – Friday 8 July:
Le Mans–Châteauroux, 218km

My dad has a saying: 'To finish first, first you have to finish.' Looking at the amount of casualties already on this Tour, he certainly has a point.

Although today wasn't as long as Thursday's stage, a block headwind in the first half of the day slowed the pace dramatically and meant I had done over five and a half hours by the time we reached the finish in Châteauroux.

There were more crashes again today. The first big one came with about 45km to go and saw Max having to get off his bike and run along the side of the peloton to get around the fallen riders and hop back on again. I was caught behind the crash but, luckily, I was one of the first to be able to stop and got around it. Séb Minard was with me and he brought me straight back into the bunch.

Shortly after that, we turned left into a narrow road through a forest and there was another big crash. Everybody wants to be near the front on these stages, as it's seen as the safest place in the bunch. All day long riders try to get through gaps in the middle or up the outside and, obviously, there isn't enough room for everyone. All it takes is a touch of wheels, a rub of an elbow and bang, there's a pile of bodies on the deck.

Today Bradley Wiggins came down in a massive pile-up. As others picked themselves off the ground around him, Wiggo could only sit there clutching his arm. A broken collarbone has robbed him of his dream of a podium spot at this Tour.

Wiggo is someone I admire in the peloton. We rode together at Cofidis in 2006 and we had good fun there. We always have a chat on the bike and I think we have a mutual respect for each other. When you ride so many races with the same guys over so many years, you often have disagreements with some of them over the smallest of incidents, but there's never been anything like that with Wiggo.

He has a mesmeric pedalling style. He's so smooth that he looks like he's part of the bike, and when he time-trials it's amazing to watch. Brad is one of those riders I was hoping would be up there fighting for the win at the end of this Tour. Even though, indirectly, I'm one of his rivals, I'm also one of his fans, and I was really looking forward to seeing how far he could go this year.

Winning the Critérium du Dauphiné before the Tour was an amazing ride for him. He was really lean, really flying and had the whole Sky team focussed around him. I think he would have had a great Tour. Instead, he's sitting in hospital tonight getting x-rayed.

I've been in that situation, at the Dauphiné, where I was in top form and a stupid crash threw everything off. It's really unfair. You can train and work hard, eat right, look after yourself as much as you like for months, maybe the whole year, but it all goes in the bin just because, at that second, somebody else was looking at a bird in the sky or something and not looking where they were going.

I hit a pothole in the Dauphiné and it was probably the only pothole on the road that day. It's the same with Brad, he probably just touched wheels today and it destroyed his race. That's one of the unfair things about cycling. You can put in so much work, so much preparation and then a small mistake by somebody else or something as simple as a badly timed puncture ruins your whole season.

After the crash there was chaos, with two big groups fighting in the crosswind to regain contact with the front of the peloton. I had Séb Minard, Jean-Christophe and Séb Hinault with me in the front group, although the constant switching and changing of teams on the front made it very hard to stay close to each other and get shelter.

Séb Minard has been fantastic for me all week. He keeps me out of the wind all day. I just sit on his wheel for the length of the stage as he wastes his energy so I can save mine. He's been amazing on this Tour. Today he was one of the last men to get back onto our group after the crash and he never recovered from the effort, so I just followed the changes of direction of the other guys at the front until the finish.

Because the three-quarter headwind was so fierce, there was no team strong enough to stay there for very long, and there was constant moving and jostling for the final 20km or so. In the last 600m, I protected Séb Hinault from the wind and got him up to Thor Hushovd's wheel for the sprint where he finished tenth, and I just rolled across the line for fifteenth. It was only a 200m effort, but it was a bit of excitement and I felt like I was doing something for the team.

I'm one of those guys in the bunch who always looks for calm. When I'm overtaking, I always try to be polite, but some guys are taking too many risks in this Tour and making other guys crash. Because it's the Tour, people want to win a stage or wear a jersey, so they dive into corners, elbow guys out of the way, lean on guys, push to open gaps that aren't there. A lot of it is totally unnecessary and causes crashes. Okay, the Tour can change your life, but you don't want it to end it.

After my opening-stage crash, I've ridden this first week with my wrist strapped and still have a cut on my shin. Because it's still open, I can't get a massage between the calf and the shinbone, so I now have a bit of contraction around the area.

Today I wore some Kinesio tape on my leg for the first time. Although it has been around for a few years now in soccer and other sports, I was a bit sceptical about it. It looks like nothing, but it's supposed to provide support for your muscle, keeping it in its usual position and stopping overcompensation, which can lead to more injury. You can get the tape in all kinds of colours, and it's nearly a fashion statement in some sports. I never felt the need to use it so far, but the team physio convinced me today, so I gave it a go. It looks ugly, because you have a big strip of tape down your leg, but it did the job. It really eased the pain around my shin and helped with the vibration. Hopefully, we won't run out of the black tape, though. I don't know if I could handle pink, which is the only other option.

Today, my legs were much better, and every day they seem to be improving, but I'm a bit anxious about tomorrow. Apparently, the third-category ascent of Super-Besse is not the hardest finish and there could be a big group of around thirty guys fighting it out for the stage, but I can't afford to do another Mûr de Bretagne and lose contact with that group in the final metres. I need to stick with those guys.

So far, most of this race has been ridden in the big chainring. The last time I used the little ring, apart from training, was about a month ago now. Even then I only got to do one mountain stage at the Dauphiné. Before that, it was the Tour of Romandie in Switzerland, which was about two months ago, so I'm a little apprehensive as to how it will go.

Like Wiggo, I've trained all year for this race. He had

his crash today, I had mine in the middle of the Dauphiné and another one last Saturday. But I can't do anything about that now. I can't train any more or give myself more time to recover. Either I have the legs or I don't. We'll soon find out.

Stage 8 – Saturday 9 July: Aigurande–Super-Besse Sancy, 189km

The plan today was to try to get Christophe, Maxime or Blel in the break. Hopefully, they could survive to the finish and have a chance of winning the stage.

Christophe is one of those riders who when he wants to get into the break, usually gets into it. Last year he made it into the race-winning move on stage fourteen and took his first ever Tour de France stage victory at Ax 3 Domaines. Today he instigated a nine-man move after just 8km and by the time they reached the biggest climb of the day, the second-category climb of the Col de la Croix Saint-Robert, with 30km to go, were still a couple of minutes clear.

In the peloton behind, there were a lot of attacks near the top and everybody was looking at each other to see who would react first. Eventually, Alexandre Vinokourov of Astana jumped clear, and that made the BMC team of second-placed Cadel Evans ride for the final kilometre of the climb.

Going through the village of Besse, 6km from the uphill finish, Christophe was still ahead with Spaniard Rui Costa, American Tejay van Garderen (HTC Highroad) and Frenchman Cyril Gautier (Europcar) while Vinokourov and Juan Antonio Flecha of

Team Sky had joined him in their lead group.

The climb to the finish was all action. I wasn't the most comfortable, but at least I hung on. I stayed in the top twenty for as long as I could. I was hoping to stay there without having to fight too much and rode the climb on the little chainring at the front. With about 600m to go, a lot of guys moved up to the big ring but I stayed with the inner ring. It was probably a mistake, though, as I was out of breath as I tried to spin my legs to keep up with the rest of the group. Usually, I do the opposite and have to grind a big gear while watching the others spin away from me. I finished nineteenth on the stage, three places behind the yellow jersey, to move up to fourteenth overall.

Cadel Evans had begun the day just a second behind race leader Thor Hushovd and, along with most of the peloton, probably expected he'd be in yellow at the finish, as the mountainous profile didn't exactly suit the big Norwegian sprinter. Today, though, Thor put in a great display to finish sixteenth and keep yellow.

I have a lot of respect for Thor. He's one of the guys in the peloton that I'm a fan of. I'd go so far as to say that he's one of my idols. It was an amazing ride today and he showed great character to hang in on the final climb and keep his yellow jersey.

Thor was my boss when we rode together at Credit Agricole a few years ago. I spent my first Giro in 2007 riding for him, helping to get him in position for the sprints, and I learned a lot from him. In the bunch, Thor is one of the good guys and is well respected. He's got a neat style of riding and moves through the peloton without aggression and is always very polite.

Christophe was only caught by the peloton with about 300m to go. Like me, Christophe likes to give out a bit. If you think I'm grumpy, you should see Christophe when he's tired. After today's stage he was sitting in the back of the bus with Jean-Christophe and Blel. Even though the rest of us were miles away from him and couldn't hear what they were talking about, we knew by the low tone of his mumblings that Christophe was giving out about something. But that's his character, and we love him for it.

Stage 9 – Sunday 10 July:
Issoire–Saint-Flour, 208km

My dad is working on this Tour in a public relations capacity for Skoda and, although he has never been too far away all week, we haven't really had time to catch up. The other day he brought a few VIP guests on to my Ag2r La Mondiale team bus to show them around, but we hadn't time to chat for long.

This morning he called over to my hotel at breakfast time, and myself and Chiara, who has arrived along with some of the guys' wives for Monday's rest day, had a quick coffee and a chat with him. We didn't talk shop, though, and just spent the time shooting the breeze.

With seven climbs on the agenda today, I wasn't too impressed to be greeted by yet more rain at the start. We've had six days out of eight in the wet now, and it takes the pleasure out of the race. You go through the whole early season in the cold rain, so when you arrive at the Tour in July you expect a little sunshine. Instead of 25 degrees and sunny, though, it's been 15 degrees and raining. I might as well be in Ireland.

A five-man breakaway group containing Spaniards Luis Léon Sánchez and Juan Antonio Flecha, French duo Sandy Casar and Thomas Voeckler and Dutchman Johnny Hoogerland were almost four minutes up the road by the time we reached the first second-category climb of the day, the Col du Pas de Peyrol. With Voeckler threatening to move into yellow if the break finished more than a minute and a half clear at the end of the stage, the climb was ridden at a pretty quick tempo with Hushovd's Garmin team setting the pace.

I was a bit further back than normal on the climb, for two reasons. The first one was that there was no real need to be in the top five or ten going across the summit and the second was that I was a bit tired. While the pace wasn't hard enough to be dropped, it was just enough to deter attacks on the way up.

The descent was very dicey, with patches of wet road on some of the corners. Going around one of the left-hand bends, there were bodies and bikes all over the place. As Andreas Klöden limped out of the ditch to my right, Belgian Jurgen van den Broeck, who was fifth last year, was lying prone in the middle of the road. I had to pull my foot out of the pedal and go up on the grass to get around him.

The bunch slowed down as I heard over the radio that Vinokourov had gone over the barriers into a forest. I later found out that he broke his pelvis and his femur. The crash also claimed Dave Zabriskie of Garmin, with a broken wrist, and lots of riders stopped to assist their various leaders while others looked down the slope into the woods in search of their teammates.

At the foot of the next climb, of the Col du Perthus, race leader Hushovd and points competition leader Philippe Gilbert had a chat at the front of the bunch, and the climb was ridden at a slower pace in order to allow the riders involved in the chaos behind to regain contact. This meant, however, that the breakaway's lead grew to seven minutes by the time we got to the top and Hushovd would lose the race lead by the end of the stage.

Up front, the break was nearly wiped out altogether when an official car tried to pass but hit Flecha, who brought down new King of the Mountains Hoogerland. I didn't find out what happened until afterwards but couldn't help notice the blood streaming down his leg as we caught him a few kilometres later. He had been catapulted on to a barbed-wire fence in the crash and would need thirty-three stitches after the stage.

With about 12km to go, and the gap still around four minutes, Hushovd's Garmin team gave up the chase and the other three stayed away to the finish, where Sanchez won the stage and Voeckler took yellow.

I had a really hard time at the bottom of the finishing climb today but then slowly found my rhythm. The group began to split in the final metres, and as I was right at the back I tried to move up the inside, but Levi Leipheimer didn't see me and closed the gap on the last bend. He took the short way around the corner and I had to go around him and lost the wheel in front of me. As on the stage to Mûr de Bretagne, I was only a couple of lengths behind the wheel in front, but with the time taken from the front of the group, I lost eight seconds, finishing seventeenth on the stage and moving up to thirteenth overall.

I'm disappointed to have thrown away another eight seconds as I definitely had the legs to stay with the front part. On the other hand, I'm happy that my condition is improving and, even though I crashed on stage one, I've got through the first week without too much trouble. I lost nineteen seconds the other day and eight seconds today. Those twenty-seven seconds won't mean much if I lose twenty minutes next week, but in the Vuelta last year there was only a minute between six of us in the last few days, so it could be important.

Rest Day – Monday 11 July: Le Lioran Cantal

Most of the guys had dinner with their families last night. Instead of sitting at one big table, we all sat with our respective wives, girlfriends and kids at separate tables dotted around the hotel dining room.

As Blel and Christophe were the only two whose families couldn't make it to the race until next weekend's second rest day, they gave everyone a good laugh by arriving into dinner holding hands and pretending they were a couple. They even got the waiter to sit them at a little candlelit table together.

It was nice to be able to take it easy and catch up with Chiara over dinner, and I even had a glass of wine with my meal. A group of Irish fans came to visit me in the hotel last night and took a few photos. I met them last year too and they drove about three and a half hours from Bergerac to get here. They even brought me a book for my birthday, which was really nice. I went to bed pretty late and caught the last forty minutes or so of *Batman Begins* on French TV before flaking out for the night.

I got up at about eight thirty this morning and went down for my three minutes of cryotherapy before breakfast. At around ten thirty, I headed out for a short training ride with the team while Chiara went grocery shopping with Sabino, one of the team masseurs, for stuff for our musettes at the feed zone on Tuesday.

Training today turned out to be shorter than I expected because of a pain in my knee. I'd first felt it at the start of Saturday's ninth stage to Super-Besse, but the adrenaline rush and the intensity of the racing put it out of my mind for most of the day. It feels like a muscle contraction around my knee, almost in the exact same place as the injury I picked up at training camp in December. With luck, it won't be as bad this time around but after twenty minutes of riding I turned around.

Usually, I do a couple of hours on the rest day, but today I didn't want to take the chance of aggravating the knee more and just rode back to the hotel at an easy pace. I'm trying not to think about it too much now. At this stage of the Tour, everybody is sore somewhere and, hopefully, it won't get any worse.

For lunch, myself and Chiara walked about a kilometre down the road to a different bar for something to eat. We're in the middle of nowhere, so there wasn't much choice of places to eat and I could have got the same ham and cheese omelette at the hotel, but it's nice to get out of the Tour bubble for a couple of hours and relax. In the three Tours I have ridden, this one has been by far the most dangerous, with crashes every day. As well as being physically tiring, it's mentally draining having to be alert every second of the stage, watching out for crashes, changes of direction in the peloton, changes of direction in the wind, so it's good to get away from the stress of the past nine days.

After lunch I had an hour's sleep and a massage before another three minutes' cryotherapy. I then spent the rest of the afternoon trying to be as quiet as possible and give myself every opportunity to recover. As I sat in the sun reading my book and drinking coffee with Chiara, it felt a little bit like being on holidays, except for the fact that there were bikes and paraphernalia everywhere and my knee was wrapped in eucalyptus and arnica.

I'm currently in thirteenth place overall, three minutes and forty-five seconds behind new race leader Thomas Voeckler and a minute and nineteen seconds behind third placed Cadel Evans. With two weeks to go, some of the guys in front of me will lose their place but some of the guys behind me, like Alberto Contador, will expect to move up, so it will be a constant battle to stay in contention. After the carnage of the first week, today was a very, very quiet day on the Tour. Hopefully, it will stay like that for a while.

Stage 10 – Tuesday 12 July:
Aurillac–Carmaux, 158km

The good news is that my knee was fine this morning when I woke up. I was a bit worried about it at the start, but it was fine all day and I had no problem. I think my easier than normal rest day paid dividends.

About half an hour before the start it began lashing hailstones. They were the size of golf balls. We all dived for the cover of the team bus and were busy changing our sunglasses to clear lenses and putting on rain jackets when Max said he still had to go and sign on.

Before, some of the big riders would just sit on their buses until the last minute if it was raining and ride off without the crowd having the opportunity to see them in the flesh signing on before the start. But there is a new rule on the Tour this year which means that if you fail to sign on by twenty minutes before the start, you are out of the race.

Because of the hailstones, the announcer had also taken shelter, and everything outside had gone very quiet, so we told Max that the sign on had closed. In blind panic at the thought of being thrown off the Tour, Max ran all the way to the sign on in the hailstones as we sat in the bus laughing our heads off.

On the bus, manager Vincent Lavenu decided it would be a good day for a breakaway to stay away and wanted somebody from our team in it. I wasn't totally convinced as I thought the stage would end in a bunch sprint. Even though there were four climbs along the way to Carmaux, they weren't hard enough to blow the race apart and I knew the sprinters would want to keep it together to give themselves every chance to go for another stage win.

What most people don't realize is that the start of each stage is really, really fast as riders try to establish breakaways early on. Today we covered 51.6km in the first hour of racing, which made it the fastest first hour so far on this Tour.

There was a massive crash after only 10km and, with bodies and bikes spread all over the road, it caused a huge split in the bunch. While groups of riders were trying to go clear up the front, I was caught in the second half of the bunch with Alberto Contador, the Schleck brothers and a lot of the GC riders. After a good 7 or 8km of hard chasing, mostly by Contador's Saxo Bank team and Alessandro Petacchi's Lampre squad, we regained contact with the back of the bunch. By then, a five-man group including my minder Séb Minard had gone clear and I stayed where I was for most of the stage.

As we were on good, wide, main roads today, and we were riding into a headwind for a lot of the stage, I could afford to stay in the final third of the bunch, as it was pretty easy to move up if need be. What kills you is going through narrow towns and villages where the bunch is strung out and everybody is in one long line. Then you have to stay near the front. On the better roads today I took it easy down the back and had Blel and Max with me for most of the day.

A lot of the guys were talking about crashes earlier today. I passed Johnny Hoogerland in the bunch at one point and had a few words. I think everybody has a bit of sympathy for him and Juan Antonio Flecha after being knocked down by the TV car while in the break on Sunday. I asked him how he was and, even though he had all those stitches in his buttocks and legs, he just shrugged and gave me a smile. He said before the start that he felt better on the bike than he did walking up the stairs but didn't know if he'd be able to finish the stage. I told him to hang in there and keep it going, which is all you can do.

It was the same with Flecha. He was probably fed up with guys asking him how he was by the time I got to him, but he just smiled and said thanks for the few words of encouragement.

In the last 30km, I moved up to the front alongside Jean-Christophe Péraud for the final climb, but I didn't think the last 20km would be so fast. The climb didn't look so hard on the profile and I thought the HTC team would string the peloton out on the ascent and keep it together on the run-in in the hope that their sprinter Mark Cavendish could get rid of some of his rivals on the hill and then take his third win of the Tour.

On the way up the climb, however, Frenchman Tony Gallopin of Cofidis attacked and when the green jersey of Belgian champion Philippe Gilbert followed him and formed a little group with yellow jersey Thomas Voeckler and Dries Devenyns of Quickstep it caused confusion in the bunch. I thought it was a good idea but there was too much of a headwind. Myself and Jean-Christophe agreed that if another group went, we had to go with them.

With some of the sprinters dropped on the hill, the top teams looked at each other to chase while they all waited for their teammates to get back to the front. Tony Martin of HTC jumped across the gap and sat on the back of the new break, hoping that teammate Cavendish would get across and knowing that if he didn't, he would have a free ride to the finish.

Cadel Evans tried to go on the top of the climb and I jumped with him, but the chase group came back to us and Sky got their guys going on the front and strung it out. It was one of those times that I wanted to go with the move but was probably better off not having gone, as we caught them in the final 5km.

I was looking forward to having a go in the sprint from the small twenty-five-man front group but then some of the guys that had been dropped on the climb made their way back on, so I asked Blel to bring me up near the front to keep out of danger. When he dropped me off, he kept going himself and went clear with Rob Ruijgh of Vaconsoleil with 4km to go, but they were soon brought back by the sprinters' teams.

The descent to the finish was very fast and I almost wiped the whole bunch out with 600m to go. I didn't know that the right-hand bend was so sharp and I tore into it on the inside behind Mark Renshaw. I swung so wide on the exit that I had to lock up the wheels and clipped a big green PMU hand that was being waved by one of the spectators inside the barrier.

It could have been worse, but after that I decided to stay where I was and forgot about sprinting. As German André Greipel took his first stage win, and Séb

Hinault took seventh, I crossed the line in nineteenth place to stay thirteenth overall.

I think I'm getting better and better each day now, definitely better than the first three days. I don't feel that I'm strong enough to be attacking and concentrating on the GC at the same time, but I'd like to be able to pull off some kind of a move this week. Today on the climb I was feeling okay, but going up 20km or 30km climbs later in the week will be a totally different effort, and hopefully I can go well.

After the stage we had another long transfer to our hotel. On the way, we were sitting in a long line of traffic waiting to get through a section of roadworks when the Radioshack team bus came up the outside of the line and tried to cut in in front of us. Our bus driver and their bus driver spent the next two minutes gesticulating and shouting abuse at each other through the window. I think this race must be rubbing off on them.

Stage 11 – Wednesday 13 July: Blaye-les-Mines–Lavaur, 167.5km

Today my Ag2r team is down to eight men. After a discussion with the *directeur sportifs* last night, John Gadret didn't take to the start this morning. John rode the three-week Giro d'Italia in May, winning a stage and finishing fourth overall. He hadn't originally planned to ride both the Giro and the Tour, as he would not have had enough time in between to recover, but the team persuaded him to try and make the most of his good form, and both he and Hubert Dupont, who finished fourteenth at the Giro, were added to the roster at the last minute.

John had been riding down the back of the peloton for most of the first week, but I thought he was just trying to stay out of trouble and waiting for his chance in the mountains. After a few days it became clear that he was struggling to recover from one of the hardest Giros in years, and I suppose the bad weather we've been having didn't exactly do his morale any good. Hubert, too, has been having a hard Tour so far but is starting to come around and hopefully will be there when we hit the big climbs on Thursday.

A six-man group went clear early on today and took four minutes on us straight away. As they were six very strong men up front, the bunch kept a really good tempo behind them for the whole stage. There was no taking it easy. In fact, we averaged 43kph for the stage which, with all the climbs and the wet roads, was pretty fast.

We had a bit of an incident at around 70km, just before the feed zone. I thought the hectic pace was slowing down, and myself and Péraud decided to stop for a much-needed wee.

Max and Hubert stopped with me and brought me back through the cars, but the pace was so fast that it took us a good while to get back into the bunch. But it could have been worse. Christophe stopped with Péraud, who took ages to answer his call of nature. As Christophe waited patiently to bring him back up, the peloton was getting further and further into the distance.

The two guys remounted and set off in pursuit, but

Péraud, who is lying twenty-seventh overall, started to panic and, instead of riding in Christophe's slipstream and saving his energy, took off on the next little hill and dropped Christophe. It took Christophe another 9km to get back and gave him another reason to be grumpy at the back of the bus today. Péraud didn't do it on purpose. He just panicked and wanted to get back into the bunch as quickly as possible, leaving the guy who was supposed to be helping him stranded behind on his own.

Six kilometres later, we went through the feed zone. Usually this kilometre-long stretch of road sees a bit of a slowdown in proceedings as we grab our musettes, or feed bags, from our team soigneurs at the side of the road. This year, though, we seem to be flying through them.

Since last year, the Tour is one of the few races to have introduced a kind of litter zone before and after the feed zone to try to make the race a bit more environmentally friendly. Everybody tries to throw their empty bottles, food wrappers and other rubbish to the side of the litter zone, where they will be collected and recycled by the race organization, but this year we've been going so fast through the feed zones that by the time you get your food into your pockets and everything sorted out and ready to throw away, we're gone past the litter zone.

Today, because the HTC team was keen to bring the gap down to the breakaways for Mark Cavendish, we whizzed through the feed zone and missed the litter zone. Most of the time, fans at the side of the road pick up the stuff as souvenirs, but I might do my little bit for the environment tomorrow and have a word with the organizers to see if they can move the litter zone back a kilometre or so to give us time to get our rubbish ready.

I ate two bananas, a cereal bar, two big jam biscuits and two slices of apple tart before the feed zone, so I wasn't that hungry for the energy gels and bars that we usually get in our musettes. I also drank four or five bottles. On a hot day, I could drink ten, or more.

I was feeling okay, but it was hard to judge how I was going as I just sat in the middle of the bunch for most of the day, before moving up towards the front near the end. With 15km to go, the break still had thirty-five seconds and, with the sprinters' teams driving along at the front, we were touching 80kph on a long flat section in the rain.

The weather on this Tour has been miserable and today was yet another wet stage. The last 10km were incredible. I couldn't see one metre in front of me. At the front there were fifteen or twenty guys preparing for the sprint but just behind that everybody was try-ing to keep their distance, praying that nobody touched a wheel in front of them. There was no way you could stop in that rain, and the slightest touch of brakes could have caused carnage.

I chose to keep my glasses on even though I couldn't see a thing through them. Imagine driving a car through a rainstorm with the windscreen fogging up and the wipers off and you get the picture, but I knew that if I took the glasses off my eyes would soon be stinging from the rooster tails of grit and dirt being thrown up by the wheels in front of me. A few times I gave them a wipe with my gloves, but it was a waste of time.

We caught the six escapees in dribs and drabs around the 5km mark. This can be dangerous, as they drift back down the outside of the peloton at a much slower pace. If you're not looking, you can slam into the back of them pretty easily. When it's raining like today, you sometimes don't see them until the last second. It's the same in the sprints. When the sprinters' lead-out men pull off the front in the final 300m or so, they often just stop pedalling, and if you're not alert or have your head down in full flight you can clip them too.

We had been told to watch out for a bend in the last kilometre over the team radio but it was more of a slight curve in the road, and nothing happened. I just rolled across the line in the middle of the bunch as Mark Cavendish repaid his team's efforts with his third stage win of this Tour.

Tomorrow is the first big mountain stage. I haven't ridden a 20km or 30km climb in a race in over a month and don't know how I will be going. It's the first stage where the big hitters will have to show their hand, and we will see who is going good and who is going bad. Hopefully I will be still in contention at the end of it.

Stage 12 – Thursday 14 July: Cugnaux–Luz-Ardiden, 211km

Sébastien Minard is very sick and has been vomiting since yesterday. He didn't come down for dinner last night and couldn't eat much at breakfast this morning.

In the first big test of this year's Tour, today we will tackle the first-category La Hourquette d'Ancizan after 141km, followed by the *hors catégorie* Col du Tourmalet at 175km with another *hors catégorie*, the tough finish to the ski station at Luz-Ardiden, after 211km. If the rest of us had a test, then Séb had a nightmare ahead of him and would end the stage over half an hour behind the stage winner.

On the Tourmalet, the Leopard Trek team of the Schleck brothers Andy and Frank set a really fast pace the whole way up. Some of the guys that were ahead of me on the GC started to get dropped. Over the team radio, I was being told that Peter Velits, who was seventh overall this morning, had two bike changes before the climb and didn't regain contact with the front of the peloton. Then Saxo Bank's Jacob Fuglslang (tenth) was also dropped, while Velits's HTC teammate Tony Martin (sixth) also lost contact with my group near the top. Andreas Klöden of Radioshack was at the back of the group suffering from a crash on the descent of the first climb.

I knew that if things stayed the way they were, I was on the way up the overall standings, but I also knew that the final climb to Luz-Ardiden was sure to see the likes of Alberto Contador and some of those behind me on GC put in an attack and possibly overtake me.

Going over the top of the Tourmalet, I was handed a newspaper by one of our Ag2r La Mondiale soigneurs who was waiting at the side of the road. We were now above the cloud line and I shoved the paper up the front of my jersey to stop my chest getting cold on the 95kph descent, which was almost as hard as the climb itself.

Yellow jersey Voeckler led us down out of the clouds before Christophe went clear on the twisting descent in a little group containing Olympic champion Sammy Sánchez and Belgian champion Philippe Gilbert. Christophe is a great descender and the idea was that if he could get a bit of a gap on the way down, he would be up the road on the last climb if I needed him.

The climb to the top of Luz-Ardiden is 15km long, but there is a 2km drag before you even reach the official slopes. Again, the Leopard Trek team set a fast tempo at the bottom and our group whittled down even more. With 10km to go, I sat in about tenth position in the group, and when there was a little lull in proceedings, as everyone looked to each other to set the pace, I moved up a few wheels behind Hubert.

Sylvester Szmyd is one of those guys that can ride really hard and steady for a long time on a mountain, and when he took over on the front of the group for his team leader Ivan Basso the pace increased ever so slightly. The extra kilometre or two an hour was enough to see more guys exit the group through the back door.

With 8km to go, I was starting to suffer too and was in danger of blowing my lights before we got near the finish. I didn't want to put myself in the red too early on the first big day, because there was a risk of losing five or six minutes, so I just let the wheel go, rode at my own pace and began to drift out the back.

Hubert came back with me and then Christophe, who had been caught, saw me and rode with me too. The two guys did an amazing job for me, leading me through the hordes of Bastille Day fans to the finish. I tried to give Hubert a hand at one point but he told me to just stay on his wheel. He set the perfect tempo and all I had to do was follow him, telling him to go slower or quicker according to how I felt. At one point I asked him to ride a bit quicker, but when he accelerated I realized I wasn't going as well as I thought and had to tell him to ease up again.

The last kilometre was really hard. We could see some of the guys – Rein Taaramäc of Cofidis and Kevin de Weert of Quickstep – getting dropped from the front group and I kept telling Hubert to go for it and try to catch them while he kept telling me to hang in behind him and encouraging me. We overtook them in the final kilometre, but when I tried to accelerate I really went into the hurt box. In the final sprint to the line, Hubert dropped me in the last few hundred metres and I finished seventeenth on the stage. I'd lost two minutes and two seconds to stage winner Sammy Sánchez.

I'd hoped to take back a bit of time on yellow jersey Voeckler today, but he put in a great display to finish ninth on the stage and put another minute into me, leaving me four minutes and fifty-seven seconds off the race lead. I don't know how long he can keep the yellow, but fair play to him for trying.

After the stage, I changed my vest and put on a thermal jacket for the 25km ride back down the mountain to the team bus. On the way up, I'd heard a familiar roar. It was my Uncle Peter cheering me on from behind the barriers. Although I didn't see him at the time, I knew he would be walking back down the climb and kept an eye out for him as we weaved our way down through the throng of spectators.

As the crowd were now using the road as a footpath, it took ages to get down the climb. Near the bottom, I spotted Peter, and myself and Hubert stopped for a two-minute chat before riding the rest of the way to the bus. I got back to the bus at six thirty and after a bit of food and a shower we had another 100km drive to the hotel. We'll be lucky to get dinner at ten.

With Hubert, myself and Jean-Christophe Péraud finishing in the top twenty-six today, our Ag2r La Mondiale squad was best team on the stage and moved up to third overall in the team classification. As we have a French sponsor, this classification is very important for the team and we have made good progress after a disastrous start saw the lot of us crash on the first day.

I'm happy to be tenth overall after the first big day in the mountains but a bit disappointed to have only finished seventeenth on the stage. I thought I would have been in the top ten or twelve, but I lost a bit of time to guys like Tom Danielson and Levi Leipheimer, who will be my direct rivals for a top-ten placing over-all. Realistically, though, with all the crashes and time off the bike I've had this year, today was my first big mountain stage since last year's Tour of Spain, almost a year ago, so I have to be pleased.

Stage 13 – Friday 15 July:
Pau–Lourdes, 152.5km

As we had won the team prize on Thursday's twelfth stage, this morning we had to go and collect it together on the podium before the start. But when it came to rounding everybody up, Jean-Christophe Péraud was nowhere to be seen.

After about ten minutes of repeatedly calling him over the team radio, Lavenu was going crazy, as there was still no sign of him.

The rest of us were getting a bit peeved too, when fifteen minutes later somebody found him in the Tour village having coffee with his wife. He was just about to get a good roasting from all of us when he explained that his kid had been playing spies with his race radio and he hadn't heard Lavenu calling him in his earpiece.

On the start line, I had a bit of a chat with French rider Amaël Moinard, one of my best friends in the peloton. When we trained together in the summer in Nice, it was often to the sound of crickets making noise in the grass in the background. Now, if we don't have time to chat during a race, myself, Amaël, and the other guys from the Côte d'Azur – Tristan Valentin from Cofidis, Geoffroy Lequatre from Radioshack and Maxime Monfort from Leopard Trek – often make the sound of the crickets when we zip past each other in the bunch. It's our little in-joke, a quick way of saying hello.

Although we've been staying in the same hotels for most of the Tour, today was the first time we've been able to have a chat since the Tour started. This year Amaël signed for the Swiss-based BMC team of Aussie

Cadel Evans, who is currently second overall. It's the first time he has ridden for a non-French team and he loves it.

As we rolled along, Amaël began to talk about my tactics in the mountains. He said that I'm often up the front on my own on the climbs and fighting out in the wind way too much; that I should have the guys around me more to shelter me. I agreed, but reminded him that we weren't Liquigas or one of these teams that has ten guys capable of riding in the wind, and the guys do the best job they can for me. I think sitting out in the wind, to the right of the group, has been a habit of mine for a long time, and maybe it's one I'll have to break myself.

The plan for my Ag2r La Mondiale team today was to get someone in the break, but that didn't happen. Christophe and Hubert got caught up in a crash going around a corner after just 30km and spent a lot of time sorting out their bikes and getting back on. After a lot of attacks and a really fast start, the break finally went clear around 60km into the stage. As we had nobody in it, the back-up plan of 'stick with Nico' was brought into action.

The break had four minutes at the foot of the Col d'Aubisque, and I was pretty convinced that was as much as they would be allowed. But, by the top, after 110km, they had eight minutes. Okay, we weren't flying up the climb, as there were still about sixty of us left in the bunch, but it was still hard, so I was pretty surprised by that news.

I rode the Aubisque in the top twenty-five or thirty

guys with my new mountain bodyguard, Hubert, alongside me. It was very warm on the way up and I think a lot of guys were trying to recover from a very hard previous stage. The sweat was rolling out of me in the clammy conditions and it was a bit of a relief to reach the mist and clouds of the summit.

I was pretty near the front on the descent, inside the top fifteen, but didn't notice Belgian champion Philippe Gilbert going clear on the way down. The first I heard of it was over the team radio in the last 20km or so. One or two of the Spanish Movistar team had by then moved up to give Voeckler's Europcar team a hand, and I heard my *directeur sportif* say, 'They are probably trying to bring back Gilbert so he won't gain any points on Rojas for the green jersey.' I thought, Shit! Gilbert is in the front again. He's going to jump over me into the top ten tonight.

I don't know whether Gilbert was riding for the GC or just going for the points towards the green jersey at the finish but the way he is riding now he seems capable of anything, and he's definitely going to be another direct rival for my top-ten place overall.

With Movistar and Leopard Trek joining in the chase with Europcar, the last 30km were really fast, but they left it way too late and stage winner Thor Hushovd finished over seven and a half minutes clear while Gilbert took back forty-nine seconds, enough to see him jump from twelfth to ninth place overall.

The last 5km were really narrow and twisty, so I just tried to stay near the front in case there was a split in the bunch. There was, but everybody else near me on

GC was in the front portion too, so none of them lost time.

I feel fairly wrecked after today, and tomorrow is extremely hard but hopefully I will be able to recover in time. Up until now, I've been rooming on my own, but as Séb Minard is sick he is quarantined in the single room tonight and I'm rooming with Max.

Max used to go to bed pretty late, but as we have roomed together a lot this year he has adapted to my earlier bedtime and we get on fine. When I say 'earlier', the transfers this year have meant that the days really drag on. Last night we didn't finish dinner until eleven, and it'll probably be the same tonight. It's hard to go to sleep with a bellyful of pasta so bedtimes have been that bit later.

The next two days are tough, especially the finish to Plateau de Beille tomorrow. I reckon Fränk Schleck, Contador or Evans are favourites now, but Basso is looking strong too. For me, the plan is simple: follow the others for as long as I can and just hang on.

Stage 14 – Saturday 16 July: Saint-Gaudens–Plateau de Beille, 168.5km

When I woke up this morning there was no inkling of the nightmare that lay ahead of me on today's stage. In fact, I was feeling good and, having started the day in eleventh place overall, I hoped to overtake at least one of my rivals and ride my way back into the top ten on the way up the tough summit finish at Plateau de Beille.

Things were going to plan as both Christophe and

my new roommate Max went clear in a twenty-four-man group early on in the stage. They would be waiting to give me a hand when we caught them later on. Although I didn't feel super, I got over the first thee climbs of the day, the second-category Col de Portet-d'Aspet, the first-category Col de la Core and second-category Col de Latrape reasonably well in the middle of the peloton. But the first signs of trouble were only a mountain away.

From the bottom of the first-category Col d'Agnes, the Leopard Trek team of the Schleck brothers hit the front of the peloton and set a blistering pace. At the bottom I was feeling okay but about halfway up the 10km ascent I knew I was in trouble. I just wasn't feeling right at all. I had begun drifting towards the back of the group and was fighting to stay on the wheels. Having struggled for almost 9km, I finally went out the back door just over a kilometre from the top.

Just before I got dropped, Max had been reeled in by our group, and he followed me out the back door and set about pacing me over the top. We rode hard together on the short descent but within minutes we hit the fifth climb of the day, the third-category Port de Lers.

As the road went skywards again, Max was having a hard time staying with me after his efforts in the early break. I was desperate to regain contact with the favourites so I dropped him on the way up the 4km climb in the hope that I could catch the group, but I was nowhere near them at the top.

As world time-trial champion Fabian Cancellara

and Stuart O'Grady, two of the best descenders in the world, led the peloton down the 20km descent that followed, I knew I'd have to take a few risks if I was to get back on.

On the way down, I was going much more quickly than the following cars. As I flew past each one at 90kph, they swerved out of my way, beeping their horns to warn the next one I was coming. I got a bit of a fright on one of the chicanes when I rounded a bend to see a bike lying in the middle of the road. With cars either side, there was nowhere for me to go but, luckily, its owner emerged from the ditch just in time to pull it out of the way. Just as I was about to make contact with the tail end of the group, about 2km from the valley floor, Max caught up with me. He must have dropped off the mountain like a stone.

The descent took a lot out of me and, with just 20km to go until the final 16km climb to Plateau de Beille, I needed to recover. Max went back to the team car and brought me some food. I crammed in three or four energy gels and gulped down a full bottle in the hope that I could recuperate in time to stay with the group on the ascent to the summit finish.

Leopard Trek continued driving at the front, leading us full pelt on to the bottom of the climb. I had Hubert and Max trying to keep me near the front, giving me a lot of moral support. Once we hit the right-hand bend at the bottom of the climb, I was determined to fight tooth and nail to hang in there. But after 2km I was out the back. I had nothing.

Hubert immediately waited for me. He kept upping

the tempo slightly, but I had nothing in my legs and he had to slow down again each time. The middle of the climb was agony for me. I was in the saddle, out of the saddle, back in the saddle, but it didn't matter. My legs were empty apart from the lactic acid that was steadily building up and burning with every pedal stroke. It was a proper nightmare. Team manager Julien Jourdie was in the car behind us and because of the noise of the crowd he had to keep beeping the horn to tell Hubert he was going too fast.

I am always wary of taking bottles from spectators on the climbs, as you never know what's in them, but I grabbed three or four bottles of Vittel from fans on the mountain. Although I spilled most of them over myself to try and keep cool, I also took a few gulps of water. It was a life-saver.

Although still suffering, towards the top I felt a little better, and we even passed a few riders. When I crossed the line, though, I was hugely disappointed to see we had lost almost seven minutes. Without speaking to anyone, I rode through the finish area, back to the car and got changed for the ride back down to the bus and the two and a half hour drive to our next hotel. Hubert followed me and gave me a hug. On the bus I told the guys I was sorry but they said, 'No worries, Nico. Just hang in there.'

As I was going backwards on the climb, Jean-Christophe was yo-yoing on and off the front group all the way to the summit. He did a great ride to finish ninth on the stage and move up to twelfth overall. He is our main man now and hopefully he can get into the top ten over the next week.

If I had an explanation for today, it would be too easy. I wasn't feeling the best in Luz-Ardiden on Thursday, but I had a decent climb. Today I was just terrible. I don't seem to be recovering as well as I usually do, even though the only time I use my legs off the bike is going down for breakfast or dinner. I suppose it would be too easy if you could have a season like mine and then ride well in the biggest race in the world. Five weeks ago, I couldn't walk for five days after a crash. Now, I was hoping the Tour would save my season, trying to convince myself this wouldn't happen, and praying that if I did have a bad day that it might come on one of the flatter days.

I haven't had many bad days in the last few years and this has been probably the worst. I dropped to eighteenth overall, eleven minutes behind yellow jersey Thomas Voeckler. It's going to be impossible to get that back and, unfortunately, my original goal of a top-ten finish in Paris is gone now.

There were a lot of Irish fans on the climbs today, and I feel sorry for them. I really wanted to achieve a good result and now I'm totally depressed. At the moment, I'm too pissed off to think about my options for the rest of this Tour. I just want to get to the hotel and forget about today.

Stage 15 – Sunday 17 July: Limoux–Montpellier, 192.5km

By now, the guys know to leave me alone after a bad day. I'm always grumpy. After a quieter than usual bus transfer to the hotel, they tried to cheer me up a bit in the hotel: 'Don't worry'; 'Keep it going'; 'The Tour is not over, we have a nice week left in the Alps'.

My dad was obviously disappointed too but also reminded me there was a week of racing left. Having lost so much time yesterday, I have no choice now but to try and get into a breakaway that stays clear. Whether I want to try and win a stage or just move back up on the GC, I know I have to do that, but today was not an option.

The last flat day of this year's Tour until we reach Paris, today was always going to be one for the sprinters, so I spent the stage recovering in the shelter of the bunch, which is a lot easier said than done. When the bunch is travelling at 50kph on the flat you don't exactly get much rest, but I stayed near the front and tried to surf the peloton to stay sheltered each time the wind changed direction. Blel was down the back and he said he spent most of the day sprinting out of corners to hold the wheel in front of him.

As Cav took his fourth stage win, I rolled across the line in twentieth place, knackered and looking forward to Monday's second rest day. I will take it very easy in the hope that I can recover and come back to some semblance of form for the rest of the race. I don't want to go through this Tour unnoticed and will revert to my pre-GC-contender days of aggressive, attacking riding if I can. I have to try something. I know next week's stages by heart, having ridden all of them at training camp with the team. Some of them might suit me, but then, I thought Plateau de Beille would suit me.

Chiara is coming to the race tonight and, although there is no room in our hotel for any of the wives or girlfriends, I'm looking forward to having dinner with her and spending some time with her tomorrow. My mum is bringing my brothers Florian and Alexis to see me too, which will be great. I haven't seen them since I spent a few days with them after the last stage of Paris–Nice in March, so I'm looking forward to that.

Rest Day – Monday 18 July: Département de la Drôme

Our post-stage hotel transfer took three and a half hours on the team bus yesterday. Every day on this Tour we seem to be stuck in an eternal traffic jam with all the other teams. Last night we didn't reach our hotel until nine thirty, which was actually early compared to some of the previous nights.

It's often a bit quicker to go in the team car, but it's more relaxing to take the bus. At least you can stretch your legs out and if you want a drink you can just grab one from the fridge.

At the back of the bus we have a seating section that can be turned into a sort of bed, and yesterday I used this space to pull on the inflatable compression boots on the drive to the hotel. I sat on the bed for forty minutes or so reading my book with the 'space boots' compressing my legs from my toes to my thighs, flushing out the toxins. It meant I didn't have to spend so long at massage before dinner, which was just as well, because I didn't get out of the dining room until past midnight.

Having taken a bit of a hammering last week, especially on the road to Plateau de Beille on Saturday, I was looking forward to taking things easy on today's second rest day. I got up around eight thirty and went out to the team's cryotherapy booth for my daily session, but the guys were obviously having a rest day too and weren't up, so I went for breakfast and didn't bother with it afterwards.

Chiara, along with some of the other wives and girlfriends, was staying in a hotel down the road, so I had a quick coffee with her before an hour and fifty minutes training spin with the team. Everyone apart from Blel was out. Blel had a very big debut season last year, and I think the fatigue of it all is beginning to set in now. He is riding his first Tour de France and was in a few moves in the first week but is struggling a bit now and getting tired. Even though we were riding at a pretty sedate pace, with a quick coffee stop at the halfway point, my legs felt terrible on the spin.

After a two-hour lunch on the terrace with Chiara, I spent a bit of time with my mum and Alexis and Florian, who came to visit me today and will watch the start of tomorrow's stage. They are big cycling fans and went on a tour of the team buses in the hotel car park, returning with big smiles and plenty of team caps and bottles as souvenirs.

Often when you take a day off work and stay in bed until midday, you feel worse than if you'd got up and went in early. I felt a bit like that today. The more I lay around resting, the more fatigued I felt. I was tired doing nothing.

Apart from the training spin and a team meeting later tonight, everybody keeps to themselves on a rest day. When you have the choice of spending the day with your girlfriend or the wife and kids who you haven't seen in a week or spending it sitting in a hotel lobby looking at the same old faces you've been staring at for the past two weeks there's only ever going to be one winner.

With one week to go in this Tour, I was expecting to be in or about the top ten. Instead I'm eighteenth overall. I'm very disappointed, but there is not much I can do about it. At the start of this Tour, Jean-Christophe Péraud was our back-up plan, the second leader of the team. After my demise on Plateau de Beille on Saturday, the roles have been reversed, but I am still a protected rider. Hubert will look after me in the mountains, while most of the other guys will look after Jean-Christophe.

Jean-Christophe is pretty happy with his twelfth place overall. He is a good time-triallist and hopefully he can hold on to it in the Alps and maybe even move up a place or two. We all have to keep an eye on him, though. Even though he is thirty-two, this is only his second year as a professional on the road, so he is still learning and makes simple mistakes sometimes like forgetting his race food, or dropping Christophe last week, but he is riding well and fair play to him for that.

There is a week of racing left but maybe only two stages where a breakaway could stay clear until the finish. Looking at the route, I think Tuesday's stage to

Gap is one of those. On a mostly uphill stage, with an intermediate sprint after 117km, Mark Cavendish's HTC team might be willing to let a big group go clear to take the green jersey points on offer, but there will be other squads wanting to use the second-category Col de Manse, 12km from the finish, as a launch pad for a late attack, so you could spend all day out front but be caught near the finish.

I can't say I'm going to be in the break tomorrow, because 150 other guys will be trying to do the same thing, but I want to give it a shot at some stage. I could just try and ride steady for the week and see if I could move up on the big mountain stages, but that would involve me having a couple of great days and some of the guys ahead of me having some really bad days.

For my Ag2r La Mondiale team, every move is going to be important from now until the finish in Paris, and we have to try to get riders into each breakaway if we want to win a stage. We will obviously look after Jean-Christophe for the GC and maybe I will be able to claw back some time.

The team classification is also very important for us. We are currently third overall, two and a half minutes behind leaders Leopard Trek. A good Tour for the team would include a stage win, a top ten for Jean-Christophe, a top fifteen for me and a top three in the team classification. With six days of racing left, anything is possible, but we have a lot of work to do.

Stage 16 – Tuesday 19 July:
Saint-Paul-Trois-Châteaux–Gap, 162.5km

Sitting in the Tour village with my brothers and my mum before the start, things didn't look good as we were lashed out of it by a thunderstorm. The sun came out before the start, though, and coaxed the peloton into a frantic first two hours of racing.

The team plan today was to have somebody – preferably me – in the break. Unfortunately, every other team had the same plan, which made the start of the stage unbelievably fast. We covered 53km in the first hour and 98km in the first two hours as dozens of groups of riders jumped clear only to be brought back again a couple of kilometres later.

I tried a fair few times. I'd jump clear in a group, ride hard for a few kilometres, get caught, drift back down the bunch to recover and then repeat the process. About halfway through the stage, on a little drag, the Canadian Ryder Hesjedal from the Garmin-Cervélo team rode off the front of the peloton, dragging a couple of riders with him. The bunch began to fragment on the climb and, as I was near the front, I went across with five or six others.

A handful more riders came across, including Christian Knees and Xabier Zandio from Sky, Rémy di Grégorio of Astana, a still-bandaged Johnny Hoogerland (Vaconsoleil), Jérôme Coppel (Saur Sojasun) and two Française des Jeux riders, Jeremy Roy and Arnold Jeannesson.

As we opened a little gap, di Grégorio, who rode with me as an amateur, came past urging me on.

'C'mon, Nico, let's go, let's go!' I told him it wasn't me he should be encouraging but the guys who were sitting at the back of the group. I was keen to keep things moving and did a few big turns on the front as others argued about who should be riding or not. Although we weren't fully cohesive, we were flying along and I hoped we would stay away as the rain started to lash down again.

It was Jeannesson's presence, however, that ultimately doomed the move. Although he was just one place ahead of me in seventeenth and no real threat in the overall standings, the young French rider lay fourth in the white jersey competition, just over two minutes down on Sky's Colombian rider Rigoberto Urán, and the rest of us knew that if he stayed in the move, we wouldn't be allowed to open a decent gap.

Christian Knees, the big German from Sky, was down the back and, after listening to his team manager in his earpiece, spoke to me in English. 'Nico, tell Jeannesson that if he stays here, they're going to keep chasing behind. He needs to sit up.'

Acting as mobile translator, I rode up to Jeannesson and told him that if he stayed in the break we were going nowhere and he might as well save his energy for another day and go back to the bunch. Jeannesson didn't want to sit up, because Coppel was sixth in contention for the white jersey and he was afraid Coppel would overtake him in the best young rider competition if the rest of us stayed clear.

I relayed the information to Knees. 'Okay, tell both of them to stop or we keep chasing.' At this point, we had ridden flat out for 17km or so, but the Sky-driven peloton was still breathing down our necks. Ultimately, neither Jeannesson nor Coppel would stop riding unless the other one did, which meant that neither of them stopped and we were caught with 65km to go, after a dogged 20km chase by Knees's teammates.

As the Sky train made contact with Jeannesson and the back of the break, some of the front portion kept going and were joined by some of the front of the peloton, including world champion Thor Hushovd and Sky's Edvald Boasson Hagen. Satisfied with catching Jeannesson and placing another man in the new move, Sky sat up and the break had 40 seconds in a flash. They were gone for the day, taking almost five minutes by the finish.

It was so frustrating. I probably missed the move by three metres. If I'd been near the front when they caught us I might have stayed away and moved back up the standings or been able to fight for a stage win. Instead, I was back in the bunch and could only watch in envy as they drifted out of sight and out of mind.

A couple of failed attempts by some of my teammates to get across the gap meant we now had nobody in the new move, so after a brief lull in proceedings for a natural break by most of the peloton, Lavenu gave the orders for the team to ride on the front of the peloton. I was hoping to be able to recover, but with two Garmin-Cervélo guys up there they would leapfrog us in the team standings and we needed to try to cut the gap down.

I don't know if it was a good idea, as we might lose more time tomorrow because of today's chase, but only a few guys can win the Tour. That's why they have other competitions within the race, and the team one is an important classification for us. The guys kept a pretty decent speed up at the front before Voeckler's Europcar team took over, and when we arrived at the bottom of the climb I was feeling okay. The first thing I did was hand my rain jacket to Séb Hinault in preparation for the change in pace, but when Contador attacked with 15km to go I had no answer.

I found myself on the front of a small chase group trying to close the gap. On my limit, I swung over in the hope that someone else would take up the chase, only to see supposed non-climber Mark Cavendish ride away from me. In fairness, Cav can climb when he wants to, but then, a kilometre from the top, a group including Italian sprinter Alessandro Petacchi caught me and I couldn't even stay with them. A real speed merchant on the flat, Petacchi can't climb out of bed, so I knew I was in trouble.

I spent the next 10km on my own. Knowing it was game over for any GC aspirations I had left, I took the descent relatively easy and then rode hard on the flat section to the finish.

I knew before the Tour that I might be in trouble physically after the interrupted season I've had but, mentally, I couldn't admit it, to myself or to anyone else. I had to convince myself that I was going to be strong, fight for the overall. The power of positive thinking. If I set my sights low, then I'd never achieve the highs. It's weird. I'm getting whipped but I don't feel that bad. Once I get on to the bus, have a bit of grub, I feel great again. I don't feel tired at night. I'm sleeping okay. I'm trying to rest. My legs just won't go any quicker.

I'm twenty-second overall now, but the GC is completely gone out of my head. I want to get a bit of pleasure out of this race now, which, to me, means getting up the road in a break. I'll need a bit of luck too. Much depends on who is in the move, the tactics of other teams. Even if I was twenty-five minutes down overall and up the road on Friday, if Contador decides he wants to win on Alpe d'Huez, he's not going to let anyone spoil that.

I'll try again tomorrow, the next day, and the next day. If I stay away to the finish, I'll be happy. If I get caught on the last climb, then tough, but I want to try and do something before the end of this Tour.

Stage 17 – Wednesday 20 July: Gap–Pinerolo, 179km

After the rain and bad weather of the second week, I now have a bout of sinusitis and a bit of a cold. My nose is blocked, my voice is going and I'm starting to cough. The team doctor put me on a course of antibiotics yesterday. They usually tire you out a bit more than usual, but I'm that tired now I don't think it will make any difference. I think it's better to take them than to get worse and be completely wrecked.

Today was another 'medium' mountain stage, as the experts like to say. We had five climbs on the road to

Gap, including the first-category ascent to the alpine village of Sestrières after 115km. With the longer, steeper climbs of Serre Chevalier and Alpe d'Huez to come on Thursday and Friday, today was another chance to try to get into the main break of the day.

After another very fast start and constant attempts to escape, a ten-man group went clear after just 10km. As they hovered forty seconds up the road, I tried to get across twice and got to within ten seconds of them with Thor Hushovd at the second attempt but never made it. We got stuck in the middle for a good while, and when the bunch caught us it took me ages to recover. I was last man in the peloton as I fought to catch my breath and find my legs again.

Those ten were caught after 40km as the constant attacking saw us cover 51.3km in the first hour again today. A kilometre later, Boasson Hagen attacked and dragged thirteen others clear. Within 20km they had two minutes, and that was it for the day and my Ag2r La Mondiale team had messed up again by not having anyone in the move.

I didn't feel right again until the feed zone at Briançon after 87km. As we hit the bottom of the 10km climb to Montgenèvre a few kilometres later, I didn't think I'd be able to fight with the top guys on the last climb, the second-category Côte de Pra Martino, so I decided to attack in the hope that I would build up a bit of a cushion before we reached it with 10km to go.

Not many people flinched when I made my move. The leading ten had seven minutes' advantage by then, so the peloton probably thought I was crazy. I was hoping a couple of guys would come with me and, while I knew we'd never make it across to the leaders, I thought we could still take four or five minutes on the rest of the race if we rode hard enough.

After I'd opened a gap, I looked back to see Johnny Hoogerland coming across to me. When I looked back a second time, I saw that Belgian Kevin de Weert was on his wheel. I couldn't have had two worse guys with me. De Weert began today's stage in eleventh place overall, just forty seconds ahead of my teammate Jean-Christophe Péraud, which meant that straight away Lavenu was in my earpiece telling me not to cooperate with the move, while Hoogerland had a teammate in the break and wouldn't ride either.

After a couple of minutes of trying to persuade us to help him, de Weert settled into a good steady pace and, slowly but surely, began to close the gap to the leaders on his own. I just sat on the wheel waiting for things to happen and hoping my boss would tell me to give him a hand at some stage.

I did think seriously about riding with the Belgian. Okay, Jean-Christophe would have lost a place overall, but I definitely think de Weert will pay for his efforts in the next two days. Even if he doesn't, I think Jean-Christophe, a former French national time-trial champion, will take five minutes out of him in the race against the clock on Saturday. But the team were not so convinced and wanted to play it safe, so I continued to ride shotgun. I didn't want to be the bastard sitting on the wheel all day, but I didn't want to mess up Péraud's chances either.

The way things turned out, if I had helped him we probably would have made contact with the lead group and been fighting for the stage win in Pinerolo. As we opened five minutes on the peloton and got to within two minutes of the break, de Weert kept plugging away on the first-category climb to Sestrières. I started riding with him a bit about 10km into the descent, with about 40km to go. When I did eventually give him a hand he wanted me to ride more because he could see we were closing the gap to the break. In the end, we got to within forty seconds of the leaders, so if I'd even just ridden on the whole descent from Sestrières we would probably have made contact.

In the last 20km, both lead groups were losing time to the peloton. On the hard bits, even if we did just 40kph, we knew the bunch would only be able to do maybe 43kph, but with the strong tailwind we could only do 53kph or 54kph on the flat whereas the bunch could hit 60/70kph and were taking back time hand over fist.

I knew the last climb and the descent. I stayed with de Weert as long as I could but, when I heard the bunch was within a minute and a half of us, I attacked him about a kilometre and a half from the top. I took about fifteen seconds on him straight away but as guys in the break and the bunch, including race leader Voeckler, were overshooting bends left, right and centre, I descended pretty carefully and de Weert and one of the crash victims caught me again with about 2km to go.

I took fourteenth on the stage and moved up a place to twenty-first overall, but it doesn't make any difference. Tomorrow is going to be a killer, and the next day is going to be even worse. I'll probably pay for today then, but we moved back up to third team overall, so my move today wasn't totally futile.

After the stage, myself and Péraud had a dope test and, as the rest of the guys had gone to the hotel when we came back, we had to get changed in the boot of the car. Jean-Christophe told me he was really worried about de Weert being up the road with me today, but I tried to put him at ease by telling him that the Belgian only gained twenty-six seconds and will definitely lose time on the Col du Galibier tomorrow.

At the team de-briefing, Lavenu said he was disappointed because we missed the last two big breakaways. He wanted to know why we didn't get in the move today. We told him the problem was that because we are going for the team prize, which adds the times of the first three riders of each team every day, Garmin, Leopard Trek and Europcar try to neutralize our moves at the start of the stage because they don't want to get overtaken in the classification, and vice versa. That's the problem with chasing different competitions. It works both ways. If another team goes, we have to ride on the front after them and it's pretty tiring.

There were loads of Irish fans on the race again today. They are so easy to spot with their massive tricolours, shamrock hats and inflatable hammers. I had a few texts from Irish Moto GP rider Eugene Laverty today. He's following the Tour in a camper van for a few days. He says he will be on the Galibier tomorrow with an Irish flag. Maybe we can switch bikes at the top!

Stage 18 – Thursday 21 July:
Pinerolo–Col du Galibier Serre Chevalier, 200.5km

As today's stage start was in Italy, just over an hour and a half from my base in Varese, Chiara drove over after work last night and we had dinner together. As our team hotel was fully booked and we are not allowed to change hotels by the Tour organization, she found a hotel 15km away, stayed the night, and also came to the start this morning, where we had a cup of coffee with my dad in the Tour village. Also there was one of the big bosses of Ag2r, Monsieur Breton, who is a big cycling fan and would be following the race in a guest car during the stage.

For the past couple of days, there has been a noise coming from my bike. Having searched everywhere for the root of it, last night the mechanics stripped it down and noticed a crack in the frame under the bottle cage. They worked late into the night to transfer my whole groupset, saddle, bars and wheels on to a new frame for this morning's start. As Trigger from *Only Fools and Horses* might say, 'It's the same bike, just a different frame.'

With three *hors catégorie* mountains en route to the highest ever Tour stage finish atop the 28km-long Col du Galibier, today was heralded as the toughest day on this Tour.

Once again, my Ag2r team wanted to have a man in the break, so I tried a couple of times before finally riding across to a big move after 35km. A few kilometres later, twenty of us began to pull away from the peloton. By the time we reached the bottom of the Col d'Agnel, we had nine minutes' lead on the peloton, but we all knew that it would be tough to survive to the finish. The fastest climbers were behind us and, after sheltering in the bunch all day, they could take minutes out of us on the final mountain.

The Leopard Trek team had two guys in the break, Maxime Monfort and Joost Posthuma. Both good climbers, they had been sent up the road so they could help their team leaders, Andy and Fränk Schleck, if they needed them later in the stage. The BMC team of Cadel Evans also had the same idea, with Brent Bookwalter and Marcus Burghardt in the group, as did Sammy Sánchez's Euskaltel squad, with Pablo Urtason and Rubén Pérez also there.

Although I was the highest placed rider on GC in the move, in twenty-first, I would need over fourteen minutes at the finish to be any threat to the yellow jersey, and was just hoping to get as much time as possible before the chase began.

As we climbed, we heard there were attacks coming from the bunch, and by the time we got to the top of the 20km-long Agnel our advantage had been cut to five minutes. Our numbers had been cut too. While the gradient and an acceleration by Posthuma in the final 3km accounted for five or six guys losing contact with my group, Mickaël Delage was almost run over by the Katusha team car before he got dropped. I heard a bang, turned around and saw the Frenchman's back wheel under the front tyre of the car. They had tipped it with the bonnet moments earlier.

On the way up the second climb, the Col d'Izoard, a

race vehicle drove by us with Monsieur Breton in it. He had his head stuck out the window. '*Allez*, Nico! *Allez!*' No pressure then!

Posthuma set an incredible tempo on the climb. His steady pace saw more guys get dropped, leaving about eight of us together before Maxim Iglinsky of Astana messed it up by attacking near the top.

Having noticed that some of the guys that were now dropped had descended better than me off the Agnel, I accelerated near the top of the Izoard to have a bit of sliding room on the way down and crested the summit in second place, with Monfort just behind me. I also knew that Andy Schleck had attacked the peloton at the bottom and was just two minutes behind us going over the top, with the peloton a further two minutes down.

I chased Iglinsky down the far side while Monfort sat up and waited for his team leader Schleck. About halfway down, these two caught me and flew past with Belgian Dries Devenyns of Quickstep and Russian Egor Silin of Katusha in tow. Now riding for the yellow jersey, the onus was on Schleck and Monfort to do all the work and apart from Devenyns, who gave them a hand now and then, the rest of us let them at it.

I was having a hard time just sitting in the wheels as Monfort drilled it in the valley, and I knew the final climb would be savage. Silin and Devenyns were dropped on the lower slopes. Shortly after, Monfort expended his last joules of energy for his leader and left Schleck alone on the front as myself and Iglinsky hung on for dear life.

We had three minutes and ten seconds with 25km to

471

go as Schleck drove on relentlessly ahead of me. After 10km of the lanky Luxembourger riding on his own, we had actually gained another minute over the disorganized yellow jersey group, who were all still waiting on each other to attack.

It was really windy on the climb, and I couldn't help but be impressed with Schleck as he made me grimace in his wake. I didn't care what was happening behind. I just wanted to hang on until as near the summit finish as possible. After 15km of slow, grinding torture, with 10km to go, I couldn't handle the searing pain in my legs any more and had to let go.

At that stage, I was third rider on the road but knew I couldn't hold off the chase group containing Contador, Evans, Fränk Schleck and Voeckler for much longer. I kept a steady pace, just trying to get as far up the mountain as I could before they caught me.

When Evans led the yellow jersey group up to me with 3km to go, I tried to hold on to them but could only last about 300m at their pace. Then another group led by American Christian Vande Velde caught me and I tried to stay with them, but couldn't manage more than 200m. With 2km to go, Hubert caught me and encouraged me to stay with him, but I lost forty seconds to him in 2,000m.

I couldn't do much more today. I completely cracked in the last 3km. When I crossed the line, I was in bits. I came to a complete standstill and prayed that someone would catch me before I fell off the bike.

I spent just short of six hours and thirteen minutes in the saddle today, five minutes more than stage winner Andy Schleck. On a day like this, though, it doesn't matter if you are in the break or in the last group on the road, there is no hiding place. You are going to suffer.

Green jersey Mark Cavendish is not built for days like this, and he finished in a large group of eighty-five riders, over thirty-five minutes down. Outside the time limit set for the stage, his group should have been sent home from this Tour, but because the stage was so hard the guys all stuck together and the group was so big the organizers couldn't throw them all out. If they did, half the peloton would be gone home. Cav was docked twenty points in the points competition, though, and will have to fight to keep his green jersey again tomorrow.

I'm trying not to think about Alpe d'Huez tomorrow. I think my legs are going to burn in the morning.

Stage 19 – Friday 22 July:
Modane Valfréjus–Alpe d'Huez, 109.5km

While waiting on the start line this morning, we were warned by team manager Vincent Lavenu that he had seen guys warming up before the start, which is always a sign to expect fireworks early.

Although we had the climbs of the Col du Télégraphe and the Col du Galibier before the summit finish at Alpe d'Huez, today's stage was pretty short at 109km and as it was the last chance for anybody to change the GC before the time trial it looked to be made for guys to go from the gun. After three days of attacking and yesterday's epic in the breakaway group,

I was expecting my legs to be sore this morning and was hoping for an easy first few kilometres. What I wasn't expecting, however, was Alberto Contador to go ballistic at the bottom of the Télégraphe and rip the race to pieces.

There had already been lots of attacks before the climb, which came after just 14km. We had Christophe in the early break and, although it was pulling clear, there was no sign of the peloton easing up at all.

When Contador jumped up the road within a kilometre and a half of climbing, all hell broke loose. Yellow jersey Thomas Voeckler jumped after him and the pace increased again.

Despite three days of antibiotics, my sinus problem hasn't got any better and I think I'm getting a chest infection. When Contador attacked for a second time, the pace increased again and I suddenly took a fit of coughing and spluttering that saw me drift quickly down the peloton and out the back.

Riders started to pass me left, right and centre and I began to get worried when the first car behind the bunch passed me shortly afterwards. I was hoping there was a big group behind me but I heard the commissaire talk into the race radio. 'Contador is pulling clear, he has twenty seconds. At the back of the peloton, Nicolas Roche is the sixth rider to be dropped.'

I thought to myself, Uh oh, this is going to be a very long day. I knew that if I didn't get into the gruppetto, the big group of non-climbers that had formed somewhere up the road ahead of me, I was in big trouble.

I climbed the whole Télégraphe on my own, still

trying to catch my breath. Near the top, the second team car pulled up alongside me. Julien Jourdie leaned out. 'Nico, what's done is done. You need to get to the gruppetto and finish.' With that, Julien drove off to look after the guys still in the action.

Although I was still riding hard, the downhill gave me some time to recover. On the way down I heard in my earpiece that the gruppetto was already three minutes behind the Contador group. I rode flat out to try and get back to them on the next climb, the 17km-long Galibier. Just a day after riding up it in the breakaway group, here I was riding up the opposite side, trying to regain contact with the last group on the road.

Going through the town at the bottom, I looked out for the following cars of the gruppetto but couldn't see them anywhere. Once we started to climb, however, I could make them out in the distance, and that spurred me on. Although I was flat out, I was flat out for a guy who was wrecked, so it took me until 3km from the summit to catch the first riders. I rode straight past Tyler Farrar, Tony Martin and Mark Renshaw because I knew they were kamikaze descenders and would catch and probably drop me on the far side of the mountain.

A kilometre and a half further up, I made contact with the back of the gruppetto. In Italian, 'gruppetto' means 'little group', but there were seventy-five riders in it, including green jersey Mark Cavendish, world champion Thor Hushovd and world time-trial champ Fabian Cancellara. Mikaël Buffaz of Cofidis did a double take when he saw me move up the group. 'What are you doing here?' he asked. 'Bad day,' I replied. He must have thought I took it the wrong way, because he came back to me a few minutes later and said, 'I wasn't trying to be cheeky, I was just surprised to see you here.' I said, 'I know, I'm just having a bad day after a hard day yesterday.'

Before the start, I had cut the top off one of my drinking bottles and stuffed a gilet into it. As I crossed the summit at the back of the group, I pulled out the sleeveless jacket, put it on and began the descent, which was ridden at a ferocious pace.

Everybody was worried about making it inside the time limit imposed by the race organizers every day. The time limit is based on a percentage of the winner's time, and if you don't finish inside the limit you're out of the Tour. The percentage changes every day, according to the perceived difficulty of the stage, so the managers work out how fast the winner will ride and add on the percentage, but it's a guessing game at best.

Today we figured we had maybe twenty-seven minutes but were already twelve minutes down going over the top of the Galibier and could easily lose another fifteen on Alpe d'Huez.

The crowds on the Alpe were incredible. We had two motorbikes acting as Moses, parting the seas of over-exuberant fans as we rounded each of the twenty-one hairpins on the way to the summit.

Although everybody wanted to get to the top as quickly as possible and get the stage over with, nobody wanted to be responsible for dropping anybody else. During an earlier bad patch, Garmin-Cervélo's David

Millar, who had been dropped before me on the Télégraphe and finished dead last at the back of the gruppetto today, told HTC rider Bernie Eisel to leave him on the road. Eisel turned to Millar and said, 'Davey, we go home together or we go to Paris together.' Anybody that went too fast out of a hairpin or on a steeper section got a bollocking from Cancellara or one of the other senior guys.

The pace was easy enough on the climb and I was pretty comfortable, but it's no great honour to be comfortable in the gruppetto. I lost more time today than I lost in my last two Tours put together, finishing twenty-five minutes and twenty-seven seconds behind stage winner Pierre Rolland.

At the summit, we were eighteen seconds outside the time limit, but we knew we had strength in numbers and they wouldn't send seventy-five of us home. The way I'm feeling at the minute, I don't know if that's a good thing or a bad thing.

Stage 20 – Saturday 23 July: Individual Time Trial, Grenoble, 42.5km

While I conked out as soon as my head hit the pillow last night, my room mate Max had trouble sleeping. It wasn't the climb to Alpe d'Huez or the thoughts of today's time trial that kept him awake, though. It was my coughing.

After a fitful night's sleep, another bout of coughing woke us both at 6 a.m. and as we couldn't go back to sleep we groggily went down for breakfast.

We had a three-hour drive to the time-trial course,

where I spent an hour on the bike to loosen up. I didn't ride the course, as I had raced the exact same route in the Critérium Dauphiné a couple of weeks before the Tour. Instead, I found a quiet road and just warmed up there instead of riding the rollers.

The time trial starts are in order of the General Classification, and while we sat on the bus for two hours waiting for our turn in the start house Jean-Christophe, Hubert and I were getting hungry, so I decided to cook a bit of pasta for us. As we had to cook it on the camping stove it took twenty minutes instead of ten, and in the end Hubert decided he didn't want any. We didn't have olive oil or anything on the bus, so we just ate it plain.

I did half an hour on the rollers to open up the lungs and get the legs ready before riding into the start house and beginning my time trial. I'd like to say that with nothing to be gained by riding flat out I took my time on the stage, but that would be a lie. I rode it pretty hard, hoping to stay within four minutes of the winner, but I wasn't expecting to lose six and a half.

I knew within two minutes of rolling down the ramp that I had nothing in my legs. On the first straight in the Dauphiné I was doing 55kph; today I was lucky to reach 48kph, so I knew I wasn't going to do anything. Sometimes you have a bad patch and a good patch but today all I had was one long bad patch. I'm at the stage now that I can't even go full gas because I just don't have the power any more. I was just empty and the whole thing was a struggle.

This morning I was actually pretty motivated about

this time trial, so I was a bit disappointed with my ride. But, if I'm honest, I was pretty empty on the home trainer before the start.

After hanging around the Tour village and the start area for most of the day, everybody was hungry for something different after the stage. I asked the team doctor if it would be okay to get one of the soigneurs to buy a couple of pizzas so that we could have a slice or two on the bus together after the stage. He agreed, so I asked two of the soigneurs to go get them for us. They were too scared they'd get in trouble and refused until the doctor came over and told them it was okay.

We bought one ham pizza and one tuna, because Blel is Muslim and can't eat ham. We had a couple of slices each on the bus and everybody was happy. When we got to the hotel, Jean-Christophe, who did a great time trial to finish sixth on the stage and keep his tenth place overall, bought a round of beer for everyone, and we had a ten-minute chat before dinner at eight.

Stage 21 – Sunday 24 July: Créteil–Paris, 95km

After breakfast we left the hotel this morning for a forty-minute bus transfer to the airport. Blel did his best to entertain us and the Euskaltel team with a game of Name That Tune using the bus stereo, but after about ten minutes everybody got fed up and did their own thing.

We hopped on a plane with the rest of the riders for a 600km flight to Paris-Orly. I spent the forty-five-minute trip down the back reading my book alongside Max while the top guys were giving interviews and having their photos taken in business class. On exiting the plane, we were all given a lunch box containing a banana, two sandwiches, an apple and a bottle of water before the short trip to the start on the team bus.

The stage itself took a while to get going, with the usual photo calls and champagne drinking in the early kilometres, but it really took off when we hit the Champs-Elysées. As usual, everybody had something to race for. Mark Cavendish needed a few more points to be sure of his green jersey while for the rest of the peloton this was a last chance for a stage win. Inevitably, though, Cav took another sprint victory, while for me it was the end of a long hard Tour and I just rode across the line in the middle of the bunch to finish twenty-sixth overall.

After 3,500km of racing, I've worn out three pairs of shorts, three long jerseys, two sleeveless gilets and seven pairs of socks. After the stage we all hopped on to the team bus for a quick shower before donning a brand new set of kit that we were given yesterday for the team's parade along the Champs-Elysées after the stage.

After our little lap of honour, my French teammates returned to the bus, put on their best suits and headed for the Elysées Palace and a meeting with President Sarkozy, while I got a lift with the mechanics and got suited and booted in the hotel for the team's big post-Tour dinner.

We always go to one of the best restaurants in Paris and can bring our wives and girlfriends. It's the sponsor's way of showing their appreciation for our efforts over the past three weeks. We always see each other in tracksuits, so it's a bit of a novelty for us to be sitting around the table in suits. The dinner usually goes on until midnight, and I'll probably have a few glasses of wine tonight.

After that, we'll head to a nightclub for the only real team night out of the year. Some guys stay out all night, some guys come home at three in the morning. I'm not big into nightclubs, but I'll probably just go for an hour to be sociable.

My Ag2r La Mondiale team came into this Tour with the aim of taking a top ten overall, finishing in the top three of the team classification and winning a stage. We have attained all of those except the stage win. We finished third in the team classification, only beaten by sixteen seconds for second place. Jean-Christophe Péraud was tenth overall. I had hoped to be in that position but, realistically, looking at my preparation and disruptions before the Tour, I was being too optimistic.

The way this Tour panned out, if I had been in the same form as this time last year, I could have been really up there in contention, but I can't let myself think like that. I have enough trouble thinking about stuff like if Hubert hadn't waited for me on Plateau de Beille we would have got second team by three minutes or so. But the guys have told me to forget about it, and reminded me that I took some time back when I went in the break a couple of days.

On this Tour, the only good thing I had was my morale. I was down physically but hoping I was going to progress as the race went on. The French call a bad day on the Tour *un jour sans,* a day without. I think, this year, I had *un Tour sans.* If cycling is poker on wheels, then I started off with a bad hand. I got away with it for nearly two weeks and then the Tour called my bluff on Plateau de Beille.

After that, I put everything into the two Alpine stages to Pinerolo and Serre Chevalier. I gave it absolutely everything on those two days, but even that was not enough.

Now, I'll take Monday and Tuesday off, but that's it. On Wednesday I'm riding a critérium in Oslo, followed by another one in Luxembourg on Thursday and the San Sebastian classic in Spain at the weekend. It sounds a bit far to go to Norway for an hour and a half of racing, but it's either that or drive eight hours to another race in the south of France, and it's easier nowadays to get to Norway from Paris than it is to get from Dublin to Cork.

Thanks to all the Irish fans who came over and shouted, cheered, waved flags or just said hello. It means a lot to me to have that kind of support. My next big stage race is the three-week Tour of Spain at the end of August. Until then I'll continue to train right, eat properly and try and stay upright in the next few races. Hopefully, my form will come back. Things are going in the right direction. It's just a matter of giving my body a chance to recover now.

19

The Cat's in the Cradle

Living the life of a professional cyclist is not easy. Apart from the battering your body takes every day on the bike, there are other things to take into consideration, like the constant travelling and being away from home. Last year, I raced around a hundred days. With training camps, meetings, functions and travel to races added in, I spent maybe two hundred and fifty days away from home, sleeping in a different bed every night. But I'm used to it now. It's habit. When I do go home, it's great for a few days, but then I can't wait to go away racing again.

Cycling is a twenty-four-hour job. When you're not racing or training, there is a constant battle to stay rested, fit, focussed and healthy. After the Tour last year, I celebrated with a pizza. Normal people eat a pizza every week, but I can't just go and have a pizza, an ice cream or a bag of chips. I can't go down the pub at the weekend and drink a couple of pints. Simple things. During stage races, I eat plain pasta, every day for three weeks. It takes a certain kind of mentality to be able to do stuff like that.

On my days off, I don't go walking around shopping

centres with my girlfriend, like most normal couples. As a cyclist, I have to stay off my legs, rest them, always thinking of the next race. Maybe in ten years or so I'll be fed up travelling and racing, but I think I will always have to keep busy. I will have to do some kind of job or something.

People say that the top cyclists in the world are often farmers' sons or, in the old days, peasants' sons, guys who were already used to a tough life, used to grafting hard for whatever they could earn, guys who don't mind getting their hands dirty, don't complain about the rain or the wind or the snow. Like a lot of top boxers, they come from poorer areas and have little or no other prospects of escaping reality and making a life for themselves.

Me, I come from a good background. I didn't have to ride my bike to make money. I could have gone to college and got a degree like my sister or I could have got a job somewhere else. But it's what I wanted to do. Maybe my dad had a lot to do with it. I wanted to be like him. Maybe I wanted to prove I could do it myself. Maybe I still do.

I've asked him to say some words here in this final chapter to give his perspective on this world of professional cycling we have inhabited in different generations.

Stephen Roche: I think Nicolas wants to make us all happy, but I think he is a bit confused himself. He knows I'm happy. I've told him loads of times. I am proud of everything Nicolas has done. All I want is for him to be happy.

When I visit my parents and my brothers and sister, I look at Alexis and Florian and see the bond they have and I'm jealous. They are really close as brothers. They're like twins, even though Alexis is two years older. You could put the two of them in an empty room for a day and they would still find something to do together. They are my biggest fans when I'm racing, and I love spending time with them when I get back to Antibes, but I still feel like I'm missing out a little on what they have together.

I'm at the stage now where the next two or three years are the most important of my career, and I want to give myself every chance I can to make the most of it. If that means moving to Italy or Switzerland to train and race, then it has to be done. As for a family of my own, I haven't really thought about it yet. I think it would be too easy for me to be away from home while my wife or partner brought up a baby. A lot of cycling marriages and sporting relationships in general end in divorce once the athlete has retired. Suddenly they have all this time on their hands and don't know what to do with it. Often their family has got used to them being away and have grown up and gone their own ways by the time retirement kicks in.

Some of the guys in the peloton have kids, and it's nice when they come to visit them during races. They have photos of their wife and kids in their suitcases. It's a lovely thing to have, and it's extra motivation as well. I miss out on stuff like that. But being married to a cyclist is hard, with all the travelling involved and days away, and both parties have to accept those terms for as long as your career lasts.

I always said I wanted to have kids while I was young. For now, it might seem selfish, but the extra stress and extra tiredness that children bring into the equation would affect my racing and training. Getting up for night feeds and nappies and worrying about them would take a lot out of me. I really want to give it everything for these next three years and then maybe think about it. But my dad was world champion and he had two kids, so it didn't stop him.

Stephen Roche: When I was a cyclist, I missed that side of it. I missed out on the family side of things because I was being egotistical, or egocentric, and focussed on what I was doing, which was racing my bike. But are the two really compatible? I had a certain amount of time to make as much money as I could so that, hopefully, we'd be able to have a good life after my career was over. Myself and Lydia were a team. When I came home, she did everything for me. I'd come home from training and she'd have my dinner ready for me. She was every bit as important in my career as my training or the food I ate or whatever. But your career is only for a short period. It could be even shorter if things are not good, but the longer and the better career you have then the better life you can have afterwards. What people don't realize is that life only starts when your career is finished, and you have to get it right.

Some people need their family around or their kids around all the time. I'm a family man, but I also like being alone. In Varese, I train sometimes with Australian professionals Simon Clarke and Leigh Howard when they are around, but mostly I train alone. I spend most of my day alone as well. That's just the way I am. I relax better on my own. While I'm still very attached to my family, I live in Italy while they live in Antibes, and I probably don't see them as often as I should.

When I was younger I would arrive to the start of a bike

race, sometimes having won a big race the week before, and the announcer would simply announce me as 'Nicolas Roche – the son of 1987 Tour de France winner Stephen Roche'. I used to get frustrated. I used to think to myself, What about the race I won last week? Why didn't he say 'Nicolas Roche – winner of the Junior Tour', or 'Nicolas Roche – winner of stage four of the Tour de l'Avenir'? I'm often asked what it would take to stop being called the son of Stephen Roche. Would I have to win a stage of the Tour de France? Would I have to win the Tour de France outright, or the world championship? But people have to understand that, whatever I do, I will always be the son of Stephen Roche.

Stephen Roche: I'm in an awkward position really. It's difficult to be in the same sport. If Nicolas was playing basketball or something, it would be brilliant. I'd be just like any other father, giving advice but without really knowing what I was talking about. But the problem is that I did the same sport.

I was a Tour rider and was strong in some classics. Nicolas has loads of class and could be a very similar type of rider to me. He has the facility to be really supple and have great power at the same time. I was always supple, but I never had the power he has. He has incredible power. He has the ability to pedal and push a big gear, so I always say he will definitely climb some day because, on the climbs, you need to be able to do both. It's the same in a time trial, so it has to be his brain or his preparation that's letting him down at the minute. Some day, if he gets it all right, he will be able to climb and time trial. He is faster than me in sprints, but he could be a Tour rider. Whether he can win the Tour de France or not, I don't know, but I think he could win a Tour of Spain.

Since I started cycling, Dad has given me advice, but he pretty much kept himself to himself. Even now, he might take a quick look over things but he leaves me to do my own thing. Only afterwards will he say, 'You should have done this or that. Next time do it that way.' He always waits for me to ask his advice first, unless he sees me doing something really stupid. Then he'll give it to me straight without the sugar coating.

He will say it once and then it's up to me to take it on board or not. A lot of the time, it takes a while to realize that some of the stuff he's saying is right. Other times, you just think, What the hell do you know? I suppose it's like any other father–son relationship. Sometimes you listen. Sometimes you don't.

Stephen Roche: I don't want to sound too much like an old guy, and kids never listen to their parents anyway. But it's frustrating for me to see Nicolas making the mistakes he makes now. Unfortunately, in cycling, you're never really at your prime. You're either young, or it's over. People say, 'Well, he's young,' but he's in his sixth year as a pro. Soon maybe he'll be too old. I'm maybe too harsh with Nicolas sometimes, but I'm purposely harsh. I tell it the way I see it. It's not beating around the bush and it's not telling him what he wants to hear either, because everyone else tells him what he wants to hear, and I can understand that.

It's brilliant what he's doing. The performances he's having are fantastic but, looking at it from the outside and having the inside perspective, seeing the effort he's putting in, the diet, the training, he does everything bang on and then it's the little things he makes the errors on.

Every time trial you do, you have to learn for the next one,
but he's been doing them for six years now and isn't learn-
ing. His position now, for example: I've been telling him he
should be sitting two millimetres higher than me. The other
day he tells me he had this guy looking at his position and it
should be 74.2. I said, 'And? I've been telling you that for the
last six years!' I understand it's difficult to hear it coming
from your old man and that's why I'd never hold it against
him. But at the same time, he can't hold it against me for not
telling him.

I could have made life easier on myself. I could have kept
up the football or the rugby, even gone into hotel management, but I caught a bug when I was a kid. I caught it from
my dad, and it has infected my whole family and, no matter
where we go, we can't get rid of it. That bug is cycling, the
hardest, most beautiful sport in the world.

Even now, at twenty-seven years of age, people still refer
to me as Stephen Roche's son. In a way, you can only disappoint everybody. Because I'm Stephen Roche's son it's like,
'Stephen won Paris–Nice when he was twenty-one, was
fourth in the Tour de France when he was twenty-five. This
guy is twenty-seven, and he's only got five pro wins.' Five pro
wins when you're just turned twenty-seven, that's not bad. It
took me a long time to understand that but, as I said before,
there's not a Stephen Roche around every corner.

My brother Alexis started his cycling career this year,
riding as an under-fourteen with my former club in Antibes.
Fifteen years after I started cycling, he now races on the same
bike that I started with, Mum's old blue Gios. Alexis and
Florian fancy themselves as the next Schleck brothers.

Sometimes I wish I could just beam them into my body *à la Star Trek*, to let them feel the suffering and pain that professional cycling brings. The lactic acid burning your legs as your heart rate stays at a constant 185bpm, the salty sweat dripping into your eyes as you gulp for air in the intense heat, and the aches and pains as you strain every muscle just to keep your bike moving forward. In fairness, my dad warned me of all of this years ago, but I wanted to find out for myself, and they will probably do the same. Alexis will find out in his first year that he too is the son of Stephen Roche.

Just a couple of weeks after the first edition of *Inside The Peloton* was published, in the autumn of 2011, I was due to fly home to Dublin for a day or two to promote the book with a series of TV and radio interviews. But as the season drew towards its conclusion, my Ag2r team was ranked number 18 in the UCI world rankings. In football terms we were in the relegation zone, and we needed every point we could get to stay in the Premiership and guarantee entry to the world's biggest races for 2012. There were only two races left to score big points: the inaugural Tour of Beijing – a new five day race on the WorldTour calendar – and the Italian one-day classic, the Tour of Lombardy.

When I told him about my book promotion plans, Vincent Lavenu reckoned that I'd be better off trying to harvest UCI points in Beijing than signing books in Dublin, and promptly dispensed me to China to do just that.

My whole aim going into the Tour of Beijing was stage three. With one second-category and three first-category climbs en route to Ying Nong, it was the toughest mountain stage of the race and the one earmarked for me. Although they'd probably heard it a hundred times before, I told the guys at the team meeting that I was really up for the stage, and that I needed them to position me well going into the final climb with about 15km to go. As we went through the feed zone after 85km, we had Lloyd Mondory about two and a half minutes up the road in a breakaway group of five riders and the rest of us near the front of the bunch. I told the guys I was going to do my best to try to win the stage and to trust me. Everything was going to plan.

Lloyd's group were caught with 30km to go, on the penultimate climb, and immediately Seb Hinault and Julien Bérard went to the front and increased the pace for me. Christophe Riblon and Mikaël Cherel led me onto the bottom of the final climb at the front of the bunch and I knew it was time to put my money where my mouth was.

As it happened, Philip Deignan went clear with 15km to go and opened up a gap of about twelve seconds. Even though I would be chasing the only other Irish rider in the race, I knew I had to follow him. Jumping clear of the peloton, I was followed by Chris Froome of Sky and we caught Philip near the summit and I led our three man group over the top with only a handful of seconds' lead over the peloton. We knew that we had to put absolutely every-thing into our attack if we wanted to stay away and agreed to ride flat out until the final kilometre.

With 3km to go, the peloton were still breathing down our necks. Our gap hovered at between five and eight seconds and each time I turned around they seemed to be getting closer and closer. My stomach was doing somersaults as we went under the red kite signalling the final kilometre with just four seconds' lead. Usually when I manage to get into this position, I somehow mess it all up in the last few metres. I looked back as we turned onto the finishing straight and saw the peloton heaving behind us. 'Not today. Please God, not today. I can't lose today.'

In my head though, I had everything calculated. Froome was the best-placed overall of our trio so I knew he would keep riding flat out to the line in the hope of taking over the race lead. I left him on the front for the final 900m or so but was still worried about Philip's sprint. It was touch and go whether we'd be caught as Froome drove towards the line in the tailwind with Philip sitting behind me ready to pounce and the bunch within touching distance. At 500m to go, all bets were off. Philip and I both knew a stage win in a WorldTour race would redeem our respective seasons and neither of us were going to let the chance go without a fight.

With 300m to go, I took one last glance behind and could almost feel the breath of the sprinters on my neck. I knew I had to go. I jumped as hard as I could and sprinted absolutely eyeballs out. I could sense Philip coming halfway up my bike as we neared the line but I kept going and just held him off to take the biggest win of my career thus far. Finally, I'd got my first victory in two years. The fact that it was in a WorldTour event made it even better.

Philip and I threw an arm around each other as we free-wheeled after the finish. The last time we'd been in Beijing, we'd shared a room in the athlete's village for the Olympics so it was fitting that the points we both earned that day qualified another Irish rider for London 2012. My mum and dad, girlfriend Chiara, plus friends and family from home all phoned me in China, delighted. They're the ones who had been trying to keep my morale up when things weren't going my way, told me to keep my head up, keep training, keep eating properly and resting properly, and that it would come right eventually. It was hard to believe them at times but thankfully they were proven right.

When I get second or third in big races, they are good moments, but there is only one moment that can make you forget about all the sacrifices you have made in the months or years before. It's the moment that makes you forget about the cold, rain-soaked days spent struggling in the gutter as the wheel in front of you sprays your eyes, nose and mouth with shit and muck from the road below. It's the moment you forget about the days when the sun shines so hard that the road melts in front of you. You forget about the days spent skidding across the tarmac on your arse with only a pair of lycra shorts for protection. You forget about the days spent vomiting on yourself in the middle of the peloton due to the hotel dinner the night before, afraid to stop pedalling because you know you won't start again. You forget about the days spent shovelling endless bowls of pasta into your mouth and nights spent lying with your legs on pillows just so that you have enough energy to do it all again the next day.

In cycling, that moment is the one when you cross the line with your hands in the air and a smile on your face.

In other sports, like football, boxing, or tennis, you start off with a 50–50 chance of winning. The thing about cycling is, only one guy can win from a bunch of two hundred riders, and there can be periods of days, weeks, months or even years in between those victories. Even if it's only a couple of days since my last victory, those couple of days will not be totally happy ones.

If I was satisfied with what I did every day, then eventually I'd just stay in bed and do nothing. But I'm a competitor. I am passionate about what I do, and every day I give one hundred per cent. But, afterwards, I will always, always, wish I could have done better.

Afterword
by Bradley Wiggins

There are not many names in cycling as big as the name Roche. When most people hear it, they think of former professional Stephen Roche. I grew up watching Stephen Roche on TV, saw him win the Giro d'Italia in 1987 and then follow it up by becoming only the second person ever to win the Tour de France and the world championships in the same season.

When I moved to the Cofidis team in 2006, they told me I'd be rooming with another Roche at our first training camp. Immediately, I had flashbacks to sitting in front of the TV as a kid and watching Nicolas, who was no more than a toddler then, being held by his mum while his dad stood on the top step of the podium on the Champs-Elysées as winner of the Tour de France.

We spent a year together at Cofidis and, as we both spoke English, we roomed together quite a bit and immediately struck up a friendship that lasts to this day.

A dedicated follower of fashion, Nicolas made me smile by turning up at races in his own clothes. Instead of the team-issue tracksuits and trainers, he'd be wearing Gucci shoes and a nice Prada shirt. I think he bought his first BMW with most of his small neo-pro's wages that year. To the outsider, the flashy clothes combined with the steely blue eyes, jet-black hair and easy smile meant Nicolas was often mistaken for just another pretty boy living off his father's name.

But as soon as he started racing in the professional peloton you could see that this kid had something. He had this raw edge that meant he wasn't frightened to just empty himself in a race, regardless of how good or bad his form was. To this day, he still has this innate ability to go into races and push himself to the point of collapse.

What struck me most about Nicolas was that he was such a gentleman off the bike. There is no ego, no big-headedness about him. As proud as he is to be Stephen Roche's son, he tries to detach himself as much as possible from that and never seeks to gain anything from it, which is something I admired in him straight away.

That year, before racing Gent–Wevelgem, his dad turned up and we went out on the bikes together. I was still a little bit in awe of Stephen and it was incredible for me to be sitting behind these two as we rode along the canal in Belgium. The pair of them looked like poetry in motion, as if they were part of the bike.

When you've got a dad as famous as Stephen Roche, it's always going to be difficult to live up to people's expectations. I know because my dad was a professional bike rider too, although I didn't grow up with my father and he was nowhere near as good as Stephen Roche.

You could see from an early age, though, that Nicolas was determined and knew exactly what he wanted to do in his career. To have that single-mindedness and not be affected by people constantly drawing comparisons to his dad is quite something.

But the comparisons are always going to be there. Any turn of the pedal you make, people are going to remember your father and speculate about how good you are now or potentially could be. 'Is he ever going to be as good as his dad?' 'He looks like he could be as good as his dad!' Those comparisons are with you continually, throughout your career. I don't think they ever go away.

Although he's trying to emulate what his father did in the Tour de France, Nicolas has forged his own path. He is such an all-rounder, he can do everything really. He's got such a stocky frame that five or six years ago I'd never have thought he'd be among the top ten in the Tour de France, but he seems drawn to the Tour and has turned himself into a bona fide GC rider.

I think he has been inhibited a bit in the team he's been in for the last few years. I don't think he gets a fair crack at the whip. I don't think he'll ever get the support that the French riders do when they're in those teams and I think he's battled with that the last two years. I've noticed it more this year with the addition of Jean-Christophe Péraud to the Ag2r roster. He seems to get all the support in the races while Nicolas is left to his own devices, maybe with one rider to look after him.

It was the same last year in the 2010 Tour where he was up against John Gadret for team leadership. Gadret would puncture and the whole team would wait. Nicolas would puncture and nobody would wait. I saw that first hand and I think with more support he's capable of better results than he's been getting.

But he's learning his trade in the French teams and still getting results with everything going against him. The minute that he gets a team that's centred solely around Nicolas Roche, like I did at Team Sky, I think the results will just start flowing. With the right route, the right run of form and a bit of luck he is certainly capable of a podium place in the Tour de France, maybe even a victory.

You forget how young Nicolas is. By the time he gets to Cadel Evans's age it's frightening to think what he could achieve. Riding GC in the Tour de France takes years and years of experience and disappointments, coming back stronger, learning what you're good at and improving in the areas you're bad at. Nicolas is still doing that, still developing those areas.

He's only ridden three Tours. He didn't get the opportunity, like some of the younger French riders, to get into the Tour early and gain experience. He had to come through the ranks, ride all the shitty little races and grab any opportunity that presented itself.

He debuted at the Tour de France in 2009, got a bit of experience under his belt, came back a year later and finished fifteenth overall. To do that in your second Tour shows something about you. 2011 was to be the year he moved up again. But for a crash, he looked like he could have moved on to another level in the Tour in the same way I had hoped to. It was such an open Tour that it was there for him to do, but a bad crash in the Dauphiné really knocked him back.

You only have to look at Cadel Evans and see how many times he had to come back from disappointments and crashes to win the 2011 Tour at thirty-four to realize that Nicolas has another seven or eight years to do that. Time is on his side and experience counts for so much in the Tour de France.

Off the bike, he's a pleasure to be around, regardless of whether he's winning or losing, and he's always gracious in defeat, a sportsman through and through. He treats everyone the same, whether you're a world champion, a multi-Tour winner or an amateur club rider. One of the nicest guys you could ever meet, he's also very professional on the bike, a fantastic teammate.

In ten years' time, it's people like Nicolas Roche who are going to mould the sport of cycling in so many ways. I think he's capable of anything he sets his mind to. I could also see him winning classics like Liège–Bastogne–Liège, a race that's really suited to him. He's already looking towards the 2011 Vuelta now and I think he'll be back to the Tour stronger next year. Whether he does or doesn't achieve anything in the Vuelta this year, you can guarantee he will give it everything every day. Someone like that, when they keep persisting, keep fighting, day in, day out, eventually they get their rewards.

Knowing Nicolas as a person, I know what he thinks is morally right, what is acceptable and what is not acceptable. If he does achieve his ambitions in the Tour de France, then he will be the kind of sportsman that people can look up to. There is no question mark about where he stands on the doping issue. It doesn't even cross my mind with him. In five or six years' time Nicolas could be winner of the Tour de France and a real role model for the next generation. He's the future of cycling in so many ways. The sport of cycling needs people like that, people like Nicolas Roche.

August, 2011

Picture Acknowledgements

Unless otherwise stated, all pictures are personally provided courtesy of the author and his family, with thanks to the cycling organizations and the photographers who have followed his life and career over the years. Every effort has been made to obtain the necessary permissions with reference to illustrative copyright material. We apologize for any omissions in this respect and will be pleased to make the appropriate acknowledgements in any future edition.

First section, p. 6: McCann and Roche; Deignan and Roche both © INPHO/Shane Stokes.

First section, p. 7: Tour de l'Avenir photographs both ©Bruno Bade; Roche father and son © Gerard Cromwell.

Second section, p. 2: Erviti and Roche © INPHO/Getty Images; Ag2r photographs both © Stephen McMahon.

Second section, p. 3: national championships photographs all © Stephen McMahon/Sportsfile.

Index

INDEX